OTHER BOOKS BY PAUL AND SARAH EDWARDS

Best Home Businesses for the 90s

Getting Business to Come to You
with Laura Clampitt Douglas

Making It on Your Own

Making Money with Your Computer at Home

Working from Home

Finding Your Perfect Work

Finding Your Perfect Work

The New Career Guide to
Making a Living, Creating a Life

Paul and Sarah Edwards

A Jeremy P. Tarcher/Putnam Book
published by
G. P. Putnam's Sons
New York

A Jeremy P. Tarcher/Putnam Book
Published by G. P. Putnam's Sons
Publishers Since 1838
200 Madison Avenue
New York, NY 10016

Most Tarcher/Putnam books are available at special quantity discounts for bulk purchases for sales promotions, premiums, fund-raising, and educational needs. Special books or book excerpts also can be created to fit specific needs.

For details, write or telephone Special markets, The Putnam Publishing Group 200 Madison Avenue, New York, NY 10016; (212) 951-8891.

Library of Congress Cataloging-in-Publication Data

Edwards, Paul, date.
    Finding your perfect work : the new career guide to making a
living, creating a life / Paul and Sarah Edwards.
        p.   cm.
    "A Jeremy P. Tarcher/Putnam book."
    Includes index.
    ISBN 0-87477-795-X
    1. Vocational guidance.   2. Vocational interests.   3. Self-realization.
4. Self-employed.   5. Home-based businesses.   I. Edwards, Sarah (Sarah A.)
II. Title.
HF5381.E467   1996   95-17939 CIP
658'.041—dc20

Design by Susan Shankin
Cover design by Mauna Eichner
Photograph of the authors by Helen K. Garber
Cover illustration © by Catherine Kanner

Printed in the United States of America

10   9   8   7   6   5   4   3   2   1

This book is printed on acid-free/recycled paper. ∞

CONTENTS

ACKNOWLEDGMENTS

FIRST WE EXPRESS OUR GRATITUDE to the men and women in our workshops on self-employment who have over the years pushed us to help them resolve their confusion, doubts, and concerns about how to find an independent means of support to live the lives they're seeking without compromise. We thank them and the thousands of other courageous and daring individuals whose commitment and determination to find their perfect work continues to inspire us and show us all the true possibilities that lie within even the most seemingly impossible of dreams.

Again we're forever grateful to Robert Welsch and Jeremy Tarcher for their vision and continuing belief in our work, and to our editor, Rick Benzel, who encouraged us to write a career book and whose insights enable us to shape and refine our ideas until they take their final form. A special thanks also to Rena Wolner for her enthusiasm and excitement about the need for this book and for spreading that excitement to others at Putnam.

Without the help of our assistant, Sheila Syracuse, we'd probably still be trying to finish this book, in which contributions of hundreds of people were important. So thank you, Sheila, for handling so many, many things and making it possible for us to keep writing. And thanks to Dr. Jessica Schairer for sharing her expertise, time, and considerable energy in working with us to develop the Doing What Comes Naturally survey and complete the self-employment career directories.

Thanks, too, to Ben Lizardi for applying his special talents to designing artwork that visually expresses the concepts we wish to communicate. And to Darcy Tom, whose line drawings so remarkably capture the special personalities of the fabulous individuals we want everyone to meet through this book. Thanks, as well, to Allen Mikaelian, who patiently guided this book through the many complexities of production, and to Susan Shankin for her amazing creativity in designing page layouts for the many facets we wanted this book to include.

Finding Your Perfect Work

Something's Happening

PERFECT WORK. There was a time when that would have meant finding the right job and building a good life around it. But something's happening. Whatever your job, if you have one, chances are you're finding that the pieces of your life don't fit together so easily around it anymore. Often there aren't enough hours in the day to fit in everything that needs to be done. Life should be more than working for a living, but often after work, there's not much left for living. There's not much time, not much money, and not much energy to spare.

Finding and holding down a job that allows you to put your life together in a way you want to live has become a puzzling challenge. Often just keeping it all together gets harder by the day. According to pollsters, too many of us are overworked or out of work, juggling shifts or patching together multiple jobs. Parents worry what their kids are up to because they rarely see them in the daylight. People everywhere spend sleepless nights wondering if they'll still have a job when they show up for work in the morning and dreading what they'll do if they don't.

Look reality in the eye and it won't take you by surprise. You can grab hold of what you see and shape it into what you would make of it.

This isn't the way life's supposed to be and, fortunately, it doesn't have to be like this. You don't have to put up with such an existence. There is a better way. Right when it seems as though life is getting completely out of control and everything is falling apart, the very changes that are wreaking such havoc in our lives are also providing an unprecedented opportunity for you to take charge of your life and start living it on your own terms. But you won't find it within the job-oriented careers we've all depended on for so long. Jobs as we have known them are no longer sufficiently dependable, flexible, or malleable to work even nearly perfectly for most people anymore. Today's new economic realities call for new solutions and new models. That's what this book is about.

We will show you how to reclaim your life, rekindle your dreams, and start putting the pieces of your life together so that what's most important to you comes first. We will explain how what's happening in our society today is making it economically possible for the first time in history to truly find your perfect work outside the confines of a job so you can build your work around your life instead of the other way around. Most of all, this book will provide you with the tools to actually earn your living in harmony with your interests, values, priorities, and dreams and thereby create a life that works the way you need and want it to.

FINDING YOUR WAY

With each passing year, greater numbers of people come to our seminars on self-employment—eager, ready, and excited to take charge of their lives. They want to start living on their own terms and they're filled with ideas, hopes, and dreams. But as eager and hungry as they are to build a new life around their dreams, they're still not sure it's really possible. They're not certain they can trust what their hearts are urging them to do. They know that to do what they want to do, they need more freedom and flexibility, but they don't know if it's practical. They don't know the type of independent work that would allow them to live the way they want to live and still provide a steady and dependable income. They can't see how their most promising and financially viable work opportunities are the ones they can create for themselves. And traditional career advice doesn't show them how. That's why we decided to write this book.

Most career books and courses are still based on the traditional job-oriented models. They're still about applying for a job, not creating one of your own. They're still about doing a job search; whereas today's search isn't just about finding work, it's about finding a way to make a life that works. Books and courses exist to help you discover your life goals, but these too don't show you how to create a living in practical terms. Trend forecasters help identify possibilities for the economic future, but reading them doesn't give you concrete direction as to how you can turn today's trends into a livelihood that will support your goals.

To find your way today, you need more than a traditional career guide, more than an inspirational program for how to live-your-dream, more than an economic trend report, and more than a self-employment manual. These are piecemeal guides to the puzzle; what's needed is an integrated, comprehensive guide that shows you how to link all the pieces. In other words, you need a master guide that shows you how to turn today's new realities into opportunities to create the perfect work for supporting yourself and the life you want to lead.

Over 14 million people have already taken the quality of their lives into their own hands by supporting themselves in a life of their own choosing. Others are joining them at the rate of over 1500 people a day.

"Hello, everyone. I have a problem I'm hoping someone can help me with. I want to go out on my own, but I don't know what line of work I should pursue. I've spent my whole life working in one field and I want out. I have a computer. There must be something else I can do."

CREATING A MASTER GUIDE

We communicate every week with hundreds of individuals who have already found a way to create work of their own and thereby realize their desires for a better life. Through our seminars, our radio and TV shows, our column in *Home Office Computing* magazine, and the *Working from Home Forum* we manage on CompuServe, we've met tens of thousands of such individuals. And, we've been living such a life ourselves for over twenty years. So we felt certain that, buried within experiences like ours and those of so many others who have successfully stepped out of old job models that no longer worked for them, we could find the new solutions and new models so many others need today if they are to create a life more to their liking.

Beginning in 1989, we began conducting and reviewing hundreds of interviews, synthesizing thousands of conversations, and analyzing stacks of national research studies. Our goal was to identify patterns that go beyond the basic steps involved in becoming self-employed, beyond how to get ample work and balance your personal and professional lives. We had already written about those things in our other books on self-employment, and we teach these practical how-to's in our seminars. What we were looking for were the patterns for how people have made decisions about the work they want to do on their own, how they've tailored these decisions to the kinds of lives they want to live, and how they've put it all together to be financially viable.

And indeed, we did find patterns that are both interesting and compelling. Although the thousands of people we've spoken with were from all walks of life, all ages, all ethnic groups and job and socioeconomic backgrounds, although the lives they'd chosen to lead varied in every way imaginable, and although they may have stumbled, sailed, flailed, or flown into their new lives by chance, by choice, or as a result of some crisis, when their new lives worked for them, there are clear patterns in terms of how they found their perfect work to put their lives together. These patterns are the basis for what we believe to be a master guide for how to live and work on your own terms in the new realities of the approaching twenty-first century. And the key to it all is:

In the future, most of us must create our own livelihoods based on our personal choices about the kind of life we want to live.

USING THIS GUIDE

Given this principle, as you read this book you, too, will be embarking on a highly personal and unique journey. Your journey won't necessarily be a logical 1-2-3-step process. You probably won't take this journey as the crow flies; in other words, don't expect it to be a straight shot from point A to point B. It seems that few such journeys have been so simple. You'll be creating both a living and a life, so in a sense your experience will be somewhat like that of an artist. You'll be drawing from what's in your heart and soul to create something new, unlike what's ever existed before. You'll be trying out first one possibility, then another, and mixing and matching possibilities until you like the look and feel of what you've created.

Also, because this journey is more like a creative process, as you proceed through this book, at times you might feel somewhat lost, confused, or even overwhelmed and a bit frustrated. Should this happen, consider it a sign that you're right on track and simply proceed, taking a breather or respite at any point you wish and returning when you're ready. Trust yourself and the process of your journey: you'll find new insights, and clarity will emerge at the most unexpected times.

But as in planning for any journey, you'll basically be addressing three issues around which this guide is organized: where you want to go, which path you want to take to get there, and how you'll pay your way. Here's a preview of what you can expect:

PART I: THE DESTINATION

The journey to your perfect work, whatever it might look like, must begin with believing you can truly create the life you want to live. You must believe that what's happening in this economy is actually making it possible for more and more people like yourself not only to survive but to thrive by creating their own livelihoods. And you must believe it's possible for *you*. So **Chapter 1, "Believing in the Possibilities,"** is packed with evidence—facts and figures that show how trends and economic forces are making it possible to start living and working the way you want. There are many, many stories about people who are already benefiting from what's happening in today's economy; these are individuals who have found the perfect work to successfully create lives of their own either by choice, by chance, or in response to a crisis. And you will see that they are doing all kinds of things that would have been considered impossible or impractical in the past.

When you finish this chapter, you will have ample ammuni-

Creating a New Life of Your Choosing

Part I. "The Destination" is designed to enable you to envision the life you want to create.

Part II. "The Path" is designed to enable you to explore many avenues that could take you to your desires and choose the most appealing path.

Part III. "The Means" is designed to enable you to evaluate the many opportunities open to you to earn a living along the path of your choice.

"I think I can."
The Little Engine That Could

"It's over. D'ya hear?
Over. Over. Over.
Build your own firm."

Tom Peters

tion for fending off your own doubts and fears as well as those of well-meaning family, friends, and peers. If at any point you start doubting that times have truly changed in favor of finding your perfect work and creating what you want from life, feel free to return to this chapter for a reminder. We agree with management consultant Tom Peters, who said about the world of work as we've known it, "It's over." You must understand that we're living on a one-way highway these days, heading for a new world; times have indeed changed, and there's no going back to the way things were. You have, however, an array of choices for how to proceed along the road that lies ahead.

There's no sense in making a plan if you don't know where you're going.

Since, clearly, it's now possible and even necessary to find your perfect work and start creating the life of your choice, you might as well decide what you actually want. In **Chapter 2, "Answering the Right Question,"** you'll have the opportunity to do just that. **Chapter 2** will provide a series of signposts to help you make sure you don't get sidetracked into settling for work or a lifestyle that will be less than what you *really* want. You'll find exercises and questions to help you clarify what's most important to you. Often people are surprised at what they discover. What you actually want may not be what first comes to mind. For example, upon reflection, it's usually not money, big cars, and big houses people yearn for most, but greater freedom, more time for family and loved ones, or the chance to do more meaningful work. But whatever it is that's most important to you, when you finish this chapter you should have a reasonably clear idea of the life your perfect work will be designed to create.

PART II: THE PATH

Given freedom of choice, when the path isn't bearable, we don't proceed.

One of the best things about finding your perfect work and taking charge of your life is that you only have to do those things you can get yourself to do. But that means it is essential that you choose a path for your work that's sufficiently bearable so you won't turn back and sufficiently enjoyable so you won't dally. Of course, the path you choose for your life work must also be a fruitful one. While there are many possible routes to personal and economic independence, we've all seen too many people struggling to make it on their own—and that's the last thing you want for yourself.

Since only the most rare venture just "takes off" on its own, you'll see how those who find their perfect work have drawn upon their own inner resources to get their new career and new life going. And, most important, you'll learn how you can find a path for your work that, like the Energizer Rabbit, will keep you charged up and motivated so you'll keep going and going and going, until you get where you want to go.

Many books have been published about how to find such a career path. Usually they're written from the traditional career paradigm of "finding a job." Some, like the popular books *Do What You Love and the Money Will Follow* and *Wishcraft*, recommend following your heart with the confidence that it will take you where you want to go. Others, like Naomi Stephan's *Finding Your Soul's Purpose,* recommend discovering your life mission. Most career experts like Richard Bolles, author of *What Color Is Your Parachute?* focus on helping you find work that best suits your aptitudes, knowledge, and skills.

While many people have been helped and inspired by these approaches and we frequently recommend these books, we've found that many people can't identify how to earn a living from a passion or a mission and still others don't want to do what their aptitudes, skills, and background would suggest for them. In fact, upon closer investigation, we've discovered that nearly half of all people who successfully create satisfying new lives on their own do so without mining a special talent, or identifying a particular passion or life mission. Many successfully carve out lives by tapping into existing skills and experiences. Others pursue hobbies or interests, while still others are successful pursuing unexpected opportunities that take them in new directions and require them to master new skills and develop new interests.

Our research shows that there are actually four distinct paths people are taking to find their perfect work and successfully make a living creating the life of their choosing. Each of these paths has the potential to enable you to tap into sufficient motivation and energy to get where you want to go and commit to getting there. Each of these paths has its advantages and disadvantages; each, its pros and cons. But most important, although many people pri-

"I have a dream about something I know I can do, but I'm afraid to leave my job."

"I have a 486 computer with a built-in hard drive and CD-ROM. What can I do with it to earn a living if I get laid off?"

"After my fifth baby, I started a desktop publishing business so I could work from home and be with my kids. The business didn't take off. What else can I do?"

"I would like to be my own boss, but doing what? I ask myself over and over…what can I do? What can I do?"

"I've been following my dream, doing what I love, for ten years. I'm glad I did it, but it's still such a struggle. My wife thinks I should give up and do something more lucrative. What do I tell her?"

marily pursue one of these paths, those who are most successful draw upon the resources and energy available from several or all of these paths to achieve their goals.

In **Part II: The Path,** you will explore these paths to finding your perfect work and how to tap into the benefits they each offer. By combining elements of the various paths, you will be able to discover a path of your own that most closely matches your goals, desires, and circumstances. Your choice will probably be unique, as are those of the many people you will meet throughout this section. Again, you will find many examples. Our belief is that as you meet the men and women who have taken these various paths to success, you will begin to see new choices and chances you might not otherwise have thought of, and new possibilities for your own path will come into focus.

PART III: THE MEANS

For many people the final stage of the journey becomes the greatest challenge of all—how to make money doing what you really want to do—without a paycheck, without a job! If only you could just do what you love and the money to support it would follow! If only finding and pursuing your chosen path could somehow, in and of itself, ensure your success. Although we all wish it could be so, in truth, we've seen far too much evidence that it simply isn't necessarily so. And chances are you have, too. Unfortunately, we've all met far too many highly gifted people who are trying to follow their hearts or pursue their passions only to end up struggling miserably, often not even understanding why.

Finding your perfect work, be it to follow your gift, passion, mission, or assets, is only one side of the coin. No matter how passionately you love what you do, no matter how deeply you care about your work or how socially important it is, or how outstanding you are at what you do, how good your intentions or what a deserving person you are, no matter how much you want a better life, if you are to have it, you must find some way to match your gifts, passions, missions, and assets to opportunities that people need and will pay for. Until you find such a match, your journey to the life of your dreams will be a long and hard one.

Without some means of transportation your journey can't begin, and without a ticket you can't get aboard.

"I know choreographers, actors, activists, poets...who give up their vocation for lack of next month's rent. The burden of the small bill, the shrill voice of the collection agent demanding the check for $200 deaden the soul. A manuscript gets put in the drawer for lack of enough money to pay the electric bill."

Richard Rodriquez, journalist

PROFILE: AMANDA MCBROOM, DREAMING

She loved to sing the songs she wrote for her friends and they loved it when she did. They would shower her with praise and exhort her to find some way to share her music with the world. But she didn't want to get involved in the music industry. All the hassle. All the distress of trying to get a record deal was so unappealing. For many years she resisted their pleas. Ultimately, however, she knew she had to honor what she had created. She owed her talent the effort to make sure it could be heard. So she began the arduous task of trying to get an album published that would showcase her songs. She found no interest. But by then, there *was* no doubt. There was to be an album. And she found the way. She raised the money herself, and produced the album *Amanda McBroom— Dreaming*. That was only the beginning. Her music has been heard on Steven Bocho's groundbreaking television series *Rock Cop* and in her own one-woman show *Heartbeats* at the world-famous Pasadena Playhouse.

Based on what we observed other people unknowingly doing, we've developed a process called *matrixing*. This process shows how you can merge your desires, resources, and opportunities into marketable work. You'll see many examples of how this process works in others' lives. And you'll see that by matrixing you won't need to "sell out" to support the life you want. There is no need to compromise the things that are most important to you in order to earn a good living.

But that needn't be. You owe it to yourself to find a match between your desires and those of others, and you'll learn there are ample opportunities for matching what you want in life and what you can provide with real-world needs of others.

> "There are no passengers on spaceship *Earth*, only crew."
> *Buckminster Fuller, engineer and philosopher*

You'll learn how to see the chances, make the choices, and turn what's happening around you into an opportunity to live the way you want. You'll have time to do the things you love with the people you love, working when you want, where you want, and how you want in accord with your goals, values, and priorities.

NO NEED TO SETTLE FOR LESS

As you can see, something really is happening. Our topsy-turvy lives are filled with the signs of some very real, but very promising, changes. And you might as well take part in them. Once you start to see the multiplicity of opportunities these changes can open up for you to find your perfect work, you'll realize you need

FEATURES OF THIS BOOK

This book is actually a personal journey and not a reference book or generic how-to manual. You undoubtedly have particular ways in which you prefer to go about learning that help you see options, make choices, and reach decisions. Some people prefer working from a conceptual framework, looking at the big picture. Others prefer many specific examples and visual illustrations. Still others want a step-by-step procedure they can follow. Most people want some combination of all these things. Therefore, we've designed this book to provide a wide variety of resources for you to draw upon. Each section has the following elements we invite you to use as fully as you find valuable.

Stories. Each section has many stories of real-life people who are making a living creating their own lives. We believe the more stories you read, the more possibilities you'll begin to see for yourself. Many of these stories are about more-unconventional and less-obvious ways people have created a living making a life. They're here to stretch your imagination and spark ideas, not so much for doing just what these people have done, but for doing what you want to do.

Profiles. Each part of this book also includes in-depth profiles of people that enable you to get to know in greater detail how others are creating new lives for themselves as a result of what's happening in the economy today. You'll learn more about what motivates them, how they think, what they've done to create the kind of life they want, and how they feel about the new lives they've created. Again, you'll find their lifestyles often quite original. No one person is quite like another. But as you get to know their stories, you'll better understand how you might create the particular and equally personal life you're seeking.

Work Sheets. Each section also has many work sheets that will enable you to capture your ideas, explore your possibilities, define your goals, and evaluate the alternatives you're generating as you read. Feel free to write on these work sheets or, if you prefer, you might want to use a separate journal or notebook so you can write and plan more extensively. Alternatively you may prefer to record your an-not settle for pursuing anything less than making your living by creating the life you truly want. And doing so can become the journey of a lifetime, filled with the surprises, the satisfactions, and the magic that make having dreams worth keeping and life worth living.

swers on tape or in your computer. Once you've completed these work sheets you will have done the planning and exploration you need to do to know what direction you want to go with your life and how to create the perfect work to get you there.

Marginalia. On most pages throughout the book, you'll find pertinent facts, quick summaries of key points, and inspirational thoughts. You can turn time and time again to these margin notes as a reminder or reference.

Figures, Boxes, Resources, and Lists. Whenever possible, we've illustrated key concepts and ideas visually to make them come alive. Each part of the book also concludes with a resource list for further reading on various subjects.

Appendices. We have developed three appendices you can use to find an array of careers you can pursue independently. This list of over 1,600 independent careers is there to stretch your mind, to enable you to see possibilities you might never otherwise consider and match them with the lifestyle you're seeking. Each career we list has been evaluated as to how well it's suited to your personal style as well as lifestyle issues like whether it can be done from home, if licensing or degrees are required, and if it's family friendly or not.

In using these resources, you should feel free to make notes and write in this book as you would a workbook, underlining, circling, or highlighting examples or ideas that appeal to you and actually using the pages to write out your thoughts, experiences, plans, and ideas. Also, at each step of the way, once you've gotten the information you need to make your decisions and reach your goals, feel free to skip or skim past any of these elements when you're ready to move on. You don't have to do every exercise, for example, if you've already reached a decision about what it covers. And, of course, you need not read all the many examples we've provided. If, at any point, however, you are feeling stuck or unclear about your next step, try reading through the material you might otherwise have skipped over or skimmed through. Going back to things you've skipped or skimmed over may just provide the fresh perspective you need at just that moment.

PART I

The Destination: Deciding Where You Want to Go

ONE

Believing in the Possibilities

FOR GENERATIONS, people have come to America to pursue a better life—and they're still coming. A million men and women from all across the world come to our shores every year with a dream in their hearts. The United States is a nation built upon dreams. When asked about their dreams, grade-school children from all walks of life talk excitedly about the interesting, rewarding, and important things they want to do when they grow up. They talk of curing cancer, exploring outer space, becoming Olympians, and saving the environment.

Whether blessed with the advantages of loving, nurturing parents or cursed with a cripplingly dysfunctional family, whether advantaged by the best of college educations or challenged by having had to drop out of high school, every American has dreams. And while not everyone achieves them, there's always been a feeling of hope that someday we might—and if not, then at least our children may be able to realize theirs. That's the great American Dream and, one way or another, we've always been able to keep that belief alive. Until lately.

We hold these Truths to be self-evident, that all Men [and Women] are created equal, that they are endowed by their Creator with certain unalienable Rights, that among these are Life, Liberty, and the Pursuit of Happiness.

The Declaration of Independence

Elio Samame

"...America is the creation of individuals ...constantly shaping one another, creating one another. A genius happens because his mother worked for the phone company to send him to school, or a grade-school teacher took dirt wages to teach him to write."

Richard Rodriquez, journalist

PROFILE: ELIO SAMAME

All his life, from the time he was a little boy in Lima, Peru, Elio Samame had a dream—to come to America and open a gym where he could share his fitness philosophy with the world and help people improve their lives. In 1985, he did it. He came here with $300, rented a tiny apartment in Venice, California, and started working as an independent fitness trainer. He trained his first client for free. Four months later, this person became a success story and his first testimonial. Her story appeared in the local paper, and the phone hasn't stopped ringing for Elio. His clientele grew, and in 1991 he opened his own 2,500-square-foot gym: Elio's Fitness for *Success*. A year later, he expanded to a 10,000-square-foot facility where he is today . . . living his American dream.

PROFILE: PHILLIP SPECTOR

Phillip Spector was determined to pursue his dream. He came to America to open his own tailor shop. We can only imagine the efforts he must have put forth to start that shop and bring his family here one by one. But the business didn't work out. He closed the door on his shop and in that one moment he let his dream die. He took a job as a tailor working for someone else. He did that job the rest of his life—over fifty years. He never talked about the dream that died. In fact, he never talked much. But from the pictures on the mantel, you knew he had dreams for his children.

FADING DREAMS

Until lately, there were always certain givens you could count on to keep the promise of your dreams alive. You could go to school and if you did your best you could get a good, steady job of some kind. Usually you could keep that job or get another one you liked as much or better. You could keep working steadily toward a good life and a secure future. If you got laid off, it was literally a temporary "layoff"; eventually you were called back. For better or worse, if you did what was expected of you everything went pretty much as would be expected. But that has changed. You can't count on those things anymore.

Chances are what you've been taught to expect is no longer what you can expect.

Jobs Are Disappearing. Even if you go to school, work hard, and do the best you can, you may or may not be able to get a job, let alone a good job, or a steady job. Paradoxically, although it takes a college education to earn a good living these days (college graduates earn 73 percent more than others), even college graduates aren't finding jobs commensurate with their education and their expectations.

One recent college graduate, for example, works as a clerk in a Rand McNally bookstore. She's a geographer; she feels lucky to be doing something related to her degree. At least it's a full-time job. Not everyone she graduated with had her luck. Last year only one in three new graduates had a job waiting. As many as 35 percent ended up with jobs that don't require a college degree, and many have settled for part-time or temporary jobs. In fact, Manpower Temporary Services has become the nation's largest single employer.

Two years ago, a Howard University graduate did find a job. He's a temp in the mail room at a major software company. "I don't like the word *temp*," he says. "It's like I don't have a name. They say, Oh, just give it to the 'temp.' I didn't graduate with a degree in business to work in the mail room. I want something more permanent." Still since it is a full-time job, he keeps it. After all, today's average service worker works only thirty-three hours a week.

And, of course, it's by no means only young workers who can't find jobs. In the past two years, there have been over ten million layoffs. And new layoffs continue to be announced every day. Nonetheless, a twenty-year veteran engineer was surprised when he got a pink slip. "I knew there would be layoffs, but I didn't think it would happen to me," he says. "They kept the younger people who are getting paid less. So much for loyalty, huh?" He's been looking for another job for eight months but finds that "they say I'm overqualified."

After having been laid off in a merger, one bank manager felt lucky to find a new job right away, but within the year, she was laid

"From now until the year 2025 college graduates will outnumber jobs available to them by 20 percent each year."

U.S. Labor Department

off again. "The first time was bad enough," she remembers, "but the second time is much worse, because if I do find another job, how do I know it won't just happen again?"

Existing Jobs Aren't So Hot. The sad truth is, regardless of salary, education, or skill levels, those who are fortunate to have a full-time job aren't doing so well either. They're putting in more hours, but they're getting fewer benefits and smaller raises, and they never know if they'll still have their job tomorrow. The old-fashioned forty-hour week has become the fifty-hour week or more for those who are working full-time, with executives putting in an average of over sixty hours each week. Forty percent of workers say their employers expect them to work an unreasonable amount of overtime hours. Half say their jobs intrude on family commitments. According to a variety of studies, workers have a third less time for leisure and family activities than they did in 1969. One survey found that half of salaried workers would be *willing* to work one day less a week at no pay just to recover some free time! It seems today that there are three types of jobs: temporary, part-time, and overtime.

Money Is Tight. Despite all these long hours, one in three adults report they have trouble paying their monthly bills; three-quarters have trouble saving for their children's education; and half have trouble saving for retirement. Perhaps this relates to the fact that 80 percent of male heads of households saw their incomes fall instead of rise during the past few years. And to make matters worse, up to 50 percent of workers who have jobs are worried that they'll lose them, especially as they near retirement. Labor Secretary Robert Reich describes this growing cadre of workers as the emerging "anxious class." They fear becoming one of a growing pool of surplus workers, people whose labor simply is not needed. Often referred to as "discouraged workers," these individuals have given up looking for a job and aren't even counted in the unemployment statistics.

Quality of Life Is Shot. All this stress affects the quality of our lives and our health. Seventy-two percent of workers are so stressed from their jobs that they experience frequent

"The amount of money allocated this year for pay raises will be the lowest since 1975."

U.S. Conference Board

"A young male high-school graduate earns 30 percent less on a job today than his counterpart earned in 1979."

New York Times

stress-related physical and mental conditions! And at the age of thirty, today's executive has a 48 percent chance of becoming disabled for at least ninety days before reaching age sixty-five.

Single parents and two-career parents, who constitute the majority of families now, are especially stressed and pressed. Studies show that the less time they spend with their children, the more they worry about them. A study conducted by Pittsburgh's Priority Management shows that the average working parent gets to have only thirty seconds of meaningful conversation with his or her children, and working couples engage in only four minutes a day of meaningful communication with each other. It's no wonder a Millman Lazarus and Lake study for Massachusetts Mutual found that the number-one cause of stress reported by workers was lack of time with their families.

To combat this, many families have resorted to piecing together multiple jobs, juggling multiple shifts, or forgoing sorely needed income so someone can be home with the children. Still, the Bureau of the Census reports, every day 1,600,000 children ages five to fourteen are left alone after school, and another half a million children start their days without adult supervision. Seventy-five percent of day-care centers are rated as providing only minimal care, and hoof-and-mouth disease, most often associated with animals, is commonly spread at these centers. Also every day, 2,200 teenagers drop out of school, 500 experiment with drugs, 1,000 turn to alcohol, and 1,200 commit suicide. So parents worry about their children and their future.

Perhaps this fear for our children's future is the greatest threat of all to our belief in the American Dream. Times have been tough before. Belief in the Dream survived a civil war, two world wars, the Great Depression, and more. But no matter how rough or hopeless times were, parents could always fall back on the belief that things would be better for their children. But now pollsters say, we're even wondering about that as well.

"When I got the pink slip, I only had four months to go before retirement."

"At work you think of the children you have left at home. At home you think of the work you've left unfinished. Such a struggle is unleashed within yourself. Your heart is rent."

Golda Meir

"My parents say, 'I'll spend time with you tomorrow,'" said a little girl whose voice was as light and high as a sparrow's... "but they don't."

REKINDLING OUR DREAMS

As bad as things may seem, though, the greatest dreams are often born in periods of the greatest distress. Times like these make people mad. We get tired of putting up with frustration and disappointment. We grow restless, discontented, dissatisfied, even desperate. Personal crises shake us from our complacency and force us to find new solutions in order not to give up our dreams. Change presents us with new choices and causes us to seek new options that fire up our dreams. And that's exactly what's happening.

Right now, over twenty-four million Americans have decided they're not willing to give up on their dreams. They've become their own bosses, creating the freedom and the flexibility they need to live and work the way they want to. For some, it took a crisis, a traumatic life-changing event, to force them into finding some new way to hold on to their dreams. For others, it was a conscious choice; they decided there had to be a better way, and they set out to create one. Still others simply stumbled quite by chance onto some new opportunity and eagerly seized the moment to give their dreams a chance.

DREAMS BORN OF CRISIS

Our research indicates that perhaps as many as 40 percent of people who have gone out on their own have done so in response to some kind of crisis that forced them to take back their dreams and find new ways to live them. They've told us:

I Had to Do Something . . .

I Got Fired. "I thought they were calling me to come in for a promotion. Instead, I got fired. I was about to feel terrible, then suddenly a wave of relief came over me and I realized it was the best thing that ever happened to me. I haven't worked for anyone else since."

My Husband Died. "My husband died and I had a new baby. I had to do something. But I never imagined I'd end up

---

Only 20 percent of people surveyed believe the American Dream is still very much alive. Sixty-four percent believe it's harder to achieve the American Dream today than in the past.

Fifty-seven percent of Americans say the outlook for the next generation's future will be worse than life today, and that number grows the further into the future one projects.

CBS News Poll

"I don't fear for myself, but I fear for my children."

USA Today

The Chinese symbol for "crisis" is also the symbol for opportunity.

earning more money than he had by doing something I like so much."

I Was Too Sick to Work. "I became ill. I couldn't work under the conditions I'd been working. It wasn't ever a healthy situation, but now I couldn't do it if I wanted to. I wouldn't go back."

I Got a Wake-up Call. "I fell off the back of a truck. When I woke up in the hospital, I knew the first thing I was going to do when I got out of the hospital was quit my job and start doing what I always wanted to do."

My Husband Divorced Me. "My husband divorced me for a younger woman, and the divorce settlement went up his nose. Because of his cocaine habit all his money was gone, his business was gone, everything was gone, and I had two teenagers to support. I had to become a person I never thought I could be: strong, independent, capable, and—best of all—happy."

My Ideas Were Rejected One Time Too Many. "When my boss turned down the best idea I've ever had, I couldn't put up with it anymore, so I left and did it myself."

My Husband Lost His Job. "My husband was out of work. We had to eat. I sat up all night thinking how I could help, what I could do and still be home with my babies. That night I would never have guessed the idea that finally came to me would become a multimillion-dollar business for the whole family."

I Couldn't Take It Any More. "I was working sixty-hour weeks just to keep my job. I never saw my family. I felt like a stranger in my own house. Now that I'm on my own, not only do my kids know who I am and what I do, I know who they are and what they do."

I Was Passed Over for Promotion Again. "After getting passed over for another promotion, I said, 'That's it! I'm going to give myself a raise.' "

I Retired with No Income. "I didn't have any retirement funds, so I've created my own Social Security."

We Were Broke. "I mostly did it out of fear. We were going broke."

"People are not idle;
they are inventive."
James Flanigan

I Married My Co-worker. "I got fired because I married a co-worker. Now we work together and we both make more money than our boss."

I Had a Crisis of Conscience. "I didn't believe in what I was doing. Their ethics were so marginal, against everything I believe in. One day I couldn't take it any more, so I just walked out on everything I'd ever worked for so I can have what I'm really working for."

My Son Needed Me. "Our son needed special education, but my husband and I both worked. Our son wasn't making progress in school. We decided to move and put him in a better program. I started a home business so I could work more closely with him. Now my husband works in the business, too, and our son has taken his first steps and spoken his first words."

The Discrimination Was Intolerable. "When I asked my boss for a raise, he said I was making enough money for a woman my age. So I quit, and I'm making six times what I was making then and more than I would have ever made working there."

We Were Losing Our Farm. "We were losing our farm. We had to do something. So we looked around and put the equipment we had to other uses. Not only do we still have our farm, we didn't have to leave this place where we grew up, and we can live here all our lives."

I Couldn't Find a Job. "I was on my third stack of résumés. I'd sent out over a hundred and gotten only eight responses, all politely saying they didn't need me. I threw them all away and asked myself why I was going begging for a job. I'm going to create my own."

Perhaps you're facing such a crisis right now in your life. Perhaps you're living with some circumstances you can no longer tolerate. Now you're willing and ready to change, but you don't know what you could do to support yourself. As you read through this book you'll find there are many ways you can turn the crises you're grappling with into a better chance to pursue your dreams. We hope you'll be able to look back on this difficult time and say,

According to an IBM study of new businesses, 38 percent were started because their owners were laid off.

as so many people we talk with do, "It turned out to be an unexpected gift."

PROFILE: CLYDE GLANDON

"When my father, Clyde Glandon, retired at sixty-five, he became a magician. His stage name was Colonel Boone. As Colonel Boone, my dad became a whole new person—a happy person. You could see the special gleam in his eye. Unfortunately, he died just four years later, but before he died, when he was too sick to get out of bed, he said to me, "If only I could be on stage one more time . . . if only I could do *one* more magic trick." In a way I knew how he felt, because I knew how much I didn't want to die without doing all the things I knew I could do if only I would. Those words were his last gift to me, and in saying them he got his wish because from that day on I started to do the things I'd been wanting to do but kept putting off. Some magic trick, huh?"

DREAMS BORN BY CHOICE

For some people, there is no crisis that catalyzes them to pursue their dreams. Quite the contrary, they simply decide they're no longer willing to compromise, delay, or forego what's in their hearts and souls. So they summon up their courage to make a specific choice that will change their lives. In fact, we've found that 40 percent of those who are going out on their own have made a conscious decision to find an independent route to their dreams. They read or heard about the many interesting and exciting opportunities other people are pursuing and were eager to do something about their situation, too. They tell us:

I Wanted More Freedom. "I was starting a family and when I saw that new technology had a perpetual problem in our industry that I could solve, I quit my job and started my own company in my spare bedroom."

I Always Wanted to Be My Own Boss. "I decided to work in every department of the company where I worked, and when I had learned about every facet of doing business, I left to start a company of my own."

We Made a Choice. "My wife and I decided that both of us wanted to be home to raise our children, so we searched

"No trumpets sound when the important decisions of our lives are made."

Agnes de Mille,
actress

until we found something we could do together working from home."

I Said, "Not Me." "The whole time I was growing up, every night I heard my father complain about how much he hated his work. So when I heard myself doing the same thing, I knew I had to make a change. But I knew no one would pay me to do what I wanted to do, so I had to go out on my own."

We Changed Our Minds. "We thought we had to live where my husband could get a job, but we missed the small-town atmosphere we grew up in. We wanted our kids to grow up with the kind of security and community feeling we had, so we actually planned out how we could create work for ourselves that we could do from anywhere, and we moved back to our hometown."

I Put My Foot Down. "When I became a single mom, everyone wanted me to go back to school and get a job. In fact, the court ordered me to do that if I wanted any alimony. But I decided that my kids were still going to come first, so I looked for what I could do at night and I started writing. I not only pay the rent but have bought a home and I still pick up my kids every day after school by working for myself."

Perhaps there's something you feel equally strongly about and have decided to find some way to do it. As you read through this book, you'll be encouraged to discover just how many creative ways others have found to follow through on their decisions by finding their perfect work and becoming self-employed.

DREAMS BORN BY CHANCE

Other than facing a crisis or making a choice, about 20 percent of people who are setting out on their own future have somehow just "fallen into" their new life by chance. Suddenly they encountered a previously nonexistent opportunity and realized it could be a route for doing what they'd always wanted to do. Or they were presented with a serendipitous event, a fortuitous happenstance, a series of coincidences that led to pursuing a completely unexpected, but welcomed, new path. In speaking of how they came to do what they're doing, they frequently say something to us like **"Who would have thought . . .":**

"I've been in the PR business for years, but there aren't any jobs open to me. All they want is freelancers. So here I am standing in the unemployment line. At this point, I'll take any job I can find."

"Not all inventions are wrought by necessity. Sometimes serendipity plays a part. The trick is recognition. All the elements were there, but chance alone had put them together in just the right way. And chance was the essential ingredient."

Jean Auel, author

I Just Fell Into It. "One day this person came up to me where I was working and asked me if I knew anyone who could organize the kind of event he needed. It wasn't what my employer did, but I realized I could do it. So I told him I could help him. Having my own business all grew from that one conversation."

People Started Asking. "People were asking if I'd help them out, so I started doing it on the side. Next thing I knew, I was making more money in my sideline business than I was on my job. So finally I just quit my job."

I Ran into This Guy. "He asked me if I wanted to be part of this project he was bidding on. I said, 'Sure.' That's how it all started."

The Idea Started to Grow on Me. "This woman told me, 'You sure are good at this. You ought to do this for a living.' I'd never thought about it before. But the more I thought about it, I decided to do it!"

It All Began as a Distraction. "At first I started writing the novel to keep myself from getting depressed about all the résumés I was sending out that weren't leading anywhere. Then I started to think maybe I could get it published and I developed a plan. But I never guessed it would become an immediate best-seller!"

This Idea Hit Me. "I was reading in the paper about what someone else was doing and I thought, 'I could do that!' And immediately I saw just what I was going to do."

I Happened to Notice. "By coincidence I noticed this machine my brother bought was just sitting around gathering dust. So I asked him if I could use it to get some work. He wasn't doing anything with it, so he said, 'Why not?' "

I Ran into Her by Accident. "I hadn't seen her for years. We started talking. Her ideas and my background were a perfect match. We looked at each other and said, 'Let's *do* it.' "

Actually, I Had This Dream. In my dream a man told me about a hair product I could use for my hair. It came from Africa, but I tracked it down and it worked for me. Then people started asking me how they could get it. And next thing you know, I had a new career."

Actually it's not unusual that so many people are experiencing unexpected and serendipitous events like these. Chances are

Some people think being able to create your own career occurs by magic; others say it comes from sophisticated planning. The truth is that many, perhaps most of such careers, arise from everyday occurrences, events large and small that people use to re-shape their lives.

they're taking place around you as well. Specific economic forces are creating a wealth of such opportunities, and as you become aware of these forces and what they can mean for your life, you won't have to wait for some crisis or change to intervene. You'll begin seeing a variety of possibilities for pursuing your dreams in ways you may never have considered before.

FOUR FORCES CHANGING
THE NATURE OF WORK

It's no accident so many people are finding that the best route for them to keep their dreams alive is to forgo the idea of having a reg-ular job in favor of working on their own. In fact, four specific changes are creating an increasing demand for people who are willing to lead a more independent lifestyle. These include de-mocratizing technologies, increasing reliance on corporate out-sourcing, expanding small-business services, and growing niche consumer markets. Let's look at them each in terms of the kind of opportunities they're creating:

1. DEMOCRATIZING TECHNOLOGIES

New office technology is dramatically changing the way we live and work. On the one hand, technology is taking away jobs by en-abling companies to downsize, restructure, and reengineer. With today's computer and telecommunications equipment, more work can be done electronically, and so companies need fewer full-time employees. We're served these days by automated tellers, voice mail, fax-on-demand, and electronic kiosks. Whole floors of fac-tories operate in the dark, housing only robots, no people. Re-motely operated TV cameras move silently around television studios without a cameraperson in sight.

On the other hand, new technology is also putting powerful tools once available only to large organizations into the hands of individuals who are using them to start home-based and other small businesses. Only a few years ago, the equivalent of the com-puters sitting on our own desks would have required a whole room and a staff of personnel to operate. The copy machine sitting nearby would have been the size of a walk-in closet. The brochure we can produce using our computer, software, and printer would have required a professional design staff and outside print shop to create. The voice-mail answering machine sitting on our bookcase is no bigger than a book but does what we would once have needed a secretary to do, and when it takes a call, the callers don't know if they've reached a large company in a chrome-and-glass high-rise or a part-time one-person firm operating in the corner of an unfinished basement.

Today with computer and telecommunications technology, we can work virtually from anywhere—in cities or suburbs, small towns or farmland, mountaintops or seaside, onshore or offshore. Our homes, cars, vans, boats, and small offices can house the capability of a Fortune 500 company. For under $4,000 we can have a telephone, computer, printer, fax, modem, and copy machine of professional quality that can all fit easily on a desk or inside a closet!

Indeed, just as some two hundred years ago democracy put political power that had once been reserved for royalty into the hands of the individual, so today's technological revolution puts economic power once reserved for corporate America right into the homes and offices of individual men and women. Today, because of technology, it's often more cost-effective and thereby preferable for big business to do business with individuals and small businesses than to hire employees. And technology is also creating many types of work people can do on their own that didn't even exist before.

Nearly 50 percent of the best home businesses
we researched for the 90s
didn't exist twenty-five years ago.

Finally technology is enabling people in even the most low-tech of endeavors to work cost-effectively on their own successfully and professionally. The artist can now send regular monthly flyers to everyone who came by his booth at an art fair. The family day-care center can send out timely professional invoices. The building contractor can schedule and track cash flow with ease. Essentially, computerized electronic technology is setting us free and providing us with tools to discover the perfect work to pursue our dreams.

2. OUTSOURCING

As companies downsize and rightsize, we've seen millions of layoffs; not a week goes by when some new restructuring isn't announced in the paper. But as distressing as these announcements are, for those who want more autonomy, more flexibility, and more opportunity to set up their lives on their own terms, these announcements can have silver linings. Every layoff means more work will be contracted out to individuals and small businesses. Many companies are actually laying off entire departments whose functions need to be contracted out to independent individuals or small companies. Notice how by *crisis, choice,* or *chance,* people are creating new and better work for themselves as a result of these changes.

For example, trainer Rita Guy lost her job when the computer store chain she worked for in Chicago was bought out by another firm. The new owner had decided to close the entire computer-training department. While for others this might have been a ***crisis,*** Rita wasn't devastated; she was elated. Instead of a career setback, she saw opportunity. The chain was still selling hundreds of computers, and their customers still needed training. So who would do it? Why not her? She talked to the company about her plan. They were pleased. After all, by sending clients who needed training to Rita, they could avoid customer complaints about not offering training and there would be no cost to them. Not only did Rita stay busy working for herself, she also contracted work out to others who had been working in her department, thereby increasing her income beyond what she could bill for her time alone and providing independent work for others in the process.

Instructional designer Mike Greer knew that the company he worked for was billing his work out to clients at nine times his hourly rate. During a typical day on the job, he could only get in about five hours of actual work because the rest of the day was spent attending meetings and dealing with office poli-

> "I'm more worried about my job every day. It used to be if you worked for several years and kept your nose clean, you could be confident you'd have a job for the rest of your life. Now you can lose your job anytime."

tics. He was convinced that by working five hours a day on his own, he could bill his clients considerably less and still triple his income. So in 1981, that's the *choice* he made. Now the entire instructional design industry is essentially composed of independent individuals like Mike who can meet the needs of large organizations more cost-effectively while still earning excellent incomes.

After having been courted into moving his family to Boston to take a management and marketing position with a semiconductor company, Henry Davis was laid off. But inspired by his wife, who had been her own boss for many years, when faced with this *crisis* Davis decided to use his contacts and knowledge to work with other large high-tech companies offering the same services he had been providing for his employer.

Senior editor Rick Benzel lost his job when the publisher he worked for was acquired by a larger firm. His layoff was also unexpected. Everyone had been assured the new owner intended to keep everything just as it had been. A month later, many of the employees were let go. With a new baby and a mortgage on a new house to provide for, Benzel turned what could have become a *crisis* into an opportunity. He now works for the same publisher as an independent contractor, but he has other publishers as clients too. And he has greater flexibility to take on writing projects of his own. He's written two books, and a third is on its way. By working from home Benzel can also squeeze in extra time with his daughters when they come home from school.

Twenty-six-year-old Mark Hankins had risen from a job in quality assurance at JCPenney to become one of the company's well-paid designers with his own clothing line. By *chance* while riding a train in upstate New York, Hankins was reading an article about how Connie Chung had turned her career around by deciding to take control and do her own thing. Hankins got off the train at the next stop to call JCPenney and quit his job. Two weeks later he'd started his own company and signed a licensing agreement with Penney that will bring a million dollars into his new venture in the first year. He has other projects under way, too, including a contract with Vogue Butterick patterns.

Rebecca Baldwin was an economist for the state of Alaska Department of Agriculture when proposed cutbacks in federal funding began threatening her job security. The mother of a two-year-old, she felt she could be more effective by operating outside the governmental system, so her *choice* was to leave the job to create her own company, EEA, Economic Environment Analyst. She now operates as a resource analyst serving clients like trade associations, state agencies, and fisheries. Her work includes such projects as writing proposals outlining the positive and negative effects of proposed legislative changes on the environment and commerce.

Hillary Morolla had been a secretary for fifteen years when she left her job to have a baby. To bring in some extra income, she posted a flyer on a local college bulletin board offering her services to type papers for students. By *chance,* someone from the Michigan Association for the Education of Young Children saw the flyer and called to ask if she would help them with registrations for an upcoming conference. That was the beginning of what has become a continuing source of income providing conference and convention registration services to her clients.

Over 40 percent of the best home businesses we researched for the 90s provide services that corporations now outsource.

PROFILE: PAMELA YARDIS: CRISIS TO TRIUMPH

Confined to her bed after a back injury sustained while delivering her seventh child, Pamela Yardis watched her husband leave on a business trip and never return. "I just wasn't happy," he said in a note he sent later. In the next month, two of her children were hospitalized, her car was repossessed, and a foreclosure notice arrived from the bank. Rather than giving up, Yardis used this *crisis* as an opportunity to do something she had only dreamed of doing. She enrolled at Columbia University, gave students free lodging in exchange for baby-sitting, and several years later graduated with two master's degrees.

After graduating, Yardis took a job and within three years rose from a computer sales rep to a company vice president. But soon after her promotion to VP, an accident involving a drunk driver landed her in bed again. Lying flat on her back, unable to continue with her job, she decided to create her own consulting firm. Her company, a home-based business, specializes in designing and implementing information environments for Fortune 500 clients like IBM, Clorox, and Bristol-Myers. It's now a $900,000-a-year business. In 1993, Yardis was named an Avon Women of Enterprise winner.

So these success stories are not unusual. Large companies are not only increasingly willing to outsource to independent individuals, in many cases that's the only way they're willing to do business. Often they also need new services that require talents and expertise that haven't been part of the corporate environment before. Actress Dorene Ludwig, for example, is teaching corporate employees how to avoid sexual harassment. Samantha Greenberg teaches corporations how to protect personnel who use computers for many hours a day from developing repetitive stress syndrome, a condition she herself developed and recovered from. Jim Hullihan creates multimedia promotional presentations directed at high-school students for clients like Pepsi and Nike through his company, Motivational Media Assemblies. Magician Bill Herz teaches magic tricks to corporate executives to help them improve their sales and management skills. Roger von Oech teaches corporate creativity skills. And through his company DocuVision, Robert Acosta produces public-service documentaries for corporate clients like MAIL BOXES ETC. and CIGNA Insurance.

Outsourcing for an array of services is becoming so prevalent that even the top corporate executive in a company may not be an employee. Robert Glendon, for example, is a freelance CEO! Also called a turnaround specialist, he takes on one ailing client company after another, nurses their financial operations back to health, and then moves on.

3. SMALL-BUSINESS SERVICES

While we think of big corporations as forming the backbone of the American economy, in fact, small business has been, is, and will continue to be the foundation of our economy. Even in 1971, Fortune 500 companies employed only 20 percent of the population.

By 1991, though, that number had dropped to 11 percent. Of the 24 million business enterprises in the U.S. only 7,000 have more than 500 employees. All the rest are small businesses with three out of five of them having fewer than 5 employees. And while the number of large businesses is shrinking, the number of small businesses is growing. Since 1980, the number of businesses with under 100 employees has grown twice as fast as companies with over 1,000 employees. In fact, a new home business opens every forty-six seconds. Virtually all small businesses need and use a variety of outside services.

Small-Business Services in Demand

Advertising
Bookkeeping
Copywriting
Business networks
Business plan writing
Computer repair
Computer consulting
Desktop publishing
Desktop video
Information broker
Janitorial services
Mailing list services
Manufacturers' agents
Mediation
Medical billing
Medical transcription
Mystery shopping
Professional organizer
Proposal and grant writing
Public relations
Technical writing
Security consulting
Word processing

Almost half of the best home businesses we've researched for the 90s primarily serve other small businesses.

Here's a sample of how by crisis, choice, or chance people are creating their perfect work by providing services primarily to small businesses:

Deborah Martin and her husband, Tom, run a million-dollar-a-year enterprise from the home they had custom-built in Belleville, Illinois. The business, an advertising specialty service, Custom Towel, began as a matter of survival when Deborah lost her job. In response to this *crisis,* Martin started contacting people she'd known from her job. In the first year, they shipped more than $300,000 worth of custom-imprinted towels. Instead of cramming their home with inventory or moving the business into a warehouse, their solution was to contract their printing out to a silk-screen shop. Thus two small businesses are supported in this way.

Tom Chapman refurbishes homes, town houses, and condos abandoned by their owners for banks and savings-and-loan companies. He got into this business by *chance.* Sensing that the company he worked for was going out of business, he started looking around for what he could do. He thought about real estate but didn't care much for the work. Then he noticed that lenders were rehabilitating property just to recover their losses, and he had an idea. He could rehab the properties for the lenders and make a profit. Since he typically works on two to three dozen properties at once, Chapman subcontracts with 250 other individuals to clean out, refurbish, and repair these properties, thus providing jobs for many other independent workers.

Thom Hartmann was publishing a newsletter for a nonprofit agency he'd founded to help care for abused children. The newsletter was the agency's principal source of income, so when Hartmann had to leave the country to do business abroad, he was shocked to discover that ad agencies would charge from $5,000 to $10,000 an issue to put out the publication in his absence. This looked like a real business opportunity to him, so upon returning from Europe, Hartmann made the *choice* to start the Newsletter Factory, which produces high-quality newsletters at affordable prices. He uses the services of six to eight freelance writers and designers to custom-design newsletters primarily for other small businesses. So Hartmann both serves and hires other small businesses.

DEGREES OF INDEPENDENT WORK

The lines between the employed and the self-employed are blurring as companies both large and small use contingent workers and adopt new payment and hiring policies like:

Temporary employees. Paying an outside agency to provide workers when needed.

Outsourcing. Using outside services of independent contractors or other businesses.

Independent contractors. Hiring outside independent individuals to carry out or complete a particular project.

Gainsharing. Calculating employee pay based on worker contribution and cost.

Commission. Paying staff a percentage of what they've sold or saved.

Charlotte Mitchell was working as a legal secretary in San Diego when an attorney asked her to place an ad in the yellow pages and line up several notaries who would serve the new clients the ad would generate. And, indeed, the ad did generate customers, but the notaries didn't come through, so the attorney turned over the work to Mitchell. This *chance* occurrence led her to start a mobile notary service, Notary on Wheels. She started part-time, doing freelance secretarial work for the first few years until she had built the notary service into a full-time income serving professionals and small businesses.

Again, the needs of small businesses are also creating opportunities for talents previously not used by businesses. Cartoonist Stu Heinecke of Seattle, for example, has created a humorous line of personalized marketing materials small businesses can use as direct-mail pieces. J. Victor Bodney literally puts his small-business customers on the map. He creates brightly colored poster maps of commercial areas that feature his clients' locations. Rita Tateel locates celebrities for nonprofit charity events. And David Kalb uses the background he gained working in government before spending cutbacks eliminated his job to provide a "red tape" service, which helps small businesses navigate the maze of governmental regulations they face.

Specialized Cleaning Services

Air duct cleaning

Auto detailing

Carpet cleaning

Ceiling cleaning

Chimney cleaning

Floor cleaning and refinishing

Furniture cleaning

Mobile power wash

Pool cleaning

Recreational vehicle cleaning

Tile cleaning

Van, boat, or plane cleaning

Window cleaning

Window blind cleaning

4. NICHE CONSUMER MARKETS

One result of the dramatic changes taking place in the way we live and work today is that people have less time for the chores of living. Almost a third of Americans say they always feel rushed for time, and 58 percent say they almost never have spare time on their hands. Rushed two-career couples and single parents don't have time to clean house, run errands, take care of pets, do their gardening, plan their weddings, or take their kids to after-school activities. But one way or another, all these things need to get done. The lack of time for cleaning alone has spawned a need for over a dozen types of specialized cleaning services.

Handyman Chas Eisner has found a unique niche consumer market. His clients are single women and widows who don't have a husband, brother, uncle, or neighbor who can do the usual repairs that need to be done around the house. Eisner not only does their repairs, he's also created a workshop called the "No Husband-Father-Brother Needed Women's Repair Workshop" in which he teaches women how to handle home-repair tasks themselves.

In response to frequent complaints from time-stressed parents, Victoria Digby has created a service called Kiddie Kab in Orange County, California. She transports kids to and from after-school events like soccer games, ballet classes, Little League, and so forth.

Maudi Evans's friends were always asking her to do them a favor by running this errand or that. So with only $20, she started an errand service, Mysti's Executive Shopping Service, in Detroit. Popular requests are to run by a client's office with an emergency pair of panty hose or, on rainy days, to deliver a spare pair of windshield wipers.

When José Vila retired as a software officer from the U.S. Air Force, he made an interesting *choice.* Instead of retiring, he started a gourmet Chinese catering service in Honolulu. About 80 percent of his business is cooking for private house parties. He prepares all the food in his customers' homes. His wife, Happy Chan, is the cook.

Being so pressed and stressed for time, people also need a little pampering, a few small indulgences to reward ourselves and a lot of personal care and attention to make ourselves *feel* better and become more successful. Here are a few of the services people want to treat themselves to that are creating opportunities for those others to find their perfect work:

- Faith Feldman of Pacific Palisades, California, is an image consultant and personal shopper. To help her clients look their best, she will either go with them to pick out their dress-for-success look or will bring wardrobe selections to their home or office.
- John and Dayna Cravens of Fitzhugh, Oklahoma, create Western Christmas cards and decorations.
- Sheryl Martel, R.N., creates healthy gift baskets. Her company is called Healthy Helpings.
- Tim Harden of Ponca City, Oklahoma, offers Farm Hayrides.
- Jonathan Goldman creates healing stress-reduction and meditation tapes. His company is Spirit Music of Boulder, Colorado.

Life Management Consumer Niches

Bill-paying service
Caterer
Cleaning service
Errand service
Family child-care provider
Gift baskets business
Hauling service
Disc jockey service
In-home health care
Interior designer
Medical claims assistance
Pet-sitting service
Personal shopper
Plant care giver
Private investigator
Repair service
Reunion planner
Wedding consultant
Wedding makeup artist

- Julius Galer of Atlanta takes people on fishing and hunting trips throughout the South.
- In Denver, James Martin is a color consultant who helps families restore Victorian homes with historical accuracy.
- Jack Canfield has created and teaches self-esteem classes.
- Nancy Bonus helps people who love to eat and hate to exercise lose weight effectively.
- Although people snickered when Tim Edison told them about what he wanted to do, he and his wife, Wendy, are busy full-time stimulating many a palate with their Mo Hotta Mo Betta mail-order catalog of spicy foods.
- Susan Pinsky and David Starkman delight the child within many a grown-up with their catalog of paraphernalia for 3-D photography. It's called Reel 3-D.

Better than a third of the home businesses
we researched for the 90s
serve special consumer niches like these.

These and the other people you'll meet in this book are like a thousand points of light showing us a new route to a better life. While once the road to the American Dream was to buy some land to farm or to open one's own retail shop, for three generations the road for most people has been to get a good job and climb the organizational ladder. Of course these routes are still possible and will continue to be the best route for some, but the four economic forces we've just described are changing the nature of work in fundamental ways that require us to adopt an entirely new way of thinking about how we'll make a living. In fact, these changes are causing a shift toward self-employment that is making it possible to find not only work, but our perfect work—that is, work that allows us to live as we want to, where we want to, doing what we want to do.

A NEW ECONOMIC IMPERATIVE

For generations, getting a regular paycheck has been the route to financial security. Supporting yourself and your family usually meant you spent most of your waking hours working for someone else. In fact, most people's lives have been organized and structured entirely around their eight-hour-a-day jobs. This lifestyle has provided a sense of security and certainty that made it attractive, desirable, and comfortable. But it offers virtually no flexibility in terms of when to work, where to work, or the pace of work. Any dreams beyond those you could pursue on your job had to be squeezed into after-work hours and weekends or delayed until retirement. In fact, an entire generation of individuals has spent a lifetime counting the days until retirement, when at last they could fill their days with what *they* wanted to do. But by the time retirement rolls around, of course, most people have long ago given up the grand dreams of their youth.

But pursuing anything other than a nine-to-five-job-to-retirement lifestyle was a risky proposition for most people and was highly discouraged by parents, teachers, and guidance counselors. There simply were too few opportunities to pursue the "folly" of a nontraditional path. Starting a business, for example, was a costly, risky, totally consuming and draining experience that required access to resources, both financial and personal, that most people simply did not possess. The two of us saw this firsthand. Paul's father had a succession of failed businesses. Sarah's dad had his own business, but he rarely made it home for dinner. And when he did get home, he was tired and grouchy; he sighed a lot and had a lot to complain about. That route didn't look at all appealing to either of us or our siblings.

Certainly taking the route of the "starving artist" was equally risky and perceived as socially undesirable—unless, by some rare chance, you happened to become famous doing it, at which point, of course, you were no longer starving and became one of the heralded elite. Generally, however, deciding to seriously pursue one's creative interests was certain to arouse the consternation of relatives and loved ones.

The prevailing advice for generations was to "settle down and get a good, steady job." This advice was not some concoction of cruel and uncaring adults. It was the economic imperative of the time. Income statistics proved it right year after year. For many generations, taking the unconventional path to pursue a lifestyle of

When the Industrial Revolution began, there were many people who feared that ordinary men and women would never be able to adjust to holding down a job. Sunday school classes were established to help adults learn the disciplined habits required of the new on-the-job work ethic.

"Chasing a stupid dream causes you and everyone around you heartache."

The father in the movie Rudy

"My mother always said I could play my music for fun just so long as I went to secretarial school."

"I know I was always a disappointment to my parents because they didn't want their son to be a hairstylist."

THE SHIFTING NATURE OF WORK

As you move from working for someone else to working for yourself, the very nature of work changes. Where you work, when you work, how you work, what you do, and whom you do it for all become more flexible and malleable to your own design and intention.

WORK FOR OTHERS	WORK FOR YOURSELF
Work is done by the clock	Work is done by the calendar
Hours are fixed	Hours are flexible
Schedule is fixed	Schedule is organic to tasks
Workload is constant	Workload varies by demands of tasks
Work locations are prescribed	Work locations are optional
Work tasks are specific	Work tasks are varied
Role is defined by job description	Role is defined by demands of tasks
Home and work are separate	Home and work can be integrated
Work habits are methodical	Work habits are flexible
Work demeanor is reserved	Work demeanor is expressive
Predictability is preferred	Spontaneity is preferred
Postpone freedom until retirement	Enjoy freedom now

"My father told me that if I wanted to be a potter I'd have to marry an accountant. So that's what I did. But I was never truly happy in my marriage until I met a fellow potter. I divorced, and now I can be happy in both my love and my work."

working on your own was simply not a viable route for most people to achieve the American Dream.

But all this has changed. It's time to update prevailing thought. Although many people don't realize it yet, the four forces we've described have created a new economic imperative in which the best route to the American Dream is no longer assuredly to get a good, steady job. Jobs are no longer good or steady. Often they're mundane or temporary or exhausting. Instead, you must rely on yourself, to create a good, steady job on your own. The job you create for yourself won't have the built-in security once provided by the traditional job, because there's no guaranteed salary or payday. But traditional jobs don't offer that security anymore, either. And on your own, every day can be payday.

Furthermore, because in the new economic imperative you must generate your own income, instead of having to fit your entire life around a job, you get to create a job that fits around your life. And instead of forgoing your personal interests and creativity until after working hours or retirement, in the new economic imperative, you *must* draw directly on your interests and creativity every day to define and succeed in your work.

Today you may have more promising opportunities to work for yourself than to find a good, well-paying job. You may have to do what you most want to do. That's the new economic imperative.

While good jobs are increasingly scarce and salaries are down, self-employment opportunities like those you've been reading about in this chapter are on the rise. In the "Alphabetical Directory of Self-Employment Careers" in Appendix II alone, you'll find over 1,600 ways people can and are working independently. And as you look through that appendix you'll notice that nearly 15 percent of them are in some kind of creative field that would have been difficult for all but the elite few to earn a decent living from in the past. And this list doesn't even include the best self-employment opportunities of all, those in which people do something so uniquely tailored to their own personal experiences, interests, and desires that no generic name has yet been given to the work they get paid to do. We call these "hybrid" careers, and in the chapters that follow you'll read about many of them and how people go about creating them.

You'll meet hundreds of people who have taken a wide variety of what would once have been considered highly unconventional and risky routes to their dreams with surprising ease. You'll discover that not only are these routes less risky than before, sometimes now they're less risky than the more conventional routes. Many people can find good sources of income on their own in less time than it would take them to aggressively pursue finding another job opportunity.

One proof of this was evident from the results of two pilot studies conducted in Massachusetts and Washington. These states offered residents who had lost their jobs the chance to use unemployment funds to pursue self-employment. The surprising result was that those who became self-employed got off unem-

"I always wondered what would have happened if I'd tried to pursue my writing. Could I have done it? I hate the thought of dying without ever knowing."

"Actually I like my work, but on this job I don't get to do much of it because I'm always in meetings or other hassles about how, if, when, or who will do what. And on top of that, it takes nearly an hour each way to get there and back and I've got to be there from eight to five whether there's anything to do or not."

"Now that I'm on my own, I really don't know how many hours a week I work. I know what I have to do and I do it. So I don't keep track of hours. I just do my work."

"When you are doing something meaningful, your capacity to replenish yourself is high."

Doug Kruscke,
management
consultant

ployment more quickly than those who continued searching for a traditional job!

PROFILE: RICHARD NEMEC, ENGINEER

"For the first time in twenty-seven years I have no employer, no office to which to go. The irony is that I am finally doing exactly what I have longed to do all my life. At the age of fifty-one, I am independent and self-employed. But I came to this experience as the result of a macroeconomic phenomenon over which I have absolutely no control. . . . The future is unclear, but I know one thing: What happens will depend entirely on me—no corporate hierarchy or fickle executive."

PROFILE: LESLIE GARDNER, TWENTY-EIGHT, CREATING YOUR OWN OPPORTUNITY

From the time she was six years old, Leslie was drawing clothing on the characters in all her books and comic books. After high school, she enrolled in the Fashion Institute of Technology in New York with the intention of becoming a fashion designer on Seventh Avenue. She soon realized, "That world was too nine-to-five for me. To compete in that world, you'd have to give up your time, your freedom, everything." So, during her last semester at the institute, Gardner had a brainstorm. She decided she'd work on her own, designing costumes for rock bands. At nineteen, she set up shop in her parents' basement, made up business cards, and resolved to become known in the field. She began by writing articles for local rock-and-roll magazines about rock fashion, including a rock fashion column on what's in and what's out.

When she moved to L.A., Gardner needed to refocus. There were no jobs in the fashion industry, but she saw someone dressing a model on the set of a rock video and realized there was a profession called wardrobe stylist. It looked perfect for her. But she had no idea how to break into the field. Instead of letting that stop her, she set out to find some way in. "It's not who you know," she told us. "It's finding the little cracks and crevices where you can get in." And she adds, "You have to remember, you're not calling God. If you don't sound desperate, people will talk to you." Her parents, whom she describes as very nine-to-five people, still can't believe her success. For many years they didn't think she had a "real" job, but after

Leslie Gardner,
wardrobe stylist

seeing her name roll by on an MTV credit they've decided her career is for real!

Be it through demands from outsourcing, small business, or special consumer niches, the number of people leaving the conventional path to seek their dream by **choice**, by **chance,** or by **crisis** is becoming the norm instead of the exception. It certainly has been the norm for twenty-eight-year-old wardrobe stylist Leslie Gardner. She has never had a job and doesn't see the need for one. "I always have work," she told us, "but I'm the boss."

For many people, this is the New American Dream. In this dream, to paraphrase English essayist J. B. Priestly, you no longer work for machines and money, but money and machines work for you. You work for **your** dreams, not for someone else's; and the work you do becomes part of the life you enjoy now, not someday. You no longer have to exchange freedom and flexibility for economic survival and security. Instead you have the freedom and flexibility to create your own security and thereby ultimately achieve greater security than you'd have today on a job. And the moment you decide to pursue this route to your dreams, your attitudes toward work and making a living shift forever. You can replace the saying "After work, there's life" with "Through work, there's life."

When people talk about working for themselves, they often use the same kind of words others use to describe especially enjoyable leisure activities. Here's what researcher Barrie Jaeger, author of *The Meaning of Work among the Self-Employed,* said people told her about their attitude toward their work:

> *It's a lot of fun.*
> *It's a way to find out how big a person I am.*
> *It's a way to see what I'm made of.*
> *It's a way for me to serve other people.*
> *It's my connection to the world.*
> *It's fulfilling.*
> *There're not enough hours in the day to have that much of a good time.*
> *It involves my soul so much.*
> *It's exhilarating.*

Just as in the past when many people could not believe that the ordinary person would ever be able to hold down a job, many people today don't believe that the ordinary person will ever be able to support himself or herself without a job. But we know they can. We've seen ample evidence that those who see the chances, make the choices, and utilize the changes facing us today can not only do it, they can relish it.

"Some of the most enjoyable moments are just out in the woods by myself marking timber and measuring the trees or just walking through the timber and getting a feel for it."

Furniture designer,
The Meaning of
Work Among the
Self-Employed

SHIFTING ATTITUDES TOWARD WORK

As people begin working for themselves, their attitudes about what constitutes work shift. There's no longer a chasm separating your "work life" and your life. You literally get a life. Instead of feeling as though your days are mortgaged to an employer, every morning you're the proud owner of your day. It becomes your responsibility to create that day as you wish, along with the means to support it.

WORK FOR OTHERS	WORK FOR YOURSELF
After work there is life	In work there is life
Work is what you do	Work is part of who you are
Work is often an unpleasant means to an end	Work itself is enjoyable and satisfying and gives your life meaning
Work is separate from your personal life	Work is integral to your personal life
What you do is assigned based on what the boss wants or company politics dictate	What you do is an expression of yourself and what your clients need
Financial gain is fixed	Financial gain depends on personal results
Freedom comes later	Freedom is now
Security is dependent on other's decisions	Security is dependent on your own initiative
Success is based on conformity and control	Success is based on creativity and adaptability
You work at the beck and call of others	Your work is self-directed
Work defines the parameters of the rest of life	Work is in perspective to the rest of life
Others control the work environment	You control the work environment
Self-expression is sacrificed for economic security	Economic security comes from self-expression
Leisure comes after work	Work can resemble leisure

It's really a great feeling.
There's a lot of personal satisfaction.
It doesn't feel like work; it seems more like fun.

"To become bigger,
we must become
smaller."

LaoTzu

OVERCOMING THE FIRST CHALLENGE

As great as the opportunities of the new economic imperative may sound, for most people heading into an unfamiliar future, no matter how promising, gives rise to many concerns. If you still have a salary, it's natural to feel hesitant about letting go of the security it provides. It's natural to resist even the prospect of doing that. You may never have had to be overly concerned with survival and security needs, so charting a more independent path can shake the very foundation of your existence. Not only are you losing a ready source of income, you also may worry about missing the familiar faces of co-workers and losing whatever prestige and self-esteem your job provided through ego-gratifying organizational titles and job descriptions.

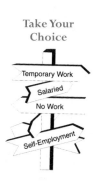

Take Your
Choice

Career paths heading
to a new century

Also any time you make a dramatic change in your life, it can feel at first like going backward instead of forward, like having to give up too much to risk what you might gain. (That's probably why so many people don't make a change until they must!) This is particularly true when the kind of work we're discussing would have been considered to be a pipe dream for most people not so long ago. In fact, others in your life who haven't realized the implications of the economic forces at work right now may still consider such things to be impractical. So believing you really can find your perfect work and achieve the life you want on your own is usually the first challenge. After all, who would have thought the following dreams could be practical?

- Rusty Berkus wants to spend her life writing poetry that heals the pain of loss and alienation and restores a sense of magic to people's lives.
- Bob Dumouchel wants to live a quiet, peaceful life in the Bahamas with his wife.
- George Hoeing wants to have his artwork seen by millions without having to starve for years in order to do it.

- Marilyn Miller wants to avoid the stress-related illness that caused her to leave a university position yet continue to pursue a successful and stimulating career.
- Anita Raatz wants her work and her daily life to reflect her spiritual beliefs.
- Jack and Elaine Wyman want to get back into the game after retiring but still have plenty of time and money to enjoy themselves.
- Jerry Jampolski wants to devote his life to helping children with terminal illnesses live the remaining days of their lives as fully as possible.
- Ralph Foreman wants to retain not only his income, which was considerable, but his self-esteem after suddenly losing a management job of twenty years.
- Jim Crotty wants to travel the world and discover some new adventure every day.
- Warren Faidley wants to spend his life photographing tornadoes, hurricanes, and other storms.
- Aaron Chang wants to spend his days surfing.

Pipe dreams? Not anymore. These individuals probably would never have found a job doing what they wanted to do, but by declaring their independence they have turned these dreams into their perfect work and have each created a livelihood that makes such dreams financially viable.

In today's economy, what would have been pipe dreams in the past are now practical realities.

"Of course I had doubts that we could do it. But I never let them enter my conscious mind. You have to throw the doubts out of your mind."

Explorer

To willingly forego whatever security and confidence you've attained from the way things have been, and set out to pursue your own such dreams, you too must believe that the dreams you're seeking are no longer pipe dreams. You must believe that times have indeed changed and that not only can others achieve such dreams, but you can as well. Demonstrating this in concrete terms is one purpose of this book. So far, having read about the changes that are taking place, what do you think? What do you believe?

DO YOU BELIEVE?

The purpose of this chapter has been to demonstrate that times have indeed changed—and changed in your favor. It's actually possible today to have the greater freedom and control you've dreamed of, the kind of work you've wanted to do, and the kind of life you've wanted to live. But you must create it from the opportunities these times present. That means you must believe it's possible. Do you? Which statement do you believe best describes today's economic reality?

___ *No change.* Things are pretty much as they've always been, and we just need to keep doing what we've always done.

___ *Temporary change.* Things will get back to the way they've always been pretty soon. We just have to wait it out.

___ *Permanent change for the worse.* Things won't go back to the way they've been, but there's nothing we can do about it. We'll just have to adjust to having less.

___ *Permanent change that will benefit some.* Things won't go back to the way they've been, and some people will be able to adjust and still have a good life, but not me. I'm losing out in this change.

___ *Permanent change with potential benefits to most people.* Things will never be the way they were, but there are many opportunities for an even better life and I can seize them.

It is our wish that with each page of this book, you will become ever more strongly convinced that the truth lies in this final statement.

We believe that once you glimpse what's truly possible by reading through the pages that follow, you will find your perfect work, as did the people we've described, and realize you have a far better chance for putting the pieces of your life together to achieve your dreams than you may ever have imagined. Of course, there will be a lot of work involved in creating dreams from today's possibilities—hard work. And it won't always be fun at the time you're doing it. In fact, some people say that going out on your own and creating your own work is too hard, and not everyone may make it. That's possible. It can be hard. But it's been hard before in other times. That's nothing new. And it's certainly not that easy these days to get and keep a good job. The point we're making is not that a new life of your own making will be a snap,

"I don't have any land to toil. They took all my land.... [So] my crops have to grow elsewhere. If I'm lucky enough to do this, then I have created an economic base by using my mind."

John Trudell,
Santee Sioux artist

"The more people who own little businesses of their own, the safer our country will be, and the better off its cities and towns, for the people who have a stake in their country and their community are its best citizens."

John Hancock

but that you can have a truly promising future to believe in and work toward. The point is there's still hope, not just for others, but for you—hope that through your own efforts you can not just hold on to the past but create something better than the past, something better than ever before.

Our challenge today is not to learn to live with less than our dreams but to dream more fully, because for the first time in history, if you define what you truly want and work consistently for it, the odds have shifted in favor of your getting it.

RESOURCES

Age of Unreason. Charles Handy. Boston: Harvard University Press, 1989.

Career Shifting. William A. Charland. Holbrook, Mass.: Bob Adams, Inc., 1993.

Coming Back, Rebuilding Lives after Crisis and Loss. Ann Kaiser. New York: Random House, 1988.

Incredible Coincidences, The Baffling World of Synchronicity. Alan Vaughan. New York: B. Lippincott, 1979.

Job Shift: How to Prosper in a Workplace without Jobs. William Bridges. Reading, Mass.: Addison-Wesley, 1994.

Take Two, True Stories of Real People Who Dared to Change Their Lives. Jo Brans. New York: Doubleday, 1989.

The Meaning of Work Among the Self-Employed. Barrie Jaeger. School of Human Sciences, Rutgers University Press, 1994.

The Survival Personality. Al Siebert. Portland, Oregon: Practical Psychology Press, 1994.

The Virtual Corporation, Structuring and Revitalizing the Corporation in the 21st Century. William H. Davidow and Michael S. Malone. New York: Harper Business, 1992.

TWO

Answering the Right Question

SO IT'S TRULY POSSIBLE TO CREATE a life of your own, doing work that's a natural expression of who you are and what you want from life. But this means, of course, that you have to decide what it is you want! That should be easy, right? Isn't that what you've always wanted? It should be a snap! But is it?

In some ways you're like trailblazers from other times in history who suddenly had the opportunity to pursue a new and better life, those who sailed off from fifteenth-century Europe to the New World or the early American pioneers who joined wagon trains for the frontier. Like these individuals from the past, you may be experiencing dissatisfaction, restlessness, and frustration with your present circumstances. Like them, something is driving, compelling, or enticing you to change—and you're feeling excited and perhaps a bit apprehensive about seizing a new opportunity for greater freedom and a better future.

In other ways, however, as challenging as those historic journeys were, what you must do to seize today's opportunities is more challenging. Those journeys were collective ones to a

We all grow up someday, so we might as well know what we want.

Mark Morgan Ford

specific destination. People who set out on those journeys may not have known just what to expect when they arrived, but at least they knew where they were going and what they would be doing if they got there. Your journey, on the other hand, is by nature a highly personal and individual one. There is no ship to sail on, no wagon train to join up with, and no one clearly defined destination to head off for. Your opportunities must not only be pursued, they must be conceived. And the possibilities are vast and varied. To pursue your dream today, you have to select a destination that exists at first in your mind only, as no more than an idea or a desire. Then you must find your way to this imagined destination, figure out how you'll get there, and decide what you'll do to support yourself both along the way and once you arrive. In other words, to follow your dream today, you have to create it from seemingly infinite choices and nearly unlimited possibilities.

THREE TRAPS TO AVOID

"I never thought about what I'd do at twenty-five because I never thought I'd live to twenty-five."

An ex–gang member

Most of us have never really taken such an option seriously. When we say we'd like to live life on our own terms, be our own boss, it's almost like saying we want to win the lottery. Of course we want it, but we don't think it will actually happen, so why should we take the time and energy to decide what we *really* want. We probably won't achieve it anyway.

Most of us have led lives that revolved around our jobs or school or family demands, squeezing everything else we want to do into "after working hours and weekends." And even in our free time, we may not get around to doing the things we'd really like to do because either we have to catch up on pressing odds and ends or we're just so worn out that we need a chance to sleep in, goof off, or live it up. Most people these days feel there just isn't enough time for many of the things they'd like to do, sometimes even the most important ones. As a result, when you set out to create a more independent life, you risk making one of three common mistakes many people make in their search for what kind of work to do: instead of finding and enjoying your perfect work,

"I never thought much about how my life would be, because I never thought what I did had much to do with it."

Thirty-three-year-old woman

you could end up stuck in a rut, getting burned by buying into some hot opportunity, or simply drawing a blank when it comes to how to proceed. As a result you could conclude that independence is not for you.

ENDING UP STUCK IN A RUT

If you don't know for sure just what you want to do or what else you could do, you might set out to simply duplicate the life you have now. You might automatically decide to basically do on your own what you've been doing, living in the same place, keeping the same hours, working with the same kind of clients, only to end up wondering why your new life isn't any better. "If it's not going to be any better than this," one woman told us, "why should I go to all this trouble? Why shouldn't I just get another job?" And that's a very good question. If the life you create for yourself is just as stressful, pressure filled, financially tight, dull, or boring as the one you had when you were working for someone else, why go to all the extra trouble of starting a new one?

"If you keep on doing what you've been doing, you'll keep on getting what you've been getting."

GETTING BURNED BY WHAT'S HOT

Or again, not knowing just what you want to do, like many others who are trying to create a life on their own, you might be tempted to look for whatever's hot and do that. One woman told us, "In the seventies I became a marriage and family counselor. That was the 'in' thing. It took me several years to get my license, but when I opened my practice it wasn't that easy to get clients. By then real estate was really hot, though. Friends of mine were making a lot of money doing that, so I decided to get my real estate license. Now the bottom has fallen out of the housing market, so I'm trying a medical billing service. It's supposed to be really good, but it's not very interesting to me and it's getting harder to get business. What do you think about 900 numbers? I hear they're hot." This woman is a classic case of chasing after what's hot. Unfortunately whenever you're chasing something, you end up at the rear and you never get a chance to go where *you* want to go.

DRAWING A BLANK

"I got these big hands. What am I gonna do with 'em?"

Boy Willie,
The Piano Lesson

Or again, not knowing just what to do, like many others, you may simply draw a blank when it comes to thinking out what you could do to create an independent living for yourself. You may not believe there's anything you can do well enough to make a living on your own. Drawing such a blank can stop you in your tracks or it can lead you back into a rut or chasing after what's hot. In fact, drawing a stubborn blank about what you could do can be so frustrating that like many people, you get hyped into buying a multilevel marketing program or a business opportunity of some kind only to discover that your spur-of-the-moment decision isn't really what you're looking for. When the "great" opportunity doesn't "take off," and most opportunities don't "take off" without some considerable effort, the search begins again for another way to make some money.

Actually the people who succeed in programs like those, or any independent venture, usually do so not because they've found something "hot" that "takes off." They succeed because they had some idea of what they were looking for. They knew where they wanted to go. In other words, they had a destination in mind. They knew what they wanted to accomplish and believed they could achieve it. As a result, they started out asking the right question— the one that led to the kind of work they could do successfully to get where they wanted to go.

ANSWERING THE QUESTION
MOST PEOPLE NEVER ASK

So if you're feeling stuck or burned out or uncertain as to how you'll be able to earn a living on your own without having to compromise the things that are most important, you're probably not asking the right questions. To find your perfect work there's really only one question you need to answer, and it's one most people never ask. Unfortunately, most people ask one of three other questions instead:

- What could I do?
- What should I do?
- What's the best thing for me to do?

All three of these questions will take you down the wrong path. Here's why:

Don't Ask What COULD I Do?
You'll Get Lost in a Forest

"What could I do?" is usually the first question people ask when they start considering going out on their own. But when you ask yourself this question, chances are you'll end up lost in a forest of endless possibilities. After all, as you can see from Appendix II, there are over 1,600 possible ways you could work independently; and this list doesn't include the literally thousands of other ways people are supporting themselves doing work that is so new, or so uniquely tailored to their background, experience, and interests that there's no name for it yet. Chances are there are hundreds of things among these possibilities that you *could* do, and still more possibilities that are unique to *you.* So while it may be interesting to consider all the possibilities, and at different times in this book we may invite you to review a number of options from the appendix, asking yourself what you *could* do is often more overwhelming than helpful.

And, of course, whenever *could* comes to mind, the *couldn'ts* rush in closely behind. Chances are you, and others you talk with, can quickly generate a long list of reasons you couldn't do just about any of the things you're considering.

So stop asking what you "could" do and if you find yourself getting hung up in *coulds* and *couldn'ts,* try this Could and Couldn't Shrinker:

> ### COULD AND COULDN'T SHRINKER
> Immediately follow thoughts or commands of overwhelming **Coulds** and limiting **Couldn't**s with the question **DO I WANT TO?** And proceed accordingly in the direction this liberating thought permits. If your answer is "yes," you then explore the option further. But if your answer is "no," or "not really," or "not sure," look elsewhere.

"I'm a multitalented person. There are so many things I could do. How do I choose?"

"I've got too many ideas for how I could proceed. I'm sitting here surrounded by books of ideas."

Don't Ask What SHOULD I Do?
You'll Get Stranded on a Barren Desert

Since there are so many possibilities for working on your own today, the next most common question people ask themselves or
those they consult with is "Well, then, what should I do?" But
chances are, this question will leave you stranded on a desert
where nothing measures up to the expectations you or those
around you have for what you should and shouldn't do based on
what you can measure up to in their eyes. You may even discover
everyone has different views about what you *should* do and that
you do, too. One day it may seem as though you should do one
thing; then the next day it seems as if you should do something
else. And you may never see how you could make what you
should do sufficiently interesting or motivating to actually do it.
If you wish, take a minute to review the things you think you
should do to support yourself and see just how it can leave you
stranded on a desert barren of sufficiently appealing ideas. Do any
thoughts like these sound familiar?

> *"Well, I should use my legal background, but I don't like
> working with lawyers."*
> *"I should make more money than the things I'm considering
> will produce."*
> *"I should make use of my government contacts, but I'm burned
> out on government."*
> *"I should be home most of the day with the baby, but I know
> I'll need to get out to do a lot of marketing for almost anything
> I could do."*
> *"I should get into this multimedia thing, but I don't have the
> money for the equipment."*
> *"My dad [or spouse] thinks I should . . ."*
> *"I've got this college degree I should do something with . . ."*

And then, of course, if your "should list" doesn't leave you entirely barren of appealing possibilities, once you start thinking
about the *should*s, the *shouldn't*s are right around the corner
eliminating another raft of possibilities. There is always some reason you shouldn't do virtually anything you'll ever think of doing.
If you look over Appendix II, you'll see over 1,600 ways you could

*"I lived all my life for
other people.
Now it's my turn to
do what I want."*

*Seventy-six-year-old
woman comedian*

make a living on your own, and undoubtedly as you peruse the list, you can think of a myriad of reasons why you shouldn't do most of them.

So stop searching for what you should do and if you find yourself getting stuck in **should**s and **shouldn't**s, try these Should and Shouldn't Busters.

SHOULD AND SHOULDN'T BUSTERS

When you hear or think the command "You should . . ." immediately ask yourself "According to whom?" What authority issued the "should"? Then ask, "What is actually likely to happen if I don't?" When you hear or think the command "You shouldn't . . ." again, immediately ask yourself "According to whom?" Followed by "What is actually likely to happen if I do?" And proceed accordingly.

DON'T ASK, WHAT'S THE BEST THING FOR ME TO DO? YOU'LL END UP IN A QUAGMIRE

"What's the **best** thing to do?" is the next most common question people ask, but it can lead you into a quagmire of seemingly impossible choices. The search for the perfect venture can be as immobilizing as the world of *should*s and *could*s. What might look like the most lucrative choice, for example, might be at odds with what you would most enjoy. Or what you would enjoy most might look too difficult. Here are just a few of the most common quagmires people get stuck in when they try to find the **best** way to support a life on their own. Check off any you may be stuck in.

___ *Fork in the Road.* Feeling that you have to choose between what you want and what you think would be most practical. (i.e., "I'd really like to travel, but bookkeeping would be much more practical.")

___ *Bed of Coals.* Thinking that doing what you really want, following your dream, will only bring poverty, pain, or heartbreak to yourself and those you love. ("I've always dreamed of doing something related to music, but most musicians are poor and miserable.")

"My friends and I are all in our twenties, and we don't have any idea where we're going. We're wandering around in the Desert of What Should I Do with My Life?"

___ *Mount Everest.* Thinking that what you really want to do would be extremely difficult if not impossible. ("I'd love to be a public speaker, but that would take years and then only the most highly gifted speakers succeed.")

___ *Detours.* Thinking you have to do something else before you can do what you really want. ("After I make a lot of money in this multilevel marketing program, then I could open the bed-and-breakfast inn I've always dreamed of.")

As you can see, trying to find what you'll do to have a life of your own by asking these questions will not lead you to the answers you're seeking. They rarely lead to choices you can wholeheartedly pursue, so chances are you won't pursue them. Or if you do, you're likely to do so only halfheartedly or just until the going gets tough. Instead of getting stuck playing these questions over and over in your head, begin your quest by asking the only question you can ever count on to get you where you want to go.

PROFILE: ROY LOPRESTI, PURSUING A CHILDHOOD DREAM

Roy LoPresti left his job as a vice president in the aerospace industry to follow his childhood dream of building airplanes. He'd heard many times "Build airplanes? You couldn't do that." But he did it anyway. Traveling coast to coast, he found the financial backing he needed and LoPresti Engineering took a year's worth of orders for his private plane the Swift Fury in a matter of days after its trade show debut. "If you focus on what you want to do, your chances of success are much, much greater," he says. "I often tell people that if I go to heaven, at best, it will be a lateral transfer."

THE QUESTION TO ASK IS "WHAT DO I REALLY WANT TO DO?"

Only he who keeps his eye on the far horizon shall find his right road.

Dag Hammarskjold

If you want to create a life on your own, stop asking questions like "What can I do?" "What's the best thing for me?" "What's hot right now?" "Would so-and-so be a good opportunity?" Begin instead by asking yourself what you're looking for in life. Where do you want your life to go? What's your destination? And be totally honest. Because within the most honest answer to that question lies the path to your perfect work.

The goal of whatever work you choose to do on your own is to enable you to achieve whatever it is you want from life.

From time to time, people will tell us, "Oh, I tried working on my own, but I didn't like it." When we ask what they didn't like about it, invariably the answers all boil down to the same thing. "I was lonely," "I didn't like the work," "I didn't get enough business," "I had to work too hard," "I didn't make enough money"—all these seemingly different problems actually come down to the same thing: the work these people were doing didn't enable them to live life the way they wanted to. In other words, they hadn't found their perfect work.

When you hire yourself, you not only get to define the kind of work you'll be doing, you also get to define all the working conditions, the salary, the fringe benefits, the locale, the people you'll be working with, and the type of lifestyle your new job will support. You get to call all the shots. So before trying to figure out what to do, figure out what you're doing it for. Decide right here and now what you want from life and what you want your life to be about. Then you can literally build your work around what's most important to you instead of the other way around.

"When you work for yourself instead of for someone else, you have to become a graduate of MSU— Make Stuff Up. All day, every day, all you do is make choices about how you will live your life. That's the fun of it. You get to do it yourself."

Chellie Campbell, bookkeeping and money management service

FOLLOWING THE SIGNPOSTS

For some people, answering the question of what they really want to do comes easily; for others, it's more difficult. Some of us have always known what we want from life. Others of us don't have a clue. Some of us knew once upon a time but have forgotten. Others have never even dared to think about what they'd really want; they just have this inner yearning for something more. If up until now your job, school, or family has pretty much determined the nature and structure of your life, or you're living life the way you

"What I want in life? That's a pretty big question!"

Engineer, twenty-eight

saw your parents living theirs, you may not have spent much time thinking about how you'd really like your life to be.

On the other hand, you may have given hours, days, even years of thought to how you'd like your life to be. You may have spent years dreaming and planning for it but don't know yet how you're going to make it a reality. Either way—whether you already know or don't have a clue—you're in the right place at the right time. Now is your chance to create what you want. You can start figuring out what you can do to live your life according to your own values, standards, preferences, priorities, and goals. Now is your opportunity to spell out just what is most important to you and make it central to your life.

If you already have a clear idea of what you want, answering the questions this chapter poses will enable you to quickly spell it out precisely. If, on the other hand, the thought of defining what you want from life sounds like a difficult undertaking, these next questions will walk you through it step-by-step. Either way, this chapter outlines six signposts to help you define your destination and discover the inner compass that will direct you there. Often these signposts have become buried under the mud and rock slides of having to deal with the pressures of everyday life. So it's no wonder we lose touch with what we really want. As you address each signpost, however, you'll find they're still there, waiting to guide you precisely to where you want to go in life.

As you read through the chapter, you can use the spaces we've provided in this book or you may prefer to use a separate notebook as you begin uncovering the signposts leading to the life that will support you in the way you want and need to be supported. Or, if you prefer, you can record your thoughts and comments on an audio- or videotape. Let's begin with the first signpost—what's foremost in your mind right now.

SIGNPOST ONE: ALL I WANT IS . . .

Early in the classic musical **My Fair Lady** Eliza Doolittle tells us exactly what she wants—a room somewhere, far away from the cold night air. In fact, as the song goes, that's all she wants. What about you? What do you want? Often the answer to that question begins with "All I want is . . ." Of course, that's not all you want. But it's what's most important to you right now.

The response "All I want is . . ." usually arises from some sense of desperation or frustration. It almost always is far less than what you really want, but it's what's foremost in your mind. As soon as you attain it, you will quickly move on to all the other far more desirable things you want.

So let's get your answer to "All I want is . . ." out of the way right from the start, because you probably won't allow yourself to consider anything that doesn't address this immediate need in some way. But don't let "All I want is . . ." determine the ultimate decisions you make about the life you want to create for yourself on your own. If you do, within no time, you'll be disappointed with your choices. Just to make sure, though, that your decisions account for "All I want is . . . ," take the time to define it now. While this is not the be-all and end-all of what you really want, often it's the front door. (See work sheet on page 58.)

SIGNPOST TWO: DISSATISFACTIONS, DISCONTENTS, RESTLESSNESS

Actually, such minimalist "All I want is . . ." expectations arise from even more fundamental desires. They're a door to the deeper restlessness, dissatisfaction, yearning, or hunger you're feeling about your life. They're a sign that you need a change. And you are in no way alone in having this "All I want is . . ." feeling. It's a symptom of our times. It's driving us to create new ways of living that will be much more rewarding and meaningful. It can help us identify our deeper desires. If we don't do something about the immediate dissatisfaction or discontent we're feeling, it will continue to haunt us. So becoming aware of what you're dissatisfied with or less than happy about is often the next step to discovering what you do truly want.

Often we don't want to think about what's missing in our lives because, after all, who wants to dwell on that stuff? And, indeed, that's the point. Dwelling on this serves no purpose. In the past, there may have been no point in thinking about what you *really*

"I knew exactly what I wanted to do. It sprang fully formed into my mind. The only thing between me and success was figuring out how to execute it."

Doll maker,
thirty-six

"In the quest for happiness, partial solutions don't work."

Mihaly
Csikszentmihalyi

WORK SHEET

"…some peace of mind."

"…a little money in the bank."

"…a little time to myself."

"…a little respect."

"…a chance to show what I can do."

"…to be there when my kids get home from school and still keep a roof over our heads and some food on the table."

"…to have a little fun."

"…to get out from under my boss's thumb."

"All I want is…"

_____

_____

_____

_____

_____

_____

_____

_____

_____

_____

_____

_____

_____

_____

---

wanted because you probably couldn't have done it anyway. There were so many fewer choices. But today, chances are strongly in your favor that by creating an independent lifestyle you will be able to design your life to your liking.

In other words, heeding feelings of dissatisfaction, discontent, and restlessness can serve to prod and guide you to what you want . . . and can have. In his book *Finding the Hat That Fits,* John Caple calls this *divine discontent* and identifies several signals that will let you know if you've got it. We've elaborated on

SIGNS OF DISCONTENT

HERE'S HOW IT FEELS WHEN THERE'S A DISCONTINUITY BETWEEN WHAT YOU WANT AND WHAT YOU HAVE. MARK ANY YOU EXPERIENCE AS (M) MILD (U) UNCOMFORTABLE OR (I) INTENSE

___ Not wanting to get out of bed

___ Difficulty motivating yourself to do routine tasks

___ Losing interest in things that once engaged you

___ Nagging doubts about yourself and the course of your life

___ Worrying about how you'll keep things together

___ Feeling bored and restless

___ Wishing you were someone else

___ Having frequent bad dreams and nightmares

___ Feeling mildly depressed for days on end

___ Overeating, using alcohol and drugs to feel better or escape

___ Feeling chronically tired, deenergized, and listless

___ Losing a sense of enthusiasm

___ Getting frequent headaches, stomach upset, and other body aches and pains

___ Difficulty sleeping, or oversleeping

___ Complaining, nagging, and bitching

that list on the above work sheet. Check off any signs of your discontent and allow them to come to the surface so they can guide you to what you truly want.

We hope that as you read this book such feelings of dissatisfaction and restlessness will surface and heighten—because as long as you dwell in complacency, as long as you won't allow yourself to feel discontent, as long as you deny that things are less than you know are possible, or you drown your dissatisfactions in diversions like drinking, doing drugs, watching hours of television, overeating, sleeping long hours, or whatever, you will never, ever connect with the desires and yearnings that can point you in the direction of what you want and need to do to make the changes it's now possible for you to make. You'll find that these feelings of discontent also become invaluable sources of energy to propel you to see possibilities, make choices, and take the action to create what you want.

As you read on, not only will you feel an increased awareness of your discontent, you will also begin noticing a growing sense of hope, a growing feeling of excitement and anticipation at the chance to reclaim the magic feeling of being alive that you've felt at special times in your life and long to feel again.

SIGNPOST THREE: A YEARNING FOR THE MAGIC

Remember when you were a little child? Remember that magic feeling you used to have sometimes when you'd first wake up in the morning on a special day? Remember that feeling of everything being fresh and new, tingling with possibility? Remember that almost electric feeling that anything could happen? Maybe it was the morning of the first day of school. Or maybe it was the morning of the first day of summer vacation. Maybe it was the night before a big game, going to summer camp, or Christmas Eve. Later in life, maybe it was getting ready for your first date with that special person who made your heart stop. Graduation day. Your wedding. The birth of your first child. Or a moment when you not only achieved a long-desired goal but also surprised yourself by surpassing even your greatest expectations of what you could do.

These are Personal Landmark Moments—the best moments in our lives when we feel most alive, most vibrant. Time seems to stand still. Everything flows effortlessly. Everyday cares fall away. You're at ease with yourself, in harmony with life around you. Perhaps you've had many such moments. Perhaps you can't remember having any. But chances are you have had some such moments sometime in your life, and it's the magic of these moments that most of us want and need to recapture in our lives.

It's the memory of such moments, however buried they may be, that lie beneath whatever restlessness and discontent we're feeling.

This is the magic most of us are yearning for, the magic that drives all dreams and has throughout all time. It's as real and as natural and as demanding as feeling hungry. And it is what you can recapture and create for yourself day after day when you decide to reclaim your time and put the sense of balance and harmony you're seeking back into your life. It's the feeling that comes from knowing that as you start each day the hours ahead are ripe with possibility, not always necessarily pleasant, but always at least potentially interesting and meaningful because you know you'll be growing and changing and evolving toward what you want in life. It's the feeling that comes from knowing you're becoming the person you know you can be and that you're doing exactly what you're meant to be doing.

Capturing and remembering such Personal Landmark Moments is important because if you are to chart the destination of your desired future, you need to have a strong sense of the magic you feel at these moments. That feeling, the feeling of magic, can serve as an inner compass for guiding the decisions and choices you make about what you want in the new life you're about to create. Take a few minutes now to recall such moments, large or small, in your own past. Record them on page 63. Sometimes, as you can see from some of the accompanying comments there, the small moments are as powerful as the large ones.

SIGNPOST FOUR: YOUR INNER COMPASS

This feeling we call the magic of life has been called many different things. Some have called it "optimal experience" or "peak experience." Behavioral researcher Mihaly Csikszentmihalyi refers to it as *flow* because that is the term people often use to describe how it feels: "It was like floating"; "I was carried by the flow." Whatever it's called, it's the way we feel during times in our life when we're free to invest ourselves fully in pursuing our chosen goals. And it's accompanied by amazing bursts of energy. It draws out abilities, courage, and strengths we didn't know we had. Surprising dedication and determination kick in. And it's almost addictive, in that we want to experience it again and again.

We refer to this unusual level of drive and determination these magic moments inspire in us as the Rudy Factor, after Rudy Ruettiger, whose legendary efforts to make the Notre Dame football team despite the seemingly impossible odds of his slight five-foot-six-inch frame and a mediocre high-school academic history inspired the movie *Rudy*. You may have seen the Rudy Factor operating in young children at play or when trying to master some

"I'm so excited I can't sit still to hold a thought in my head— the kind of excitement only a free man can feel."

Red,
The Shawshank
Redemption

PERSONAL LANDMARK MOMENTS

"Those were the days, all right. Snapping the ball around the infield. Stirring up the chatter in the outfield. Running after fly balls until my legs hurt. Playing heads-up ball. Looking alive. That's it. That's being alive!"

"My grandmother and I would sit on the big swing on the front porch, and she would tell me stories about the teddy bear who traveled to China in an underground elevator. The locusts would be singing and the crickets would be chirping and she would braid my hair. Summer afternoons on Grandma's porch. Time would stand still."

"When I was little, I used to dream of being a circus star. My dad would take me to the circus every year and we'd walk through the tents and I'd close my eyes and smell the hay and the canvas and the rope and the animals and I could see myself on the high wire. I still have all the old programs on the top shelf of my closet. Want to see them?"

"She asked me what I'd want if I could have anything and I said I'd love to have the bathroom redone with a Jacuzzi and she said, 'That's it? That's what you want most?' And I started to cry as I thought about all the dreams I had lost."

"I was standing at the newsstand when I saw an article about model trains. Suddenly the feelings came flooding back to me of the magic I had felt playing with model trains when I was a boy. That, that was the feeling I wanted back in my life."

"The room was electric. Suddenly all my fear disappeared and I climbed up on the platform and took the microphone and started talking. The crowd began to calm down, and slowly people began talking to one another instead of screaming. And my heart was pounding, not with fear, but with joy."

"It was like a sneak preview of how my life would be one day. I felt confident and at ease. I was so alive. I just went up to people I didn't know and started talking and I knew just what to say. And after I left the room, the hostess said people kept asking her, 'Who was that person?'"

"As I watched him skating, tears came to my eyes and my heart began to ache, not because I ever wanted to be an ice skater, but because I had forgotten how much I wanted to be as good at anything as he was at that one moment."

"I'd like to have one more of those hollyhock days. Playing in the alley with the hollyhocks and morning glories, chasing squirrels and looking for four-leaf clovers. Making clover chains. And riding my bike down Harrison's Hill. It was so steep it would take my breath away. I still have a scar on my knee from one of those trips, and I like that scar because it reminds me of a time when I had no fear."

YOUR LANDMARK MOMENTS WORK SHEET

NOTE: NOT EVERYONE HAS POSITIVE MEMORIES AT FIRST

To get to positive landmark memories, start writing about what you're experiencing as you do this exercise and work your way through to your landmarks like this:

"At first I didn't want to remember the magic times of my youth. All I could think of were the disappointments, all the things that didn't work out, the embarrassments. But then I started to remember the magic I used to feel exploring new ways to get to school. I found at least ten different ways to walk that ten blocks and I remember the alleys and roundabout shortcuts that made me late to school so many mornings. I remembered how excited I felt every year opening brand-new textbooks. They smelled so good and were filled with the promise of so many things I didn't know. I remembered how excited I was to wake up and see the first snow of the year—and how we'd all head for Chelsea Park with our sleds and pile on and streak down the steepest hill, and almost slide right into the Jersey Creek, how the snow would cake on our mittens and we'd always have to taste it."

desired activity like walking or riding a bike, jumping rope, skateboarding, or playing jacks. They do it over and over, falling and tipping over and tripping and floundering, again and again, but undaunted and oblivious to time or who's watching. This is precisely the kind of energy "that magic feeling" can release. It transforms us into someone who can do just about anything we set our mind to. And it's just what we need to create a new life for ourselves.

So the more any activity you're considering in your life captures the magic feelings of your Personal Landmark Moments, the more likely the Rudy Factor will start working for you, and your chances of getting where you want to go in life will go up dramatically. And vice versa. The less an activity or the prospect of an activity feels like these magic moments, the better served you will be to steer in another direction. You can consider this feeling of magic to be like a barometer, or better yet, an inner compass.

Throughout this book there will be many opportunities to weigh how you feel about one direction over another, compare one option to another, or consider one path against another. In weighing your choices, you can return every time to this inner compass. You can use it as a reference point to compare all options you consider in charting your future. Just as in the children's game of searching for a hidden object and having the person who knows where it is call out "You're getting warm" as you approach the object or "You're getting cool" when you're going in the wrong direction, give your choices the "Magic Test." Poet Rusty Berkus calls it the Goose Bump Test. "When I get goose bumps from an idea or possibility," she says, "I know I better proceed that way."

Ignoring the desire for this magic feeling is what gets us into dull, mundane, and intolerable lives. Heeding it is what takes us to places better than we could ever dream of. It's the natural high of life that leaves us feeling fulfilled—so full, in fact, that we're overflowing with energy and we want to reach out and give to others. It's the feeling that leads directly to comments you often hear highly successful people make like "My life has been so good, I

HERE'S HOW IT FEELS WHEN LIFE IS WORKING. THIS IS WHAT WE'RE AIMING FOR!

___ You feel energized, vibrant, and alive

___ Your confidence and capability grow from each experience

___ Time flies by or is suspended

___ You feel in control of your fate

___ You experience a sense of mastery having accomplished something

___ You're in harmony or at one with all around you, at ease and natural

___ Everyday concerns drop away

___ You discover what you didn't know you could do

___ You're highly focused and intensely involved

___ Your sense of well-being increases

___ Enjoyment replaces boredom

___ Nothing much seems to distract you

___ Although your work is sometimes difficult and challenging, you don't want to stop

___ Your abilities are tested and stretched to the limit

___ You can't wait to feel this way again

___ While fully conscious and aware, self-consciousness dissolves

___ Each day seems new and fresh, filled with possibility

want to give back to others." It's a feeling we all deserve and are meant to have.

SIGNPOST FIVE: SOURCE DREAMS

As naive or grandiose as they may be, our dreams arise from a natural human craving to experience the magic life can offer. We're born into a history of dreams, both living and dead, that all came from this same innate desire. In many ways, you can think of human evolution as a great generational relay race of dreams. At birth, we're each passed a baton of dreams that has been carried throughout the generations before us. Your grandparents passed the baton they received from their parents before them to your parents, who have passed it on to you. You've taken up the baton and are running the next leg in the race called life.

Each generation runs the race as best they can. But they each can carry the baton only so far. For better or worse, you've begun your leg of the race from wherever your ancestors' blood, sweat, and tears left off. You've begun where they brought you, with whatever advantages and disadvantages, opportunities or challenges they handed you. Your earliest dreams grew amidst the temples or shacks of theirs. To this day, inside you, buried within your dreams, beat their hopes, their dreams, their hungers and desires along with those of their parents and their parents' parents—all those both met and unmet, achieved or long forgotten.

You began the journey toward your dreams standing on their achievements and stumbling over their handicaps. What were those dreams, the source dreams, that came with you into this world? What became of them? What dreams did you begin to form in your early years because of or despite theirs?

At first you may resist looking at the hopes and dreams of your parents and ancestors. You may feel angry at their shortcomings, sad about their squandered potential, resentful that they had it so easy and have made it so hard for you, or scared that you may be repeating aspects of their lives. But until we face our past, we cannot avoid repeating it or at least being limited by it. And unless we claim it, we can never draw upon the powerful lessons and energy their struggles, trials, tribulations, failures, and triumphs can provide us. So, as you read ahead, explore your Source Dreams using the work sheet on pages 67–69.

PROFILE: MAYTA VILAN

Mayta came to America a Cuban refugee at the age of fifteen. She couldn't speak a word of English. "Even in Cuba," she remembers, "I wanted to act, but by the time I arrived here I had to put away that dream and lock it up. I thought I had to study something more practical and earn good money and help my family. I had to say over and over, 'This is just a dream and face reality.' " But in college when she heard about an acting program run by a Spanish-speaking teacher she enrolled. You can see her now in movies like *The Specialist* with James Woods and on TV in Aaron Spelling's series *Robin's Hoods*.

Sometimes also it seems silly to think back to our childhood dreams, as frivolous, grandiose, or naive as they may seem. But re-

THE DREAMS OF YOUR ANCESTORS WORK SHEET

Write about what dreams or circumstances brought your ancestors to America. How long have they been here? Are you the first generation in your family to come to America? What do you know about your ancestors, your grandparents and great-grandparents? What were their dreams? What happened to those dreams? If you don't know much about these people, you might ask your living relatives what they know about them or even do some genealogical research.

_____

_____

_____

_____

_____

_____

_____

_____

_____

SAMPLE: SOME ANCESTRAL DREAMS ARE DIFFICULT TO RECALL

Sometimes it seems there were no noteworthy ancestral dreams. If so, start writing whatever you're experiencing as you start to think about your ancestors and work your way to possible dreams like this:

"At first I didn't want to think about my parents and my ancestors. I don't know anything about them. I didn't want to. They had no dreams. They're miserable, incompetent people. My father was a failure. My mother was always unhappy. She still is. How could thinking about these people help me define what I want from life? But then I remembered one night my father was talking about doctors and I said I wanted to be one. I remember how suddenly his eyes lit up at that thought. I could see how much he wanted me to be somebody. I wonder now what it was about their lives that made things so difficult for them. What happened? Was there a time when it was different? Maybe once upon a time they had dreams. They must have. I remember my mother had an old scrapbook with drawings she'd done when she was young. Maybe she dreamed about being a sketch artist."

THE DREAMS OF YOUR PARENTS WORK SHEET

Where do your parents fit in? What are/were their dreams? What has happened to them? If you don't know much about your parents' dreams and they are still living, you might ask them about what they dreamed of doing when they were young and at different times in their lives. Or you might talk with relatives or search through family photo albums or other mementos for clues about their lives.

"I dropped out of dance school when I didn't get the lead role in a performance. I might not have gone that far, but I'll never know now. Be smarter than your mother. Promise me you won't give up your dream. Do this for me."

A dying mother speaking to her daughter

membering them could lead directly to what you need to start doing now. It did for Jim Haggerty. Recalling the magical feelings he had as a child playing with his model trains provided the impetus for him to leave behind his paycheck and the world of mortgage brokering thirteen years ago to build limited-edition railroad buildings for HO-scale model-train kits, which he sells to collectors and hobbyists. He makes a good income now reliving the magic of his childhood every day.

Childhood memories also lured Diane Vitorino from her position in a child-welfare agency to become a colorist. Throughout her childhood Vitorino loved to play with colors, mixing paints for hours on end. Now she's a partner in her own hair salon where she spends her days customizing colors for her clients' hair. If you watched her at work, you would think she was a child at play.

THE DREAMS OF YOUR YOUTH WORK SHEET

Even as a very small child, you began formulating what your life would be like when you grew up. For some of us these intentions have been very clear. For others they are more vague. But most of us have some memory of answering the age-old question all children are asked: "What do you want to do when you grow up?" How did you answer that question? What were your dreams at various times in your young life? How were they similar to those of your family? How were they different? What has happened to those dreams? Are there elements of these early fantasies in your life today? Are there elements you wish were there?

_____

_____

_____

_____

_____

_____

_____

_____

SAMPLE: DREAMS OF YOUTH

"As a child I dreamed of being a doctor but I hated biology and chemistry and premed classes, so I pursued an entirely different direction with my career. Thinking back on my childhood dream, I realize my interest in medicine had nothing to do with science. I'm interested in healing, and that can take many forms."

"Remembering how much I wanted to be an opera singer as a little girl brought back painful memories. From the time I learned my voice would never be good enough for professional opera, I buried the hunger I felt to express myself through music. Now I want that back. I want to find another way to express the beauty I feel inside."

"Although it's always been a little too embarrassing to admit, as a little boy I actually dreamed of becoming president of the United States. But when I don't think of this dream in the literal sense, I can see it's a reflection of how much I've always wanted to make a major difference in the world. I don't want to sit around anymore administering what is; I want to influence what could be. As an environmental consultant, I can do that by educating the public and particularly my clients."

Childhood memories were the salvation of Jules Joyner of Royal Oak, Minnesota. After graduating from college, she went to work in the world of finance but found the corporate life stifling. Since the age of twelve designing and sewing her own clothes had been her love. Now it's her livelihood. She left the corporate world and, using a borrowed sewing machine, began creating custom-designed wedding gowns and evening dresses.

Usually, however, childhood dreams are more symbolic than literal expressions of what we need to pursue today. I, Sarah, for example, wanted to be a trapeze artist in the circus when I was a little girl. So, does that mean that to fulfill myself as an adult, I should run away and join the circus? That's pretty much what Mary Garvey did at age sixty-plus when she started a troupe of traveling clowns, Classical Clowns. In my case, however, that's definitely not what I needed to do. My dream of being a trapeze artist, however, had a great deal to do symbolically with discovering what I truly wanted to pursue in my life.

At the time I remembered it, my work had become dreadfully dull. Sometimes, to my embarrassment, I would almost fall asleep on the job. I thought I loved my work; it was important and meaningful, but something was wrong. I was missing the excitement, the flair, the drama, the risk, the lights, the audience, the applause, and the daring talent I had dreamed of having as a circus performer. Although many years had passed since the time I used to fantasize about flying across the big top while turning flips on my backyard swing set, in my heart, I was still craving those elements. And believe me, since the prospect of speaking before a group of people made my knees wobble and my palms sweat, it was years before I would be able to enjoy any of them. Today, however, I do. Today many aspects of my life provide me with the feelings I used to dream about while twirling around on that swing set. In doing our radio and television shows, in giving the speeches and seminars we offer around the country, I often feel a similar sense of excitement, drama, and fulfillment that I dreamed the flying trapeze would provide. And I love the applause we get when we have pleased an audience, not with our dazzling feats, but with the message we have to help others accomplish all that they can.

So usually our childhood fantasies are metaphors of the person we know we are inside—the person we can become. They provide clues about what we can contribute, the ways in which we can help, create, build, lead, problem-solve, or better organize the world around us. But like many people, you may find that your seminal dreams have become eroded by compromises you think you need to make, compromises that can cut you off from the sense of magic you may crave. Instead your life becomes disjointed.

SIGNPOST SIX: CORRECTING COMPROMISES

Whatever dreams we came from or start out with, as our lives unfold we all spend our days devoted to something. We're all striving for something—be it love, money, power, fame, acceptance, a good time, independence, peace, beauty, survival—whatever we value most. Until recently, however, the demands of earning a living put serious limitations on what life could entail. For most people, pursuing any one thing usually meant sacrificing others. Earning a living required making compromises of many kinds. We had to choose between our various needs and values, putting some over others. Only the luckiest of individuals could find a way to balance all the key needs and values we long to fulfill in some way.

That's why the magic slowly seeps from our lives.

YOUR FUTURE

Our lives take place on a continuum of time. Our present becomes our past. Our past then serves as a reference for what we think is possible in the future. The present we are living in today is the result of the future we imagined yesterday. To see a new future, we must unlock ourselves from the limits of the futures we've imagined in the past. To intentionally create the life we want, we must conceive a future that's sufficiently desirable to motivate and compel us to undertake the things we need to do today to live in a tomorrow more to our liking.

If you recall, the magic and harmony you crave comes during times in your life when you're free to invest fully in pursuing chosen goals you value. So in order to be most fully alive and fulfilled in your daily life, not just during a crisis or for an occasional lucky moment now and then, you need to structure your life to support, not thwart or battle with, achieving your goals and pursuing those things you value most. To recapture the magic, your most desired goals and values need to become central to your life—not squeezed in here, or tagged on there, or pushed through after your energy has been spent on everything else. If you are to be truly fulfilled, you cannot live in a state of constant compromise. You must find some way to earn a living that will provide for and support your needs for the things you value in the three key areas of life while simultaneously allowing you to pursue your goals in each:

Your personal needs. Nurturing, enjoying, and developing your mental, physical, and spiritual well-being.

Your needs for others. Loving, caring, and sharing with the significant others in your life.

Your needs for meaningful work. Contributing to the world in a gratifying way that supports you and those you love.

In the past, one way to accommodate these needs was to divide the demands and the rewards of meeting them along the line of sex roles. Women primarily had the opportunity to devote time to caring for and about significant others while men primarily got the chance to contribute to the world through work. Although perhaps functional, such divisions of labor led to highly unbalanced lives for both sexes:

P = Personal
O = Others
W = Work

Traditional Male Role

Traditional Female Role

All that, of course, has changed. Now men and women alike are struggling with juggling these aspects of their lives. And in a job-oriented lifestyle achieving success in one area has usually meant making significant sacrifices in others. Those who devote their lives to material or career success often have had to sacrifice their relationships or their health. Those who devote their lives to loved ones often have had to forego developing their skills and talents. Either way, personal needs in a job-oriented world often get squeezed out altogether, and imbalance in any area erodes the quality of the others . . . and dispels the magic. Without balance we are not free to pursue our goals with the kind of uninterrupted, stress-free, uncompromised focus and dedication that allows us to stay true to our dreams and feel fulfilled.

According to reports from the Department of Labor, the number-one difficulty expressed most often by both men and women is trying to balance work and family. Clearly to survive and provide security for themselves and their families, most people holding jobs today lead lives that are severely out of balance and they are feeling the pain. So although they may be earning a living, they are not supporting themselves.

> "All my life there's been one little rule that has worked wonderfully for me: If there's any area of your life in which you are less than 50 percent happy, make an immediate change."
> *Mike Carlson, age eighty-seven*

Typical Two-Career Couples

Typical Single Parent

P = Personal
O = Others
W = Work

Only in very recent years has personal fulfillment become a priority for men or women. Although our lives today are probably no more or less lopsided than in previous times, today we have new options. The world is no longer a world of either/or's. As we have described in **Chapter 1**, there are many new options that free us to shape our lives as we choose, living where we want, doing what we want. We no longer have to settle for experiencing only part of our lives, only part of our personalities. We no longer need to try to be someone we're not and have no desire to become. We no longer have to settle for the compromises of the past. We can customize our lives to meet our needs like a custom-made suit of clothes.

P = Personal
O = Others
W = Work

A More Balanced Life

"Once you learn what your life is about there is no way to erase the knowledge. No matter how afraid you become you have no choice. If you try to do something different with your life, you will always sense there is something missing."
The Celestine Prophecy

Start with the assumption that anything is possible.
Gene Bua

"When I decided I was going to do what I really wanted to do, that's when things started happening in my life."

In fact, we're seeing a steady evolution toward the desire for more personal choices, and the new economy is providing options for people to fulfill a broader spectrum of their desires. That's why so many people feel dissatisfied and yet their parents tell them, "You have everything a person could ever want. Why aren't you happy?" Most people tend to make the same compromises their parents have made, however, without actually realizing it. With this in mind, think back to your parents' lives. What compromises did you grow up watching them* make? What were their lives devoted to? Reviewing their stories on the work sheets on pages 75–83 can provide valuable insights into the decisions you've made and help you understand more clearly what you want to do from now on.

DECIDING WHAT YOU REALLY WANT

Have you ever noticed how sometimes people say they want to do one thing, but they do another? That happens because at any point in our lives we're doing whatever our life is about at that time. Whether your life is about working at a job, playing tennis or golf, watching TV, helping the poor, raising your kids, getting rich, looking great, whatever it is about, you're going to be pulled in that direction no matter what else you try doing, no matter what anyone else tries to get you to do, no matter what else you have to do. And if you're prevented from doing whatever it is you're about or you won't allow yourself to do it, your life will become empty, frustrating, and unpleasant.

Having followed the preceding signposts, you should have a pretty good idea about what your life has been about, what it is

---

*If you were not raised by your parents, complete these work sheets for the adults or older siblings who raised you.

YOUR MOTHER'S STORY WORK SHEET

What is/was your mother's life devoted to? What was her life about? What sacrifices did she make? What price did she pay?

_____

_____

_____

_____

Draw a pie showing the proportions of time she devoted to various aspects of her life:

P = Personal
O = Others
W = Work

How would you improve on her life?

_____

_____

_____

_____

What meaning, strengths, lessons, values, and messages do you take from her life?

_____

_____

_____

_____

YOUR FATHER'S STORY WORK SHEET

What is/was your father's life devoted to? What was his life about? What sacrifices did he make? What price did he pay?

_____

_____

_____

_____

Draw a pie showing the proportions of time he devoted to various aspects of his life:

P = Personal
O = Others
W = Work

How would you improve on his life?

_____

_____

_____

_____

What meaning, strengths, lessons, values, and messages do you take from his life?

_____

_____

_____

_____

"I remember sitting by my father on his deathbed. Each breath was a struggle. I was struck by the fact that in his battle with death he was more alive than I'd ever remembered him. My father had spent his entire life doing everything that was expected of him. He was a quiet man. He rarely spoke, except in euphemisms like 'Keep up the good work,' or 'Atta boy.' His face had become set into a familiar mask-like half smile. He would nod his head as we talked, his eyes often blank and dull. Until that night he died. That night he looked at me with a passion I'd only glimpsed in childhood pictures from the family album. 'I'm dying,' he said with such urgency, such alarm. 'I'll miss you.' And that's the way I'll remember him. At the funeral everyone said he was a 'good man.' I wish I'd known him. But I do know I want to be as alive every day now as he was that night while I still have the chance."

"My dad was a perfectionist. He worked all the time and was very demanding. With my mom, though, we could get away with anything. 'Don't listen to your dad,' she'd say. 'You've got to have a good time in life.' I know I listened more to my mom, but as a result I haven't accomplished what I know I could. I think the balance I'm seeking is to find a way I can become more successful but still enjoy myself."

"My mother ran a retail shop. It seemed as though she was never home. I was alone a lot. I decided when I had a family I wouldn't work. I wanted to be there for my kids the way my mother wasn't there for me. But now that I'm home with three kids, I need to find a better balance. I don't want to live my life through them. I want to have my own life, too. So that's my challenge."

"My mother lived her life for us kids. She had her hands in every aspect of my life. What I wore. What I did. My friends were her friends. She even flirted with my boyfriends. I resented it. I wanted to tell her to 'get a life.' With my kids, I want to show them that being grown-up is something to look forward to, that life doesn't end with childhood. But now I'm so involved in my career I'm afraid I'm neglecting them."

"The moment my son was born, I knew that he was what I was here to do. He's only three years old, so I don't know what his life will be about, but whatever it is, I know it's my job to make that possible. In fact, that explains why I married his dad. Now, though it's hard, being a divorced, single mother. I have to find a way to support us and still be available for him. Right now I'm temping and I never know where I'll be or what my hours are. I'm dragging him here and there. One night he's at his dad's. One night he's at Grandma's. One night he's with me. I have to find a more stable situation that is flexible enough for me to take care of him but stable enough to make our lives more secure and predictable."

"My parents came to this country as teenagers with their families to escape oppression and persecution and poverty. They wanted freedom and the opportunity for a better life. They worked very hard, and I have what they came here for. They gave this to me. Now I'm able to live the dream they worked for. My goals are to enjoy life, to travel, to be with my family and have fun in my work."

"The choices my parents made caused all of us a lot of hardships. My father tried to be an actor but wasn't very successful. He left my mother, my sisters, and me to fend for ourselves. I don't want to give up my own goals, but I don't want to hurt the other people in my life the way my father did."

CHANGING NEEDS

Interestingly enough, eight of the things people say they want most from their work, according to a Yankelovich study, would not have been high priorities for workers just one generation ago—and they all become immediately possible the moment you go out on your own:

1. Working with people who treat you with respect
2. Interesting work
3. Recognition for good work
4. Chance to develop your skills
5. Working for people who listen to your ideas about how things should be done
6. A chance to think for yourself rather than mindlessly carrying out orders
7. Seeing the end results of your work
8. A job that's not too easy

YOUR STORY **WORK SHEET**

1. Up to this point what has your life been devoted to? Review your own life. What are the catalytic events—the pivotal turning points, the high points, and the low points, that have made you the person you are today? Plot these events on your life line, putting the high points to the right of the life line and the low points to the left of the line. Make notes alongside these events summarizing the decisions you made about yourself, your life, and your future based on these events. What lessons did you learn from them? Here's an example:

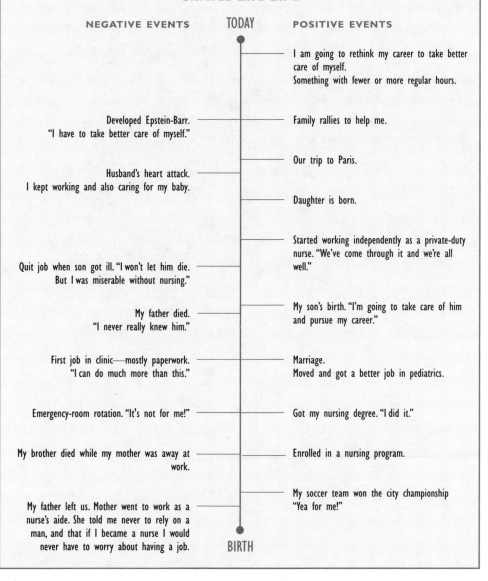

SAMPLE LIFE LINE

NEGATIVE EVENTS | TODAY | POSITIVE EVENTS

I am going to rethink my career to take better care of myself.
Something with fewer or more regular hours.

Developed Epstein-Barr.
"I have to take better care of myself."

Family rallies to help me.

Our trip to Paris.

Husband's heart attack.
I kept working and also caring for my baby.

Daughter is born.

Started working independently as a private-duty nurse. "We've come through it and we're all well."

Quit job when son got ill. "I won't let him die. But I was miserable without nursing."

My son's birth. "I'm going to take care of him and pursue my career."

My father died.
"I never really knew him."

First job in clinic—mostly paperwork.
"I can do much more than this."

Marriage.
Moved and got a better job in pediatrics.

Emergency-room rotation. "It's not for me!"

Got my nursing degree. "I did it."

My brother died while my mother was away at work.

Enrolled in a nursing program.

My soccer team won the city championship "Yea for me!"

My father left us. Mother went to work as a nurse's aide. She told me never to rely on a man, and that if I became a nurse I would never have to worry about having a job.

BIRTH

Patterns. "My life seems to have been about illness and about taking care of others and protecting them. But now it's about my illness and how I'm going to take care of me. I have to make a change. I want to work in the health field, but the long hours at the hospital or in other people's homes aren't working for me. I've made myself sick, helping other people get well.

"But I have so many more choices than my parents had. After my father left us, my mother decided to become a nurse, but when my older brother died while my mother was at work, she gave up on that dream and continued as a nurse's aide working night shifts to support us while my sister and I slept at Grandma's. Now she tries to live her life through us and our children. We are her life. But we have our own lives, so we can never give her the time and attention she craves.

"My father never held a good job, but all he did was work. He drank and smoked a lot even though he had high blood pressure. I guess that's how he got through the day. He died of a stroke."

Conclusions. "My task is to find balance in my life, to take care of my family and make a contribution to society but still take care of myself and be true to my needs."

HOW IT HAS BEEN   **HOW IT NEEDS TO BE**

P = Personal
O = Others
W = Work

YOUR LIFE LINE

NEGATIVE EVENTS   TODAY   POSITIVE EVENTS

BIRTH

In reviewing your life, what patterns do you see? What would you say your life has been about? Is there a thread running through your life? What sacrifices have you made? What price have you paid?

_____

_____

_____

_____

_____

2.Draw a pie showing the proportions of time you are devoting to various aspects of your life:

P = Personal
O = Others
W = Work

3. Is this the way you imagined your life would be when you grew up? ___ Yes ___ No. How similar is your life to what you intended or hoped for? To what you feared? What surprises have you had? How did you end up here?

_____

_____

_____

_____

4. The lessons and experiences of your parents' lives provide you with a perspective they didn't have, couldn't have had. As you look over your life, what can you see that you've been able to do or could do now that they could not? What decisions have you made for your life based on their experiences and how have you made sense of their two different perspectives on life? What do you need to accomplish in your life that your parents have been unable to accomplish in theirs? What issues and tasks must you master now that they could not?

_____

_____

_____

5. Can you see more clearly now why you are feeling a hunger to make changes in your life? ___Yes ___ No. How would you improve your life to be more supportive of your goals? Draw a pie chart reflecting the proportion of time you'd like to devote to the various areas of your life and describe the changes you would like to make in your life.

P = Personal
O = Others
W = Work

_____

_____

_____

_____

_____

_____

_____

_____

_____

_____

_____

YOUR IDEAL LIFESTYLE WORK SHEET

Imagine that you are in charge. You can do what you want, the way you want. What is important to you? Check those aspects that are important. Then create a list of what you value most. Since today's world of self-employment is a world of "ands" not "either/ors," there is no need to force-rank these values. Instead of trying to weigh one against another, assume you could have them all and indicate the priority you put on each.

A: Essential　**B:** Important　**C:** Desirable　**N:** Neutral　**U:** Undesirable

In a life with many options, you can have as many **A**'s as is the truth for you. Someone may have only one or two **A**'s. Another will have ten to fifteen and won't be happy settling for fewer.

__ Acceptance	__ Appreciation	__ Challenge	__ Health
__ Admiration	__ Quality	__ Uniqueness	__ Ethics
__ Mastery	__ Excellence	__ Casualness	__ Morality
__ Creativity	__ Originality	__ Social and civic	__ Surprise
__ Comfort	__ Informality	contribution	__ Freedom
__ Fitness	__ Community	__ Variety	__ Fame
__ Honesty	service	__ Activity	__ Financial
__ Spirituality	__ Excitement	__ Independence	security
__ Stimulation	__ Risk	__ Respect	__ Fun
__ Choice	__ Flexibility	__ Fortune	__ Relaxation
__ Prestige	__ Recognition	__ Prosperity	__ Making a lasting
__ Stability	__ Certainty	__ Leisure	contribution
__ Wealth	__ Being well	__ Making a	__ Peace
__ Enjoyment	compensated	worthwhile	__ Personal
__ Making a	__ Helping and	contribution	development
difference	caring for	__ Calm	__ Relationships
__ Pleasure	others	__ Wisdom	__ Time for your
__ Harmony	__ Beauty	__ Authority	partner, lover,
__ Growth	__ Fulfilling your	__ Solitude	or spouse
__ Power	potential	__ Being liked	__ Time for friends
__ Privacy	__ Status	__ Accomplishment	__ Time for your
__ Pets	__ Popularity	__ Competition	children
__ Nature	__ Achievement	__ Novelty	

Make a list that summarizes the aspects you most want your lifestyle to reflect. Feel free to add others not listed above.

ESSENTIAL   IMPORTANT   DESIRABLE

What's important to me in life is...

about, and what you want it to be about. As we said at the beginning of this book, it's no accident that you want to find your perfect work so you can make certain changes in your life. Actually, your entire life up to this point has prepared you to do precisely whatever you are to do next. Even if it doesn't seem like it right now, everything you've done so far, including the lessons and experiences you've seen your family cope with, has positioned you for the next steps you're ready and wanting to take.

Knowing what your life is about clarifies what's most important to you so you can decide what path will take you there and the type of work you need to create to support yourself in doing what matters most. Use the checklist on page 84 to identify and sum-

"All I know is that the first step is to create the vision, because when you see the vision there—the beautiful vision—that creates the want power."
Arnold Schwarzenegger

I don't remember anyone ever encouraging me to try to do the things I really wanted to do. No one seemed to think I could, or even care whether I did. Not even my therapist. When I told her about the various things I wanted to do, she asked me why I was always so grandiose."

marize the values, priorities, goals, and preferences that are important to you at this time in your life.

IF YOU COULD HAVE ANYTHING . . .

Despite the fact that this is a nation of dreams, the idea that most people can't have all they truly want is very deeply ingrained in our culture, having been transferred from generation to generation throughout our history. This skepticism is evidenced by the ambivalence you hear and see when someone appears to be truly happy or to have become truly successful. It's not uncommon, for example, upon hearing about someone's success, for people to roll their eyes and make comments like "Boy, I bet he made a killing on that!" or "I wonder what she had to do to get that!" Also it seems that, as a public, we have a nearly insatiable desire to uncover scandals, problems, and miseries in the lives of apparently successful people. Lots of times it looks as if they aren't that happy. We see and read about their shattered families, arrests, and addictions.

We've all grown up experiencing this type of ambivalence. We're not so sure we really like Horatio Algers. And it's enough to make anyone wonder if ordinary, honest, hardworking people can really achieve what they want and be truly happy living a good life. But to achieve what *you* truly want in life, you have to step outside of these cultural limitations and believe it is possible for ordinary, honest, hardworking individuals to be happy and successful.

So, if you dare, if you're willing, step this very moment outside all your own doubts, all your familial misgivings, and all your cultural disbelief. Believe that it's possible—possible to live a fully balanced, fully satisfying life of your choice. Reflect upon the priorities you've chosen above and imagine that you could have life the way you want it. How would it be? Think of it like a movie in which you are the main character. Where are you living? What are your days filled with? What kind of people? What kind of activities? What is your lifestyle? There is every reason to believe that as you complete this book, you will discover you can create a livelihood for yourself that will support a life that's filled with what you truly

YOUR DESTINATION WORK SHEET

Reflecting upon the priorities you've chosen throughout this chapter, imagine that you could have life the way you truly want it. How would it be? Where are you living? What are your days filled with? What kind of people? What kind of activities? What is your lifestyle? Describe your ideal life in detail, here.

"One dream calls out
your name."

"The future belongs
to those who believe
in the beauty of their
dreams."

Eleanor Roosevelt

hunger for. Describe that on the work sheet above. Think of it as the destination you're headed for. Dare to imagine. You don't need to know how you'll get there. That's what the rest of the book is designed to help you discover.

If you'd like, before filling out the work sheet, read the sampling of profiles that follows. They exemplify the choices other people have made to live their dreams fully without compromise. Read through their stories as inspiration for imagining your own ideal life.

PROFILE: DONALD MARRS, "I COULDN'T DO IT ANYMORE"

As vice president, creative director for Leo Burnett Company, one of the largest advertising agencies in the world, Donald Marrs had it all—a fruitful career, the money "success" brings, a lovely family, social standing, and political savvy. His clients were among the top companies in this country. He was a strategist and media consultant to U.S. senatorial, congressional, and gubernatorial political campaigns.

Donald Marrs, author

But it wasn't right. Marrs grew tired of living a masquerade. He was anguished by the split between his values and his career. "I wouldn't let my kids eat sugary breakfast cereals, but at the office I was dreaming up ads for Kellogg's Frosted Flakes. I quit smoking, but my job had me creating cigarette commercials for Philip Morris. Then, in the middle of the fuel crunch, I was asked to work on an ad campaign to sell gas-guzzling luxury cars for GM."

When he actually looked at what he was selling, he got a knot in his stomach. The recognition of how he'd denied his true feelings horrified him, and he knew the pain wouldn't stop until he took his life back in his own hands. "It felt strange to be going through a crisis of 'values,' when values had never seemed to be an issue before," he remembers. But the time came when money, power, social position, even security paled next to his desire to create something of more personal worth. He gave up everything to reach his destination, but he's quick to point out that you don't have to lose everything before you can create the life you truly want—especially if you have an overview of the journey you're undertaking.

After several tortuous years searching for how to integrate his values into his daily work, Marrs put his ideas to work in the marketplace and created Marketing Partners, offering small socially and environmentally conscious businesses the level of marketing support that is usually available only to large corporations. He also wrote and published *Executive in Passage, The Door to Uncommon Fulfillment,* the courageous story of his journey to a more fulfilling life. He concluded that "anyone who tells you that you have to compromise your principles to 'make it' in business obviously doesn't know what's possible. You can satisfy your desire for material success and personal fulfillment." Marrs knows because his earnings now have surpassed the hefty salary he gave up to pursue a life of his own. But he wouldn't trade it even if they didn't.

PROFILE: TOM AND MARILYN ROSS, "WE WERE PINING FOR ONE PLACE AND LIVING IN ANOTHER"

In 1980, Tom and Marilyn Ross had a thriving consulting business in San Diego with an office overlooking the Pacific Ocean. But a vacation to a mountain cabin on Big Bear Lake changed all that. There, surrounded by the wonders of nature, the blessed silence, the friendly squirrels playing on the roof, and the deer grazing next door, they decided they could operate their business from anywhere and set out to answer a call to nature.

They moved to a remote 320-acre ranch nestled in the Rocky Mountains. Finding that too isolating, they moved to Buena Vista, Colorado, a town of about two thousand people nestled in a beautiful valley surrounded by 14,000-foot-high mountain peaks. "Pining for one place and living in another is a typical American state of mind," Tom says. "Rootlessness is one of the most pervasive, and least publicized, problems in modern life." But Marilyn adds, "When we moved, it was major culture shock, a real socioquake! We had some frustrating, funny, and humbling experiences. Being a city girl, I have proved myself in ways I wouldn't have dreamed of."

In addition to being an incredible adventure and learning experience, their new life has provided the Rosses with a new sense of community and connectedness and several special treasures they had been missing from urban living—things that were once taken for granted like trust, honesty, safe streets, clean air, and friendly neighbors. The Rosses now share their experiences and expertise about country living with other urban dwellers who dream of getting away from it all in their book *Country Bound, Trade Your Business Suit Blues for Blue Jean Dreams* and in training workshops and retreats for individuals who want to relocate and company employees near retirement.

PROFILE: RICH POPE, "WE WERE LOSING OUR CHILDREN"

Rich Pope was a high-school science teacher. His wife also is a teacher. They both worked long hours. "Our kids were at the baby-sitter's from six-thirty in the morning until five-thirty at night," Rich told us. "We felt like we were losing them." The best way to

Rich Pope, indexer

get them back, he decided, was to reorganize his life so the kids could come first. So he began the long and hard process of looking for a new profession that would match his needs. "I needed something I could do from home that would give me personal freedom. We still had two kids in preschool, so I needed a job where I wouldn't be constantly interrupted by clients and footwork." His choice was to become a freelance indexer of science books.

"This has given me total flexibility to be with my kids whenever they need me, be it for a school picnic at noon, to coach soccer after school, or attend a play at night. I can always be there." His day starts at 4 A.M. (which he says he truly enjoys!). He works for a couple of hours before he makes breakfast and gets everyone off to school and work. Then he works until the school bus pulls up at 2:45. "That gives me several hours with the kids and a couple more with my wife. The kids can be in extracurricular activities now, because I can take them. We have plenty of time to discuss any problem they have. They can have friends over and do their homework without being alone or at the baby-sitter's. And my wife is more relaxed because I can take care of the laundry, pack lunches, and make dinner. We feel like a family now."

Rich believes this is the perfect system for his family right now. Once he made the commitment, he was surprised the transition was so easy. He no longer has the benefits and retirement plan he had on the job, but his income has climbed back up to about two-thirds of what he was making on the job. He points out, however, that, considering the fact that they no longer need to pay child care at $600 a month and his gasoline bills have dropped $150 a month now that he's not driving to work, they're breaking even financially.

The change is paying off in ways money can't buy, though. His youngest son, who's six years old now, started reading two years earlier than his older sisters because of their daily reading ritual after lunch right before afternoon nap. His oldest daughter's grades have jumped from C's to A's. "My only challenge now comes in the summer when everyone else is home on vacation and I have a deadline to meet when they all want to go camping and horseback riding. I have to use a little discipline then, but the peace of mind is worth the price."

PROFILE: MARTHA SAHN, "RECLAIMING MY LIFE"

Twelve years ago, Martha Sahn left her job to pursue her dream. She had worked in the retail business all her life, and her dream was to open her own gift shop. Drawing upon the many good things she'd learned from the large retailers she'd worked for, she and her husband, Ken, opened a 600-square-foot mall store selling ceramics, art deco reproductions, and cards. Her husband's background was in wholesale, so they made a great team, and the first store quickly grew into six stores in six malls.

Martha Sahn, accessorizer

At first the gift business was new and exciting. Her dream had become a reality. But as time passed, it turned into a nightmare. "The business," she told us, "became a bottomless pit." She was on call twenty-four hours a day, working twelve-hour days, seven days a week. "I wasn't running the business. The business was running me." Overhead costs were tremendous, and rents kept going up. So three years ago they closed their stores to reclaim their lives.

Sahn went back to work for another retailer, and her husband also took a job. But for Sahn a new job wasn't any better. The hours were still long and other than not having to pay the bills or run a business, she still had the same responsibilities, just for less compensation. In trying to gain greater control over her life, she had actually forfeited the little control she had. "Working for someone else, you have no control over when you're expected to work. Even when you define what you can and can't do, they expect whatever they need from you."

So Sahn and her employer decided on a parting of the ways, and she took a six-month hiatus to think about what she wanted to do. She found that "being at home opened my eyes to what life is all about. I took a look at my home life and my personal life for the first time and realized what I was missing out on." Everyone else in the family liked her being at home, too. "Your being at home here really raises the quality of our lives," her husband and their three children, ages twenty, sixteen, and eleven, told her. "In retail, you're working during the times everyone else is playing," she told us, "so they enjoyed the fact that I was home before ten o'clock at night. We could go to movies, celebrate holidays together—all things I'd never been able to do.

"I realized I really liked being home. I decided I wanted to create a home-based business of some kind." Drawing upon her background, she began looking for merchandise to build a private line of accessories. Called Martha Sahn's Private Collections of Bloomfield Hills, Michigan, her line includes many one-of-a-kind clothing, accessory, and gift items from the several well-known artists she represents. Her line is sold strictly by private appointment, trunk showings, or open houses. And it's a win-win arrangement for everyone. The artists love working with Martha because when they place their creations in the top nationwide chain stores, the markup is so high that sales are low. Because Martha has virtually no overhead, however, she can sell these top-of-the-line creations at discount prices people can afford.

Sahn now feels she has the best of both worlds. She gets up early, does her work, and then she's free for her family. "I like this life because of what it gives me," she says. Twice over the last two years her new life has turned out to be a blessing in ways she would never have expected. Two years ago her husband had a heart attack, and she realizes, "I'm able to be here for him." When he had to go in for emergency surgery recently, she could call her customers and reschedule a showing without inconveniencing anyone. Last January, her sixteen-year-old son had a wrestling accident that left him homebound in a cast and a wheelchair for several months. "Thank God I was here," she says.

"In growing my home business, I'm planting a seed, growing a new way of life, and I feel grateful every day. I can't believe how beautiful the sky is, for example. I've been in a mall all my life!" At forty-four, she finds that "the best years in my life are now! I say to my kids, You can do anything you want.... And they can see it's true, because I'm doing it."

PROFILE: ROBBIE BOGUE, "FIRED INTO A BETTER LIFE"
In January 1987, Robbie Bogue was a sales executive for one of the largest printing companies in the nation when, as he puts it, "I was

canned along with the president and fifteen other people in a corporate takeover." He knew the company was in trouble, but he says,
"You're never really ready for the hammer to fall." After having been
a corporate executive for twenty-five years, he didn't know what he
wanted to do next. He could do many things well. What should he
pursue at this point in his life? To find the answer, he spent $3,500
for the advice of an industrial psychologist. One of the possibilities
that came up during these discussions was that of starting a marketing consulting practice. Bogue had never seriously thought of going out on his own, and he continued sending out résumés in search
of another position. But when an interview led to a job offer, he realized he had to give the opportunity to go out on his own a try.
"Otherwise," he says, "I would never have known what I could have
done."

Robbie Bogue,
Certified
Management
Consultant

So he turned down the job offer and became a marketing
consultant. A week later, to his surprise and delight, his potential employer called and asked to become his first customer!
He was hired to do on his own what he would have done on the
job.

When starting out Bogue remembers, "Fear was my single
strongest motivating force: fear of failure, fear of not being able to
make the mortgage payments, fear of not being able to support my
family, which included being the sole support of my mother, who
was seriously ill." Although he started out with a network of hundreds of key contacts developed over his twenty-five-plus-year career, "I didn't get one lick of business from any of them. Being a
consultant," he discovered, "was the corporate version of leprosy."
His contacts looked on him as a person who was between jobs.
But that all changed when he incorporated as Marketing Excellence
and became a certified management consultant.

After two years of success, Bogue had carved out a specialty,
counseling injured workers who want to start or purchase a business. For the past seven years, he's earned his living helping others
become successful. And the living has been a good one. Although
it took him three and a half years to get back to the $100,000
income he was making with salary and bonuses, he's now doing
over a quarter of a million a year and has two employees. Much
of his profits go right back into his company. "We want to have

state-of-the-art equipment and software," he says, "so we can show our clients we can do a little more than they could do for themselves." He sums up this formula for success with one word of Cajun philosophy: *Lagniappe*. It means "doing just a little bit more."

Bogue now enjoys what he calls a boutique lifestyle. Every morning he gets dressed professionally for work and goes to his office 100 feet away in a converted pool house on his property. It's a lovely, shaded walk down a stone pathway alongside a swimming pool complete with a gurgling waterfall. The walkway is canopied by an ancient live oak tree so large and lush Bogue and his clients don't even get wet walking to the office in the rain. "I don't drive a Mercedes," Bogue says. "I spend my money on art." And his office is decorated with the art he collects. Music from his jazz collection can be heard in the background while he works. On the Fourth of July every year, he holds a live Jazz Fest around the pool for his clients and friends. And, of course, he's never far from his wife and foster daughters.

"I'm unemployable now," he claims, "because I've become an absolute free thinker. I have all the confidence that comes from being a CEO, and I surround myself with other people who have built something significant by making a contribution to the world and by pursuing life with vigor. His advice to others is: "Always be seeking to improve someone else's situation. If you have that concept constantly in mind, you will be provided with opportunity. It can be as simple as recommending a Chinese restaurant or as complicated as putting your signature on a million-dollar contract that will increase a client's competitiveness. It all comes down to improving life for others."

PROFILE: BRENDON ETTER, "LIVING THE IMPOSSIBLE DREAM"

From the time he was four years old, Brendon Etter has loved playing music. He started out playing the piano, but by the age of eight he was tired of practicing and his interest shifted to drumming. His parents bought him a used drum set and by the age of thirteen, despite other interests in skiing and motorcross racing, he found music was the one thing that was always on his mind, and so he decided to take it more seriously. He played with a number of high-school bands, and his mother ran the band like a little business complete with a contract for their performances at school events and clubs, where in order to play Etter had to use a fake ID. The other band members were all older than Etter, though, so when they graduated he was left behind. But by then, though, he had decided to become a professional drummer.

That's when his parents, who had always been supportive of his music, started impressing upon him how difficult it would be to make it in the music industry. They began urging him to have a backup plan of some kind. But Etter says, "I just didn't want to hear about that. I didn't want to have a backup plan. Everyone I ever knew who had a backup plan ended up using it. I wanted to put one hundred percent into my music. I didn't want there to be any other way out. I wanted to have to put everything I had into making it work."

So he and a friend followed their dreams and moved from Cincinnati to California, where Etter applied and was accepted at the Applied Musicians Institute. There he met many of the drummers he had admired for years, but when he graduated no job was waiting. He had to take day jobs to make ends meet. Then one day he saw a note on the school bulletin board in yellow crayon seeking someone who could play like the legendary drummer John Bonham of Led Zeppelin. Bonham had always been one of Etter's idols, so he responded to the notice and hit it off immediately with guitarist Andrew Parsons. They communicated right away through their music and began looking for others they would click with to form their own band. It took some effort, and they didn't find anyone for some time. At one point Etter felt burned-out by the search and signed on with another band. It wasn't what he was looking for, though, so after six months he quit to continue his search with Parsons.

Through club contacts, they met bass guitarist Hugh Bonner and singer and lyricist Brian Taylor, and the four of them formed the band Nature and rented a practice facility together. "I really believed we could take it all the way," Etter says. A lot of effort was required to keep everyone motivated while working their day jobs, but finally,

"You are what your deep, driving desire is. As your desire is, so is your will. As your will is, so is your deed. As your deed is, so is your destiny."

Upanishad

a year later, they played their first gig. Their performances at local clubs began attracting a small, but growing, fan base. And one night their break came at an unexpected moment.

They were playing at a little club in Hollywood at one o'clock in the morning. The performance hadn't been well promoted, so there were only about five people in the audience. With such a small crowd they weren't that eager to do the show. But three of their friends had shown up and paid $5 to get in, so they decided to play anyway. Thank goodness, because one of the five people was someone from a record company who offered them a contract. Their album was in production at the time of this interview for release last summer.

So Etter says, "You've got to do the best job you can in any forum that opens up to you and approach it as if you were performing for a national audience. You never know who will be listening." At twenty-four, he quit his day job to devote full time to the first demo and says of their future, "I know we're going to take off, eventually. So if this album isn't a hit, well, we'll go on for the next one."

ONE FINAL TEST

Looking over what you've defined to be what you truly want in life—just to be sure you haven't sold your future short—ask yourself: Would your dreams be more desirable if you had grown up in a different family? If so, how? Would your imagined future be more desirable to you if somehow you were someone else? If so, how? While you can't change the family you were born into, as the profiles so clearly show, you can most certainly change the person you can become. So before going on, using your inner compass, the Magic Test, fine-tune your definition of what you want most to reflect any changes that feel sufficiently more desirable to you until it's what you truly desire.

With this destination in mind, you're ready to discover the path that will take you there.

RESOURCES

The Celestine Prophecy. James Redfield. New York: Warner, 1993.

Executive in Passage. Donald Marrs. Barrington Sky Publications, P.O. Box 4928, Los Angeles, CA 90049, 1990.

Finding the Hat That Fits. John Caple. New York: Plume, 1993.

Flow, The Psychology of Optimal Experience. Mihaly Csilszentmihalyi. New York: Harper Perennial, 1990.

The Seven Spiritual Laws of Success. Deepak Chopra. San Rafael, CA: New World Library, 1995.

PART II

The Path:
Choosing How to Get There

THREE

Finding Your Way

THERE ARE MANY POTENTIAL paths to any destination, but not all are desirable ones. And so it is with choosing a path that will take you to your perfect work and the life you've just defined as wanting for yourself. Some paths to making a living by having the life of your choice are rocky and barren, others long and winding. Some lead to dead ends. Obviously the harder and harsher the path, the less pleasant the journey and the more likely you'll become discouraged. If you begin disliking a particular path or doubting it will actually get you where you want to go, you may want to turn back, give up, and settle once again for less than what you really want. So you need to find a path that's relatively smooth, lush, and even scenic that will take you as directly as possible to where you want to go.

The most successful paths, the truly fertile ones, actually feed and energize you along the way. A fertile path to self-employment will propel you toward your destination by enabling you to tap into the magic it brings into your life each day. It will release inner reserves of energy that like the current of a river will carry

From where does the strength come to finish the race? It comes from within.
Eric Liddell,
Chariots of Fire

"The river flows along the path of least resistance and carves itself deep into the earth to travel unerringly and inevitably to the sea."

you toward your goals. The right path will ignite you with an electrical charge that is like the wind beneath your wings.

And that's precisely what you will need because when you're on your own, there will be no one prodding and nudging you. There will be no boss's wrath to face if you don't get up and out of bed. There will be no time clock to pull you away from the morning newspaper. No one to keep you working when you'd rather play with the kids, shoot some hoops, watch TV, talk on the phone, or putter around in the garage with the car. And there will be no one else to put up, cover up, or pick up for you when you misstep or stumble. So you need to select a path that will be sufficiently appealing to keep you motivated and energized.

You'll want to find a path that assures you the highest possible degree of success, because research shows that most people need to be successful in their efforts about 75 percent of the time in order to sustain their motivation. When we're successful even as little as only 50 percent of the time, most of us begin to feel despair. So while no path will be totally without challenge or completely free of all difficulty, the path you choose should energize and intrigue you, enable you to tap into your strengths, predispose you to success, and provide its own intrinsic rewards. Otherwise working for yourself will feel much like working for someone else, only possibly worse. Without a truly desirable path, even though you'll be traveling toward a better life, you could start to feel as if getting there involves one sacrifice after another and an arduous journey of waiting for "someday" when you'll finally be able to enjoy yourself.

The Fertile Path

- Is consistent with your dreams
- Suits your temperament
- Calls upon your talents and skills
- Feeds your confidence
- Builds your self-esteem along the way
- Keeps you motivated
- Primarily provides an enjoyable experience
- Holds your interest
- Energizes and fulfills you
- Increases your chances for success.

Often we're asked, "But now that I know what I want from life, can't I just find something people will pay for and do whatever's in demand?" Or they'll inquire, "Can't I just find some need, whatever it is, and fill it?" And indeed, that would seem logical. In fact, it's what many experts recommend. We don't, however. We think that approach leads far too many people down discouraging and desolate paths. It's like the advice we once got from a would-be mentor who told us, "Figure out which way the wind is blowing and go stand in it." That advice might get you somewhere, but will it be where *you* want to go?

We find that becoming successfully self-employed is much

more like sailing than surfing. Instead of waiting for a wave that will carry you somewhere, you must seek out and use the wind that will carry you to the destination of your choice. The work you choose to support yourself and attain your ideal life should be sufficiently enjoyable and consistent in and of itself with what you want so that it's not only worth the effort but actually meets your needs along the way. That's what finding your perfect work is all about.

The path of your perfect work will charge you up like your own Energizer Rabbit, generating within you the steam, the juice, the gusto, the pizzazz, the drive to push you through the inevitable fears and doubts of stepping into the unknown and keep you going and going. Otherwise you'll be forever scrambling, stumbling, juggling, and struggling to keep yourself afloat.

To find such a fertile path, you must begin first by looking within at what you have to offer that will feed, energize, and propel you while you're doing it. That's what Part II is designed to help you do. Then, once you've discovered what you will enjoy offering, what will be most engaging and natural for you, then, you'll be well positioned to start looking outward to find who needs and will pay for what you can most successfully offer. That's what **Part III** will help you do.

Over the past fifteen years we have conducted and analyzed over a thousand interviews with self-employed individuals to determine how they found what they could do to support themselves. We've found that invariably those who were successful could be identified as having taken one or a combination of four specific paths to self-employment.

- *Harvesting a Gift.* For some, the path of choice is to harvest a gift, ignite an innate talent or an acquired skill at which they shine.
- *Pursuing a Passion.* For others it's to follow their heart, earning a living doing something they love passionately.
- *Following a Mission.* For still others the path of choice is to answer a calling, follow a mission or a sense of destiny they believe it's their role and purpose to undertake.
- *Capitalizing on Your Assets.* And finally, for some, in fact

many if not most, their path is to capitalize upon their assets and current circumstances, doing what comes most naturally to achieve the other important goals in their lives.

As you read about each of these paths in the next four chapters you'll come to know their pros and cons, advantages and disadvantages, traps and pitfalls, as well as their needed safeguards. You'll see, however, that all these paths have characteristics that can enhance your chances for success and enable you to go from dream to action. Each taps into some internal source of energy that will help carry you toward your destination.

Four Paths to Independence

Gifts. Following your talent

Passions. Following your heart

Missions. Following your gut

Assets. Following your nature

You will meet people who have successfully pursued each of these paths. Work sheets in the upcoming chapters will provide you with the opportunity to weigh the value of each path to your situation. As you respond to these work sheets, be sure to elaborate fully on your answers and provide as much detail about the ideas as the space permits; or, if you prefer, use a separate notebook or audiotape to explore your answers. Force yourself to go beyond a one- or two-word response; such limited answers rarely provide you with the insights you need to discover the richness of choices that you actually have.

We urge that you read and explore all four paths thoroughly even if you are strongly inclined already to a particular one, because, as you will see, we have discovered that those who find their perfect work and pursue it successfully usually combine several paths into one that's custom suited to them. Your goal should be to find such a custom-designed path—an independent career that meets your needs, fulfills your desires, and involves those things that come most naturally to you. In other words, discovering your path is like weaving a tapestry, braiding a cord, intertwining vines along a trellis, or interconnecting strands in a fiber-optic cable—one cord of multiple fibers of varying widths and colors—through which you link your desires, your energy, and your capabilities to the needs of the world and receive in return, through that same cord of life, the rewards and satisfaction you seek.

WEAVING A PATH TO YOUR PERFECT WORK

The path to your perfect work will spring from within your
deepest desires and be woven from the gifts, passions, missions,
and assets that live in your heart, your mind, and your very nature.

FOUR

Harvesting a Gift

Each of us has our own special gift from God, one of one kind and one of another.

1 Corinthians 7:7

ABOUT ONE OUT OF SIX PEOPLE becomes successfully self-employed by taking advantage of a special talent or skill he or she has that others value and willingly pay for. These people have tapped into a gift, something at which they shine, that others can readily recognize and want. Such a built-in demand makes this path a particularly desirable one because in a normal economy, marketing a business based on a gift is usually not a problem.

Many people, however, miss out on the opportunity to harvest their gift, because they don't recognize it or they discount its value. In fact, a gift often comes so easily or naturally that those who have it that they either assume everyone can do it or that it has no particular value. It's so much a part of who they are and what they do that they think there's nothing to it. That's undoubtedly why, unlike the other paths, people most often discover this route to independence only by accident, happenstance, or serendipity.

At first glance, perhaps you too may be thinking, "Oh, I don't have any particularly valuable talent." But like the individuals below, you could be surprised to discover the income-producing opportunities latent in skills and abilities you've long forgotten or taken for granted over the years.

"For so many years I felt like I was selling my soul at the company store, and people kept telling me I didn't have to put up with this job. 'Your designs are so good,' they'd say, 'you ought to just do it on your own.' Finally I took their advice. I don't know why it took me so long."
GRAPHIC DESIGNER

"An old friend from school asked me to help him set up his computer system. Then someone else he knew called me. Then someone else. And the next thing I knew I was busy all the time helping people out. I realized all I had to do was start charging for it and I'd have a full-time job."
COMPUTER CONSULTANT

"I couldn't help but notice the growing number of customer complaints at the company where I was working. I could see so many ways they were doing a really poor job that I knew I had a real knack for what I do. I could do a better job than they ever did!"
COMMODITIES TRADER

"I was desperate to do something different, anything. I just didn't know what. Then one night I was showing my old high-school yearbooks to my son, and I noticed what so many people had written on those pages. 'Talking to you has made me feel so good.' 'I don't know how I would have gotten through this year without our long talks.' 'You are the best listener.' There it was in black and white. My gift. I'm always listening to people's troubles and helping them feel better. As my aunt was always saying, I should be a therapist! I opened my practice seven years ago."
MARRIAGE AND FAMILY COUNSELOR

"I was the wife of an executive. My job was to entertain and look great. I did it well. But when my husband died I had two small children to raise, and all I knew was fashion. I did what I knew how to do well, dress people so they'd look fabulous."
WARDROBE CONSULTANT

"When the training company I was working for went out of business, the clients turned to me: Help us, please. I realized that for them I was the company. So I said okay and became my own company."
CORPORATE TRAINER

"When she showed me her beautiful surrealistic oil paintings, they took my breath away. When I complimented her on them, she said, 'Oh, it's just a hobby. Anyone can do that.' Today she's one of the nation's few professional matte artists."

"I was forever helping my friends out with their makeup—for their proms, for their weddings, for their special dates. Then one time I did makeup for a friend of my sister-in-law and she said, 'I look so great, I really should pay you for this.' And you know, she was right. I'd been running a not-for-profit business for years. I just didn't know it was a business."
MAKEUP ARTIST

"When my husband's back went out his disability insurance ran out after a while, and I wanted to help bring in some money while still taking care of him. I was racking my brain thinking of what I could do. I hadn't ever actually had a job, but one night I remembered I got a national journalism award in college. I could write! I still can. But now I get paid for it!"
FREELANCE WRITER

"People were always telling me, 'Please bring your pies. Please bring your pies. Your pies make our dinner parties.' How many times had I heard that before it occurred to me I could make money doing this!"
DESSERT CATERER

"When I got my first standing ovation I realized I had the power to say something in a way people would understand, and I realized I could earn a living doing it."
MOTIVATIONAL SPEAKER

As you can see from these examples, some people don't consider earning a living from their gifts unless by chance they're invited, encouraged, or pressed into discovering them. You, too, could be overlooking the income potential of one of your talents to free you to live the life of your choice.

PROFILE: MICHAEL W. DAVIDSON, BIOPHYSICS RESEARCHER AND PHOTOMICROGRAPHER

While working as a research scientist in the field of optical and scanning probe microscopy with Florida State University and the University of Florida, Michael Davidson had some of his microscopic photographs of vitamins, flavors, sweeteners, and hormones published in several journals. One day a man called asking to license Davidson's photography for greeting cards, posters, wrapping paper, calendars, journals, T-shirts, refrigerator magnets, you name it. And that's where you can see it today. The company is called Mi-

Michael Davidson,
Biophysics Researcher

croscapes. You can also see Davidson's photographic art in his book *Magical Display*. "I would never have imagined all this was possible," says Davidson. "I'm just a researcher."

PROFILE: LILLIAN HAMMER ROSS, WRITER OF JEWISH FOLK TALES FOR CHILDREN

Ross discovered her exceptional talent late in life. It arose from an accumulation of painful life experiences. Jewish by birth, she was raised and educated as a Catholic, cut off from her Jewish cultural heritage. A retired kindergarten teacher, now seventy, she began undergoing Jungian analysis after a family crisis. In analysis she wrote down her dreams and created dialogue between the characters. Impressed with the seeds of talent he saw in her journals, the therapist suggested she take a creative writing class. The writing teacher saw the talent too and her encouragement motivated Ross to send her first manuscript to publishers. Her first book, *The Little Old Man and His Dreams,* came out on her sixty-fifth birthday. Her second book, *Buba Leah and Her Paper Children,* was published in 1991. Since then there have been more. *Sarah, Also Known as Hannah* is the story of her mother's journey from Europe to America at age twelve. As Ross shares her children's tales, she's reclaiming her own heritage.

RECLAIMING UNRECOGNIZED, UNAPPRECIATED, OR DISPARAGED GIFTS

Often gifts are those talents that we have been using and enjoying since we were children. Linda Ronstadt, for example, began singing harmony naturally at the age of four. Sculptor Louise Nevelson also knew she was going to be an artist from early childhood on. Colorist Diane Vitorino began mixing paints while playing as a child. At an early age she knew how to distinguish subtle differences between shades and hue and how to change and enhance them. Other gifts are the skills we've spent many years developing. Michelangelo reportedly said, "If people knew how hard I worked to get my mastery, it wouldn't seem so wonderful."

Many things can happen in the course of growing up, however, that can block us from recognizing, valuing, claiming, or believing in our talents. These experiences can even affect our ability

Deliver us to our brilliance.

Marianne Williamson

to recognize or pursue outstanding skills we develop later in life. If, for example, everyone in your family, school, or job is brilliant at a given talent or skill, you may not realize how good you are at it too. A software engineer, for instance, who consistently got B's at Stanford University, once told us he wasn't sure how well he'd do out on his own because he was only an average programmer. This was his view despite the fact that he was already one of the top designers at the high-tech company where he worked.

A young girl who grew up in a family of talented artists decided her artistic ability was strictly run-of-the-mill, something that would come naturally to everyone. Growing up in the shadow of an acclaimed financier, a brilliant analyst didn't realize he too had outstanding analytical abilities, albeit not yet as well developed as those of his famous father.

Even more likely, however, your family, teachers, or bosses may never have recognized or pointed out your talents and skills because these weren't ones they put a value on or had the ability to see budding in you. So having never had these abilities called to your attention, you may not have noticed them either.

It might also be that you were discouraged from pursuing your talent. Myra Davis, for example, was a very talented artist from a very early age. While in high school, she won a blue ribbon at the county fair for her oil paintings. But her parents never encouraged her to pursue her talents. Being from a more traditional upbringing, they insisted that her role in life was to get married and have a family. She was never provided with the guidance, encouragement, or tools to seriously consider pursuing her inner gifts. But today, at the age of fifty-one, she has finally decided to turn the crafts she has been making for family and friends into a serious business.

Milton Lipinski literally had his talent beaten out of him. He was a born "tinkerer." He could take anything apart and put it back together again. If it wasn't working, he'd have it operating in no time. He'd even invented some clever gadgets in the process. But Lipinski grew up as the third of six children in an intellectual midwestern household. His parents considered his tinkering to be a messy, embarrassing diversion to be discouraged at all costs. Often he was spanked for sneaking down to the basement to tinker

"Capacities clamor to be used and cease their clamor only when they are well used."

Abraham Maslow

around instead of doing his homework. "Stop puttering and do your homework," his parents would yell at him. Or "Get up here and make yourself presentable for dinner," he was told. Around the dinner table his siblings were encouraged to discuss the academic subjects they'd been studying in school that day. The conversations would be animated and clever. Milton would eat in silence.

Later his brothers and sisters went on to college, but Lipinski dropped out of school. In disgust, his father got him a job as a store clerk. While his siblings became accomplished professionals and college professors, throughout his life Lipinski wandered from one dead-end job to another, none of which related in any way to his remarkable "tinkering" talent. He was a lost man, cut off from his gift. He died in poverty.

While Lipinski's may be an extreme circumstance, many people—because of the households they grew up in, the neighborhoods where they lived, the schools they attended, even the time in history when they were born—have lost touch with their talents or simply never recognized them because no one else has. Women born in the 1920s and 1930s, for example, were rarely acknowledged for their leadership skills, and the math ability of women growing up in the 1950s was often minimized or overlooked. In some communities, teenagers with brains go unrecognized when compared to sports stars or muscle men. But in another time or place, or another family, such talents might have been recognized and encouraged at an early age.

If Lipinski had been born to another family, for example, he could have enjoyed a similar level of success as has one of our radio listeners who called in to tell us that he earns his living gluing things together. The caller told us he began seven years ago in his basement charging $3 to glue together any broken item. "I've had a knack for putting things back together all my life," he said, and his knack has paid off. When he called us, he was making $65,000 a year still gluing things together in his basement. His minimum charge had gone from $3 to $75, however, and he specializes in fixing antiques and collectibles. And that's not all Lipinski could have done. There are over forty occupations listed in **Appendix II** for people with skills in the fields of repair and restoration. If only Lipinski had known!

"Your talents can hardly wait to be expressed. They are itching to get out and about. To go through life without releasing your strongest talents leads to feelings of frustration, resentment, even depression. You feel bottled up, envious, and discouraged. You may even question if you should exist at all."

Laurence G. Boldt

PROFILE: STEVE EHLERS, DESIGNER

Ehlers was designing amusement parks when a friend's gun went off accidentally. The bullet went through Ehlers's head, leaving him instantly blind. He learned Braille, got a guide dog, and began looking for a job. But no one would hire him. "So," he says, "I started my own company. I had no choice." A friend asked him to design a shooting gallery for a circus. He did and has become one of the nation's leading shooting gallery designers. Though he's lost his sight, he hasn't lost his vision. He has a vivid picture of his one-of-a-kind galleries in his mind.

IDENTIFYING YOUR GIFT

So even if you are unaware of having any one outstanding talent, do not overlook the gifts you do have. We each have a variety of natural abilities that are an expression of our personalities. Sometimes by nurturing, polishing, and using these abilities, you can develop them into special gifts, talents, or skills at which you truly shine. Some of us develop exceptional physical skills, for example, like Ann Ferre, who discovered she can help people push past physical limitations by leading them through dangerous wilderness adventures. Others have physical skills for sports, dancing, singing, operating or repairing machinery and equipment, building and maintaining physical structures, or working with taste, color, light, sight, hearing, or touch.

Some of us, like information broker Seena Sharp, are exceptional problem-solvers with intellectual prowess for analyzing, decision making, planning, and researching. Sharp, whose company is called Sharp Information, does strategic intelligence research for her clients. She's like an information-age private eye, tracking down, analyzing, and synthesizing myriads of information her clients wouldn't know how to find, or have the time to dig through and make sense of. Seena's intellectual and analytical ability is just one of the seven different types of intellectual prowess Thomas Armstrong identifies in his book *7 Kinds of Smart, Identifying and Developing Your Many Intelligences.* Armstrong points out that some intelligences are less appreciated in our society than others, but that does not make them less valuable. We simply need to recognize and capitalize upon them on our own.

Many of us have outstanding creative skills, producing heart-stopping artwork, crafts, paintings, sculptures, ad copy, screen-plays, choreography, food, decorations, designs, creative writing, poetry, or inventions. But we may doubt that we could actually earn a living using these talents, so we discount their potential for supporting us in creating a better life for ourselves. We shouldn't. We can harvest them however small they may seem to us. That's what Jim Pelle of Sacramento, California, did with his home-based company Laughter Works. Pelle has turned his gift for humor into a unique business teaching organizations how to enhance their creativity through laughter. His clients include some of the nation's biggest companies.

Sharon Leeds uses her creativity to design English gardens on her clients' patios and porches. She calls her one-woman company Secret Gardens. It all started from a hobby for which she had such a gift that when her friends admired her own tiny garden, they began asking her if she would help create one for them.

Some of us shine at interpersonal skills like listening, under-standing, consoling, teaching, healing, helping, or team building. Rona Bartelstone of Miami, for example, began applying her gift for taking care of others twelve years ago when she realized how miserable and inadequate sons and daughters feel when they can't help their ailing elderly parents. As a social worker, she saw such misery often and understood the feelings of helplessness. She decided to do something about it; she left her job to pioneer an entirely new field, home geriatric care. She serves as the liaison for long-distance children, helping their ailing parents at times of crisis such as the death of one parent that leaves the other alone and grieving, or the development of a chronic illness, a stroke, or dementia that leaves an elderly parent unable to care for him- or herself.

PROFILE: MARTY GRODER, PSYCHIATRIST

He sits with his eyes closed listening as a client tells him about the anguish in her life. Images begin to form in Groder's mind. It's a special gift; he's unaware of how or why they appear. Experiences from the client's past, long buried and forgotten, flash in his mind's eye— a fire, a burning room. He shares the image and suddenly the client remembers in horror the night her father died trapped in a house fire. She had seen and forgotten it all as a four-year-old child. Although without fault, in her young mind she had blamed herself for not being able to save her father. She and Groder talk until she absolves her guilt and feels at peace for the first time in forty-some years.

Still others have outstanding communication skills for persuading, motivating, debating, negotiating, mediating, explaining ideas and concepts, writing, and speaking. That's David Kalb's gift. He knows how to cut red tape. He was mediating problems for a state governor's office that received hundreds of calls and thousands of letters every week from unhappy citizens who were ensnarled in bureaucratic red tape. "Suddenly a lightbulb went off in my head," Kalb says. "People desperately need help understanding the complexities of dozens of state agencies." Nine years ago he began Capital Services to simplify state government for his clients. "Basically I run interference for them."

Still others have a special ability to make order out of chaos. They have a knack for organizing the world for others. Tom Neverman is such a person. Organizing things has always come easily for him, so six years ago when a friend asked for help moving into a new apartment, he found handling the move was a snap. In the process, he noticed all the many little things that needed to be done that can turn moving into a stressful, gut-wrenching experience for so many people. Now as the Moving Doctor, Neverman is a professional organizer with a special niche—planning and orchestrating stress-free moves for his clients. He locates the moving company, arranges for the utility services, organizes the kitchen and closets, and puts everything in order down to the last detail— including installing new shelf paper in all the drawers and cabinets!

A talent is a gift you are born with;
a skill is a gift you give yourself.

So as you can see, special gifts or talents and skills of any kind can become a route to a satisfying livelihood, so it's important not to discount or overlook yours simply because no one has as yet called them to your attention or encouraged you to use them. Fortunately, you don't have to wait until crisis hits or someone calls you into service to recognize and start tapping into a gift that could become your path to making a living creating the life of your choice. In fact, like so many of the individuals we've described, people may already have been calling you and you just haven't heard the call. Think about it. What do people readily and spontaneously compliment, praise, or appreciate you for? Is there something people often ask you to help them with? What kind of favors are you frequently doing for people? Use the work sheet that follows on the next page to identify your gifts and the interest you might have in pursuing them.

Don't worry at this point if you don't know how you would earn a living using your gifts; and if you have trouble connecting with your special talents, taking the Doing What Comes Naturally survey in Appendix I may help you recognize possible gifts you're overlooking because they've been unrecognized, unappreciated, or disparaged by your family, peers, teachers, employers, or the culture you've grown up and worked in.

UNUSUAL TALENTS
PROFILE: BARBARA BOWERS, CORPORATE AURA READER

For the past nine years Barbara Bowers has traveled the country reading electromagnetic auras for her clients, which include major corporations like Blue Cross/Blue Shield, Lorimar, and Brink's. Bowers believes each organization emits an energy she can see as a color that permeates the corporate environment. "Each...has a spectrum of attitudes and behaviors," she explains. Her workshops, readings, and consultations help companies with management issues like morale and team building.

FINDING YOUR GIFT TO HARVEST WORK SHEET

Your talent or skill may be something that goes back to your childhood or something you developed later in life. Often people will have commented on these special abilities. They may frequently ask you to volunteer to help them because you are so good at using your gift, or you may have received a direct compliment that you just let slide by, such as "You sure are good at this! You ought to start a business doing that." Can you recall such comments?

Use the following questions to identify your talents and skills. Then rate each gift on a scale of 1 to 10 as to your interest in pursuing it as a livelihood.

1	2	3	4	5	6	7	8	9	10
NOT VERY INTERESTED				SOMEWHAT INTERESTED					VERY INTERESTED

Base your ratings on **1)** the Magic Factor each item has for you—that is, how energizing and compelling it would be for you to earn a living using this gift and **2)** how closely pursuing this gift as a livelihood would match the type of life you want to create for yourself.

Do not base your evaluation on whether
or not you think you could make enough money using this gift.
You'll be able to evaluate that in Part III.

Things I'm most frequently complimented on and praised for:	MAGIC FACTOR RATING	LIFESTYLE MATCH RATING

Things people ask me to help them with or do for them:	MAGIC FACTOR RATING	LIFESTYLE MATCH RATING

Things people have told me I'm so good at I ought to get paid for doing them:		

I've always thought I'm good at:		

GIFTS I MIGHT WANT TO HARVEST WORK SHEET

Review your lists and write here any gifts that appeal to you at a 7 rating or above on each scale, along with any ideas you have for how you could support yourself using them. Look through Appendix II: "An Alphabetical Directory of Self-Employment Careers" for ideas of ways you can make a living on your own using these gifts: You may also want to use Appendices I and III to make sure that you'll be comfortable doing the things you'll need to do to turn your gift into a livelihood.

GIFTS   POSSIBLE SELF-EMPLOYMENT OCCUPATIONS

1. _____   _____

   _____   _____

2. _____   _____

   _____   _____

3. _____   _____

   _____   _____

4. _____   _____

   _____   _____

5. _____   _____

   _____   _____

6. _____   _____

   _____   _____

7. _____   _____

   _____   _____

PROFILE: BOB WALTERS, PARKING-METER BEATER

Private investigator Bob Walters has a most unusual talent—he's never paid a parking ticket fine for any of the over forty parking violations he's collected over his lifetime. All his parking tickets have been officially and legally dismissed through a series of letters, $2 checks, and a copy machine. He shares the secrets of this peculiar talent in a book entitled *How to Get Your Parking Ticket Dismissed by Mail,* which he sells for the price of a ticket where he lives in Modesto, California: $15. It's all on the up and up and he carries a parking meter and a copy of the California Vehicle Code with him when he goes to speak about his amazing talent.

PROFILE: SUSAN BENCUYA, FACT CHECKER

Having worked as a research editor for *Inc.* magazine, Susan Bencuya now is an independent fact checker, verifying and confirming facts in reports, articles, books, and other documents through interviews and print research. Her clients include magazines, journals, scientists, and researchers.

PROFILE: CHRISTOPHER DARRYN, TALK SHOW REGISTRY

Christopher Darryn has always had an appreciation for unique individuals. He goes to a baseball game, and instead of watching the game, he watches the people. Now he earns his living collecting interesting experiences of offbeat people for his company, the National Talk Show Guest Registry. So far he has 1,800 people in his database, each of whom pays $3 a month for the chance to tell his or her unique story on TV. His registrants include an Idaho man who swapped places with a buddy to get his friend a medical deferment from the Army and then went to Vietnam in his place, and an Arizona homeowner who's haunted by the ghost of a woman who lived in the house where he now lives. Darryn is a clearinghouse for the types of unusual guests talk show producers have to find day after day. "Everybody has a story," he says, and he can condense it into a paragraph that will catch the eye of a producer.

PROFILE: EVE SHERWOOD, NEW-STORE OPENING EXPERT

Eve Sherwood has turned the skills she's gained from thirty years of retail experience in department and specialty stores in Chicago,

New York, and Los Angeles into a unique business. She teaches new specialty retailers how to open their stores. Her consulting and seminars include information on scouting locations, negotiating leases, planning store layouts, establishing credit, advertising, and marketing.

THE PROS AND CONS OF HARVESTING A GIFT

If you have one or more gifts you could enjoy as a livelihood, there are a number of strong reasons that pursuing one of them would be an excellent choice. First, you're good at these things! This means you will probably have more self-confidence in your ability to do them well, making it easier for you to market and sell yourself successfully. In addition, since you are gifted in these areas, you'll most likely have a shorter learning curve and do an excellent job for your initial clients right off the bat. Your happy clientele will begin eagerly spreading the word about you, making it easier to quickly build a good reputation for yourself.

So harvesting a gift can get you off to a great start, which will feed your self-esteem and help keep you motivated. That's important because, remember, research has shown we do best when we're successful at least 75 percent of the time. This is the most important advantage of harvesting a gift. Also, if your talent is already something people have been asking for, you already have a built-in market. You may even get badgered into harvesting your gift. For example, Abbe Gail Eckstein literally began selling the hats she was making right off her head. Strangers would stop her on the street to ask where they could buy a hat like the one she was wearing. When they found out she'd made it, they'd beg her to sell the one she was wearing or at least make one for them. Now her Abbe Hats are sold in shops nationwide.

Although certainly not everyone who harvests a gift has quite this dramatic a reaction, the value of even a small built-in market cannot be underestimated. It's what we all dream of. It makes this path the most charmed of routes to self-employment and finding one's perfect work. But this blessing can also be a trap. Sometimes your gifts can actually get in the way of finding and committing to the kind of work you really want to pursue. Just because you're very good at keeping files organized, ironing, or doing the taxes, for example, doesn't mean that you necessarily enjoy doing these things. Even if you do enjoy them, you might not want to do them day in and day out. Just because everyone says "You're so good at this, please do it for me" doesn't mean you should feel compelled to earn your living from it, unless it's something you genuinely want to do. So if there are other things you'd rather be doing, the pull to harvest your gift can become like a tar baby. That's why we had you rate your talent on two scales, the magic factor it offers and how well it matches your desired lifestyle.

"Every artist was an amateur."
Ralph Waldo Emerson

A man in one of our seminars told us, "I know I'm an accounting whiz, but I'm sick and tired of accounting. I don't want to do it anymore. But it's like honey, and I'm the bee. As soon as I decide I want to do something else, someone comes along willing to pay me a bunch of money to handle their accounting and I get stuck doing it again."

Someone else complained, "I'm great with kids. Teaching and taking care of them is truly a gift of mine, but I'm tired of being with kids all day long. I want a life centered on grown-ups for a change. But running family day care is so easy. It seems as though there's always another parent standing at my doorstep begging me to take care of her kids. Doing something else would take a lot more effort. I'm trapped by my talent."

A software engineer told us, "Programming has always come so easily to me, and there is such a demand for it. I know I should feel grateful that I have so many opportunities, but I want to try something new. It's just that in trying something new I feel so awkward. I won't be especially good at it for a while. How will I be able to compete? I'll be starting over, and I won't be paid as much as I can get now. It's a hard decision to follow my heart instead of my head."

Granted there are worse problems to have than these. You may be thinking that you would gladly trade places with any of these people, but when you're hungering to do something else, the talents and skills you've mastered feel like a prison, albeit a tempting one. I, Paul, know personally just how tempting. I have a talent for mediation. It comes naturally to me, and I do it very well—so well that invariably someone calls upon me to step in and do it again.

So building a business as a mediator wouldn't be difficult, but it's just not what I want to spend my life doing.

Creating a job for yourself based on your talent but involving something you don't enjoy won't feel much better than staying in a job you can't stand. So while it may take courage to turn your back on a gift you've outgrown or dislike, it's worth it. Again that's one reason we stress that you make sure to give any gift you're considering the Magic Test and the Lifestyle Test. Remember, you're not aiming to just make a living; you're creating a life. So just how much juice, pizzazz, or charge will you get from harvesting a particular gift? Unless your work is simply a means to some other end, in order to create the life you want to live, you'll be best served by pursuing those talents and gifts you enjoy doing at a 7 or above.

Another drawback this path presents is that the market demand that can get you going so successfully can also make you vulnerable because it can desert you as well. What starts out hot can cool. And if you've come to rely on the ease of having people flock to you without putting out much effort to attract them, it can be quite a shock when you suddenly have to get out and start promoting yourself the way others have to do. Again, remember self-esteem begins to erode when your success rate drops closer to only 50 percent. So if you've been flying on rapid and easy success, a sudden unexpected drop in the demand for what you offer can send your self-esteem into a tailspin.

Many different things can cause your built-in demand to cool, and you have to be able and ready to weather any sudden shift in climate. The economy might change, for example. A brilliant interior designer, who had been snowed under with work from the time he first went out on his own, became despondent in the early nineties when clients who still wanted his services could no longer afford to redecorate their homes. It took him several months to learn how to repackage and market himself, something those who start out on the other three paths usually have to learn before they can even get started.

Another reason an initially eager market may cool is competition. By having blazed such a glorious trail you may open doors to imitators who can offer a low-cost rendition of what you do. This

happened to one of the nation's premier customer-service trainers. Having always been in demand, she was initially baffled when
clients began buying services from cheaper competitors. She knew
her material was much better, because her programs were truly
brilliant. But the day came when she had to find ways to demonstrate why her brilliance was worth a premium price.

It's at a point like this that anyone who has chosen this path
will be confronted with needing to decide how much they really
want to earn a living by harvesting their gift. So as with the other
three paths, before you even start, we strongly urge you to pursue
this path only if it fits with what you want to do at a 7 or above on
your work sheets, because at some point you may need to tap into
a high level of magic and energy to keep yourself confident and
motivated when success isn't automatic.

Also instead of just jumping right into harvesting some highly
sought-after gift, you can circumvent later problems by learning
how to target and package what you offer in the ways you will discover in **Part III: "The Means".** This is an especially important
section if your special gift is one that's not so highly sought after
because you're a brilliant fish in a pool of so many other brilliant
fish that it's hard to get the right people to see you shine. This is
the case with many highly talented actors, speakers, and artists. If
that is your situation, you may find yourself sharing some of the
same challenges as those who want to pursue a passion. But as you
will see, we agree with actress Annette Benning, who believes that
ultimately talent can always find a way to shine through. It may not
be the traditional avenue. In fact, often it's not, but there is a way,
and **Part III** can help you find it.

PROFILE: MONICA MEDINA-AZPURUA, IMAGE DESIGN CONSULTANTS

"My professional life was going well," Monica Medina-Azpurua
wrote. "My job was exciting but very unstable, and ever since I was
a little girl, I wanted to have my own business. I grew up with that
flame inside me. I would do crafts and sell them to my friends, but
after graduating from college I did what almost everyone does, 'got
a job.'

"Although I was doing my job, sometimes working ten hours a

day, many times after getting home, I would feel a sense of emptiness. I felt as if I was wasting my time and my energies working for someone else. I wanted to do something on my own, but what? What would it be? That's when I found your book *Best Home Businesses for the 90s,* and it was almost like magic. I began reading it right there in the bookstore. After I bought it and took it home, I started devouring it like someone who had never read a book before. One business caught my attention—'image consultant.' I have two years of experience in fashion design, a degree in broadcast communication, and I love the world of fashion. Image consulting is the perfect choice for me! I am so proud telling you I founded my own company specializing in corporate image consulting. I am accomplishing my dreams."

Medina-Azpurua presents workshops on image, business protocol, and verbal and nonverbal communication, and her business is doing great. "I work many hours each week," she says, "but it doesn't matter because I am so happy. Finally I am working for myself."

HARVESTING A GIFT

Goal. Discovering what you do very well that people need and will pay for.

Driving force. Usually driven by people asking, urging, or encouraging you to start using your gift to make a living, although you might also begin from an inner desire to pursue a particular gift and seek out those who need it.

Pros. Built-in recognition of and demand for your talent or skill and your ability to do well right from the start predispose you to success.

Con. You may be drawn into doing something you don't like doing. Ease of entry may leave you unprepared for and vulnerable to marketing challenges when the economy or tastes change.

FIVE

Pursuing a Passion

ABOUT ONE IN FOUR PEOPLE who go out on their own are driven by the desire to pursue what sometimes is called a "fire in the belly." They want to earn their living doing something they love. Artists and entertainers of all kinds are perhaps the most familiar examples of people who will make whatever sacrifices they must in order to earn a living doing what they passionately cherish. But many other people are supporting themselves pursuing passions that range from the exotic to the mundane. Some arise from lifelong hobbies and pastimes; others spring from interests developed later in life.

On the more unconventional side, Craig Hosada has long been a movie buff who especially enjoys watching his favorite well-known movie stars in classic nude love scenes. While reviewing one of his favorite scenes in a screening room where he worked, he was asked by a colleague if he knew of any other love scenes the actress they were watching had done. Right then and there, Hosada had an idea of how he could earn a living pursuing one of his favorite pastimes. His idea was to publish a directory of nude

What has not burst forth from your own soul will never refresh you.

Goethe

Often people expect that Clarissa Frasier finds her work as an independent medical claims processor to be boring. They couldn't be more wrong. "I love to do things other people hate. Usually my clients are already hurting, and by processing their claims I can make their lives a little easier. It makes my day to see their eyes light up when they realize I've done all the stuff they'd dreaded having to do."

"I love reading court transcripts," says transcriptionist Martina Szlova. "I learn so much every day about things I'd never otherwise encounter. And it's like reading a soap opera, but it's better than TV, because it's real life."

scenes well-known actors and actresses had appeared in. While it may sound like a bizarre idea, it's become a booming success. Called *The Bare Facts,* his directory caught on immediately. Now in its third edition, it has been publicized in *Video Movie Review* and *Playboy* magazines. Hosada has even been a guest on the *Joan Rivers Show.* And the best thing for him about his new business is that it is something he can do from home where he can spend time with his family and his new baby.

On a more conventional side, Constance Briggett told us, "I love to type. I can type for hours and never get tired. I've enjoyed it all my life, ever since I took typing in junior high school. For me, it's almost like being in a meditative state." Having worked as a secretary for years, Briggett became disillusioned by the low pay, lack of respect, and overtime she experienced on the job, so she went out on her own. You can surely guess what she decided to do for a living.

Because we are naturally drawn to do things we most enjoy, it's not surprising that once people decide to work for themselves, many of them find their perfect work involves earning a living by doing what they truly love. After all, if you're going to create a job for yourself, why not create one you really enjoy? This choice nevertheless often goes unrecognized. Many more people would undoubtedly pursue their passion for a living if they could just believe it's actually possible. Unfortunately, most of us have been taught to think of work as something that's supposed to be unpleasant and not for our own enjoyment. This archaic idea of work is beginning to change, but it's still sufficiently pervasive that far too many people summarily dismiss the possibility they could find their perfect work and create a job for themselves doing the things they most enjoy.

Just in case you have any doubts about being able to support yourself perfectly well doing something you thoroughly enjoy, here are some mind-bending real-life examples that we hope will stretch your idea of what's possible. These profiles provide a glimpse of the broad spectrum of ways people have turned something unconventional they enjoy into a living.

SOMEONE'S REALLY MAKING A LIVING DOING THIS!

These mind-bending examples are reflective of the economic changes we described in Chapter 1. If people like the following can actually make a living doing what they love, should you wish to, surely you too can find a way to make a living pursuing your passion.

Antique Office Furniture. Thor and GiGi Konwin love old things, but not just any old things; specifically, they're fascinated by old office technology. Always interested in antiques, they developed a particular passion for finding and restoring old office equipment. They decided to devote a year and a half to tracking down rare office artifacts and restoring them. Then they opened This Old Office, a catalog and retail store specializing in fully restored technologies like typewriters, calculators, telephones, check protectors, etc., circa 1882–1924. (One of the calculators has more moving parts than an airplane of the same vintage and cost more than a Cadillac in its time.) They sell mostly to private individuals; but if you look closely, you'll see some of the Konwins' period pieces on television and movie sets too!

Backcountry Adventures. Debra Mounla fell in love with the backcountry of Arizona—its history, landscapes, legends, coyote trails, streams, cattle passes, cactus-covered mountains, panoramic waterfalls, arroyos, and mesas. Today as Soaring Eagle Adventures, a day-tour service, she earns her living sharing all these hidden treasures with others, taking families and tourists on daily treks hiking, panning for gold, picnicking, playing in hundred-foot waterfalls, horseback riding, or touring all her favorite places in all-weather jeeps.

Bad Weather. Photographer Warren Faidley is obsessed with bad weather. As a boy he dreamed of being a Navy pilot, but his eyesight kept him from achieving that dream. His second love was photography, so after studying journalism he began doing freelance photography for a wire service and local papers. His life took a strange twist in 1983, however, when southern Arizona was hit by a major flood and Faidley was assigned to his first bad-

> Is not life a thousand times too short for us to bore ourselves?
> *Friedrich Nietzsche*

weather shoot. Houses were collapsing into a river, the world was deluged by water, and he was transfixed. Soon after that a freak thunderstorm came to Tucson, and his newly acquired fascination for bad weather led him to capture the picture of a lifetime. A light pole twenty feet from him was struck by a lightning bolt so powerful that it knocked Faidley off his feet and nearly kicked his camera over. The light blinded him. He could smell the ozone and feel the shock wave of electricity. All he could think about, though, was getting the shot—which he did. It turned out to be the closest high-quality photo ever taken of lightning, and *Life* magazine published it in 1989. Now every morning Faidley listens for the weather report on the Weather Channel and other sources and heads off for the worst weather around. Some days he'll drive 500 to 600 miles for the chance to get a great shot. He shoots hurricanes, tornadoes, and disasters of all kinds. His photos are represented by twelve photo agents around the world and a film agent in Los Angeles who markets 35-millimeter film. "I think the secret to life," he says, "is to have one goal that's always eluding you." For the past three years for him that goal has been to get a shot from inside the eye of a tornado. "Maybe next year," he says.

Baseball. Although Henry Stephenson's talents lie on the computer keyboard instead of the playing field, he earns his living at the center of professional baseball. He and his wife, Holly, draw up the playing schedule for the major-league baseball season. "In the computer field," Henry says, "you tend to do fairly boring things or just one aspect of something. This is interesting because we follow through on the whole process—analyzing the system, doing the programming, and working on the schedule. Then at the end of the process, we get to go to the games and actually see our work." At first Holly and Henry were trying to develop software so sports leagues could do their own scheduling, but they found too many human judgments were needed. So instead they quit their jobs as a systems analyst and urban planner, respectively, and began offering a scheduling service for professional sports leagues. They prepare all these league schedules right from an office in their three-story Staten Island home. So if your favorite team is on the road when you're in town, you now know who's to blame.

Big Murals. Kent Twitchell paints murals, BIG murals—four, five, twelve stories high—on freeway walls, underpasses, and buildings. Now fifty-three, Twitchell did not originally expect to become a renowned outdoor muralist. As a kid growing up in a small Michigan town, though, he was already painting big roosters on the side of the barn. In fact, he's always been a big thinker. Images like Stonehenge and Mount Rushmore have always danced in his head. He says he "just has this thing for big things." Despite his love for creating large images, at first he had a fear of heights. Now, however, he buckles himself into a harness, climbs the swaying scaffolding of his "canvas" walls, and works above the roar of the freeway or clatter of street traffic below. These days, however, he isn't actually painting the murals up there anymore. Instead Twitchell paints from his home so he can be with his family. Through a process he's developed, the mural is actually created in his home studio where he does the graphics, photographs every section, then enlarges them into long strips of material that he glues together on their intended location.

Castles in the Sand. It's jokingly said that people who dream grand dreams but never achieve them are building castles in the sand. Well, Bob Bell and Ted Seibert dream of building grand castles in the sand, and they actually do it. Their castles aren't washed away by the tide, however, because they build them in shopping malls, at trade shows, fairs, and festivals throughout North America and around the world. Their company, The Sand Castle, builds massive thirty-five-ton, two-story sand castles, indoors or out, of just about whatever their clients want, be it scenes from *The Wizard of Oz* or Santa's village. Their sand sculptures last about three months.

Celebrities. Karen Hebert was a first-grade teacher, but her interest in authors and celebrities led her to create a job for herself as a freelance media escort. Working on her own now for fourteen years, Hebert spends her days shepherding authors and celebrities around town to book signings, media interviews, and talk-show appearances. Her clients are the publishers or studios

"If you have built castles in the air, your work need not be lost; that is where they should be. Now put foundations under them."

Henry David Thoreau

who send their authors and stars out on the media circuit, and Hebert has now guided hundreds of them through their arduous schedules. She's escorted Clive Barker, Ken Follett, Carrie Fisher, Bob Woodward, Muhammad Ali, Dom DeLuise, Shirley Mac-Laine, and many more whose names you'd recognize. You may be surprised to learn there are freelance media escorts like Hebert in every major metropolitan area.

Exotic Reptiles. Former camp counselor Teresa Pollack has a strange passion—reptiles. She's turned that love into an intriguing livelihood entertaining kids and adults from age four and up. For each appearance she's hired to do, she brings her collection of snakes, frogs, turtles, and lizards for an hour-long presentation in which she introduces up to twenty-five species and discusses where they come from, how they live, what they eat, and so forth. Her reptilian friends include an eleven-foot Burmese python and a basilisk, which is a type of iguana.

Folklore. Bill Wellington moved to the mountains of West Virginia in the mid 1970s to follow what he calls "an uncontrollable interest in fiddle and banjo music." There he was welcomed by the older musicians, who had seen a decline in community interest in the old-time music. They felt Bill captured the spirit as well as the tunes of their music. He played his banjo throughout the state and became Old-Time Banjo Champion of West Virginia in 1987. While in the mountains, however, Bill also became impressed with the power and importance of the folklore of the region, and today Wellington is a virtual ambassador of its folklore. He believes it is something parents and children can share together, and that's what he does for a living through concerts, children's programs, and recordings.

Gargoyles. Marla Harper has been fascinated with gargoyles since she was a child. Several years ago she had an idea for how to turn this passion into a livelihood. She hand-draws gargoyles from famous buildings around the world and transfers them onto T-shirts, tote bags, sweatshirts, and other items that she sells directly or through tourist sites. Her company is called Building Creatures. While this is a part-time venture now, she plans for this work to grow into a full-time living.

"...do that which best stirs you to love."
Saint Teresa of Avila

Marla Harper,
Building Creatures

Horror. Del Howison and partner, Sue Duncan, have both been fascinated by horror movies, comics, and books all their lives. Last year they turned that passion into a part-time, soon-to-be full-time livelihood creating Dark Delicacies, a catalog of horror gifts and books. In addition to books, comics, and movies, their catalog includes horror candelabras, horror place mats and quilts, horror Christmas stockings, and more. Another especially enjoyable aspect of their work is that Dark Delicacies has become an interest the family can share together.

At first Del and Sue sold their favorite horror paraphernalia strictly by mail order using lists like the Horror Writers of America or at conventions like the World Horror Convention. They have over a thousand horror devotees on their mailing list. Recently, however, they've opened a retail horror shop, adding new items on consignment from horror artists. The shop has enabled them to reclaim their home, 90 percent of which had been taken over by merchandise. Already they're averaging $250 a day in sales at their bookstore alone. "It's our niche!" Del says. To promote the store they've created a bulletin board listing upcoming horror events in the community, and they host a horror event every month at the store. A hearse club was featured one month, and Sarah Karloff (daughter of Boris) was once a guest speaker for an event. Not surprisingly Del says, "We're scared to death, but we're having a great time!"

Hot-Air Ballooning. Mike Bundgaard developed his love for hot-air ballooning rather late in life. At age forty-eight, he bought a balloon to help advertise his marginally profitable bicycle sales and repair shop. Once he had the balloon, he started participating in ballooning events where he met and fell in love not only with his partner and wife-to-be, Joyce, but also with ballooning. He sold the bicycle shop and opened the Lifecycle Balloon School Unlimited, providing balloon rides, selling balloons, and teaching people how to pilot them. He says it's a lot of work but a lot of fun, because sailing over the earth in a balloon is a lifetime dream for many people. As interest in ballooning is growing, the Bundgaards' livelihood is soaring right along with their balloons.

Musical Instruments. The Clark brothers, Dave, Phil, and Wayne, love folk instruments of all kinds—like dulcimers, hammerettes, Swedish humles, German zithers, Irish bodhrens, ancient medieval psalteries, guitars, Celtic harps, lyres, lutes, mandolins, Indian tanburs, and many others. To assure the availability of these rare instruments at reasonable prices, they created Rocky Mountain Enterprises in 1985. Many of the instruments in their catalog couldn't be obtained anywhere at any price before they began making them. Their business supports four families, and they run it from their three houses, which are situated side by side on a street in Homestead, Pennsylvania, a bedroom community of Pittsburgh. Dave points out that most hand-crafted musical instruments are made in someone's basement. "What's unique about our company," he explains, "is the variety of instruments we make from scratch and the volume." Rocky Mountain Enterprises produces from 1,000 to 1,500 instruments a year. Nonetheless, having left his job as corporate controller for an oil company, Dave says, "I'm much freer doing what I love. I don't make quite as much money, but every dollar we spend goes directly to our families or our business. I have everything I need and almost everything I want. I'm much happier."

Neon. Daniel Sullivan's passion is neon. As a neon artist he creates art and signs for restaurants, nightclubs, entertainment centers, small businesses, and private individuals. His company is called Thunder & Neon, and in the summer of 1990 his entire factory and office were destroyed by fire. (He's quick to point out, though, that the fire wasn't caused by the neon.) After the fire, rather than being discouraged, he just kept going. By moving his entire operation into his home, he never missed a beat or lost a client.

New Ideas. Like her growing following of radio listeners, Laura Lee is interested in cutting-edge ideas. She's fascinated by alternative views and mental adventures into uncharted conceptual territory. She recognized, however, that in many fields some of the most exciting discoveries, theories, stories, concepts, and developments just never get heard. So she decided to create a radio show dedicated to trying on and discussing new ideas with leading-edge thinkers in a wide range of fields. Her show, *The Laura Lee Show,* airs nationwide every night on the Business Radio Network. Lee broadcasts live from her home in Belleview, Washington. She also sells tapes of her shows through a mail-order catalog. Subjects include ancient history, new science, alternative health, brain/mind research, living mythology, ecology and nature, and much more. In response to listener demand, her catalog also includes the books, videos, and audiotapes of the authorities she interviews.

People. Videobiographer Bruce Long has been interested in personal stories since he was a child growing up in tiny Spur, Texas. To this day, he recalls that the town was filled with unforgettable characters. "Everybody's story is fascinating, full of high drama, agony, and ecstasy," says Long. "We all have our own journey and it has its unique perils, joys, and pleasures. If you get below the facts, the dates and place of birth, where you went to college and how many kids you have, you get to the soap opera." And that's what Long captures—the extraordinary life stories of ordinary people, the seamstresses, the aerospace workers, the insurance salesmen, who otherwise might die without anyone ever knowing their stories. His clients are usually those who want to preserve their family histories. After about two and a half hours of video interviewing their aging parents, Long gives them each more than Andy Warhol's fifteen minutes of fame—a full hour to be remembered by.

Rock Carvings. Mary Maturi and her family lived for one year on Wrangell Island in southeast Alaska. One day she traveled to Petroglyph Beach, an area of massive rocks grooved with carvings from an ancient unknown tribe. She fell in love with these beautiful carvings and wanted to preserve them. Using rice paper and different colored ferns, she rubbed the petroglyphs to transfer their images onto the paper. When she showed her tracings to friends, they too were fascinated and she decided she wanted to share their beauty with others. The tracings were many feet long, however, so she had to figure how to create them in a more accessible form; that's how her company, Killer Whale note cards, was born. Using the rubbings as her guide, she created smaller pen-and-ink drawings for her cards, which she now sells in Alaskan gift shops and natural-history museums nationwide. Her petroglyphs are also available on T-shirts and sweatshirts.

Roaming. Michael Lane, a former music company executive, and Jim Crotty, a former publicist, are modern-day vagabonds. In

1986 they set out on an open-ended journey in their twenty-six-foot mobile home with their two cats. They've been traveling around the United States for ten years, living like virtual monks. Along the way they started writing a newsletter to share their unique perspective of this American journey with their friends and family. Their tales were so hilarious that Michael's mother suggested they sell subscriptions to help support their travels. Taking up the idea, they began supporting the publication at first with health food and New Age advertising. Their advertising base has grown to include record companies, book publishers, and liquor manufacturers. From their humble beginnings, *Monk* has become a 100-page glossy four-color quarterly magazine with 40,000 subscribers, read by over 140,000 readers, and brings in $40,000 per issue in ad revenue. Written in a Christmas-letter, round-robin-like fashion, *Monk* is truly a dashboard publication, written entirely on their solar-powered Macintosh. Now Lane and Crotty also have a book, *Mad Monks on the Road,* published by Simon & Schuster. They are most certainly making a living creating a life.

Rowing. Former Harvard sculling coach Buz Tarlow started the Southern California Boat Club to teach rowing, sailing, and kayaking to writers, truck drivers, doctors, lawyers, and other men and women looking for an alternative way to exercise and socialize. He opened the school in 1992 with three shells, put ads in several local papers, and then began earning a living teaching the sports he loves to people who would otherwise never experience these fascinating sports. The club now has 100 members.

Spices. It seems that more than some like it hot these days. Numbers of people are turning their love for the spice of life into a good living. Newlyweds Tim and Wendy Eidson, for example, had a burning desire to flee the rat race of urban living and their high-pressure jobs. One of Tim's lifelong passions, hot sauce, became their ticket out. Knowing they could run a mail-order business from anywhere, they selected the oceanside community of San Luis Obispo, California, as their new home and started Mo Hotta-Mo Betta, a funky-style mail-order catalog of hot and spicy items like Hell in a Bottle and Cowboy Caviar. They sent their first catalog to 300 friends and family members despite advice from

business "experts" who told them the idea would never work—
"too small a niche" they were told. The response was great, however; sales jumped from $27,000 the first year to close to $2
million in 1993, four years later.

Robert Spiegel also turned his love for hot stuff into a living
by publishing *Chile Pepper* magazine. His Albuquerque-based bimonthly publication is in such demand that revenues will top $1
million this year. Jeff McFadden also tapped into his passion for a
spicy palette. He turned his salsa recipe, which he calls Religious
Experience, into an instant hit around his hometown of Grand
Junction, Colorado. Its reputation has spread far and wide, and his
sales have grown 60 to 70 percent a year since he started in 1988
to over a half million dollars a year.

Spinning Wheels. Florence Feldman-Wood is *The Spinning
Wheel Sleuth.* That's the name of her newsletter, but it's also how
she thinks of herself because she tracks down unusual spinning
wheels and information about them which she publishes in her
newsletter before these rare wheels and their histories are lost
forever. Each issue focuses on one or two types of wheels, their
locations, and what they are known for. She also takes listings from
dealers or collectors seeking or selling interesting spinning
wheels. As a teacher of spinning and weaving herself, she wants to
share her knowledge and enjoyment of textiles with others as do
her friends who are quilters, knitters, and other textile crafters.
Realizing that many crafts groups are constantly seeking speakers and instructors for lectures and workshops, she created her
specialized registry service to help link these fiber and fabric
enthusiasts.

Surfing. Aaron Chang has become one of the world's top surf
photographers. Surfing is his passion. In fact, becoming a professional surfing photographer was primarily a route for Chang to
continue surfing full-time without starving. He was given a camera by his father, and he put it to work pursuing his passion. As a
surfing photographer he could travel the world from Australia to
Hawaii, Bali to South Africa, surfing the best places and making
top money riding the top waves. At thirty-three, Chang secured a
retainer from a surfing magazine and many other freelance jobs.
Now he also has a line of T-shirts and sweatshirts featuring black-

and-white reproductions of his photos, and he's expanded his work to other lines of professional photography.

Tearing Paper. Marlene Stephenson is a medical technician by background, but one night while attending a coffee klatch with a group of friends who meet weekly to explore new craft ideas, she fell in love with a unique form of making torn-paper sculptured jewelry. She began wearing her handmade creations, and people who saw them asked her to make some for them. She now creates custom-made one-of-a-kind pieces for her clients that match their clothing ensembles.

Toy Cars. Three years ago Stephen Yoke could only hope to live until retirement to do what he really wanted to do. Now he says, "I feel retired and still have the rest of my life to look forward to. Each new day is a new vista. I don't ever want to quit working if this is the way it's going to be for me." Three years ago, Yoke decided to turn his hobby of collecting toy cars into his livelihood. He started on the side, keeping his job as an Oldsmobile salesman, until by 1992 he was earning over $90,000 a year selling his collections of miniature cars at car shows, swap meets, and toy shows. Then he decided to "cut the cord of occupational bondage," as he puts it, and quit his job. Within twenty months of leaving his job, his sales have grown to exceed $200,000, and at forty-seven he says, "I've found my ultimate source of income for life."

> To love what you do and feel it matters—how could anything be more fun?
>
> *Katharine Graham*

IDENTIFYING YOUR PASSION TO PURSUE

As you can see from these examples, there seems to be no end to the possibilities for earning a living doing something you love. The only barrier is suspending your disbelief that you could do it, too, if you wish. Use the following work sheets on pages 137–139 to begin exploring the possibilities for pursuing your own passions.

PROS AND CONS OF PURSUING A PASSION

If you have one or more passions you would strongly enjoy pursuing as your livelihood, you will find doing so has a definite advantage: you won't have trouble motivating yourself to get to work

PURSUING YOUR PASSION WORK SHEET

Is there anything you especially enjoy or have a fascination for? It might be some aspect of your current work. It might be something you'd never dream you could get paid for like playing golf or tennis, writing children's stories, making people laugh, matchmaking, even going to parties. Actually, as you will see, there is usually some way to turn your greatest passion into a living, so don't be concerned at this point about how you would do it. Think instead of those things about which you can truly say "I'd do this even if I weren't being paid!" Think of those things you'd leap out of bed on Monday morning to do even if you were still tired and worn out from an exhausting weekend. What things, if any, do you feel that way about? What would you do with your days if you could spend them doing anything you want? Make a list of these things here, and to help you decide if you'd like to pursue any of them as your livelihood, rate each passion on a scale of 1 to 10 as to how interested you would be in making your living doing it.

1	2	3	4	5	6	7	8	9	10
NOT VERY INTERESTED				SOMEWHAT INTERESTED					VERY INTERESTED

Base your ratings on **1)** the Magic Factor pursuing each passion as a livelihood has for you, how energizing and compelling it would be, and **2)** how closely pursuing it would match with the type of life you want to create for yourself.

*Do not base your evaluation on whether
or not you think you could make enough money using this gift.
You'll be able to evaluate that in Part III.*

PASSIONS *The Things I Enjoy Most*	MAGIC FACTOR RATING	LIFESTYLE MATCH RATING

PASSIONS _The Things I Enjoy Most_	MAGIC FACTOR RATING	LIFESTYLE MATCH RATING

Now list below any passions that appeal to you based on a 7 rating or above along with any ideas you have for pursuing these passions as a way to make a living. Look through Appendix II: "An Alphabetical Directory of Self-Employment Careers" for other possible ideas on how you might support yourself pursuing these passions and list any appealing ideas here.

PASSIONS   POSSIBLE SELF-EMPLOYMENT OCCUPATIONS

1. _____   _____

   _____   _____

2. _____   _____

   _____   _____

3. _____   _____

   _____   _____

4. _____   _____

   _____   _____

5. _____   _____

   _____   _____

6. _____   _____

   _____   _____

7. _____   _____

   _____   _____

8. _____   _____

TWO FOR ONE IS MORE FUN

Some people combine two or more passions into a livelihood:

Joshua Grenrock loves pets, people, and photography. So that's the name of his company: Pets, People, and Photography. He says, "I create fine-art portraits of the entire family."

Kent Kachigian combines his love for doing fine-art watercolors with his love for gourmet cuisine. He does paintings of the top chefs in the country as they are at work in their kitchens.

Lauren Hefferon began a love affair with Italy when she won a Rotary scholarship to study there. Now she has combined her passion for Italy with her love of cycling and outdoor education. She takes people on cycling and walking tours of Italy.

Jeff Caneis is a self-proclaimed scribe. Inspired by the illuminated manuscripts of the Middle Ages, he transforms letters, poetry, and documents into works of art. For $300 he will combine his love of history, poetry, and art into unique handmade communiqués for his clients complete with ribbons, wax seals, and parchment paper.

Sig Unander combines his love of aviation with his love for art. He sells prints, posters, paintings, and sculptures of classic airplanes. His company is Air Art Northwest.

and keep at it! Your passion is intrinsically motivating. In other words, your work is rewarding in and of itself. And because you like doing it so much, pursuing a passion provides you with a level of endurance and perseverance that other paths may not. If the going gets tough, you'll be more likely to keep going because you have such a passion for what you're doing.

Three Reasons You Don't Have to Be Exceptionally Gifted When You're Exceptionally Motivated

As many golfers will testify, just because you have a passion for something doesn't mean you're gifted at it. You may love it but not necessarily be the very best at it. So if you're not particularly outstanding at what you're most interested in, don't think that means you can't earn a living doing it. You can. To pursue your passion as a livelihood, you don't have to be excellent at it already in order to succeed. If you are the best, that's great. That means you have both a gift and a passion! That's a powerful combination. But it isn't necessary for three reasons:

1. To succeed on your own, you only need to be sufficiently competent to inspire sufficient confidence to attract clients and customers and to deliver a satisfactory result for them. And fortunately competence is usually something you can acquire through experience.

In this sense, creating a job for yourself is like finding employment with someone else. Employers must hire the best they can get, but that doesn't mean they can always hire the very best. Often they can't. Most independent careers aren't like professional sports. You don't need to be among the elite to do perfectly well.

If you don't believe this, just think about your own experience as a consumer. Haven't you seen people who are extremely successful at something who aren't the very best there is at it? Surely you have. These people are successful because they're so motivated by their work that they will go the extra mile to win the trust and support of loyal clients and customers. You probably use many such services yourself. Do you only use the very, very best printer in the city? Do you go to only the very, very best lawyer or accountant? Is your dentist the very best in the field? Are your appliances always the top of the line? There is ample evidence that there's plenty of room for mere competence in the marketplace.

2. You can educate yourself and build your competence. When you love what you're doing, usually you're automatically motivated to work at it long enough and frequently enough to develop sufficient competence. When you love what you do, usually you want to learn from every mistake and correct it to do better. This will help you grow into the kind of person who can attract and satisfy clients and customers.

Remember Abbe Gail Eckstein, the woman who had people buying hats right off her head? Well, her talent for hats began as a passion. She loved hats because her favorite memories from childhood were the times when she and her grandmother would play

There is nothing so easy but that it becomes difficult when you do it reluctantly.

Terence

"You are good at
what you enjoy with
the possible exception
of golf and tennis."
Richard Bolles

- Fred Astaire was
  once told he
  couldn't dance.
- Phyllis Diller was
  told to go home
  during rehearsal the
  first time she had a
  chance to appear
  on TV.
- Paul Newman was
  told he couldn't act.
- Sir Laurence Olivier
  tripped over the
  scenery and fell into
  the footlights on his
  stage debut. The au-
  dience and cast
  laughed at him.
- Joan Rivers was
  booed off the stage
  during one of her
  earliest perfor-
  mances.

dress-up and her grandmother would let her wear the most unusual and beautiful hats. As an adult Abbe Gail decided she wanted
to learn how to make hats as a hobby, so she took a class in hat
making—but she failed it. So she took the class again—but she
failed it again. By the third time, however, she could make a decent
hat and the teacher was truly proud of her progress. Of course,
Eckstein didn't stop there. Her hat-making abilities continued to
improve as she pursued her hobby until the time came when people would literally stop her on the street to admire and inquire
about her hats.

In this information-intensive age, there are books, tapes, seminars, workshops, videos, and every other conceivable means for
educating yourself to become competent in some aspect of whatever passion you want to pursue.

3. In some cases, you don't have to do what you love to be
part of what you love. Of course there are some limitations you
can't or won't want to surmount with education. If you are tone
deaf, chances are you won't be able to support yourself as an opera
singer. But if opera is your passion there is still a myriad of ways
you can be involved in earning a living from opera even if you can't
sing. Below is a range of ways you can become involved in earning
a living pursuing any passion.

Deborah Blum's father was a well-known entomologist, and
she dreamed of following in his footsteps into a career in science.
Early in her education, however, it became clear she was not cut
out for a career in research. "Klutzes don't make very good scien-

TEN DIFFERENT WAYS TO DO WHATEVER YOU LOVE	
1. Do what you love.	6. Create a product related to what you love.
2. Provide a service to others who do what you love.	7. Sell or broker what you love.
3. Teach others to do what you love.	8. Promote what you love.
4. Write about what you love.	9. Organize what you love.
5. Speak about what you love.	10. Set up, repair, restore, fix, or maintain what you love.

tists," she says, remembering how she knocked over the Bunsen burner in freshman chemistry and almost burned down the lab. Her abilities lay elsewhere, in the field of writing and journalism. But she still pursues her love for science as a science writer, a field in which she has excelled, writing many prize-winning stories and even winning a Pulitzer Prize. Now she has a critically acclaimed book entitled *The Monkey Wars,* a study of the controversy over the use of primates in scientific research.

Like Blum, you can undoubtedly find various ways in which to apply your own natural abilities to whatever the things you love most. To explore those possibilities, take the Doing What Comes Naturally survey in **Appendix I** and then explore the types of self-employment occupations best suited to your top three abilities by referring to **Appendix III: "A Directory of Self-Employment Careers by Personal Style."** Here's a few examples of the kinds of options others have found:

EXAMPLE

Do What You Love One Way or Another
A Love For Law

Do it:	Practice, mediate, or arbitrate law	*Sell:*	Prepaid legal services
Help others do it:	Become a paralegal	*Write:*	Books, articles, or newsletter on legal issues
	Do legal transcription		Edit legal textbooks
	Become a court reporter, scopist, or proofreader	*Product:*	Produce do-it-yourself legal kits
	Digest depositions and transcripts	*Organize:*	Professional organizer for law firms
	Serve as an expert witness		Law library management
	Make videos for negotiations and trials		Private practice consultant for lawyers
Teach or speak:	How to find a lawyer		Set up a referral service
	Selecting legal contract software	*Promote:*	Do public relations for lawyers or law firms
	When to do it yourself versus hire an attorney		Create networking groups for lawyers

MATCH DOING WHAT YOU LOVE WITH WHAT COMES NATURALLY

A LOVE OF ROMANCE		LOVE TO TRAVEL	
Creator:	Wedding photography	*Creator:*	Develop unusual
	Designing evening dresses		packaged tours
	Gift baskets		
Improver:	Marriage and family	*Improver:*	Publish a newsletter
	counseling		to help people live
	Matchmaking service		abroad
	Couples enrichment groups		
Organizer:	Romantic travel excursions	*Organizer:*	Become a tour
	Romantic trade shows		organizer and guide
	Romantic dinners for		
	couples		
Builder:	Massage for couples	*Builder:*	Become an outdoor
	Teaching yoga for partners		adventure guide
	Sailing excursions for lovers		
Leader:	Teach flirting classes	*Leader:*	Speak, write, and
	Speaking on restoring		promote particular
	romance		aspects of travel
	A radio show on romance		
Problem solver:	Private investigator	*Problem solver:*	Best travel buys
	Find-your-lost-lover service		referral service
	Research romance novels		

PROFILE: JIM STRAWN, LOVES TENNIS

Jim Strawn is a certified tennis professional. He operates a part-time home-based racquet-restringing and repair service. He also teaches tennis at a local tennis club twelve to fourteen hours a week and has built a substantial client base of tennis and racquetball players in Roanoke, Virginia.

In **Part III: "The Means"** you will learn more about how you can package what you love to do to fit your personality and the marketplace and how to make a choice from the myriad of possibilities.

FIND VARIED AVENUES TO PURSUE YOUR PASSION

John Nagy runs a historical database of nineteenth-century newspapers.

Mark Detwiller collects and sells rare records.

Allegra Yust, twenty-five, publishes a Blue Book Social Registry that began in 1917. She didn't want to see its tradition die.

Mary and Richard Haggerty use their computer and a database to tell people what happened 100 years ago on their birthday or any other given date they request.

Wendy Elliot is an oral historian and author of several books on how to preserve your family's history.

James Martin researches and mixes paints for renovating historic buildings.

Suzanne Koblentz-Goodman and her husband loved restoring their turn-of-the-century duplex. They live in a neighborhood of historic New York brownstones. Now she pursues her love of history using architectural skills to help others renovate their brownstones.

Tori Kovach is restoring historic buildings in his hometown of Aberdeen, Oregon.

WHEN THIS ROAD IS AN UNUSUALLY EASY OR INTRIGUING CHALLENGE

If what you love doing is something people dearly want or need but absolutely hate or have no time to do, pursuing your passion could be remarkably easy. That has certainly been the case for Ron Aslett. He loves something most people abhor, housecleaning. Aslett founded his own cleaning company over thirty years ago to pay his way through Idaho State University. He found he could reduce the time involved in housecleaning by 75 percent and soon expanded his business to other states and added other services like home repair, floor refinishing, paperhanging, painting, even rebuilding and landscaping. Eventually he began writing and consulting on ways to cut cleaning costs in home and commercial

Deliver us to our passion.

Marianne Williamson

LOVE ANIMALS?

TWENTY WAYS YOU CAN TURN A LOVE OF ANIMALS INTO
A FULL- OR PART-TIME LIVING:

- Keep pedigree records by computer
- Provide inventory for pet shops
- Develop a mail-order business for pet owners
- Create pet novelties
- Operate a pet-sitting service
- Provide a pet taxi service
- Groom pets from a van that goes to the pet's door
- Catalogue and track pet diseases by breed for vets and breeders
- Train pets and their owners
- Breed pets
- Photograph pets
- Create videotape histories or life stories of family pets and notable animals
- Offer counseling to grieving pet owners
- Write books on the nature, history, and care of pets
- Create multimedia products featuring pets, perhaps pet histories for families
- Cook gourmet foods for pampered pets
- Operate a dog-walking service
- Create a database of characteristics of winning animals organized by judge and sell the information to owners and handlers
- Operate a pet lost-and-found service on the Internet, which forms the foundation for a store selling pet items or services to grateful owners you have helped
- Provide a taxidermy service for owners of pets who wish to keep their loved creatures around

---

buildings and has since become known as America's #1 Cleaning Expert, having written dozens of books on how to save housecleaning time and money. He now travels the country speaking, conducting seminars and workshops, and, of course, selling his many books.

If your passion coincides with some latent or growing hunger or craving people have, then you, too, may find yourself catapulted to success along this path with a speed and ease you would never have imagined. That's what happened to Bev Wood, whose passion is psychology. Bev's interest coincided with the emerging Human Potential Movement of the early 1960s, so when she decided to conduct a seminar in her hometown of St. Louis on one of the newest psychological techniques, she was overwhelmed with registrants. Hundreds of people turned out, and suddenly she had a flourishing occupation.

If your passion is sufficiently in tune with the times, you may even have the opportunity to pioneer in an entirely new field. Julia Child, for example, fell in love with French cooking at a time when very few Americans knew much about it. When she began writing and speaking on French cuisine, the American public became as enchanted and intrigued with it as Child was. They devoured her cookbooks and flocked to see, hear, and learn from her.

PROFILE: RICHARD BANGS

Thirty years ago, whoever had heard of white-river rafting? Fewer than 100 people had rafted down the Colorado River, and "adventure travel" was not part of the travel vacationer's vocabulary.

That was before Richard Bangs pioneered what has become a burgeoning field. Twenty-one years ago Bangs began taking people on river-rafting trips. He fell in love with rafting as a teenager cruising the Potomac outside Washington, D.C. During college, he spent summers as a guide on the Colorado River. Then, as a last fling before settling down to the "real" world and getting a job, he convinced some friends to join him on an African river-rafting trip.

It was such an overwhelming experience for him that on his way home he decided rafting and adventure travels had to be his life work. So in 1973, he cofounded a company that is now called Mountain Travel-Sobek. He never really intended to go into business, so much as to find a way to support himself so he could keep rafting.

Now of course, he's only one of many, many rafting and adventure companies; but he's still the world's largest, taking customers down the Amazon, up Mount Everest, even to the North

Passion persuades.
Anita Roddick

Pole. And while many areas are overrun with "adventurers," he's still finding new worlds to explore such as Mozambique, Angola, Cuba, Afghanistan. He says, "Every time I look at a map, I'm still amazed at how much has yet to be explored." And you can bet if there's a way to get there, Bangs will be willing to take you.

WHEN THIS ROAD IS PARTICULARLY CHALLENGING

On the other hand, as is all too often the case, if what you love doing is something many others would love to do and the readily available opportunities to pursue it are limited, then choosing this path can become a more challenging one. For example, if your passion is acting, dancing, oil painting, fly fishing, playing golf, or writing poetry, you will no doubt have to be more creative and ingenious in discovering how you can package what you want to do so that you'll actually be able to earn a living at it. We truly do not want you to have the experience of trying to do what you love only to discover the money just doesn't follow. We have seen so many people beat their heads bloody against closed doors while trying to do what they love most. We've spoken with a man who lost his family, his home, and finally even his car trying to do what he loved. We've talked with a woman who was abandoned by her husband because year after year she refused to give up her dream and take a paying job. We've seen marriages break up over failed ventures, met people who lost their homes trying to finance their passion, people who returned in despair to jobs they hated because their egos had been severely battered and wounded by years of failure. We don't want that to happen to you, and it doesn't have to. There is another way.

> "If you want to succeed, you should strike out on new paths rather than travel the worn paths of accepted success."
> *John D. Rockefeller*

FINDING OPEN DOORS

For some people, the biggest challenge of choosing this path will be finding how to make it financially secure. Your challenge, if you choose to pursue this path, could be to find some way to do what you love that plenty of people will willingly pay for or one that others have not already snapped up. In some cases, it may feel as if you're trying to get into an auditorium that hordes of others are also flocking to but there's only one access door. Meanwhile the gatekeeper is only letting in one or two people every so often. It may look as though you will have to stand in line a long, long time before you'll even get a chance to get in. Or it may seem as if you're going to have to jostle, push, and shove your way through the door, trampling everyone else to get where you want to go. Neither the endless wait nor the knock-down-drag-out battle is a very appealing path for most people. That's why many of us give up on taking the path of our passion without even giving it a chance.

But you don't need to. Nine out of ten people who successfully pursue what they love don't even try getting in the same door everyone else is pushing to go through. They find an alternative route, an alternative entrance, sometimes even an alternative auditorium where they can just walk right in. Often success involves connecting the activities you enjoy with activities they're not usually associated with. Here are just a few examples:

Body Designs. When George Hoeing graduated from the Chicago Art Institute, he saw two equally unappealing paths open before him. On the one hand, he could go the starving-artist route, struggle to get his original work placed in a gallery somewhere, and hope to sell enough pieces to live on someday, or he could take a job in a commercial agency creating artwork for advertising copy. Not content to choose either of these routes, he looked for an alternative. His goals were twofold: 1) to have as many people see his artwork as possible and 2) to earn a good living creating his own designs. A bodybuilder himself, one day at the gym he had an idea. Bodybuilders love to show off their bodies in colorful workout garb. Why not create a line of clothing displaying his designs! That's exactly what he did. The workout clothes are his canvas, and you can see his art worn in style in gyms across America.

Radio Theater. Susan Albert Loewenberg had a dream of creating a theater company where top actors and actresses could return to their roots in the theater between television and film projects. She began building a repertory company. Performing initially in prisons, she wanted her troupe to evolve into the L.A. Classical Theater Works, but she couldn't raise the money needed to bring that project together. Undeterred, Loewenberg found an unusual alternative route to her dreams.

She took theater to an unaccustomed medium. As part of her fund-raising effort, she put on a benefit in the form of a live in-studio performance radio show starring most of thirty-four actors in the company. It was so successful that she kept doing radio productions, hoping to keep the company alive until other funds materialized. But before long her radio work had a life of its own.

"I do love it," Susan says of her radio theater. "I wouldn't do it if it weren't fun."

Loewenberg has created the nation's leading contemporary radio drama series, *The Play's the Thing,* heard weekly on KCRW FM radio, a PBS station in Los Angeles, and on the BBC in London. The plays are recorded in a Santa Monica hotel before a live paying audience of about 1,500 people, many of whom have season tickets. Each play runs for four nights and is broadcast on a subsequent Saturday or Sunday. Now she has productions in Chicago and Boston as well. Participating in her productions are such actors as Annette Benning, Joe Mantegna, John Goodman, Ed Begley, Jr., Jo Beth Williams, Tyne Daly, and Ed Asner. L.A. Theater Works is also expanding into audiotapes. They have a 120-play audiotape library, which is sold through a catalog and on the Internet. "We're always looking for new frontiers," Loewenberg says. "Who knows where it will lead."

Knit Picks. Brenda French learned to knit in grade school and in 1978 began making scarves at home with yarn she bought at Woolworth's. Through contacts she's made working in various merchandising roles, she was able to get her scarves placed in stores that soon were begging her for sweaters to go with them. So, dying the yarns in the kitchen sink, she began designing and making the sweaters that have become known as French Rags. Sold in top stores across the country like Saks Fifth Avenue and Bloomingdale's, her original sweater collections expanded into coats, jackets, skirts, and pants and boomed into a major industry employing 300 people in a 25,000-square-foot factory. Sales approached $10 million a year. Then it all began to unravel. Financially troubled department stores needed such high markups that increasingly financially strapped customers could no longer afford to buy French Rags. Some of her knitwear ensembles were being ticketed at $1,000. French thought about going out of business, but then a customer in New York called complaining she could no longer find French Rags and proposed a novel alternative. The customer wanted French to let her sell the knitwear collection in her home at a party for her friends. At first French was skeptical. "Is this what I've come to, the Tupperware Party?" she wondered. But she gave her okay, and at the first in-home trunk showing she sold $80,000 worth of knit sweaters, dresses, and coats in five days. Soon afterward a call came from a customer in Chicago wanting to do the same. And now she has sixty agents around the country who make a 15 percent commission from their sales to women in their region who, by the overwhelming growing response, seem to be clamoring for more. French Rags sales are surging again and at $5 million a year the company is more profitable than ever before. Gone, however, is the headache of running a huge factory and workforce. French uses state-of-the-art electronic knitting machines run by computers, which has cut her need for a large workforce, but she retains a small crew of hand knitters. French has found another way to continue doing what she loves.

Performing for Kids. Tom Stewart, twenty-seven, has been interested in the performing arts for years, but he admits he didn't think he'd end up as a Teenage Ninja Turtle, Superman, Elvis Presley, PeeWee Herman, or Batman. But that's how he earns his living, pulling costumes from the trunk of his car to perform at kids' parties. Although he never gets a weekend off, he grossed over $100,000 last year. Sometimes he drives several hundred miles for a party, so he's put 141,000 miles on his car in four years. His wife also is a party performer. She's a balloonist, certified by the National Association of Balloon Artists in Jacksonville, Florida, and she creates dogs and other animals and objects by blowing up and tying her balloon art into colorful party favors.

Each of these alternatives is unique. Probably none of them would work for you. But that's the key—finding the alternative that will be an open door for you. In **Part III: "The Means,"** you will learn how you can personalize an alternative route for yourself, one that will predispose you to success doing what you love.

REFUSING TO WORK FOR PENNIES

Another trap you will want to avoid in choosing this path is the temptation to work for pennies. If you truly love doing something, you may be willing to virtually give it away just for the chance to

The time has come when we must start believing people will gladly pay us to do what we most enjoy doing. Then we have to find out how to make what we enjoy so appealing that they will do so.

do it. We strongly urge you to avoid this pitfall. First, unless earning a reasonably good living is a very low priority in your life, you will be trading doing what you want to do for having a decent lifestyle. This is a trade you do not have to make unless you want to. Granted, for some people, material possessions are unimportant and if that's true for you, then fine. But if you are someone who aspires to a higher level of material comfort, working for pennies will turn you into an embittered, unhappy person. It may all too quickly take the joy out of your passion. It may even create discord in your relationships as spouses and children feel overburdened with having to provide more than their share of the household income or feel angry about being deprived of what they see others around them enjoying.

The people we introduced you to in the above examples are doing what they love but they are not working for pennies. In fact, George Hoeing finds that the more he charges for his workout clothes, the more he sells; the radio theater seats are no less expensive than any other good-quality theater performances; French Rags creations still cost from $85 to $565 each; and Tom Stewart is performing for $90 an hour. These people are successful because they've carved out their path and are making sure their way is paid.

While people who set out to make a living doing what they love may experience a dip in income at first as they start to build up their new livelihood, this dip, if necessary at all, needs to be only temporary. You must refuse to work for pennies. You must find a way to charge what you're worth and what you need. Fortunately, you can. It's a choice you can make.

Susan Schatz,
Wedding-cake
specialist

PROFILE: SUZAN SCHATZ, DOING WHAT SHE LOVES AND GETTING PAID WHAT SHE'S WORTH

Suzan Schatz fell in love with cooking while traveling and decided she wanted to make food her vocation. But she also wanted to be able to take care of her family, which includes two children who are now growing up while Schatz works from home. She decided to specialize in making gourmet wedding cakes, but, by law, she couldn't make them in her kitchen. So she developed a plan, which took two years to implement. First she and her husband, a geophysicist, had an addition built onto their home and turned it into a state-approved second kitchen. "Specializing in wedding cakes and desserts gives me tremendous flexibility and helps me plan time with the kids. I know how long tasks like preparing ingredients and decorating will take. I can put something in the oven and go over to the house for an hour. Best of all, I don't have to go out at night as I would in the catering business." And the kids can see what she does for a living. Also, because people will pay more for a wedding cake, she never has to work for pennies; her cakes average $450. And they're worth every penny, because each one is truly a one-of-a-kind work of art.

"Most of my performances are still for free" a middle-aged musician told us, his eyes weary, his clothing worn. "People just don't have the money for live performances. But I love music so much, I'd rather starve than stop playing." "I'm getting paid more for each performance I do," another musician told us. We could hear the excitement in his voice. "I'm more and more in demand. Each performance seems to lead to more. And I have a concert coming up in Hawaii." We've been utterly dismayed to discover how often we about such contrasting experiences from equally capable people who are pursuing their passions. Often these differences are written off as being a matter of self-esteem. While that is undoubtedly sometimes the case, we've found that more often, it's a matter of not knowing how to package what one loves to do in a way that people will pay for it. It's amazing how quickly success can bolster someone's self-esteem.

In **Part III: "The Means,"** you will learn how you can position what you love to do so there will be no need to work for pennies. You'll discover why the one musician was struggling while the other was thriving and what you can do to thrive, too.

WARDING OFF BLOWS TO SELF-ESTEEM

Whenever we care passionately about something, we become more vulnerable to blows to our self-esteem. When we've intensely invested in something, and care about it passionately, we tend to identify with it. It's our "baby," so to speak. An attack on it feels like an attack on us. If our work is rejected, we may feel as though we've been rejected. If it's a failure, we may feel like a failure. As a result, some business experts actually argue against ever getting into any kind of business you really care about. We think that's ridiculous advice—at least for the self-employed, because of the enormous energy, determination, endurance, and gratification that doing what you love can provide. After all, you don't abandon your "baby"; you do what it takes to keep it alive and healthy. And so it can be for those of us who choose this path.

The critics do have a point, however, in that if we take what happens in our work too personally we can lose our objectivity and make unwise decisions. Therefore, if we are to succeed on this path we must make ourselves strong. We can't let ourselves *be* babies. If our passion is our "baby," we have to be the adults, the parents. We have to take care of business. Whatever it is, we have to get over it, get past it, let go of it, so we can get on with it. We owe that to ourselves and to the work we so much love doing.

In observing successful people handle rejections, roadblocks, and setbacks, we've noticed that they often overcome them by redefining success. We were intrigued, for example, when musician Brian Taylor redefined what others would consider to be the difficulty of breaking into the music business as enabling him to be in control. We've been impressed when we've noticed how often some people will evaluate their worth not by how many sales they've made or how many clients they have, but by how many calls they've made this week or how many appointments they've set up. We've also noticed how people who are successfully doing what they love say something like what weather photographer Warren Faidley said when he didn't get his tornado shot this year: "Maybe next year."

Perhaps that's one of the greatest blessings of taking this path. Doing what we love is such a joy that we can put up with a little more or wait longer for success if need be.

One final thought about choosing this route: Not everyone wants to earn a livelihood doing what they enjoy as their pastime, hobby, or interest. Sometimes we enjoy these things **because** they are a diversion, an escape, or a novelty in contrast to the rest of our life. If this is the case, trying to turn these pursuits into a livelihood would take all the joy out of them for you and they'd just become another form of work you can't wait to get away from. So it's best to test out how much you would enjoy working at your play before making a full-blown commitment to it. Give it a try on a one-time basis, for example, and see how you feel about it. And if you do decide to pursue something you have loved as a hobby, make sure you allow yourself to develop new diversions, escapes, and ways to relax after your old treats have become your daily bread.

"Sports is my greatest love," said the medical writer.

"So why don't you write about sports?" we asked.

"Because I don't want to write about sports. I just want to enjoy them!" he answered with a smile.

PURSUING YOUR PASSION

Goal. Discovering what you love most and finding a way that people will gladly pay you to do it.

Driving Force. Usually pursuing this path has to be driven by your own inner desire, although sometimes your desire will match up with a strong external demand that can help propel you.

Pros. You probably won't have any problems staying motivated because just doing your work will give you so much enjoyment. This can also help you persevere and endure when needed. You don't have to be the best at what you do as long as you're competent and there are many ways to match what you love with the abilities you have.

Cons. Sometimes you will have to be most ingenious in figuring out how to package what you love doing so people will pay, and pay well, for it. Because you care so passionately about what you're doing, your self-esteem may become vulnerable to the ups and downs in your work—so you'll have to toughen up.

SIX

Following a Mission

You have a calling
which exists only for
you and which only
you can fulfill.

Naomi Stephan,
Ph.D.

FOLLOWING A MISSION is by far the least-traveled path people take to begin making a living creating a life. Fewer than one in six people go out on their own along this path to their perfect work. But for those who do, it can be a highly rewarding and deeply meaningful way to live. And we predict that as our economy comes to rely more heavily on self-employed individuals who are providing information and personal and creative services of all kinds, this path will become an increasingly popular one. We believe this to be true because we sense a growing hunger in people to do work that makes a difference, that fulfills some higher purpose, that makes a significant contribution to the world around us. And that's what following a mission is all about.

In many ways, following a mission is a hybrid of pursuing a passion. All the people we've met who are following a mission of some kind have a great passion for what they're doing. The difference between these two paths, however, lies in the source of the primary reward. Those pursuing a passion usually find the act of doing what they do to be personally enjoyable. Following a mission, however, is not always personally enjoyable. The enjoyment often comes not so much from what you're doing as from the ultimate benefits or results others derive from your work.

We define a mission as a cause or task or duty someone feels destined, moved, or called upon to undertake. This definition seems to capture the way people talk with us as they describe earning their living by following a mission. Often those who've chosen this path will make comments like:

"This work gives purpose to my life."
"I didn't choose this work; it chose me."
"It's my calling."
"This is my destiny."
"I'm sure this is why I was put on this Earth."
"This is what I'm here to do."
"This is my life. This is me."
"It's almost like an obsession. I just have to do this."
"I couldn't quit if I wanted to."

They may call what they're doing a mission or refer to it as a life purpose, a calling, a destiny, or a cause. But whatever it's called, following a mission involves knowing that you're doing something that goes far beyond making a living. It might involve righting a wrong, championing a cause, or creating something new and original that no one believes is possible. Earning your living following a mission provides you with the satisfaction of knowing that the world is a better place because of your work and because of what you've contributed.

A mission may spring from an inspiration, a deeply held social belief, a traumatic life experience, a problem you've overcome, or an injustice you want to correct. You may have such concerns, beliefs, and experiences in your life but not have realized you can actually support yourself devoting your life to doing something about them. Here are five ways people have set out to earn their living from a mission:

"One of the most difficult requirements of the explorer's life is to adapt to extreme and often intolerable conditions. The price of entering the unknown is misery in many forms."
Douchan Gersi, explorer

"Yeah, it's a gamble, but it's the path I'm on. I mean, this is bigger than I am. It's like, I have to go this way. This is the direction."
David Caruso, actor

1. Surviving Personal Tragedy or Overcoming Difficulty

Perhaps the most common way someone decides to follow a mission is as a result of experiencing a personal tragedy of some type, an overwhelming loss, an illness, a lifelong problem they've overcome, even a life-threatening situation. Such a mission may be fueled by a conviction that something must be done about what they've experienced, that the situation they've faced cannot be allowed to happen again, that others must know about it and be protected from it. Sometimes, however, it's simply a desire to help ease the way for others who are suffering what they have gone through. Here are some examples of people who now earn their livelihood following such a mission.

Healing the Grief of Loss. Bette Claire Moffat lost a son to AIDS. In her grief, she became inspired to begin writing and publishing books to help others better understand and cope with this tragic disease. Her first books were *When Someone You Love Has AIDS, a Book of Hope for Family & Friends* (Plume) and *AIDS: A Self-Care Manual* (IBS Press/APLA), which has sold 60,000 copies. Moffat has gone on to write other books on surviving grief and loss including *Gifts for the Living, Conversations with Caregivers on Death & Dying* (IBS Press), and *SoulWork: Clearing the Mind, Opening the Heart, Replenishing the Spirit* (Wildcat Canyon Press/New World Library). Her newest book is *Opening to Miracles: True Stories of Blessings & Renewal* (Wildcat Canyon Press/New World Library).

Putting an End to Drunk Driving. Real estate saleswoman Candy Lightner's daughter was killed by a drunk driver. This tragedy galvanized Lightner into a new career as a political activist. She created Mothers Against Drunk Driving (MADD) and launched a national campaign speaking, writing, and educating people about drunk driving. Her efforts have contributed new state laws that criminalize drunk driving and have resulted in many innovative programs that make it socially unacceptable today to drink and drive.

Research suggests that those who have made it through tough experiences are more likely to become highly successful in life.

PROFILE: JIM AND NANCY CHUDA: A MISSION OF LOVE

Jim and Nancy Chuda seemed to be leading a charmed life. Both strikingly attractive, they were happily married, blessed with an angelic young daughter named Collette, and equally successful in their careers: Jim as an architect; Nancy as a broadcast journalist and writer. They both had long shared a concern for the environment.

As a teenager, Nancy had worked as a model and wrote a cookbook containing low-fat recipes. While on a media tour for her book, she became aware of food, pollution, and pesticides. Her slogan became: A slim solution for fat pollution. As a mother, Nancy led nature walks for children through the park in her neighborhood. In 1990, with Jim, she became involved in working for the California Green Initiative and coproduced the ABC-TV special "An Evening with Friends of the Environment."

Jim came by his interest in the environment more traumatically. His daughter from an earlier marriage was born with severe mental and physical disabilities. Then Jim was diagnosed as having melanoma, a life-threatening skin cancer. After undergoing various surgeries, he came to the conclusion that he had a choice. He could allow his environment to poison him or he could put good things into his life that would nurture him. He rejected chemotherapy in favor of his Buddhist faith, nature, and a nutrient-intensive diet. The cancer never returned, and Jim began specializing his architectural practice to build environmentally safe and ecologically sound homes and offices.

Nothing could have prepared the Chudas, however, for what was to come. Jim's eighteen-year-old son died in a surfing accident and, within a year, Collette developed a rare form of cancer that has no genetic origin. Since Jim had built their home himself devoid of all toxic building materials and the family ate only organic foods, they had no idea how Collette could have developed this cancer. Doctors could provide no answers, although one doctor did tell them that no doubt there is an environmental factor in these cancers.

"When Collette died," Nancy says, "there was only one way to cope and that was to do something about the fact that there is no testing being done, no environmental research on the effects of toxins and pollution on children." That has become her mission: to bring attention to the environmental health needs of children and the creation of environmental regulations that will protect our children's health.

Together the Chudas have created the Collette Chuda Environmental Fund and its offshoot, the Children's Health and Environmental Coalition (CHEC), both of which are headquartered in a home office that was once Collette's bedroom. Through the fund Nancy and Jim have raised money to underwrite new studies on the impact of environmental pollutants on children. And through CHEC they have created a national network uniting hundreds of grassroots groups and thousands of concerned parents and others who are working on children's environmental health issues.

Their commitment to these goals is as strong as their love for their daughter. They are certain that public pressure will lead to change. Nancy says of their work, "Collette did have a mission. When she died she was saying, 'I'm going, but you've got some work ahead of you, Mom and Dad, and you had better do it.' This is a mission of love. It's something we have to do to honor her."

Safeguarding the Workplace. As a bookkeeper and accountant, Samantha Greenberg had used a typewriter or computer keyboard for a quarter of a century when something started going very wrong. She was punching entries into her VDT for many hours a day without breaks, and within months she became one of the 73,000 cases of repetitive-stress illness on record at that time with the Labor Department. Within three years the number of such cases has more than doubled, but at the time neither Greenberg nor her employer knew about this problem or how to prevent it. She began wearing splints and taking cortisone shots and pills, but ultimately she couldn't work any longer and had to quit her job. Gradually Greenberg educated herself about the problem and decided to do something about it. She created the Computer Injury Network, devoting herself full-time to educating employers about how to prevent these problems in the workplace and providing information to individuals who are already suffering from these technology-related injuries.

"That which does not kill me makes me stronger."

Friedrich Nietzsche

Providing Hope by Knowing One's Options. Janice Guthrie was diagnosed with a rare form of ovarian cancer, but she was left in the dark about the nature of her illness and her treatment options. A treatment was recommended; however, she grew increasingly concerned as to whether it was the best medical science had to offer. So she went to the medical library and began reading everything she could find about her illness. This research led her to a specialist who initiated a different type of treatment that ultimately was successful. As she was healing, however, Guthrie started thinking about her life, and it became clear that her calling was to do such research for other people. There is so much information available today that even doctors can't keep up with it all, so Guthrie does the in-depth research her ailing clients need to feel assured they know about the latest breakthroughs and possibilities open to them. Her company, The Health Resource, Inc., researches the diagnosis and compiles a 50- to 250-page report of all recent data on a client's illness.

Reclaiming Our Birthright to Defend Ourselves. For years, Ellen Snortland thought, "I should take a self-defense course." But like so many people she didn't get around to it until something happened to change her life: she and her husband came home to find a burglary in progress. The burglar surprised her, knife in hand. She screamed; he ran; and shortly thereafter she finally took that self-defense class. Through this experience, Snortland discovered that "instead of teaching women and children to fight for and protect themselves, our society teaches us to be helpless," and she's determined to change that. "I consider self-protection skills to be essential to well-being," Snortland says, and "I'm actively on a mission to encourage other women to learn how to defend themselves."

She joined the Impact Foundation as a board member and conducts self-defense workshops for women and children. Snortland is a weekly columnist writing about self-defense and is writing a book entitled *Beauty Bites Beast*. "It is our birthright to fight back," she writes, "just as any other animal would when threatened with injury or death. If men have the 'right' and are, in fact, expected to protect themselves and their families, we of the 'fair sex' should claim the same right."

"The first three years were tough. I didn't take a salary—any profit was turned directly back into the business. After five years, though, we really turned the corner and have become very profitable."

Janice Guthrie,
The Health
Resource, Inc.

Breaking the Silence. Former therapist Joan Avna had a problem no one ever talked about: she lived for 12 years in a sexless and passionateless marriage. But she decided to break the silence. She felt it was time for her to begin a new life and bring this problem out into the open. With Diana Waltz, she wrote *Celibate Wives* (Lowell House), a clarion call to all women who have been living without sex in their marriage. Avna now devotes her life to spreading the word to the many women who have chosen to ignore or suffer this problem in silence because they do not know they are not alone. "The first thing a woman needs to do," Avna says, "is realize there are many others who are struggling with the same issues. Each has her own reasons, her own story, and what she can do to cope." But most important, she wants women who are facing what she's faced to know there are ways to find answers and fulfillment in their lives.

Healing Pain through Art. Riua Akinshegun was the first in her family of ten children to break out of a "welfare mentality" and pursue higher education. While in college, she became involved in the black separatist movement in Berkeley, California, and during the turmoil of those times was shot in the spine by a fellow activist. The injury left her a paraplegic and she spent the next seventeen years in a wheelchair, living daily with constant chronic pain.

After a protracted depression Akinshegun realized, "I don't have to change my life and my dreams just because I'm a paraplegic. I have the same kind of personality and other traits that I had before the injury." So she went on to continue her studies in art at the University of Ife in Nigeria, and as an educator and artist has become an authority on living as an "abled" disabled person. Her mission is to teach people how to manage both spiritual and physical pain and to reach their full potential in spite of their circumstances. Using sculpture, ceramic masks, batik, and African wrap dolls she does this through classes, workshops, and exhibits that explore art as a healing force.

Putting an End to the Deprivation and Desperation of Dieting. Nancy Bonus had tried just about everything to lose weight: liquid diets, diet pills, fasting, hypnosis, etc., etc. Nothing worked. In fact, every time she lost weight on one of the many diets she tried, she'd gain it back plus some. Finally she gave up on dieting and started researching why she was overweight and why diets don't work. Completing a Ph.D. in psychology, she specialized in the psychobiology of weight loss, all the while searching for a personal solution. Gradually she developed her own philosophy on eating and a way of thinking about food that enabled her to lose the weight she wanted permanently without diet or exercise. "At last," she says, "I felt like a 'normal' person, free to eat whatever I want when I'm hungry and then forget about food." Still a trim size 6, Nancy has been sharing her no-diet, no-exercise weight-loss program, The Bonus Plan, with others for the past years through seminars, a home-study course, a weekly radio show, and recently a national television program.

2. FIGHTING INJUSTICES

Another common way people choose to follow a mission stems from outrage, from a desire to correct an injustice they've seen or experienced. They decide such injustice simply cannot be tolerated or ignored and that they must do something about it. Here are examples of several people who are earning a living fighting to right what's wrong.

Making Happier Employees. "I got mad!" Shelley Espanosa told us in explaining why she started her business, Working Solutions. Having worked as both a secretary and a professional social worker, she saw how badly administrative staff were treated in many organizations. "There was no one going to bat for them," she found, "and as a result both the organizations and employees were losing out due to low morale, decreased productivity, and high turnover." She became so disturbed by the situation that she decided to do something about it. She researched and wrote a book called *Working Solutions from Working Secretaries.* The book provides practical solutions from the point of view of the people who are doing the work. This book and the research she did to write it became the building block for her company. "Usually support staff attend one series of training programs and managers and technical staff attend others," Espanosa points out.

"No one is useless who in the world lightens the burden of another."
Marcus Aurelius, Roman emperor

But in her Working Solutions seminars, both groups are trained together. "This way they can be walking down the same path," she says. Her clients are the types of large organizations she once worked for.

Creating Equal Access for All. Patricia Moore is an industrial designer and consumer advocate. She is incensed by the way our modern world has been designed with only the young, healthy, and agile in mind. "It's not enough to assume that if well-bodied individuals can use a certain piece of equipment, then it is properly designed," she tells her audiences of architects, planners, designers, and engineers from coast to coast. And she is convinced this is unnecessary because she herself has designed the eating utensils, pill bottles, and other household items to prove it. Moore is a leading advocate for what's called "universal design," products that address the needs of all consumers including those like the elderly grandmother, the latchkey child, the person in a wheelchair, or someone who's physically challenged by crippling arthritis.

Working as a product designer in New York, by the age of twenty-six Moore had discovered no employer was going to listen to her ideas about universal design, so she left her job to set up her own design firm. To research and develop her concepts and ideas, she literally went undercover, disguising herself as an eighty-five-year-old woman trying to navigate the world. She wrapped her body to create a hunch, she used knee splints to stiffen her walk, plugged her ears to dampen her hearing, used Vaseline and modified contact lenses to blur her eyesight, and taped her thumbs to simulate arthritis. Her experiences were life changing and have been described in her book *Disguised: A True Story* (World Books).

Now she and her husband and partner, David Guynes, together in their company Guynes Design, are getting attention in top corporate boardrooms. Universal design is becoming a hot trend, and Moore has a long list of problems for designers to tackle. Her list of features for the universally designed home would help any occupant reach high things, clean bathtubs and sinks, carry purchases, use tools, go up and down stairs, and traverse the household without slipping or falling.

Standing up to the IRS. Richard Schonfeld has dedicated his life to rescuing people from the IRS. He knows how to do it because he began his career working for them. "I was young and inexperienced," he remembers, "but I didn't like being the bad guy and felt the IRS was often unfair. They placed liens on houses, they garnished wages. Lives were being ruined, and I couldn't be part of that." Years after leaving the IRS, he was laid off from the aerospace industry where he had worked as a senior executive, so he took a few years off to do some soul-searching. "I was fed up with corporate accounting. I wanted to do something meaningful." The result was a decision to dedicate his practice to the underdog, protecting the average guy who's being hounded by the IRS.

"When people come to me they're often paralyzed with fear. Some have considered suicide, or their marriages are breaking up. What I do brings a sense of calm to their lives." And when it comes to defending his clients against the IRS, Schonfeld won't take no for an answer. "I make it my business to interpret for the IRS, and my clients almost always end up winning."

Pets Are Wonderful Support. Five years ago a friend with AIDS told Nadia Sutton that his family had given away his cats while he was hospitalized. "He was devastated and didn't even want to go home," she remembers. But she soon learned her friend's experience was not uncommon. Actually it was just the tip of a daily nightmare in the lives of persons living with AIDS. Some, she learned, were even going without eating so they could feed their animals. Some were using money that could go to their own medical care to pay vet bills. Others were refusing to go into the hospital because they couldn't afford to board their pets. "How could I not do something?" Sutton asked. "For a lot of people with HIV, their pets have become their chosen family. When you've lost a lot from your life—your job, your home, some friends, some family—it's your animal who is there for you. That little creature is your lifeline." So she founded PAWS (Pets Are Wonderful Support), a group that helps people with AIDS keep their pets. With 650 volunteers, including 14 vets who work for reduced fees, Sutton serves over 800 clients and a growing demand of 35 to 40 new requests for help every month. She has raised enough to keep PAWS going on a $200,000 annual budget.

"Sometimes I go home at night and cry from the grief I see, but if you don't have love from the only living creature in your life, why stick around? What we're doing here is the stuff of life, the stuff of love."

Nadia Sutton, PAWS

Defending Burned Investors. Working as a compliance and corporate officer for brokerage firms, Paul Young saw firsthand the conflicts played out daily between the duty of security investment brokers to do what's right for their clients versus their desire to make a higher commission. Too often, he says, the latter wins out. Hence he left his job to take on a mission. He created Securities Arbitration Group, a company that represents "burned" investors. Young helps people recover money they've lost due to fraud and abuse perpetrated by licensed stockbrokers and firms. And he does so with a missionary zeal, eagerly carrying his message to radio and television and operating a Securities Fraud Hotline as a clearinghouse for information on investment fraud. "I represent the victimized individual investor in binding arbitration," he says. And the cases are pathetic. One client lost a $31,000 inheritance. Another lost a $50,000 investment he was making for his children's education. Still another lost his life savings of $100,000 and was living on Social Security. But Young asserts, "I recover these losses. I have an eighty-five percent victory rate!"

PROFILE: JO QUINN, REPAIRING FAMILIES BY ASSISTING PARENTS IN COLLECTING COURT-ORDERED CHILD SUPPORT

Jo Quinn wasn't looking for a mission. In fact, she thought she'd be working for her employer as an account manager until the day she retired. Instead, she lost her job. The company she worked for was downsized after having been purchased by a larger company. Quinn set out to become an independent contractor hiring herself out to other companies, but then a friend asked her for help. The friend, who had been divorced, needed help locating her ex-husband who, by court order, owed child-support payments. As her friend explained all the efforts and money she'd spent trying to collect the money she was owed to support her family, Jo began to realize the seriousness of this problem. "All of a sudden, every time I picked up a magazine or newspaper or turned on the television, someone was talking about the twenty-four billion dollars of unpaid child support in the U.S. and the billions of tax dollars spent on welfare to support these financially abandoned children." Using the same skills she had used on her job, Quinn found her friend's husband. But she says, "More important, I found a new purpose in life.

"I started ATPC (Assistance to Parents Collecting Court Ordered Child Support)," she says, "as a mission to help children have a better life." Unlike other collection agencies, ATPC works to regain not only monetary but also emotional child support. "Experience shows," Quinn finds, "there are very few deadbeats." There are ex-spouses who are still carrying emotional baggage from the marriage. There are parents in financial crisis who don't see a way out and so they walk away from the problem. "We try to solve the existing problems," she says, "and help parents clean up their past record and start over with their children."

Since 1991, Quinn believes she's been through the learning curve and has found the way to accomplish this mission. Now she's teaching it to others through the ATPC franchise network she's building nationwide.

Getting the Picture on Abuse. Donna Ferrato came upon her mission quite by accident, but it has become her self-proclaimed obsession. While taking photographs for an article on perfect couples, to her amazement she found herself shooting a terrifying act of spouse abuse in the glamorous home of an "ideal" couple. This experience changed her life. While working on other assignments to pay the bills, she began documenting domestic violence on film. At first, however, she couldn't find anyone who would publish her disturbing, violent photos. But determined that people get the picture, she began actively lecturing on the topic. In 1991, she opened the nonprofit Domestic Abuse Awareness Project in Manhattan. The project takes two fifty-photograph exhibitions around the country to raise funds for battered-women's shelters. And since her book, *Living with the Enemy* (Aperture, 1991), was published, she has become established as the nation's leading photographer of spouse abuse. After thirteen years, her pictures have appeared in magazines like *Life* and newspapers like the *New York Times* and the *Philadelphia Inquirer.* Ironically, after she started gaining fame for her photos her father told her that her grandmother had been beaten regularly by her late grandfather.

3. FINDING A BETTER WAY AND MAKING A BETTER WORLD

Another reason people decide to pursue a mission is because they believe they have found a better way. They have a vision of what's possible that others haven't seen, and they're determined to prove it can be done. Here are several unique examples:

Green Cotton. Sally Fox foresees the day when cotton will grow in many colors. At the time she developed her hobby of hand-spinning cloth, cotton grew naturally in only one color: brown. For years cotton growers have experimented with growing various other hues, but the colored fibers were always too short for weaving machines. So ten years ago, Fox decided to challenge this situation. A biological insecticide researcher, she set out to create a machine-spinnable, colored cotton plant. This mission became a long and arduous one. For years, she says, her vacations have been spent in cotton fields. Her friends thought she was crazy. But they don't now. Fox made a breakthrough. She's growing green cotton! The twenty-five acres she bought to begin this experiment have grown to 160 acres and she has turned her first profit, harvesting and selling woven green cotton through a mail-order company and several well-known national retail chains! Her mission isn't finished yet, though. She's busily creating red, yellow, gray, and orange cotton fibers.

Getting Back to the Land. "I'm part of the back-to-the-land movement," says Tom Roberts. He was working for a state planning office when he realized he felt he was just going to work out of habit. "I wanted to do work I could believe in," he said. For Roberts that had to do with proving we don't have to poison our foods with insecticides. "I wanted to demonstrate that a person could make a living from organic farming." Although he'd never done any organic farming, he had grown blueberries and made maple syrup, so he joined with an existing farmer and created PeaceMeal Farm where he raises 147 varieties of organic vegetables on an eleven-acre hillside farm. During growing season Roberts works ninety-hour weeks, but he says, "I don't mind."

Teaching People to Read. Gwen Thomas's personal mission sprang forth spontaneously in the aftermath of the 1992 Los An-

"Where there is no vision, the people perish."

Proverbs 29:18

geles riots. A former IBM sales representative, she was attending a meeting of civic leaders when, seized by a sudden inspiration, she rose to her feet and announced to the group that she was going to start a literacy program. "I had no experience of any kind with such a program, but I deeply believed that the economic survival of the African American is based on literacy," she says. So she began studying existing literacy programs and then created her own, WALET (West Los Angeles Literacy Empowerment Team). Run by Thomas, WALET is staffed entirely by 100 volunteers who meet with their students in libraries, homes, and restaurants. "Our headquarters," Thomas says, "is the Crenshaw Burger King."

Personalizing Entertainment. Jeannine Frank was frustrated. She hated the fact that to go out for an evening's entertainment, she was forced to order a certain number of drinks, sit in a smoke-filled room, and be subjected to performers who were pitching their acts to the lowest common denominator. There had to be a better way, she figured, and she found it. Frank, a former teacher, paralegal, and university researcher, hosts performance parties. They began in her apartment in 1990. Soon she was getting eight to ten calls a week from all over the U.S. and Canada from people wanting to participate in these private gatherings and her mission, Party Performances, was born. The parties quickly outgrew her apartment, so people in the audience began volunteering their larger homes. She had very little overhead other than public relations and incidentals. She splits the ticket sales with the performers. And she makes sure every entertainer has a full house, even if she has to give out complimentary tickets. Each experience is unique. The performances are more like an intimate family affair. People get to know one another and the performers. "It's a communal experience," she says. "The thing that thrills me most is going out and finding gifted people no one knows about and giving others a chance to experience their talents."

Playing with a Purpose. Jacob Miles III wants to teach American children how to get along with one another, and he won't be deterred from that mission even though it has meant turning down multimillion-dollar deals with big national toy companies. "My social agenda is as big as my financial agenda," says Miles, who with his partner and wife, Rosalind Bell, has created the nation's first African-owned full-line multicultural toy company, Cultural Toys. Now in its second year with millions of dollars in orders coming in, Cultural Toys is breaking ground as the nation's leading manufacturer of multicultural toys. Miles's vision is to create nonviolent, self-reflective, culturally correct dolls, books, games, videos, and other toys that reflect a broad array of physical abilities, personality types, and races. And the line, which includes a doll in a wheelchair and an African American girl "doctor," is winning accolades from parents, educators, and children. They're available nationwide at stores like Target, Toys "Я" Us, Wal-Mart, and Kaybee.

Bringing TV to the People. Nancy Cain finds network TV boring. "It's the same things on every channel," she says. But since over fourteen million people in the U.S. own camcorders and over 75 percent of homes have VCRs, Nancy Cain and partner, Judith Binder, had an innovative idea—a camcorder-generated television network featuring footage from a nationwide network of camcorder correspondents! Although it may sound farfetched, they've taken this idea on as a mission and when we last spoke with them CamNet, The Camcorder Network, was playing continuously two weeks a month on cable channels in ten cities with almost a million subscribers. "We're really the opposite of what you see on television; we're trying to show events, issues, and lifestyles that haven't had their say-so before. We want to be a real alternative. Very real, very intimate. Real life!" CamNet footage has included a defense of cigars, fire dancing in Bali, homeless people living in a tunnel, urban wildlife, thrift fashion, local heroes, world-class street music, and much more. Reviews have been good: "MTV with a conscience," said *TV Guide;* "a show that does all the things television was meant to do but never does," reported *Billboard.* Although advertising is scarce and it's an uphill battle keeping the fledgling network afloat, Cain says, "CamNet is the best job I've ever had."

PROFILE: JACK AND ELAINE WYMAN,
WANTED BACK IN THE GAME

Jack and Elaine Wyman had been looking forward to a relaxing, fun-filled retirement in Scottsdale, Arizona, after having operated a San

Francisco advertising agency for thirty-three years. When they sold it, the company had grown to include over thirty staff members and served retail clients, banks, savings and loan associations, and insurance companies. They were ready to start their new life away from the stress and strain of so much responsibility. But during the first year of retirement, they felt something very important was lacking. Retirement had no Saturdays and Sundays. All the days were just the same. They were suffering from what they call retirement blues. "We missed the inner drive to accomplish something," Jack says. "We missed the involvement with clients, learning about their marketing problems, finding creative solutions to help them."

Wyman tried going to work at a large company in a top marketing position, but after one month, he says, "I realized it would never work. I ran my own company for over thirty years and here I was in a big organization whose modus operandi wasn't anything like what I was accustomed to. For over thirty years, if I wanted to take a certain action, I took it, but not there. I just wasn't cut out to work for a big company." At night Elaine noticed Jack was looking very tired and unhappy. "It was something I hadn't seen before," she says. So Jack resigned. But clearly, they agree, "Retirement is just not for us."

"For me, there's nothing like the feeling of wearing a smart dark suit and a red tie striding down San Francisco's Montgomery Street heading for a meeting where I'm going to help a client," Jack admits. So he went back in business with Elaine as administrative assistant. But now they operate their business from home—actually two homes: a home office in Scottsdale and an outpost apartment in San Francisco. They have clients in California, write and publish in Arizona, and feel they now have the best of both worlds. In Scottsdale, they relax; in San Francisco they rejuvenate.

"This time around," Jack points out, "we only work for clients with whom we get along very well, and we're not building up a large staff again." Finding a lifestyle that works has been, he says, "interesting, at times exhilarating, at times exasperating, but life's at its best right now." So good, in fact, that Elaine and Jack now share a new mission: telling other retirees how to get back in the game on their own terms. Together they've written a book called *Retired? Get Back in the Game*. It profiles thirty-seven vibrant men and women from sixty to ninety who are zealously productive. And whenever they get the chance, the Wymans travel across the country speaking and appearing on radio and television to let others know that retirement need not be the end of the road. Says the seventy-four-year-old Wyman about his new cause, "I feel like a kid."

Building Self-Esteem. Jim Hullihan was on his way to becoming a math and P.E. teacher, when during his student teaching assignment he noticed a problem. The kids in his classes were having a tough time learning algebra and geometry when their minds were preoccupied with personal and family problems. They couldn't learn if they felt bad about themselves and their lives. Besides, these kids were used to being exposed to movies, sitcoms, and MTV. The classroom was boring in comparison. Having an interest in the emerging field of multimedia, Jim took several students he was working with to a multimedia presentation, then just a fancy slide show. They loved it—so much so that they wanted to do one themselves. Jim thought that was a great idea, and that was the beginning of Motivational Multimedia Assemblies.

Motivational Multimedia Assemblies now produces big-scale, big-time multimedia presentations that teach self-esteem, values, and character development to high-school students. Over the past nine years, these multimedia extravaganzas, the costs for which are either fully or partially underwritten by sponsors like Pepsi, the Bose Corporation, and Johnstone's Yogurt, have been featured at assemblies in over 34,000 schools and have reached thirty-two million students. Hullihan's productions are shown in from 3,000 to 5,000 high-school assemblies a year.

The business expanded into the corporate arena when the son of a Memorex executive came home and told his dad about the multimedia event he'd seen at school. The executive thought such productions would be ideal for management-training programs as well. And indeed, Hullihan has developed presentations for many corporate-training programs, and Motivational Multimedia Assemblies has now expanded into Canada, Australia, and recently Taiwan.

4. PRESERVING WHAT COULD BE LOST FOREVER

Saving a Dying Art. When Valerie Justine needed a rug for her apartment, she went to an auction house. Little did she know she'd find much more than the rug she was looking for. Although Justine had no previous background or interest in rugs, there it was—a kilim, not just a rug but a piece of folk art and the birth of a mission. Justine was so taken by this unknown flat woven rug that she began exploring its history and learned that weaving is among the oldest of crafts, and among the oldest of weavers are those from vanishing pastoral societies in countries like Turkey and Central Asia where most kilims are made. To preserve this craft and share its beauty Justine has written a book about kilims and created a traveling exhibition entitled Textiles from Vanishing Cultures, to which she will be adding new tribal pieces from other cultures. She has also cofounded a textile gallery, the Pillowry, in the Pacific Design Center specializing in woven goods including kilims, pillows fashioned from kilims, Oriental rugs, saddle and food bags, shawls, and blankets. Justine's goal is to expose more people to these textiles. "By preserving these pieces," she says, "at least the world will remember some part of this tradition."

Restoring Civility and Service. As a little girl, Kathryn Dager remembers a time when shopping was an elegant experience. The doorman welcomed you in white gloves and held open the door for you. The clerks greeted you by name. They took time to get to know you personally and kept a record of your likes and dislikes. They sent notes to let you know of items you might be interested in and called you with news of new arrivals you might like. Service was the name of the game. Her memories stood out in sharp contrast to the rude salesclerks she would meet in today's malls, too busy chatting with one another to answer customers' questions, too unfamiliar with the merchandise to answer questions about it if they tried, and always a new face, never the same person from one visit to the next.

Dager felt a great sorrow about the elegance and lost civility in retail service, and she decided it didn't have to be that way. She felt sure shops were losing money as the result of poor customer

"To work for the common good is the greatest creed."
Albert Schweitzer

service. She felt certain one reason for such poor service is that few of today's clerks have ever experienced real service, so they have no frame of reference for knowing how to provide it. With this vision in mind, she has created Profitivity, a company dedicated to teaching the highest quality of customer service. Her theme is profit through positivity. And her vision was indeed right-on. Her business has grown by leaps and bounds. Clients are malls, retail chains, and department stores, and they see tangible results from her training sessions and consultations. Staff morale and sales go up. Complaints and turnover go down. Everywhere she goes she's able to restore just a bit of the best of an era she so fondly remembers from so long ago.

Preserving the Prairie. B. C. LaBelle describes herself as a prairie artist and preservationist. Her mission comes from a passionate desire to preserve the prairie lands around her home in Hickman, Nebraska, which are being sorely neglected. If they are to be preserved, these prairies must be burned periodically. So her efforts involve planting community prairie gardens and actually moving prairies that are being replaced by road expansions. As a result of her efforts she has been nominated to receive a national conservation award.

For LaBelle, however, this work is her life. All her art, including her oil paintings, is inspired by the prairies. Her pottery and dried-flower arrangements are created from the Nebraska clay, dried grass, and wildflowers from her backyard. They enable her to earn a living learning and sharing things that will otherwise be lost. "Each flower and grass on the prairie," she points out, "has a name." And she's learning that the prairie plants have many medicinal uses. "Living with the land keeps me focused and in harmony," she told us. "I've found my place. I'm perfectly happy."

Establishing Neighborhood Landmarks. James Sazevich is an architectural historian. He was working for the Minnesota welfare department in 1974, when he got his first commission to research the history of a house that was being restored. He went on to research and identify so many historic buildings and get so many of them nominated for the National Register of Historic Places that the *St. Paul Pioneer Press* has dubbed Sazevich "The House Detective." In 1978, he was able to leave the welfare department and pursue this lifelong mission full-time.

Of this mission he says, "If I died tomorrow I would feel completely fulfilled because I'm surrounded by the success of my work. I've helped people understand their community. Every neighborhood deserves a landmark. A landmark gives a neighborhood a sense of pride. People who may not have a sense of history are painting their homes and patching their chimneys. That brings about community." To round out his businesses, he leads architectural tours, does genealogical research, and participates in restoration of historic buildings. He hopes to expand his teaching because, he says, "If we can instill values and pride in children with something as simple as their homes, we will see less vandalism and graffiti."

PROFILE: MICHAEL ROZEK, CREATING A MAGAZINE THAT LEAVES YOU FEELING AS SATISFIED AS A FINE FULL-COURSE, SIT-DOWN DINNER

"I'm Michael Rozek, the writer, editor, and publisher of *Rozek's*. Over the last ten years, I've written nearly two thousand magazine articles, for many of the top publications in America. But all along I've wanted to do longer, more fully researched, more in-depth stories, about really substantial people—the kind of nonfiction that, these days, you rarely find in any magazine. Stories that, to put it more simply, are true. So true, the people they're about can say, 'He got it right. He captured who I am.' "

That's an example of how Rozek introduces his monthly magazine, each issue of which contains one article of from 6,000 to 7,000 words in length. Preserving this type of in-depth journalism is Rozek's mission. *Rozek's* contains no pictures; his words create those in your mind. And there are no ads to distract from his stories. *Rozek's* is only you, the printed page, and the people you meet there. Other than in Rozek's opening greeting, you don't even get to know his perspective. "The writer should not be the star," he asserts. "I don't put myself in the story." Instead he's the conduit, literally the medium, through which his readers can explore a new world in each issue and make a new friend. Later in this chapter you'll meet one of the new friends we met through *Rozek's*. In other words, *Rozek's* is the antithesis of the glitzy, tabloid, sound-bite sensationalism we see so much of in today's media. Rozek spends four hundred hours researching each story. Forgoing notes as too inaccurate, he also tapes all his interviews and allows the subjects to read the articles for accuracy before publication.

Rozek gave up a $100,000-a-year freelance writing career to pursue this mission and after two and a half years, his brainchild has grown from 250 to 1,400 incredibly loyal subscribers and an almost unheard of 60 percent subscription renewal rate. But his road has not been an easy one. He's peddling against the stream of thirty-second sound bites and celebrity mania, but he doesn't care because, as he points out, everyone doesn't need to read *Rozek's*. He only needs to find 5,000 subscribers who relish this kind of journalism he's working to keep alive. Nearly $75,000 in debt, he is undaunted, because he's sure those 5,000 people are out there. He just has to keep going until they find him, and they are. A recent article by the Associated Press generated 600 new subscriptions and more are coming from the great reviews he gets in publications like the *Christian Science Monitor* and *USA Today*.

And *Rozek's* is perhaps the only magazine whose subscribers have donated $50,000 out of their own generosity just to keep it going. *Rozek's* is published now from Michael's Seattle, Washington, home, twelve issues for $78. In each issue he offers this simple hope: "That in a day of fast-food magazines, *Rozek's* will be much more satisfying to you."

5. LISTENING TO AN INNER VOICE

Sometimes pursuing a mission comes from a highly personal, even deeply spiritual, journey revealed through prayer, a dream, an inner vision, or an inner voice that directs and inspires you to undertake certain work. Here are some examples of how that can happen.

Sharing the Arts of African Cultures. Vera Yahanna was born and raised in Liberia, Africa. But in 1990 she had to flee her homeland in the midst of civil strife. She left with only the clothes on her back and came to the United States where she began working at survival jobs. One evening while meditating, she had a revelation, a vision, that she was to share with others the experience of African culture—its art, its food, and, most important, its communal sense of personal sharing. So she started holding events in her home, each featuring the culture of a different African country, serving its traditional food and featuring its dances, music, and spiritual teachings. At first she had only twenty people at each gathering but within the first year, the events grew to over one hundred each. People seem to have a hunger to share with one another, and Vera says of her events, "They're about experiencing the harmony of the human spirit."

Making Computers Fun. Jeffrey Armstrong had worked as a computer salesman for six years. While between jobs, living on credit cards, he started accepting invitations to give speeches about the new computer technologies flooding the workplace. On the way home from one such speech, he was feeling especially grateful for having just earned $400 talking about something he knew so well that he began to pray. Joyfully expressing his gratitude, the prayer spontaneously took on a whimsical note that was to change his life.

Amused by his prayer, once home, he wrote down what has become known as "The Keyboard Prayer" and began sharing it with others. Everyone who saw it wanted a copy of this humorous take on the overly serious world of computers, so Armstrong decided to have 1,000 copies printed and take them to a computer expo. The posters sold so quickly, he realized he'd hit upon a need—bringing a little levity to an increasingly high-tech society. Overnight, he had a mission—to become the world's first high-tech comedian. Calling on inspiration from the initial prayer, he created an entire persona for himself as St. Silicon—a hooded, robed guru with a silicon chip on his forehead.

As St. Silicon, Armstrong found he was able to satirize technology. He could get away with saying things no computer expert could say. "Follow me and I will make you fetchers of data" has become one of his customary greetings. With the help of a friend who raised $40,000 for him, he became a professional speaker. Later he published *The Binary Bible,* which has been called the funniest computer book you'll ever read. Eight years later, he's still

The Keyboard Prayer

"Our program who are in Memory

Hello be Thy Name

Thy Operating System come.

Thy commands be done,

at the Printer as it is on the Screen.

Give us this day our daily Data

and forgive us our I/O Errors

as we forgive those whose Logic Circuits are faulty.

Lead us not into frustration,

and deliver us from Power Surges.

For Thine is the Algorithm, the Application,

and the Solution, looping forever and ever

Return."

"We strive for excellence, yet at times we may not see that invisible barrier to our advancement...the Glass Ceiling! It takes belief in ourselves and a leap of faith. For then we make a difference and reach our vision of breakthru beyond the Glass Ceiling!"

earning his living as St. Silicon. "That's longer," he jokes, "than many high-tech companies have been around."

Armstrong thinks of himself as the Mark Twain or Will Rogers of the computer age, commenting in his Sermon on the Monitor about the consequences of technology in our daily lives and getting his audiences laughing at the absurdity of it all. "If you say something that can't be forgotten," he says, "you live in people's minds." And that's his goal—to get his light and humorous approach to our high-tech world permanently imprinted in people's minds. He's sold 13,000 copies of his *Binary Bible* without distribution in a single bookstore, and he's earned $130,000 on the book alone. His speaking fees have gone from $400 to $4,000, lightening up Fortune 500 and Silicon Valley audiences in companies like IBM, United Way, Visa International, Chevron, and AT&T.

Breaking Glass Ceilings. "It all started with wanting to do something positive for the women's movement," says Vivian Shimoyama. At the time Shimoyama was running her own management-consulting firm, but she wanted to do something to encourage people to be aware of the invisible barriers that limit women and minorities, to enable them to reach out to help one another break through these barriers and take a leap of faith. From this desire grew an inspiration—a line of glass jewelry that would be symbolic of breaking through the "glass ceiling."

She calls her work "Glass with a Cause!" and it has become a mission not only for her but for all those who buy and wear her jewelry, including Senator Carol Mosley Braun and Hillary Rodham Clinton. "It is our hope," Shimoyama says in a note accompanying each piece of jewelry, "that this jewelry will be a visual representation of your vision, a conversation piece, an encouragement to strive for excellence while breaking through the invisible barriers that could hold us back."

Although Shimoyama knew nothing about creating jewelry when she started, her new company, Breakthru Unlimited, has become her full-time occupation. She designs the jewelry and each piece of glass is broken and fused back together into a work of art created by a woman artist. "Wearing this jewelry," she says, "is a

Vivian
Shimoyama,
Breakthru
Unlimited

chance for people from all walks of life to become part of something bigger than themselves and to agree that we can each make a difference."

Creating Miracles. Rusty Berkus was going through a divorce and trying to complete a master's degree in marriage and family counseling in order to support herself and her children when suddenly, midway in the program, she stopped everything. "I had to stop and assess my life," she remembers. "All I wanted to do was just stare at a tree." Feeling sad and painfully burdened, one night she sat in her living room and began talking to herself as a nurturing parent might talk to a child. "With those words, I began healing myself," she says. The next morning she awoke with a joyous feeling and said to herself, "Life is truly a gift!"

She decided to write down what she had told herself the night before and began sharing it with others, who also found it healing. They encouraged her to have these thoughts published. Thus her first book, *Life Is a Gift,* was born.

She knew exactly how she wanted the book to look. She engaged an artist to illustrate it and began the rounds of going from publisher to publisher. But no one was interested in producing a four-color illustrated book of inspirational poetry. Many friends and supporters, however, wanted to help Rusty publish her book. So she chose one, who became an investor, and *Life Is a Gift* was published in 1992. Once the book was published, knowing nothing about the book industry, Berkus personally carried her books to bookstores and thus Red Rose Press got underway.

Now Berkus has national distribution for her seven books with 400,000 copies in print. "This is my calling," she says, "and it all began from an act of self-love, a decision to take care of myself." She acknowledges that when she decided to take a step in self-love and self-care, it felt like a very daring thing to do. So much so, in fact, that at the time, she went to her mother. "Mother," she asked, "did you ever have to stop everything in your life as an act of self-love?" "Rusty," her mother replied, "you were born from an act of self-love." Berkus was surprised to learn that as a young, single woman, her mother had started to feel overwhelmed on her job and summoned the courage to tell her boss she had to take some time off.

"There comes that mysterious meeting in life, when someone acknowledges who we are and what we can be, igniting the circuits of our highest potential."

"Life allows you to be the writer, director, choreographer, editor, and star of your own scenario—and you don't have to sleep with the producer to get the job."

"Life gives you a chance at the brass ring. And, if you miss it—gives you another and another ad infinitum."

Life Is a Gift, Rusty Berkus, poet (Red Rose Press)

She traveled to visit with an aunt and uncle who took her to dinner at a fine restaurant where unexpectedly they met a friend of the family, a young man who was to become her husband and Rusty's father. "It was love at first sight!" her mother said. For Berkus, this coincidence is just one more amazing example of how life works.

PROFILE: JONATHAN STORM, PUBLISHING THE SHEET MUSIC OF THE WIND

Jonathan Storm,
modern composer

We met Jonathan Storm through *Rozek's* magazine, and so before we ever spoke with him personally we felt as if we knew him well. It was on the pages of *Rozek's* that we learned Storm is a nature sound recording artist with a mission inspired by naturalist John Muir, whose works he had read avidly as a young man.

Although Storm had always favored spending time outdoors, like so many of us when entering college, he set out on a more "practical" course. He thought he would prepare himself to become an architect. But during a three-month summer vacation traveling throughout Europe and in the wilds of Alaska, he began to contemplate changing the course of his life. And while sitting on a glacier, taking in the sounds and sights of nature around him, he realized what he wanted and needed to do—to be in nature, listen to its sounds, and record and capture its music to share with others.

So after having left college and apprenticed with Dan Gibson, one of the best-known nature sound artists, that's what he does. He spends many, many hours out of doors recording the sounds of nature and then creates virtual symphonies from these recordings, which he has published on tapes and CDs. He now has ten albums. *River of Life,* his first, is melodies of water sounds, rivers, oceans, and streams; *River of Ice* is songs of glacier sounds; *Seastream* captures the voice of surf sounds; *Ancient Forest Still Small Voice and Ancient Forest Spring Chorus* introduce the listener to forest sounds.

Storm's albums all have two purposes: one, to convey the beauty of nature for relaxation and entertainment; and two, to provide education about the sounds of nature. Therefore each album is accompanied by a twelve-page booklet that educates the listener about what they're hearing. This dual mission has distinguished Storm as an artistic leader in his field.

His mission is one of sunny meadows, dewy forests, windy seas, and many bright, cold days and long, dark nights. He spends at least two months a year outdoors recording, four months in his studio creating the albums, and the rest of the time administering his business, which includes selling wind chimes, some of which are included in his recordings. But it's the field time that Storm lives for. At first, though, he had to work at a job in order to pursue this mission. He and his wife, Laura, have lived simply in a meadow near Port Ludlum, Washington, investing everything they have been able to spare over the last ten years in this dream. To their joy, for the last two years most of their income has come from his recordings, which he sells through his catalog *Earthtunes,* in gift shops nationwide, and through the Cornell Laboratory of Ornithology.

In the future Storm dreams of going on to do bioacoustic recordings of vanishing tropical ecosystems. By recording the sounds of these waning biological systems, he believes his ecological bioscapes will enable people to better understand ecosystems, how they work and how we can recreate or reproduce them.

Lamenting how little note is taken of the deeds of nature, John Muir asked in his book *The Wilderness World of John Muir* (Houghton Mifflin), "Who publishes the sheet music of winds or the music of the water written in river-lines?" Surely were he still alive, Muir would agree that today that publisher is Jonathan Storm.

In nothing do we approach so nearly to the gods as in doing good to others.
adapted from Cicero

IDENTIFYING YOUR MISSION TO FOLLOW

Once again, as you can see from these examples, there are seemingly endless possibilities for earning a living following a mission or calling. To identify if there is a mission you would like to follow, use the following work sheet to begin exploring what life has presented to you that is calling out in some way for you to address.

FOLLOWING A MISSION **WORK SHEET**

Answer the following questions to help you decide if you'd like to actually pursue any of the missions they might suggest as a livelihood; rate each idea you identify on a scale of 1 to 10 as to how interested you would be in making your living taking on this cause.

1	2	3	4	5	6	7	8	9	10
NOT VERY INTERESTED				SOMEWHAT INTERESTED					VERY INTERESTED

Do two ratings: **1)** the Magic Factor following each mission would provide for you, how energizing and compelling it would be; and **2)** how closely following such a mission would match the type of life you want to create for yourself.

*Do not base your evaluation of these ideas on whether
or not you think you could make enough money following such a
mission. You'll be able to evaluate that in Part III.*

	MAGIC FACTOR RATING	LIFESTYLE MATCH RATING
1. What personal tragedy, illness, or loss have you experienced that you could educate or otherwise help others to avoid or cope with?		
2. What problems have you overcome and see others struggling through that you could help them with?		

3. What injustices have you experienced or seen that bother you so much you'd like to do something about them?	MAGIC FACTOR RATING	LIFESTYLE MATCH RATING

4. What ideas do you have for doing something a better way?		

5. What would you like to prove is possible?		

6. What could you do to make the world a better place?	MAGIC FACTOR RATING	LIFESTYLE MATCH RATING
7. What do you feel strongly about wanting to preserve or restore that is being lost in our world today?		
8. What has your inner vision or inner voice been inspiring you to do?		

COMPLETE THESE SENTENCES:

This shouldn't be . . . _____

_____

_____

No one should have to endure . . . _____

_____

_____

There has to be a better way to . . . _____

_____

_____

What the world needs now is . . . _____

_____

_____

If I were in charge, here's how things would change . . . _____

_____

_____

If only . . . _____

_____

_____

WORK SHEET SUMMARY

Now review your answers to these questions and write below any possible missions that appeal to you at a 7 rating or above, along with any ideas you have for how you might make a living following them. Also look through appendices I and II for other possible ideas of how you could support yourself pursuing the missions and list any appealing ideas here.

MISSIONS   POSSIBLE SELF-EMPLOYMENT OCCUPATIONS

1. _____   _____

   _____   _____

2. _____   _____

   _____   _____

3. _____   _____

   _____   _____

4. _____   _____

   _____   _____

5. _____   _____

   _____   _____

6. _____   _____

   _____   _____

7. _____   _____

   _____   _____

THE PROS AND CONS OF FOLLOWING A MISSION

While this is the least-common path to one's perfect work, when traveled successfully, following a mission can be one of the most rewarding. The gratification that comes from knowing you're making a difference in the world, the sense of achievement that comes from doing something no one else has been able or willing to do, the peace that comes from knowing you're following a destiny of some kind, that you've been called and answered that call, the knowledge that your efforts are changing or preserving the world in a positive way can bring quite remarkable satisfaction. These are the rewards people talk about as a result of following this path. We commonly hear comments like:

"Sometimes I get very tired, but then I see the joy in my clients' eyes as they leave my office and my fatigue fades away and I feel like the luckiest person in the world."

"I feel very blessed to be able to do something that can make such a difference. I am happy to know what I do truly counts."

"Just to watch their faces, to see them enjoying themselves, appreciating new things, and to know I made it possible . . . that's enough in and of itself."

"There are times I wonder why I keep doing all this, but then at night when I'm in bed I remember why. This is what I'm here to do. No one else is doing this, and someone has to do it."

"I know I'm doing God's work through what I do each day."

Also this path, perhaps more than any other, seems to inspire a dogged determination and perseverance that keeps you motivated and moving ahead despite even apparently insurmountable odds. In fact, it's the only one of the four paths where it doesn't seem to matter whether doing it comes naturally to you. Valerie Justine, for example, knew nothing about art or weaving when she started her mission preserving kilims. Jeffrey Armstrong had never thought of himself as a comedian until he became St. Silicon. Tom Roberts had never done organic farming when he decided to make it his cause. Gwen Thomas knew nothing about teaching literacy when she started WALET. Vivian Shimoyama had no knowledge of how to create jewelry. To this day, she doesn't make it; she

The highest level of meaning possible for work is in a calling where humanity finds its true purpose.

G. E. Pence

designs it for others to make. Rusty Berkus knew nothing about and had no interest in the publishing world before creating her first book of poems.

Since a mission often arises from a crisis, injustice, or problem we have overcome, such adversity has made us strong and gives us a greater sense of capability thereafter in all things we set out to do. In pursuing a mission we further build our confidence and grow still stronger.

"I learned to master the tremblings of my limbs, to control my heartbeat and my breathing, to wipe away the sweat that burned my eyes."

Douchan Gersi,
explorer

In fact, in following a mission some people are willing to go to extreme efforts to master something that pursuing that mission requires of them. Poet and publisher Rusty Berkus, for example, is still terrified of public speaking and making radio and television appearances to promote her books. "My heart beats so fast. My palms sweat. I feel like I'm going to die," she confides, "but if I'm provided with the opportunity to tell people about my books, I must do it."

So another real benefit of choosing this path is that motivation is usually not a problem. Even major obstacles don't seem to be a deterrent. No matter how difficult or seemingly impossible it becomes, people traveling this path often still feel a compulsion to keep going. But as you may have noticed from some of the above comments, fatigue and burnout can be a problem. Overworking is one trap people can fall into all too easily along this path. And yet, oddly, often they don't seem to mind this either—but they should.

Avoiding Burnout. Taking steps to avoid burnout along this path is essential. Because as with Nadia Sutton or Jo Quinn, there may be such a need for what you're doing or because you are so driven to pursue your mission, you may actually have to consciously force yourself to restrain your dedication. Otherwise you'll defeat yourself. You cannot do your best work when you're constantly exhausted. Years of weariness can sneak up on you and erode your ability to continue or complete your efforts. Extreme overworking can literally cut short the years you'll have to make the contribution you've undertaken. And family and loved ones may suffer from your overdedication. So if you choose this path,

"I have no idea where I will go on this journey, but I know I must take it."

Martin Luther
King, Jr.

take precautions to assure that you get sufficient rest and take time to eat, to play, and to nurture yourself so you can give your best and enjoy your life in the process.

Remembering You Have to Make Money. Another common trap along this path is that it may become a sacrificial one. Money is often not the highest priority for those who choose this path and, as a result, sometimes they forget to think about how they will actually be able to support themselves. But if you want to follow your mission, you must think about money, even if you have to force yourself to do so. Unless you have some other independent means of support, you'll have to find a way to make money from the pursuit of your mission or you won't get to do it.

Also, because your mission often involves a cause of some kind, turning it into a livelihood can, at times, present a unique challenge. For example, those who need what you offer the most may also be the least able to pay for it. Or what you want to do may not yet have any immediate apparent commercial value. But there is usually a way to find that value so that you can support yourself.

- APTC has been able to price its services so that the people who need them most can still afford them.
- Janice Guthrie relied upon support from her husband's salary for the three years it took before her mission became a financial success.
- Gwen Thomas and Nadia Sutton rely on volunteers to make their work possible.
- Paul Young can charge a percentage of the money he returns to his clients.
- Shelley Espanosa gets business through two local training brokers.
- Jim Hullihan has found corporate sponsors to underwrite much of the cost of his productions.
- Jeffrey Armstrong and Rusty Berkus got financial backing from family and friends.
- Michael Rozek identified precisely how many people he needs to make his venture viable and has solicited and received donations to keep him going while he finds them.

"When you are really doing something meaningful, your capacity to replenish yourself is high."
Doug Kruschke,
management
consultant

"What I'm doing has never been about money. That's not why I do it. But if I don't earn a living from it I don't get to do this work, so I actually had to train myself to remember to ask my clients to pay me at the end of the hour. Otherwise I would let them walk right out the door."

▪ Vera Yahanna, Sally Fox, and Jonathan Storm have relied on an outside job while working to build their mission.

Making sure you will be able to make a living may be the greatest challenge in following a mission. Reading and mastering the matrixing system in Part III: "The Means," may be more important for those along this path than any other.

Succumbing to My Way or Die. Because, like most people who take this path, you undoubtedly have strong beliefs about your mission, another trap it may present is rigidity. You can let rigor mortis set in in what you're undertaking by holding rigidly to exactly what you'll do and exactly how you'll do it. If you're too rigid, however, you'll lose the flexibility you need to discover how you can package what you want to do in a way that will meet someone's needs sufficiently to enable you to pay your bills. Being flexible does not have to mean selling out or compromising your goals, standards, or beliefs; but to succeed as a self-employed individual, it will mean being open to the needs, concerns, and circumstances of others. And you will probably need to consider alternatives that were not part of your original idea for what you would be doing. In other words, a "my way or die" attitude usually won't fly. Let those things about which you must be totally rigid remain as hobbies or volunteer activities.

Signing on for the Long Haul. The other possible drawback to taking this path is that because you're pioneering, or because you're doing something with no built-in demand, or something with so much demand that it requires special funds or personnel, becoming successful along this path can take longer than other routes. So, if you decide to proceed, you must be prepared for the long haul. Therefore, no matter how great an idea you may have for taking on a mission, unless you care about it at a 7 or above on the evaluation scale, don't even think about pursuing it as a livelihood. And likewise, if an idea you have for pursuing a mission doesn't match your lifestyle needs at a 7 or above, let it pass. Let someone else do it. Or wait until a time when you can be that committed.

AVOIDING MY-WAY-OR-DIE THINKING

"I was going to humanize the American corporation. I thought I knew everything they were doing wrong. But they weren't interested in hearing about it. I couldn't make any real change—or get any real work—until I started listening to their needs. Then I could start to show them how what I wanted to do could help."

"I wasn't going to be like all the others and price what I did so high that most people couldn't afford it. I wanted to help the people who haven't been able to use services like mine. But after I started out on my own, I realized why other people charge what they do—all the costs involved—and I had to rethink what I could do to actually be able to serve the people who need me."

And although you may feel willing to go to any extreme to follow a mission, the road will be considerably easier and shorter if you're willing to build what you do around the natural abilities you possess. So, use appendices I and III to help structure ideas for how you might pursue your mission with the greatest degree of success. (Also **Part III** will help you find how to tailor your mission to assure its financial success.)

Here are two examples of how a mission can be tailored to one's personal style to increase the chances of success.

Jane and Karen both have experienced the heartbreak of infertility and although they both were able ultimately to have children, they now want to help others who are experiencing the difficulties they faced. They have quite different personal styles, however, and therefore would make life much more difficult for themselves if they tried to pursue their shared mission in the same way.

Looking in **Appendix III**, Jane, whose personal style is Leader/Improver/Builder, will find careers like newsletter publishing, copywriting, and self-publishing, consulting, and training to be well suited to her. So she might pursue her mission to help other infertile couples by writing a newsletter on infertility and giving speeches and seminars on coping with the traumas of try-

"Anyone who proposes to do good must not expect people to roll stones out of his way, but must accept his lot calmly, even if they roll a few more upon it."

Albert Schweitzer

FOLLOWING A MISSION

Goal. Finding the work you feel uniquely called to do to make a contribution to improve the world and make it a better place.

Driving Force. Pursuing this path is driven by an inner commitment so strong that it may feel like an obsession or compulsion about which you have no choice. If you truly discover one, you will probably pursue it one way or another even if you earn your living some other way. If you discover such a mission but don't pursue it, you will probably feel a deep sense of regret, deprivation, or disappointment.

Pros. Successfully following a mission is usually highly satisfying and deeply gratifying. It is likely to infuse you with a dogged determination and propel you onward against even the most challenging of odds. It can inspire you to master abilities and talents you would never have thought you had the ability or courage to undertake or put up with.

Cons. Fatigue and burnout can be a risk. You may be tempted to forget that if you are to keep going you must find a way to make money from what your work is. Sometimes finding how to do that can be more challenging than on other paths and because you care so much about your mission, you might become too rigid about how to make that possible. And you may have to sign on for a long haul before you become successful.

---

ing to conceive a child against the odds. In contrast, Karen's personal style is Organizer/Improver/Builder, and just the idea of speaking before a group scares her. She knows she wouldn't feel comfortable doing what comes easily to Jane, and she doesn't have to. She can pursue her mission in another way that's better suited to her. Looking in Appendix III under her personal style, she'll find careers like running a referral service or event clearinghouse. So she might decide to start an infertility referral service, referring couples to professionals, written materials, events, and other resources that could be useful to them.

SEVEN

Capitalizing on Your Assets

ALTHOUGH CAPITALIZING on whatever assets you have—be they your previous job experiences, your contacts, or other resources you have available to you—can be useful no matter what path you take, this is by far the most popular path people take to making a living creating a life of their choosing. Almost one of every two people who becomes self-employed choose this path at least initially. They don't begin in response to demands for some special gift they have. They don't set out to pursue a personal passion, nor do they feel compelled to follow a particular mission. For them, and perhaps for you, becoming self-sufficient is a means to some other end. It might be economic survival, having greater flexibility and more control over your life, working from home, having more time for your children, pursuing some other aspect of your life, or living and working in some location or way that better suits you.

For Al and Anita Robertson of Tulsa, Oklahoma, it was a matter of survival. When Al lost his job, they decided to turn what had once been Anita's hobby—calligraphy—into their full-time means of support. Friends and family had asked Anita to do callig-

> It doesn't matter so much what you do in particular, so long as you have your life.
>
> *Henry James*

raphy pieces for them so frequently that she was already supplementing the family income with her skill. When Al lost his job, however, they both started working at the business, full-time. But to generate the income they needed, they took The Scribe & Scroll on the road selling Anita's calligraphy matted and framed at craft shows from coast to coast. By home-schooling their two children on the road, they are able to travel three months a year, then return home to create new products.

Nathan Connors needed a way to support himself as a means to achieving his dream, to create original oil paintings. Connors knew it would be some time before he could earn a full-time living from his paintings, so picture framing became a way for him to make a living while he developed his artistic skills and built his reputation as an artist. Ultimately he was able to open his own art gallery next to his frame shop, which his wife continues to operate.

For twenty-eight-year-old housewife and mother of three daughters Leone Ackerly, the idea of becoming her own boss began when she decided she wanted to buy a new car. To earn the extra income, Ackerly took a look at her own life to identify what she knew how to do best. She decided to hire herself out as a cleaning woman with a system for cleaning a house quickly and thoroughly at a reasonable price. She's literally been cleaning up ever since. Twenty-years later, she's the head of the multimillion-dollar national franchise MiniMaid.

For Ann McIndoo, thirty-two and divorced, it all began with the desire to own her own home. Working as a secretary in a law firm, McIndoo remembers taping a picture of her dream house to the front of the refrigerator door as a reminder of her goal. Her employer had recently computerized and since McIndoo caught on quickly to using a personal computer, she was asked to help train the others in the office. It didn't take long for her to figure out that if her firm needed help computerizing, others would, too. She left her job to become a computer tutor and her company, Computer Training Services, took off quickly. Soon she was earning over $100,000 a year and working from the home of her dreams.

> "I'm proud that I'm able to make a living on my own. My biggest achievement is having ten of the most prestigious law firms in the area as clients. I'm sorry I didn't start sooner."
>
> *Ann McIndoo,*
> *Computer Training*
> *Services*

Each of these individuals was able to create an independent livelihood by capitalizing on some asset that was available to them. We all have many such assets we can capitalize upon. Many of these assets are right under our noses, but all too often we simply overlook them or take them for granted. José Villa didn't, however. Villa's asset is his wife. "Most people know somebody who makes the best cookies," he told us, "but I have a wife who makes the best Chinese food they've ever tasted." He decided that instead of working sixty hours a week for the Air Force, he would use the management skills he gained in the military to join efforts with his wife, Happy Chan, and start a gourmet Chinese catering service primarily doing private house parties. Now even their Chinese restaurant competitors pay them to cater parties.

If you're beginning to think you can't imagine any assets you could turn into an independent income, just consider "Lucky" Eddie Mauss. Mauss has identified perhaps the most unusual asset we've encountered anyone turning into an income: bad luck. Mauss describes himself as a "misfortune magnet." On the first day of one of his first jobs selling insulation, for example, he fell through the ceiling. But, as usual, he recovered ably, announcing to his astonished customer that he had good news: she didn't need any insulation!

At his grandfather's funeral, Mauss realized that his whole family had a history of bad luck but that they shared a weird, rich sense of humor that kept them all going. So he decided to capitalize on this unusual asset by starting a newsletter that "proves any hapless clod can muddle through life." Called the *Hard Luck Gazette,* Mauss publishes his monthly newsletter from his bedroom with the computer and printer beside his bed. The newsletter is filled with hapless hard-luck stories submitted mostly by subscribers. The best story of each month wins a $15 cash prize or a one-year free subscription. Right now the publication is still a part-time venture, but the *Hard Luck Gazette* has over five hundred subscribers and the number is growing.

If Mauss can capitalize on *this* asset, there has to be a myriad of assets you could capitalize on as well. The key is to begin assessing and exploring your many possibilities. And the place to begin is with the obvious and not-so-obvious resources available right around you. Even if you're already committed to pursuing one of the other paths, we urge you to read this chapter and assess your assets because what you discover could make your journey easier and more successful. Here are several places to look for assets you can capitalize on.

1. PREVIOUS JOB EXPERIENCE, EDUCATION, AND TRAINING

Previous job experience, education, and training are probably the most common and obvious assets people can capitalize on to create a successful new life on their own. In looking through **Appendix II, "An Alphabetical Directory of Self-Employment Careers,"** you'll notice literally hundreds of traditional careers people now work independently, from accounting and abstracting to writing and working as an X-ray technician. Kelle Harris is an example of someone who has capitalized on the trend for companies to outsource work that might once have been done in-house. To find a better balance between her career and her role as a mother of three, Harris uses her training and experience in marketing to operate her own marketing-consulting firm, Market Spark. Sixty-year-old Judith Cohen drew upon her background and work experience as an engineer to become a part-time writer. Her first book, *You Can Be a Woman Engineer,* written for elementary-school students, has led to a series of other books she's writing about women in other traditionally male-dominated fields. Each book is colorfully illustrated by Cohen's husband, David Katz.

PROFILE: DAVID ELIASON, AUDIO ENGINEER

When David Eliason's position as news director for a Dubuque radio station was eliminated in 1986, he had the choice of either leaving town to find a similar position or staying there where he wanted to live and finding something else to do. He chose to stay in Dubuque and turned a part-time business he'd run more like a hobby since college into a full-time business as an audio engineer, designing and installing sound systems for churches, auditoriums, racetracks, theaters, and office buildings.

Ray Jassen had worked for twenty years as a law librarian when he decided to start Law Library Management, Inc., which provides full-time law library services for small law firms. Jassen says, "I went on my own primarily because I wanted the satisfaction of being my own boss." Wayne Toliver had worked as a tile setter and general flooring mechanic when he decided he'd rather do it on his own. When Alan Kaplan decided he wanted to be the one to call the shots, he drew on his experience as an intelligence agent in the Air Force and the chief investigator for Summa Corporation. In his business, Attorney's Investigative Consultants, Kaplan is now a private investigator and engages in sixty categories of investigations with his wife, also a licensed P.I. Lewis Mann had worked as an agent for a variety of insurance companies when he became frustrated with the limitations of working for someone else, so he decided to start his own agency, Mann & Company, which brokers life, health, and disability insurance, plus annuities and retirement plans. "I wanted the freedom to choose the best possible policies for my clients, which I couldn't do with the products of only one company," he says.

While these example may seem like obvious transitions to make, others have used their background, education, and training to go out on their own doing less-obvious things. Debra Craig was a supermarket checker, for example, when she saw the many oversights and opportunities people miss out on while shopping. So she got the idea of creating a newsletter for supermarket shoppers. Marcia Layton was a marketing communications director for Eastman Kodak for four years when, inspired by her father's artistic talents, she set out to specialize in helping artists manage and market their work. Layton has written the book *Successful Fine Art Marketing.*

PROFILE: MARCIA LAYTON

"One need only recall that Van Gogh never sold a painting to recognize that talent alone is not sufficient for success," says fine-arts marketing specialist and business plan writer Marcia Layton. She grew up spellbound by her father's artistic talents. "In just hours it seemed he could create a vibrant watercolor landscape or rich pastel still life." Although she tried to develop her own artistic talents through art lessons, "I was more drawn to business," Layton explains. Through Layton and Company, she uses her experience in business to pursue her lifelong interest. "The consensus is that good artwork should be able to sell itself, but art historians can attest to the fact that many genius painters and sculptors have died penniless," Layton says in describing the need for her work.

Similarly Dennis and David Singsank wanted to reconnect with their childhood growing up on a farm. They found a way. They use the experience they gained working in the health-food packaging business to help organic farmers. They contract and sell just about every organically produced grain crop there is from soybeans to sunflowers and millet to flax, serving over 150 organic growers. As president of a manufacturing company, Suzanne Caplan experienced the trials and tribulations of dealing with the prejudice facing women entrepreneurs, so when she left her position she founded a women's entrepreneurial training center in Pittsburgh and created Safety Exchange, a database information network for her clients and others. Economist Jennifer Folhemus wanted to be able to spend more time doing community service than a full-time position would allow her. So she used her background to create Precision Research and work from her home doing microeconomic analysis of problems and issues facing businesses and individuals like lost profits, lost earnings, and business valuation.

Former editor of *Orleans* magazine and a local newspaper, Gisele Grignon became a freelance writer as was her husband, Morley Seaver. But they found they were still spending too much time working and too little time with their three young children, so they decided to shift what they did. They launched The Word Farm, publishing their own newsletters that capitalize on their personal experiences. The *Pennywise Parent* makes use of what they've learned from living, as so many families do these days, on a tight budget. *Simply Seniors* draws on Grignon's experience writing for *Today's Seniors* magazine. Gisele and Morley live outside the village of Moose Creek, Ontario, Canada, with their three kids, two angora goats, some cats, and a dog in a century-old farmhouse on twenty-three acres of property that includes a barn and a one-room schoolhouse.

Claudia Shear has turned an array of sixty-four miserable job experiences, from waiting tables at dozens of restaurants to an-

"Using the time I save by not commuting, avoiding office interruptions, and dressing up only for meetings, I'm able to maintain the earnings level I require and still fulfill my desire for community service," says economist Jennifer Folhemus. "I volunteer in my child's classroom, join the class for field trips, and serve on the PTA. I'm active in my neighborhood association and recently concluded a three-year term on the city planning commission. The personal rewards from this volunteer service are as important to me as the pecuniary rewards from my profession."

swering telephones on the graveyard shift, into unexpected fame and fortune. With no previous theater credits or writing background, Shear has written a one-woman play called *Blown Sideways* and turned her oddball life and career into a runaway Off-Broadway hit. "It's funny," she told the *Los Angeles Times* when her play opened there, "but everything that made me a misfit in the world made me just right to belong in the theater."

2. LIFE EXPERIENCES AND CIRCUMSTANCES

Sometimes it's not our job experiences or educational backgrounds that provide the most promising assets for us to capitalize on so we can do the things we most want to do. Often other life experiences and life circumstances can provide us with a rich array of assets. Here are a few examples of how others have capitalized on assets they discovered while going about their daily lives.

Helping an Ill Daughter. Programmer David Brace was looking for a way to help his daughter. She had suffered a brain trauma in an accident, so he developed some software designed to enable her to retrain her brain and regain normal functioning. His success in aiding her recovery led to requests from others for specialized computer programs. Brace suffers from a hearing loss himself, so his circumstances have prepared him to create products that will help others deal with disabilities.

Watching Your Parents Work. When Patricia Plank's husband died, she had to find a way to support herself. Although only a hobbyist at photography, she did know how to run a photography business, because she'd grown up in one. Her parents were both professional photographers and had their own studio. Initially Plank took a job, but when the job ended she decided to open a photography studio specializing in glamorous head shots for women. Using her own experience, Plank does her clients' hair and makeup to make them feel and look fabulous for their glamour photos.

Daily Duties. Marty Palmer Sprague's husband is a campus minister, and they're raising three children. She didn't want to go out to work; she wanted to be home with her kids. So it occurred to her that she could help bring in extra income by capitalizing on the things she knew best, things that could be helpful to other

"The latest price tag for raising a child to legal age is pegged at $100,000 (not counting day-care fees). We've got three children, but we come up a few bucks short of the prescribed $300,000," jokes Gisele Grignon, publisher of *Pennywise Parent* newsletter. "Turns out there is something we can do to be effective parents without remortgaging the house. In fact, there's a whole slew of things we can do," she says of the many money-saving ideas in her newsletter.

"Nobody is just a typist, just a dishwasher, just a cook, just a porter...Everyone has at least one story that would stop your heart."

Claudia Shear

mothers like herself. First she turned to her experience of having to come up with a tasty meal for her family every evening. Although she had no experience as a professional writer, Sprague wrote *Menus and Meals in Minutes.* Then she turned to her experience entertaining family and friends and wrote her newest book, *The 35 Best Christmas Party Ideas.* Through her practical advice, she's developing a reputation as the "Poor Woman's Martha Stewart."

Creating a Backwoods Home. Steve Willey wanted to live on a mountaintop in the woods. Relying on his lifelong hobby, electronics, he worked at a number of jobs, first at the telephone company, then repairing TVs and installing microwaves until he had enough money to build a solar-powered home in a remote mountain range. Others wanting to follow in his footsteps were so curious as to how he'd built a home using an alternative energy source that he realized he could capitalize on the experience he'd gained building his home. He created Backwoods Solar Electric Equipment Systems and sells equipment that enables others to live in the remote locations of their dreams using sun, water, and wind to create electric power instead of having to face the often-prohibitive cost of getting an electric power line extended onto their property.

Tagging. Yes, tagging, as in graffiti. Twenty-two-year-old Ash Hudson was once a graffiti vandal until he turned that experience into Conart (the name is a wedding of *convict* and *art)* and became a clothing distributor designing graffiti images on T-shirts and caps. Hudson started out designing and selling one-of-a-kind shirts on the streets in front of high schools. The response led him to realize he could sell a lot of shirts if he reproduced many copies of each design. Since then graffiti art clothing has become a hot item, and Conart now has over a million dollars in orders. Working in his eight-room studio, he now employs other ex-taggers, who are too busy designing to do any more tagging.

A Hot Christmas. Getting into the Christmas spirit can be difficult in Southern California when it's a balmy 70+ degrees outside. To help her friends get into a holiday mood, five years ago Jeanne Benedict started making festive, but inexpensive, edible gingerbread houses as Christmas presents. You might say that this aspiring actress is capitalizing on the good weather. Her idea has turned into a successful sideline business. Benedict's handmade houses sell from $100 on up. At the high end she'll customize a gingerbread house to look like the customer's home. She also has produced a how-to video, *Gingerbread Party House,* that shows people how to make their own edible winter wonderlands. "Half the fun is in making the houses," she says, and anyone can create their own holiday cheer no matter how good the weather may be.

A Religious Tradition. When Miss Irene came to this country from Hungary, she needed money to pay the tuition for her children to attend Hebrew school, but she wanted to stay home and make money. As an Orthodox Jewish woman in Los Angeles, she had learned how to dress attractively while following her religion's sacred dress codes, so she decided to put this knowledge to work. She converted her garage into Irene's Boutique, providing carefully chosen modest, but fashionable, clothing for Orthodox Jewish women.

3. YOUR CONTACTS

While the saying "It's all in who you know" is sometimes used in a pejorative way, the people we know and the contacts we have can truly be valuable and important assets. They can provide us with ideas and share experiences. They can serve as role models. They can open doors for us we could not open on our own. They can become our first clients or customers or introduce us to others who will be. They can serve as our cheerleaders and urge us to do key things we might not otherwise think of or wouldn't believe we could do. In fact, for many people, personal contacts become the primary avenue through which they are able to create the independent lives they've been wanting. Here are a few examples:

Elizabeth Rosenberg was working as a legal secretary while her husband was in law school. Of course, it wasn't long before she gladly began typing his schoolwork and offering editorial advice. Her help proved so useful that other law students started calling asking her for help with their work. Living on a secretary's salary, the couple needed some extra income, so Rosenberg set up her own word-processing service with a ready supply of steady customers waiting. Now she says, "I can't imagine wearing panty hose again every day. I wouldn't do anything else."

Vivian Haworth was working for a company selling comput-

Support Yourself with a Car, Pickup Truck, or Van*

Gardening or yard service

Carpentry

Housepainting

Swimming pool maintenance service

Home maintenance and repair

Mobile lunch wagon

Party sales (cosmetics, clothing, housewares)

Plant-care service

Computer repair service

Mobile auto detailing

Hauling service

Errand service

Messenger service

Pet taxi or grooming van

Car-pool service

Elder taxi

Pet-sitting service

Driving instructor

Mobile notary

Tree service

As subject to local zoning and state licensing: For example, catering services often require licensed kitchens; zoning laws may prohibit use of residential property for bed-and-breakfast inns or other commercial use of your land.

ers when she realized she needed to make a career change. She was thinking about getting a real estate license when friends in the relocation consulting business introduced her to that field and she found it to be more to her liking. They showed her the ropes and helped her get started. Now as Corporate Network Relation Services, she makes moving easier for transferred employees and their families.

Robin Roberts had always created newsletters as part of whatever jobs she held in sales, marketing, and computer support. Often she'd thought about how much she'd like to produce newsletters full-time on her own, but she kept thinking, "No one would pay me to do that." Then one day while talking to her mother, who is a legal nurse consultant providing litigation support to lawyers, Roberts realized otherwise. Having had a background in business, she could see that her mother needed a newsletter to help market her business. Roberts now spends her time producing stock newsletters for legal nurse consultants, which she customizes to meet each client's needs. Her company is called Uptime. The newsletter is *Privileged Communication*. Her mother was her first client and has since opened the door to many others.

Daryn Ross was in college when a local store offered him a part-time job selling T-shirts on campus. The pay they proposed wasn't enough to be tempting, but the idea was. He started researching the possibility of imprinting specialty items and decided to start his own line of T-shirts and sweatshirts for fraternities, sororities, and other campus organizations. As you can imagine, his contacts on campus came in handy and he says sales for his company, Innovative Concepts, have doubled every year for the past eight years. The company he uses to do most of his imprinting is owned by none other than his parents. Ross's father, an industrial arts teacher, was about to retire from teaching just as Daryn was getting his business under way. So they had the opportunity to begin their companies at the same time and work together.

4. EQUIPMENT, FACILITIES, AND OTHER POSSESSIONS YOU OWN

Sometimes our best assets are literally right at hand—under our noses—or even underfoot. Remember, for example, how prairie

---

Earn a Living from Your Land or Property*

Organic gardening

Growing edible flowers

Growing mushrooms

Growing sprouts

Hayrides

Growing exotic plants

Growing herbs

Dried flowers

Balloon school

Breeding animals

Boarding animals

Training animals

Repair shop

Nursery

As subject to local zoning and state licensing: For example, catering services often require licensed kitchens; zoning laws may prohibit use of residential property for bed-and-breakfast inns or other commercial use of your land.

artist B. C. LaBelle creates all her art from the Nebraska clay, dried grass, and wildflowers in her backyard? Well, often we have access to some type of equipment, facilities, possessions, or other resources we can utilize to help us earn a viable income. As you can see from Appendix II, "An Alphabetical Directory of Self-Employment Careers," a personal computer, for example, can become the basis for seventy-five computer-based businesses we selected to feature in our book **Making Money with Your Computer at Home.** As you look through the appendices, you'll see how many other things around the house or in your life can become income-generating assets.

Georgia Thomas's car became her salvation when she was laid off from her job in the oil fields and had to figure out how she was going to support herself and keep her son in college. She opened a messenger service. A bulldozer saved John and Lynn Klink's farm. They turned it into Klink Excavation, which has grown into a million-dollar business they still operate from their farm. For Charlene Anderson-Shea the doorway to opportunity was a birthday gift from her husband. He bought her a loom, and she set out to prove she could support herself by weaving. That was more than seven years ago. She creates one-of-a-kind handwoven clothing for women under her In Stitches label. She also teaches workshops on weaving and publishes a newsletter about weaving called *Teaching for Learning.*

Margaret Ringer turned her two-car garage into a sprout shop, Sweet Water Sprouts of Concordia, California. She has two beds of sprouts growing there at all times and produces 400 pounds of alfalfa sprouts a week. Twenty-two years ago, Anstace and Larry Esmonde-White purchased five acres of property. Little did they know that after they retired and restored the century-old house there this land would open doors to a budding second career as do-it-yourself horticulturists. To the couple's surprise, after they created a garden similar to the ones they'd loved in Ireland, the interest the garden generated spurred the Esmonde-Whites to become writers and speakers on horticulture. Now they appear regularly on radio and television on a host of home and gardening shows.

Use the Rooms or Other Space in Your Home*

Bed-and-breakfast inn

Family day care

In-home health care

Personal chef

Catering service

Canning gourmet food gifts

Cooking school

Homemade cakes and cookies

Pet treats

Breeding exotic fish

Microbrewer

Photography studio

Beauty salon

Arts or crafts studio

Shipping and packaging service

Self-help classes

Counseling

Massage therapy

*As subject to local zoning and state licensing: For example, catering services often require licensed kitchens; zoning laws may prohibit use of residential property for bed-and-breakfast inns or other commercial use of your land.

PROFILE: GREG SOUSER, TRI-STATE MOBILE POWER WASH COMPANY

Greg Souser was working his way through college, but his job of three twelve-hour days a week for Sprint was not ideal. He tried telephone sales for a carpet-cleaning company but didn't like that any better. He wanted to be his own boss based at home where he could work in peace and get away from office politics. He felt stuck where he was, however, until one day he noticed an unused asset sitting around his cousin's house. Some time before, his cousin had purchased a mobile power wash unit but hadn't gotten any business using it. It was just sitting there and Souser thought, "I'll get some business!" He did. Right away he started picking up $100 to $150 a week, and only a year later he was making over $100,000.

While attending a trade show Elsie and Ted McConnell stumbled onto an asset they knew they could capitalize on. Having been building managers in Lake Worth, Florida, the McConnells knew the cost involved in replacing a roof could run to $100,000 or more, so when they saw a nuclear roof-moisture detector gauge at the show, they recognized its potential for inspecting the over one million condominiums in Florida. They bought one, got licensed to use it, and started the Roof Leak Detection Company. With their leak detector, they can locate the precise spot where a roof is leaking; and instead of having to replace the whole roof, property owners can simply have specific leaks repaired, saving tens of thousands of dollars.

Consider Other Potentially Profitable Possessions

Computer

Piano for lessons

Swimming pool for swimming or scuba-diving lessons

Lawn mower

Bulldozer

Vacuum cleaner

Camera

Camcorder

Home-repair tool kit

Boat

Airplane

Sewing machine

IDENTIFYING YOUR ASSETS

What are you positioned to do? What resources do you have available to you? Assess your assets on the following work sheet and list possible ways you can think of for using them to support yourself in pursuing your goals. Use **Appendix II, "An Alphabetical Directory of Self-Employment Careers,"** as a source for identifying other possibilities to consider. Star (**) any possibilities you might enjoy that would be consistent with your desired lifestyle.

CAPITALIZING ON YOUR ASSETS WORK SHEET

PREVIOUS JOB EXPERIENCE, EDUCATION, AND TRAINING

What job experience, education, or training have you had? All such experience can be useful in finding and pursuing your path to independence. List your experiences and possibilities you might want to consider for capitalizing on them here:

JOB EXPERIENCE   POSSIBLE SELF-EMPLOYMENT CAREERS

_____   _____

_____   _____

_____   _____

EDUCATION   POSSIBLE SELF-EMPLOYMENT CAREERS

_____   _____

_____   _____

_____   _____

TRAINING   POSSIBLE SELF-EMPLOYMENT CAREERS

_____   _____

_____   _____

_____   _____

LIFE EXPERIENCES AND CIRCUMSTANCES

What kind of life experiences have you had? What type of things have you done outside your educational and job experiences? What kind of circumstances have you found yourself in that others may also experience? Any such experiences and circumstances could be useful in finding and pursuing a path to independence. List your experiences and any possibilities you might want to consider for capitalizing on them here:

LIFE EXPERIENCES AND CIRCUMSTANCES   POSSIBLE SELF-EMPLOYMENT CAREERS

_____   _____

_____   _____

_____   _____

PERSONAL CONTACTS

What contacts have you made through previous jobs or other activities? What circles of friends or associates are you affiliated with? Also consider the contacts available to you through your spouse, friends, or relatives. How might you serve or relate to these contacts as a self-employed individual? List your contacts and possibilities to consider pursuing here:

WHOM YOU KNOW   POSSIBLE SELF-EMPLOYMENT CAREERS

_____   _____

_____   _____

_____   _____

EQUIPMENT, FACILITIES, AND OTHER POSSESSIONS

What equipment, facilities, property, tools, or other possessions do you own or have access to? How might you use these in the process of supporting yourself?

EQUIPMENT   POSSIBLE SELF-EMPLOYMENT CAREERS

_____   _____

_____   _____

_____   _____

FACILITIES OR PROPERTY   POSSIBLE SELF-EMPLOYMENT CAREERS

_____   _____

_____   _____

_____   _____

OTHER POSSESSIONS   POSSIBLE SELF-EMPLOYMENT CAREERS

_____   _____

_____   _____

_____   _____

SUMMARY OF YOUR ASSETS

Review your assets and list those that would be of particular interest to you to use in some way as a means of supporting yourself and attaining your goals.

ASSET   POSSIBLE SELF-EMPLOYMENT CAREERS

1. _____   _____

2. _____   _____

3. _____   _____

PROS AND CONS OF CAPITALIZING
ON YOUR ASSETS

As you can see, your assets present many possibilities for success-fully supporting yourself. And no matter what you do in life, you will be well served by capitalizing on the assets available to you. In fact, if you choose to pursue one or any combination of the other three paths, you will benefit by tying in and drawing on whatever assets you have that can assist your progress. Choosing this path as your primary route to self-employment, however, has its own unique advantages and disadvantages.

First, this path is inherently different from the others. Each of the other paths provides its own built-in source of motivation, its own magic, or drive, that can propel you forward and keep you going toward your destination:

- The brilliance of a gift is continually reflected back to you, reminding and beckoning you to harvest it.
- The joy one receives from a passion keeps pulling you to return to it again and again.
- The drive and sense of destiny that emanate from a mission call to you, compelling you to follow it, even sometimes to the point of obsession.

It's as if these other paths ignite some life force of their own within you. In contrast, an asset is inert. A resource is waiting to be used, an asset has to be acted upon. A computer, for example, can sit forever on the desk or in the closet, unused. A garage will be there as is, used or not. And so it is with your past job or life experiences and circumstances. They are simply available. They don't pester you like a mission. They don't delight you like a passion. They don't yearn to be expressed like a talent. You have to plug them in and use them for something for some reason. That means you have to have some other motivation, some use to put them in service to. And therein lie both the strength and weakness of this path.

Its strength is that it can enable you to do other important things you want to do in your life; its weakness is that by necessity your energy will be divided between using your assets to make a living and doing the other important things that your income will enable you to do. A woman, for example, whose goal is to be home with her young children can earn an income working from home capitalizing on the family's personal computer, her word-processing experience, and previous job contacts, but her energies will be divided between what she truly wants to do (be with her children) and what she must do so that she can run the word processing service. The artist who creates a sideline livelihood so he can pursue his art may use his garage to restore antiques, but again, his energy will be divided between his art, which he most wants to pursue, and the restoration service with all its business demands that will pull him away from his art. This built-in pull on one's energy can create a variety of traps you'll want to avoid if you're considering this path:

The Easy-Way Trap. Taking this path may tempt you to grab for the "easy way," a way to make money that supposedly won't really involve much time or energy. People who choose this path, for example, are more likely than any other group to fall prey to "get rich quick" scams, cons, and schemes. By seeking the so-called easy way, people who try to take this path may be tempted, for example, to get involved with some multilevel selling program or to buy some business opportunity or franchise because they assume it will be an automatic "moneymaker."

As we have pointed out, however, it's virtually impossible to make money from an income opportunity without an investment of your time, energy, and knowledge. It's like any other asset; you have to do something with it before it will produce anything. Usually far more time and energy is involved in starting a business than the descriptions of these income opportunities imply. Therefore another tempting trap is to flit from one seemingly "easy" answer to the next, or to be forever looking for a business where the grass is greener. Some people try capitalizing on one asset, for example, while always looking for another that would be easier. Others try capitalizing on several at once, hoping at least one will "catch on." Actually all this does is further divide your energy and decrease the chances of successfully capitalizing on one activity.

But as you will find on the next few pages, while there is rarely an "easy" way, there is definitely an "easier" way. There is a way to match what you capitalize on so closely with what you want from it that you'll find it relatively easy because doing it facilitates rather than detracts from your real goals. There are ways to choose and use assets that will predispose you to success with much less time and effort because you'll feel more as though you're going in one direction rather than in two.

The Always Talking, Never Doing Trap. Because you'll have to expend the energy to get something going along this path that

"They said it was a turnkey operation. Maybe I was naive, but I took that to mean all I'd have to do was turn the key, and the business would run itself."

"They told me this would be a source of passive income. But it was far from that."

"They suggested that someone could live on the beach and the checks would just arrive in the mail."

"They said it was a business in a box, just add water."

leads only indirectly to where you really want to go, another common trap is to be forever talking about what you're going to do, but actually never doing it. The computer you bought to start that sideline business may sit unopened in the closet. The great idea you had on one New Year's Day may still be simply a great *idea* next January first. And we understand that 50 percent of business opportunities people buy aren't even opened once the buyer gets them home.

If any of these delays has happened or is happening to you, you can stop wondering what's wrong with you and stop berating yourself. It's a normal occurrence along this path. But as you will see on the pages that follow, if you can capitalize on assets that will generate enough internal resonance or are sufficiently compatible with your goals, you'll be able to get going more quickly. Then once you start being able to enjoy the other things you're able to do by working, you'll feel eager to actually keep doing what you've been talking about.

The Getting Distracted, Limping Along, Petering Out, or Quitting Trap. Again since you'll have to put energy into this path that leads only indirectly to where you want to go, you're more likely to become frustrated with delays or setbacks. It may be easier to get distracted, limp along, or even give up. Other things in your life may more easily intervene. You may be tempted to get by, put off, let slide. And, unfortunately, if you do this, it will become self-defeating because people will notice and be less likely to take your work seriously. Your reputation among clients may suffer— and that will make getting new clients all the more difficult. But once again, as you will see, if the assets you choose to capitalize on dovetail well with your other objectives, you can avoid this temptation because you'll be getting what you want. That will keep you motivated to keep going, and you won't want to do anything to jeopardize what you've been able to create for yourself.

The Resentment and Burnout Trap. If the work you get involved with becomes too demanding, it can begin to interfere with your being able to do or enjoy the other things that led you to pursue working on your own in the first place. You may find yourself resenting appropriate demands from your clients, sabotaging your ability to attract new clients, and even disliking your work as much as, or more than, if you had an unfulfilling job. You could also find yourself burning the candle at both ends, putting in double duty, to the point of exhaustion. Sometimes this happens because you're expecting too much of yourself. Or it may be a sign that the work you've selected to capitalize on doesn't dovetail well enough with your other objectives, which, as you'll see, can be avoided by knowing what you want, what you can expect, and then planning carefully for how to get it.

THE FORMULA FOR AVOIDING THE TRAPS

Oddly enough, when you find your perfect work along this path of capitalizing on your assets, it can also be the easiest path to travel and just as rewarding as the other three. But as we've just described, this path does have a unique set of challenges. So understanding the formula that can make it work will help you to avoid the traps and overcome the most common problems. Here is the seven-part formula for success along this path:

1. Know what you're working for. Since this path is a means to some other end, it's important to know just what that end is. What **compelling personal goal or desire** is motivating you to create a new independent life? Both in choosing what you will do and in pursuing it, it's essential to know and keep this compelling personal desire in the front of your mind at all times. Otherwise you won't be able to tailor the decisions you make to be most compatible with these goals. Instead the demands of your work will start defining your life once again. Remember, for example:

"I was trying very hard not to be what I most wanted to be, which was a pretty limiting way to live."

Al and Anita Robertson were motivated by survival. Al had lost his job.

Nathan Connors set himself up to do picture framing so he could pursue his career as an artist.

Leona Ackery wanted to buy a new car.

Ann McIndoo wanted to own her own home.

David Eliason wanted to stay in Dubuque.

Ray Jassin wanted to be his own boss.

Lewis Mann wanted the freedom to choose the best policies for his clients.

Jennifer Folhemus wanted more time for community service.

Marty Palmer Sprague wanted to be home with her children and supplement the family income
Steve Willey wanted to live on a mountaintop.
Vivian Haworth was looking for a more gratifying career.

All these individuals were able to be successful along this path because they found ways to capitalize on their assets that both were compatible with their other goals and actually enabled them to achieve those goals. As you can see, the Robertsons' decision to take their calligraphy business on the road worked perfectly for them but would have been completely incompatible with Willey's goal to live on a mountaintop or Folhemus's goal to be free for more community service. McIndoo's decision to become a computer tutor traveling from law firm to law firm would be at odds with Connor's goal to be able to work on his artwork during free moments of the workday or with Sprague's goal to be home with her children. So if you're considering this path, clearly define what you are doing it for.

WHAT ARE YOU DOING THIS FOR? **WORK SHEET**

Define here your compelling personal goal, desire, or outcome that's motivating you:

_____

_____

_____

_____

_____

---

2. Determine if you want this goal enough for it to be worth the effort involved in achieving it. Just how important to you is whatever you're doing this for? For Patricia Plank, whose husband had died leaving her with a child in college to support, achieving her goals was *very* important. It was a matter of survival, which would highly motivate most people. While buying a home or a new car was sufficiently motivational for McIndoo and Ackerley, it may or may not be sufficiently motivational for others, or for you, to actually invest the amount of time and energy they had to expend in order to reach these goals. As a rule of thumb:

The more compelling your reason for wanting to take this path is to you, the easier and more likely it will be for you to succeed.

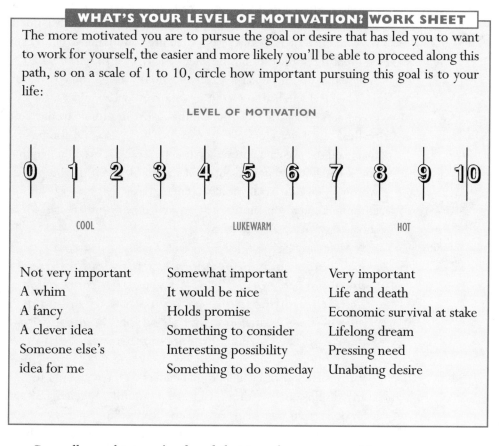

WHAT'S YOUR LEVEL OF MOTIVATION? WORK SHEET

The more motivated you are to pursue the goal or desire that has led you to want to work for yourself, the easier and more likely you'll be able to proceed along this path, so on a scale of 1 to 10, circle how important pursuing this goal is to your life:

LEVEL OF MOTIVATION

0   1   2   3   4   5   6   7   8   9   10

COOL   LUKEWARM   HOT

Not very important	Somewhat important	Very important
A whim	It would be nice	Life and death
A fancy	Holds promise	Economic survival at stake
A clever idea	Something to consider	Lifelong dream
Someone else's idea for me	Interesting possibility	Pressing need
	Something to do someday	Unabating desire

Generally speaking, we've found that in order to pursue this path successfully, you need to rate the reason you're doing it at a seven (7) or above. Otherwise you probably won't have sufficient drive or motivation to get started and keep going. That, of course, also depends on how much effort it will require.

Your
Personal
Style

What types of activities come most naturally to you? Check your three top styles after taking the survey in Appendix I, "Doing What Comes Naturally."

_ Leading
_ Improving
_ Building
_ Organizing
_ Creating
_ Problem solving

3. Make success as effortless as possible. Obviously the less effort capitalizing on your assets requires the better, because that will leave you more time and energy to pursue and enjoy the other things that are motivating you to do it. And this is precisely why people traveling along this path are so vulnerable to finding the "easy way." But since chasing what's hot is never as easy as it sounds, the following four elements of the formula can make capitalizing on an asset as effortless as possible.

4. Do What Comes Naturally. Whatever you decide to do to capitalize upon a particular asset, make sure it's something that's so well suited to your personality that doing it feels totally natural for you. Often a "hot" idea or opportunity that sounds so good may be great for someone, but not necessarily well suited to you. Of course that doesn't mean you *couldn't* do it. Maybe you could, but *would* you? If you had to go out of your comfort zone day after day doing something that you find difficult or unnatural, would you really do it? If, for example, your cousin knows several companies that need to have data entered on computer disks, even though this could become a regular source of income for you, if you prefer working outdoors while doing detail work drives you crazy, this is an opportunity you should just as well pass on other than for a short-term make-do situation.

> *Having to master or adapt to activities that are uncomfortable or difficult for you is not compatible with this path because it's a means to an end and your attention and energy will be focused mainly on reaching the end, not having to master the means.*

It's this kind of challenge that causes so many people to become disillusioned with a business like multilevel selling. Those who do well in that field have strong leadership abilities and are good at communicating and motivating people. They enjoy selling and are comfortable organizing both people and things. In other words, their personal style is what we would call Leader/Improver/Organizer. If you're more comfortable creating, building things, or solving problems, however, you probably won't be particularly successful in a multilevel business because the skills involved are at odds with your natural style of doing things. There's no reason to wonder why. It's all quite natural. Fortunately there are plenty of things you can do that are suited to you. To find out the type of things that come most naturally to your personality,

FIFTY WAYS TO MAKE MONEY WITH A COMPUTER

DOING WHAT COMES NATURALLY

LEADER
Computer sales and service
Public-relations specialist
Coupon newspaper publishing
Software publishing service
Association management service
Employee trainer
Temporary-help service
Collection agency

IMPROVER
Diet and nutrition–planning service
Astrology-charting service
Computer tutor
Computer-assisted instructional design
Documentation writer
Newsletter publisher
Professional reminder service
Answering service

BUILDER
Property-management service
Used-computer broker
Remote management
Drafting service
Desktop publishing
Computer-repair service
Scanning service
Sign making

ORGANIZER
Indexing service
Inventory-control service
Medical-transcription service
Note reader scopist
Payroll preparation
Medical-billing service
Mortgage-auditing service
Bookkeeping service

CREATOR
Computer-aided design
Clip-art service
Desktop video
Copywriter
Creativity consultant
Self-publishing
Business plan writer
Multimedia production

PROBLEM SOLVER
Computer consultant
Proposal writer
Information brokering
Financial-planning service
Professional practice management
Expert brokering service
Mailing list service
Database marketing service

complete the survey in **Appendix I, "Doing What Comes Naturally,"** if you haven't already.

Appendix I actually walks you through the steps of finding the self-employment careers that are best suited to you. It shows you how to use **Appendix III, "A Directory of Self-Employment Careers by Personal Style"** to identify the kind of self-employment options that will draw upon what you can do to capitalize on your assets most naturally. If you have contacts, for example, in the medical field, here are several examples from the appendix that illustrate how you could capitalize on those contacts by providing services based on what comes most naturally to you:

___ *Leader.* Provide marketing services for medical offices and hospitals or sell medical equipment and supplies.

___ *Improver.* Become a nurse consultant or an executive recruiter for hospitals and other medical groups.

___ *Builder.* Offer a taxi service for taking the elderly or disabled to medical appointments.

___ *Organizer.* Open a medical transcription service or medical claims processing service.

___ *Creator.* Become a medical illustrator or do interior design for medical facilities.

___ *Problem solver.* Do medical research as an information broker or become a private-duty nurse.

Here is a variety of ways you could use a computer to make money doing the kind of things that come most naturally to you as you can see on the previous page.

So use **Appendix III** to identify the self-employment occupations that are compatible with what comes naturally to you and list those you might want to consider on the "Possible Self-Employment Careers That Come Naturally to You" work sheet on page 222.

YOUR PERSONALITY IS ONE OF YOUR STRONGEST ASSETS: CAPITALIZE ON IT

Each of these individuals has created a livelihood that draws on the strengths of their personalities. Your personal style predisposes you for success in independent careers that call upon you to do the things that come most naturally to you.

LEADER/IMPROVER/ORGANIZER: BUSINESS NETWORK ORGANIZER

PROFILE: IVAN MISNER, BUSINESS NETWORK INTERNATIONAL

After working in management positions for several corporations, Ivan Misner wanted to be his own boss, so he established a management consulting firm. To get referrals, he started networking in various organizations and found that none of them was set up to truly facilitate businesspeople helping one another get business. So Misner organized his own networking group for the sole purpose of enabling members to give and get leads from one another. Soon his group was full but the word was spreading and so many others wanted to join that Misner set up another group, and then another and another. Suddenly he had a new business.

Ivan Misner, Business Network International

As a leader with a strong desire to help others succeed and the ability to help them organize to achieve their goals, Misner is ideally suited to be a business network organizer. He established Business Network International in 1985 and now has three hundred thriving chapters in North America.

IMPROVER/LEADER/ORGANIZER: TEACHING NURSE

PROFILE: VICKIE CORICH NENNER, TEACHING NURSE, MARVIK EDUCATIONAL SERVICES, INC.

Vickie Corich Nenner was burned-out. She was working as director of continuing education at a major hospital and wanted to continue teaching and helping people learn about health, but she also wanted the challenge and the excitement of developing new programs of her own. From her background she already had credibility and contacts in the health field. And with her strong desire to serve, her natural ability to communicate and lead, and her skill at organizing information in understandable ways, she was well suited for what she wanted to do.

Vickie Nenner, Teaching Nurse

Nenner's first challenge was literally to find her audience. At the hospital, of course, she had a built-in audience, but on her own she had to define and find the people who needed her seminars. Drawing on her contacts, she decided to continue giving educational programs for nurses and to start offering seminars at small companies to help people stop smoking.

BUILDER/ORGANIZER/IMPROVER: PARKING LOT MAINTENANCE
PROFILE: ROLAND SUTTON, ROLAND'S PARKING LOT MAINTENANCE, INC.

Roland Sutton was working in a small machine business when a customer asked him if he'd like to work less and make more money. His answer, of course, was yes, so the customer proceeded to make Sutton an offer he couldn't refuse: the chance to buy the customer's parking-lot-maintenance business. Sutton had only enough money to buy half the business, so the owner split the business and Sutton had a business of his own.

It was a business well suited to him. He likes working outside. He's good with his hands, likes working with materials, can get and keep things organized, and likes to satisfy his customers. So he now spends his time sweeping parking lots, cutting grass, and patching holes. His motto is "We sweep while you sleep," and he says of his business, "I'm making more money than I ever did without killing myself."

ORGANIZER/IMPROVER/BUILDER: PROFESSIONAL ORGANIZER
PROFILE: KAREN RUBIN, ORGANIZER EXTRAORDINAIRE

At the age of thirty-five, Karen Rubin had worked at more than 150 jobs but had never been fired. She had been laid off or a casualty of downsizing from one reorganization or buyout after another. Finally she figured being self-employed couldn't be any less secure than her job opportunities. So she reviewed her job history and noticed that in many of her jobs she'd been a troubleshooter, stepping in to get things organized. After being laid off from one last job she decided to do what came naturally and started offering her services to individuals as a professional organizer.

Rubin is an organizer by nature. She likes to help people, and she's willing to get in and roll up her sleeves to do whatever work needs to be done. She says, "I deal with the two most intimate parts of people's lives—their closets and their checkbooks"—so trust is the most important aspect of her work. "I wanted to create an experience for myself and others that was totally the opposite of all the negative jobs I've had. When I leave a job, people give me a hug and a kiss."

CREATOR/LEADER/ORGANIZER: REUNION PLANNER

PROFILE: SHELL AND JUDY NORRIS, CLASS REUNIONS, INC.

Judy Norris had frequently talked with her husband, Shell, about how much she'd like to start her own business. Then Shell volunteered to serve on his high-school reunion planning committee. The committee was very disorganized, and he thought reunion planning would be the perfect business for Judy. Although at that time there were no professional reunion planners, Judy, who was working for an ad agency, had the very skills the committee needed most. She is creative, good at managing people, and a great organizer.

They intended for the business to be a part-time venture, but after an article about their new business appeared in the *Wall Street Journal,* they were inundated with calls for help from desperate planning committees all over the country. Not only did Judy go full-time in the business, Shell quit his job too. Together they went on to launch this new field, having now provided training for many other reunion planners nationwide.

PROBLEM SOLVER/IMPROVER/BUILDER: MANUFACTURER

PROFILE: GEORGE BEAN, G.G. BEAN INC.

In college George Bean had majored in chemistry; at heart he's a problem solver. He wanted a profitable business that didn't involve many employees and a lot of overhead, so he started inventing chemical products that would solve various household cleaning problems. He'd develop and test first one product then another, selling them in retail stores throughout the Northeast.

Bean claims the secret to his success is that he listens. Right from the beginning, he called on all the stores in person to find out what people need. "I don't want to put things out on the market that don't work. If they don't sell, I'm dead." Clearly, helping people solve problems comes naturally to Bean, and he's willing to get in there and work at it until he comes up with something that meets a need.

5. Pick Something You Don't Mind Doing That's Suited to Your Situation. Although earning a living from capitalizing on an asset doesn't require you to feel passionately about what you do, the more enjoyable or pleasant the activity is, or at least the more tolerable, the better your chances of success will be. Usually do-ing things that come naturally to you feels sufficiently enjoyable to pursue as long as they also suit your needs and situation. But as you consider your possibilities, avoid any particular activity that holds little or no appeal to you or that would ultimately interfere with the reasons you want to create a job for yourself.

If you recall, Anita Robertson not only enjoyed calligraphy enough that it had become a hobby, she also wanted to home-school her children, so traveling to craft shows was feasible for her. Steve Willey had always enjoyed electronics, and by selling equipment for alternative-energy sources by mail-order catalog he could capitalize on that asset without having to leave the moun-taintop he was living on. Marcia Layton had been attracted to the art world since childhood, so she could meld a long-lost interest with a current ability.

So evaluate the possibilities you're considering in terms of their enjoyment level and their suitability to your situation. Again you can do this on the "Possible Self-Employment Careers That Come Naturally to You" work sheet on page 222.

6. *Pick Something You Do Sufficiently Well and Are Posi-tioned to Do.* As with pursuing a passion or following a mission, you don't have to be the best at what you do to successfully cap-italize on an asset, but the better you are at it the easier it will be. And remember, along this path, the easier you make it on your-self the more likely you will be able to succeed. So for the best and quickest results, avoid choosing things that will require a sub-stantial learning curve. Likewise, pick something that you are al-ready positioned to do. McIndoo could break into doing computer training in law firms because, having worked in a law firm, she already had the contacts. Plank knew the photography business because she had grown up in it, even though she had had little experience with a camera. Miss Irene was a member of the Orthodox Jewish community she was to serve. Although Marcia Layton was venturing anew into the art world, she was working in her own field of marketing. So was economist Jennifer Folhe-mus and law librarian Ray Jassin. The McConnells had been prop-erty managers, so they knew how to talk about leak detection to

property owners. Daryn Ross was in school on the campus where he began imprinting T-shirts for fraternities and sororities.

As you can see, they were each positioned for success. Although both the McConnells and Ross were comfortable selling, think of how much longer it would have taken or how much more challenging it would have been for the McConnells to sell novelties to fraternities or for Ross to sell leak detection to property owners. And think about how long it would have been before Folhemus had free time for the community service she wanted to do if she had been trying to open a photo shop instead of doing the economic research her background had prepared her to do.

So evaluate what you're considering doing with your assets in terms of how accomplished you already are at doing it and how well positioned you are for getting under way.

7. Pick Something with a Proven Demand and a Track Record. Finally, this path will be much easier if you do something that has a built-in demand and a proven track record. This will help you earn income more quickly and avoid the struggle of having to convince clients to buy from you. Think, for example, of the kind of things people who are following a mission are doing. Rusty Berkus is a poet. Michael Rozek is publishing an alternative magazine. Jonathan Storm is creating nature tapes. B. C. LaBelle is producing prairie art. There was no ready-made demand for these products. People weren't standing in line waiting to get them. No one was calling to ask for them. No one even knew such products existed. Letting people know about their products and building a demand for them has been their greatest challenge. But many kinds of things people are doing successfully on this path—like an errand service, law library management, a marketing firm, a word-processing service, an excavation service, power washing, computer tutoring, leak detection—have potential customers who already know about, need, and use these services. And many others have demonstrated a long track record of providing these services successfully.

So be sure to evaluate the demand and prior track record of the way you're planning to use your assets. Check out the experi-

---

┌─ **WORK SHEET** ───

POSSIBLE SELF-EMPLOYMENT CAREERS THAT COME NATURALLY TO YOU

Using **Appendix III**, list possible careers that are compatible with your top three personal styles. Rate them on a scale of 1 to 10 for each of the following factors that will make your success in pursuing them most likely:

POSSIBLE OCCUPATION	ENJOYMENT SUITABILITY	MASTERY LEVEL	POSITIONED FOR	DEMAND AND TRACK RECORD

ences others have had in earning an independent living that way. In **Appendix II, "An Alphabetical Directory of Self-Employment Careers,"** look for the over one hundred businesses we selected for *Best Home Businesses for the 90s* or *Making Money with Your Computer at Home*. Each of these businesses was screened to be sure there was a general demand for it and that there was a reason to expect the demand to continue. We also sought to make sure that there were people who had a track record of successfully pursuing these businesses. One caution, though: you will still need to check whether any particular business has become oversaturated in your community or marketplace with others doing the same thing you want to do. If so, it doesn't mean you can't do it, too; it just means that carving out your niche will be more challenging and involve more effort than when there's an untapped supply of needy customers.

The level of effort that will be required to succeed in an independent career you're considering along this path will be directly related to how high the career scores on each of these factors. The easiest things for you to pursue will be those that come most naturally to you, those you enjoy and are well positioned for, have a high level of mastery at, and can see a high level of demand for. So rate the level of effort for any career you're considering on the scale along this page based on how strongly it meets these criteria.

LEVEL OF EFFORT

0
1
2
3
4
5
6
7
8
9
10

To be a winner for you along this path, a career can't just be in demand; it must also be something you do well and naturally, and are positioned to do with ease.

WEIGHING YOUR OPTIONS

Essentially, the key to making this path a success is knowing what you want to accomplish and then finding the right balance between your level of motivation for achieving that goal and the level of effort it will involve. As you review your various assets and the options they present for earning a living, you can pretty well predict how wise you'd be to pursue any one of them by seeing where they fall in relation to these two factors: your Level of Motivation and The Level of Effort involved.

To get where you want to go, you have to start from where you are.

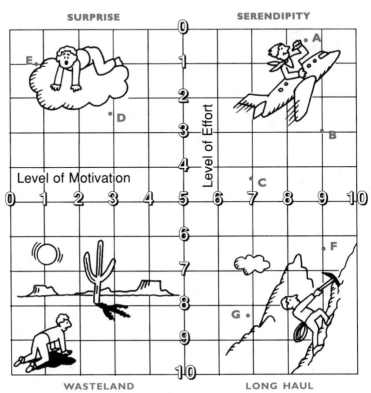

VIABILITY GRID

Finding the balance between motivation and level of effort

Using this viability grid, you can see, on the one hand, why the people we've been telling you about have been successful along this path; on the other hand, you can see how someone might also get into trouble taking this route. Here's our analysis of how the grid demonstrates the wisdom of several choices and what each quadrant could mean for you.

Serendipity! Most of the people we've described in this section fall into this quadrant. So if what you're considering falls into the upper right-hand quadrant, go for it! It means you've put together all the elements to be well positioned to attain your goal—be it to own a car, become your own boss, or boost your income. It means you're well positioned to use the assets you're wanting to capitalize on, you would enjoy doing the work, and you have the personality that's required to be successful.

Serendipity: Good fortune. When everything comes together as if by luck.

Elizabeth Rosenberg's idea to start a word-processing service is a prime example (Point *A* on the Viability Grid). She and her husband needed additional income. The demand for her services was high at the law school her husband attended, so she was well positioned to meet it. In fact, other students were begging her to help them. She has very good word-processing and editorial skills and job experience in the legal field. She enjoys doing what the work demands: helping others handle detail work and defining and advising her clients as to what they need to do to have the kind of documents they want (Organizer/Improver/Leader).

The Robertsons (Point *B*) were even more highly motivated when they turned to Anita's calligraphy as a means of support for the whole family. But they had a somewhat more difficult challenge than Rosenberg, because although Anita enjoys calligraphy and does it well, the local demand she was already well positioned for wasn't sufficient to support the entire family. They had to break into the national craft show circuit, which they were able to do by going on the road.

While Marty Palmer Sprague (Point *C*) wanted to work from home, the family's survival didn't depend on her success. So she had more time to ease into her career as a writer while continuing to put her family's needs first. She has experiences people want to know about and the ability to write about them. But she didn't start with background, experience, or contacts in the world of publishing, so while there's a need for her books, she has to find ways to make herself and her books better known to those who would want to buy them.

Surprise! If what you're considering falls in this quadrant, you're faced with an intriguing opportunity. It means you're well positioned to take advantage of a demand you're not particularly motivated to do, but the choice is yours!

This was the situation presented to Margaret Ringer (Point *D*) when she was first asked to start supplying sprouts. It took her two years to decide if she really wanted to, but when she did, the demand was still high and she had the space and the disposition to capitalize on it; and her interest and enjoyment have grown along with her success. Anstance and Larry Esmonde-White (Point *E*) had an even more surprising invitation. Having just settled into retirement, you may recall, they had no interest at all in developing a second career, but the response to their expertise and originality in the field of horticulture was so strong that it pulled them into unsolicited success. Of course, Larry's previous experience with the media and broadcasting added to their immediate success; now that they're doing it, they certainly seem to be having a good time.

Long Haul. If what you're thinking about falls into this quadrant, be prepared to work long and hard before you succeed. How long and how hard will depend on how far down into the lower right-hand corner of this quadrant your option is. Many times people traveling along the other three paths find themselves in this quadrant, especially those who are following a mission; their missionary zeal can keep them motivated and help them stick it out. Without the drive of a special gift, talent, or mission, however, you may not feel up to taking on such a challenge. Thus, if you want to remain focused on your ultimate goal, you may want to pursue some other asset if you have a choice.

Psychologist Conrad Christian (Point *F*) didn't think he really had any other viable choice. He had just moved his family to a new state in order to take a job directing a clinic for emotionally disturbed teenagers. After only six months, the clinic closed and there he was with a new mortgage, no job, a wife, and a family—in the heart of a recession. Other jobs in his field were practically nonexistent in the area, but he was not without assets. He was highly motivated to go into private practice, a good psychotherapist, and well suited for his career, which he enjoyed. But being so new in town, he had very few contacts, there were already many other therapists, and due to the recession health-insurance programs were being cut back and fewer people had discretionary income to pay for psychotherapy. This put him clearly in the Long Haul quadrant, but he felt it was his best shot. He went for it with a vengeance. With the help of his wife's salary, the family rode out the three-to-five-year process of building a practice from scratch. Within three and a half years he had replaced his salary. "Now that it's all over, I'm glad it happened," he says, "because I'm not sure I would have ever done this if I'd seen any other way out. But I've accomplished something I only dreamed about."

We think Lucky Eddie Mauss's *Hard Luck Gazette* (Point *G*) would also fall in this quadrant. Mauss had no experience or background in newsletter publishing and certainly no ready and waiting demand, but he did have enough inspiration to get started. Most important, because he has a good job, he has the time to let his idea develop and see what will come from it. Also, he's willing for it to be no more than a hobby that pays for itself if necessary. He enjoys doing it.

Wasteland. Just forget about anything that falls in this quadrant. There's not much demand and you're not sufficiently motivated, positioned, or suited to go to the trouble of trying to develop one.

If you're at an impasse trying to decide which options to pursue, use the grid to help you make a choice. Doug Cartwright's two top choices are plotted below. Doug, an architect, was ready to be his own boss, but he wasn't so sure he wanted to open his own firm. It seemed like a lot of work and a big risk. He'd be competing with big firms like the ones he worked for. But at a business opportunity expo he was attracted by the possibility of buying a turnkey sign-making business. It seemed as though it would be an easier option until he plotted it on the grid. Certainly he was motivated to do either one at a seven (7) or above, but he thought that since there was a higher demand for sign making, that would take it up into the Serendipity quadrant and put architecture into the Long Haul, but he discovered he was wrong because:

VIABILITY GRID
COMPARING OPTIONS

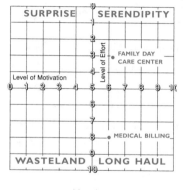

Katrina

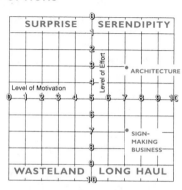

Doug

> *Demand only gets you one-third of the way up the Effort Index.*

To get up any higher, you also need to be positioned and suited to take advantage of the demand. Doug had very little interest in making signs when compared with the enjoyment he gets from architecture. Although, as an architect, he could certainly design adequate-to-great signs, he had no experience or contacts in that business. And lots of other people at the show were buying the same sign business package. Also he would be starting from scratch doing something he felt lukewarm about. As an architect, however, while the demand was somewhat lower, Cartwright had his training and ten years of experience, many contacts, and a good reputation to capitalize on. Here was the pivotal factor. Although at first glance it seemed that he was just as suited for sign making as for architecture, in fact, he would probably have been disappointed with sign making. While architecture primarily draws most heavily on the creative aspects of his personality (Creator/Problem Solver/Builder), sign making calls primarily on other traits (Builder/Problem Solver/Organizer). Doug dislikes details and loves the creative side of architecture. So he's ideally suited to continue in architecture and not as well suited for the day-in, day-out demands of sign making. This means that, despite the lower demand, architecture pops into the Serendipity quadrant, while sign making falls smack in the middle of the Long Haul. A year later, Doug's architectural firm is growing steadily and he says, "I'm a believer. You saved my skin."

Katrina Wells had a similar experience when plotting her choices. (See page 227.) She loves kids and has three of them, but with their budget getting tighter by the month and the possibility that her husband could be laid off, they both thought Katrina should start a home business. Her sister Rose had just bought a medical billing program and asked Katrina to go into business with her. Rose had already done her homework and determined there was a need for medical billing in their community, so it sounded like a perfect solution. Katrina could be home with the kids and use the computer they'd gotten for Christmas. The medical billing program included training, so the sisters could learn what they needed to know to get into this popular, well-paying field. But as Katrina began evaluating this option, she too realized that demand alone takes you only one-third of the way up the Effort Index.

Neither Katrina nor Rose had any experience or contacts in the medical field, and while Rose is a born organizer and detail person, Katrina's strongest natural abilities are communicating, teaching, and working with people (Improver/Leader/Organizer). So that means Katrina isn't particularly suited for medical billing (Organizer/Improver/Builder). And she wasn't really all that motivated in the first place, not even up to the recommended seven (7) on the Motivation Index. So for her this line of work falls deep into the Long Haul, and Katrina knew she wasn't up to it. Looking through **Appendix III**, though, under her personal style, she knew immediately what she wanted to do—family day care (Improver/Leader/Organizer). Not only would she be home with her kids, she'd actually be interacting with them along with the other children. The demand for good child care is just as high as or higher than the demand for medical billing, and through contact with other parents she knew she was much better positioned to get started. While she probably won't ever make as much money doing family day care as she could make from a successful medical billing service, since she probably wouldn't have been motivated enough to actually succeed at a billing service, realistically she's earning more money and a lot happier with day care.

KNOW WHAT TO EXPECT

Plot the various options you're considering here to see what you can expect and compare their success potential.

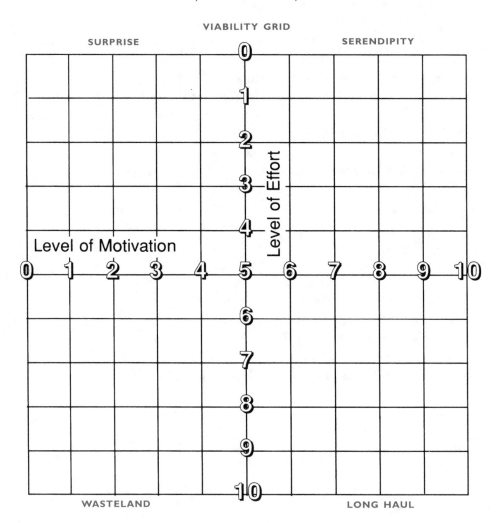

VIABILITY GRID

CAPITALIZING ON YOUR ASSETS

Goal. Defining what you want and using the assets you have to make a living so you can have it with as little effort and as much enjoyment as possible.

Driving Force. The goals you want to accomplish outside your work must serve as the driving force along this path. These goals must be sufficiently important to you that you will invest sufficient energy in using your assets in order to achieve them.

Pros. This path enables you to do other important things in your life that you would not be able to do as well within the limits of the job market or in a traditional job. When done successfully this path can be the easiest to pursue because you're doing something people readily need that comes naturally to you and you can concentrate on the other things you enjoy in your life.

Cons. Your energy is always divided along this path between doing what it takes to capitalize on your assets to make a living and doing the other important things your income is designed to help you do. As a result you may be vulnerable to taking the "easy" way out. You may have difficulty staying motivated, burn out from dividing your energy, or start to resent your work because it takes away too much time and energy from what you really want to do.

Choosing a Path

AT THIS POINT, you probably have a pretty good idea of what paths hold the most appeal to you. You probably have some ideas about how you might weave the potential of those paths together to create the perfect work to support what you want in life and enjoy the journey along the way. As we said at the beginning of this section, you are not so much choosing a path as creating one, drawing from the many possibilities that best fit your needs, desires, and circumstances. Your path will probably not look just like any of those you've read about throughout this section. Yours will be as unique to you as theirs is to each of those we've profiled. In a sense, you are creating a path only you can travel because it leads to where only you want to go, doing what only you can do in the ways only you can do it.

As you begin reviewing and selecting among your choices, keep in mind that whatever is primarily propelling you, the more of your gifts, the more of your passion, the more of your sense of mission, and the more of your assets you can draw upon, the easier it will be for you to step into the unknown and to proceed un-

daunted through any twists and turns or peaks and valleys you encounter along your journey. Use the following work sheet to help
you weave a path that draws most fully upon your desires and resources.

CHOOSING YOUR PATH | A SUMMARY WORK SHEET

Having explored the gifts, passions, missions, and assets that could serve as your
path to independence and your chosen life, you probably have some idea of what
path or combination of paths are most appealing and appropriate for you. Review
the possibilities here listing all the options you have evaluated to be at a 7 or
above. Then see how you might draw upon various combinations of all these possibilities to create your own personal path.

GIFTS	PASSIONS
MISSIONS	ASSETS

List ways you might combine these possibilities into a livelihood. Put an asterisk
by ones that appeal to you most in terms of the enjoyment you would get from
them and the degree to which they're compatible with what you want from life.

_____   _____   _____

_____   _____   _____

*Do not base your evaluation of these ideas on whether or not you
think you could make enough money by pursuing them. You'll be
able to evaluate how to do that in Part III.*

As you complete this section, you may still feel uncertain as to just what your perfect work will be. This is to be expected because in order to find your perfect work, you must take the next step. You must now find the means by which you will assure your success. You must find the way to link your unique combination of gifts, passions, missions, and assets to what's needed and wanted in the world. You must answer the question we have purposely postponed throughout this section—How will I make enough money to support myself in the lifestyle I have chosen? Right now that link may or may not be apparent to you. It may even look unrealistic. But as you move into the next section, **"The Means,"** you will see that you won't need to compromise. You will just need to be open to creating such a link—perhaps one that you've never considered before but that nonetheless will provide you with what you're seeking. Once again, you will see that if others can do the seemingly impossible things they've done in this time of new economic realities, you too can accomplish your goals.

WEAVING TAPESTRIES OF DREAMS

PROFILE: CHELLIE CAMPBELL, LEADER/IMPROVER/ORGANIZER

Chellie Campbell,
Financial Stress
Reduction

Gift. Managing money

Passion. Performing

Mission. Freeing people from financial distress

Assets. Background in acting; experience in bookkeeping

Means. A bookkeeping service offering financial awareness seminars

"All day, every day, we make choices about how our life is going to be. That's the fun of life. You get to do it yourself."

PROFILE: JAI JOSEFS, CREATOR/IMPROVER/LEADER

Gift. Songwriting

Passion. Singing

Mission. Healing through music

Assets. Computer equipment and contacts in both commercial music and new-age circles

Means. Writing and performing music for spiritual- and personal-growth events nationwide

"In writing my music, I feel guided. I find that when I shut up and listen, I produce great results."

PROFILE: EILEEN LIZER, PROBLEM SOLVER/IMPROVER/LEADER

Gift. An extraordinary photographic memory

Passion. The thrill of hunting something down

Mission. A near-compulsion to find the answers

Assets. Seven years' experience booking guests for a popular radio talk show

Means. The new field she's created: findology, researching esoteric or obscure information that's needed immediately

"There's no special genius involved. I'll tell you what it is. I will not stop until I find it. It's as simple as that." **LOS ANGELES TIMES**

PROFILE: BETTE PERRY, CREATOR/LEADER/IMPROVER

Bette Perry, Comedian

Gift. Boundless energy

Passion. Life

Mission. Proving we can do anything we give ourselves permission to do

Assets. Sixtysomething years of experience in a variety of pursuits from being a tank driver and mechanic to doing payroll preparation, cutting hair, and having her own cable TV show to farming and being crowned third runner-up in the Ms. Senior America Pageant

Means. Motivational comedian

"The greatest fear I had was standing up in front of an audience. The few steps to the microphone seemed like miles. I barely remember speaking my monologue, but I'll never forget the applause. I knew this was what I had dreamed of doing." **NEW TIMES, SEATTLE**

RESOURCES

7 Kinds of Smart: Identifying and Developing Your Many Intelligences. Thomas Armstrong. New York: Plume, 1993.

What Color Is Your Parachute? Richard Bolles. Berkeley, Calif.: Ten Speed Press, 1995.

Ending the Struggle Against Yourself. Stan Taubman, D.S.W. New York: Tarcher/Putnam, 1994.

Working with Passion. Nancy Anderson. San Rafael, Calif.: New World Library, 1995.

Finding the Hat that Fits: How to Turn Your Life's Desire into Your Life's Work. John Caple. New York: Plume, 1993.

Zen and the Art of Making a Living, a Practical Guide to Creative Career Design. Lawrence G. Boldt. New York: Penguin, 1993.

Finding Your Life Mission. Naomi Stephan. Walpole, New Hampshire: Stillpoint, 1989.

Do What You Love and the Money Will Follow. Marsha Sinetar. New York: Dell, 1989.

PART III

The Means: Discovering How to Pay the Way Every Day

NINE

Getting Connected

AT LAST, we come to the question that usually causes the greatest distress: How will you make enough money to support yourself along the path you've chosen for yourself? How will you finance your journey? How will you find the means to live your dreams? We have purposely delayed addressing this question because as soon as money comes into the picture, it's too easy for the picture to get distorted. It's too easy to stop thinking about what you want and start thinking about what you can get. For most people, how they will get what they need from doing what they want is the greatest stumbling block to proceeding with confidence toward their perfect work.

From the customary salary mentality, we're used to thinking that money is about getting. How much salary can I get? How many fringe benefits can I get? How many stock options can I get? So we start thinking, If I go out on my own, what can I get? How much can I make? Will it be enough? Thinking about money in this way, however, won't get us where we want to go. To get where you want to go, you have to stop thinking about what you can get and

> One of the greatest things in life is to take any talent you have and any opportunity you have and do something really good for people.
>
> *Joseph Califano, former Secretary of Health Education and Welfare*

start thinking about what you can give—without disconnecting from what you want, without leaving the path. That's the challenge and the opportunity of these times.

To support ourselves along our chosen path, we have to get connected. We have to find a way to connect what we want to what others value sufficiently to pay for.

We like to put it this way: To make a living creating the life you desire, the question is not What can I get? It's What can I give? How can I use my gifts and assets to achieve my desires by providing something people need or want? How can I connect what I'm motivated to do and have the ability to offer to what people desire? That question lies at the heart of finding your perfect work. To create the means to support yourself along the path you seek, you must find a link between your desires and the needs of others.

Too often, instead of finding this link, people get hung up making one of two crucial errors. Either they connect with what other people need or want and disconnect from what they desire, or they connect with what they desire and fail to connect with what others need or want. Either error will leave you flailing. When you observe other self-employed people having difficulty, it's this flailing that you're seeing. You may see someone, for example, who's doing okay financially but working longer hours doing the same work she used to complain about when she was employed. Or you may see someone who's veering closer to the edge of financial ruin while struggling to follow his lifelong dream of becoming a scriptwriter.

GETTING CONNECTED FOR SUCCESS

Your perfect work will connect your desire with the needs of others. Until you find ways to address your gifts, passions, missions, and assets to real needs of others, your work will go unappreciated and unrewarded. On the other hand, if you respond only to the demands of others' needs without regard to your own desires, whatever rewards you receive will feel somehow hollow and unfulfilling.

"Ultimately your only source of funding is satisfied customers."
Tim Mullen, home-business owner

Needs Other People Will Pay You For

- What they need to live or function adequately
- What they need for enjoyment, satisfaction, and solace
- What they need to make money and meet their goals

"Success occurs when desire meets opportunity."

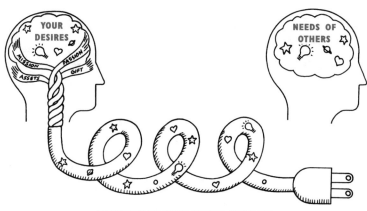

DISCONNECTED FROM OTHERS

"I won't compromise my music. I have a very clear idea about
what good music is, and I won't sell out to commercial tastes. I
won't pander to the industry. Of course, I'm not getting any
bookings. Well, so be it. I think it's a shame, but that's life. There are
other ways to make a living."

DISCONNECTED FROM OURSELVES

"I wanted my music to heal the world. That was my plan,
but that's not what people want to buy. So I'm doing other stuff.
It's okay, I guess. I'm working, mostly piano bars and clubs.
I'm making a living. Someday, I'll produce a CD of the kind
of music I really want to do."

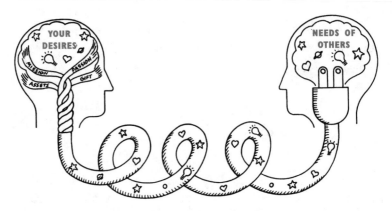

CONNECTED

"My music is different. I know that. But I'm not interested in having a hit song; I'm interested in the effects of music on the body and the mind. I know sound and tempo and rhythms affect us on a cellular level. I compose and play to help people feel good, relax, be more productive, get in harmony with themselves. That's why I have my own line of tapes. I sell exclusively through doctors, hospitals, chiropractors, psychotherapists—professionals who are committed to helping people. Lately I'm performing at quite a few holistic health conferences."

Ultimately neither of these situations will work adequately because when we disconnect with what we want, we either won't be sufficiently motivated to do it well enough to succeed, or we may push through to financial success but wonder why life still feels so stressful, empty, and meaningless. On the other hand, if we don't connect with something people need, we won't have enough paying opportunities to keep going and we'll grow increasingly embittered and angry that the world won't support us in doing what we truly want to do.

When you're connected to what you want to do, your drive, your desire will carry you a long way. Your efforts become alive, desirable, and productive. But unless you connect what you're producing with something that's wanted or needed in the outside world, nothing much will come back to you from those efforts. The work may be initially gratifying, but ultimately barren. On the other hand, when you're connected to some need or desire in the outside world, your efforts immediately bear fruit, but unless they're connected to some desire within you, that fruit may soon wither and die on the vine.

When you find a way to use your talents and assets to connect your desires to the real needs of others, however, the results are dramatically different. Your desires provide you with the energy you need to apply your talents, skills, and assets most artfully and arduously; and as you continue pumping your energy through this connection, it's returned to you in the form of money, satisfaction, and other rewards that literally "feed" you on every level: physically, emotionally, and spiritually. So finding the means to support your dreams is a matter of finding opportunities to give to others in a way that brings what you need back to you. That's what finding your perfect work is all about.

The best connection will match the things you most need to do with the very things the world most needs to have done. Your ideal connection will capitalize on your uniqueness, your thumbprint, your DNA, your way of thinking, perceiving, feeling, doing, and expressing. Literally millions of people have found opportunities for making such a connection, and in this section you'll meet some of them. You'll discover the rich variety of ways they've gone about connecting their desires with what's needed and wanted by others by doing what we call *matrixing*. And you'll learn how you can do that as well.

> "Being an artist doesn't make you broke. Giving up your dreams makes you broke."
> *Julia Cameron,*
> The Artist's Way

FINDING OPPORTUNITIES

The world is full of opportunities to do the things that need to be done. Such opportunities are all around us. We can *stumble over them* like photographer Warren Faidley did when he went on his first weather assignment. We can *create them* like Aaron Chang did when he used the camera his father gave him to start taking and selling photos of surfers. Or we can *seek them out* as engineer Chuck Berman did when his hobby became so expensive, he decided it had to start paying for itself and he began offering the commercial photography services that now support him full-time after corporate downsizing eliminated his job.

However we encounter opportunities, to actually connect

> "There is no security in life, only opportunity."
> *Mark Twain*

The time has come that we must start believing people will gladly pay us to do what we most enjoy doing. Then we have to find out how to make what we enjoy so appealing that they will do so.

THINKING OUTSIDE THE BOX

•   •   •

•   •   •

•   •   •

Can you connect all these dots in four or fewer straight lines without picking up your pencil or retracing your steps? (See pages 246–247 for the customary solution and three others few people go on to discover.)

with them, we have to recognize them. And often we don't. Often instead we look right past them, all the while wishing we could find the right opportunity. In reading *Trend Trackings,* by Gerald Celente, we discovered that there's a concept in field biology that explains why this happens. As biologists go out into the field to study animals in their area of specialization, they adopt what's called a "search image": that is, each biologist will have an image in mind of the kind of animal he or she is looking for. As a result, a biologist looking for baboons will spot many baboons amidst the flora and fauna of their habitat; the biologist looking for snakes in the same territory, however, will most likely overlook the baboons but see lots of snakes. Were the snake biologist to go into the field with the baboon biologist, she might be amazed to discover so many baboons around and vice versa.

That's exactly what we all do when it comes to overlooking opportunities. If you know the things you're looking for, and have a search image in mind, you'll see them. If not, you'll probably overlook them. They'll just fade into the background. So, to find opportunities that will match your desires, you've got to develop a "search image" for opportunity. From the past two chapters, you've already begun forming a clear image of what you want and the variety of things you can offer. Once you start seeing opportunities, you'll be able to see possible matches.

But what does opportunity look like? What are you looking for? What follows in this chapter are six signs of opportunity and examples of how others have seized upon them to do what they wanted to do. Be alert for these signs. Have your mental antenna set to recognize them and tag them so that, when you encounter them, bright lights, clanging bells and loud whistles go off in your mind, flashing: "Opportunity Alert! Opportunity Alert!" Most important, keep your mind open to the opportunities you see and hear even if at first they don't seem like an ideal match. Explore first; then evaluate. As career coach Naomi Stephan points out, the best match is not always the one you've been thinking about. In fact, you'll find that often your best matches come from "thinking outside the box," so to speak, going beyond the obvious solutions and imagining possibilities that may not have occurred to you before.

THINKING OUTSIDE THE BOX

**PROFILE: NAOMI STEPHAN,
CAREER COUNSELOR AND AUTHOR**

Imagine you are forty-seven years old and, after five years of hard work, you have established yourself as a career coach, with a successful private practice on the West Coast. You think you are pursuing your life mission, just as you help others to do. Then you begin to realize that as much as you enjoy your work, like many of your clients, you had almost given up the possibility of fully pursuing your deepest passion: music. It had been a garnish in your life instead of a main course.

Naomi Stephan, career
counselor

That's the situation Naomi Stephan faced nine years ago. How easy it would have been to decide that it was far too late to go off after some long-lost craving. It simply didn't seem practical. All her music training had been in voice. How could she pursue a singing career at her age? How could she desert the clients she'd so carefully worked to cultivate, the reputation she'd taken so long to build? But Stephan says, "It's never too late. You don't have to do it the way you had once imagined it. But you can find a way."

And Stephan has. She has reconfigured her life. She listened carefully to her inner desires and realized she had a talent for composing choral music, gained through her many years singing with choral groups. To better afford a new life in which more of her time would be spent writing music, she moved to North Carolina. But she didn't close her career counseling practice. In fact, she expanded it. Now it's nationwide because she provides counseling to her clients by phone, something she's perfectly suited to do, because of her special ear for the human voice. She says of her work, "I'm here to create a sound world through the sound of my music, the sound of my voice, and the sound of my written word."

Her first choral composition was performed in Los Angeles in 1993. She has found a connection others would have said was at least impractical, if not impossible.

PROFILE: SUZI WEISS-FISCHMANN, FROM DENTURES TO FINGERNAILS

Suzi Weiss-Fischmann was working as vice president and creative director of a dental-supply business she started with her brother when she began to notice a score of little nail salons opening in the area offering to do acrylic nails. Weiss-Fischmann realized the acrylic used in these shops is similar to the material used in dentures. So with only slight chemical revisions, she developed and packaged three products for nail salons, thinking they could be a sideline business for her. That "sideline" has turned into an international business, and her company, OPI, is a leader within the nail industry.

PROFILE: MYRON STEIN, FROM TALK RADIO TO AIR-CONDITIONING CLEANSER

When the recession hit, Myron Stein lost his job as the host of a radio talk show about autos, but having owned an auto-repair garage, he had an idea. He thought a product hospitals were using to combat mildew could help car dealerships clean air-conditioning units so used cars could smell as fresh as new. His wife, Dolly Becker, thought this was a great idea. Having a background in real estate sales, she thought, "I could sell that!" So with his knowledge of the auto industry and her selling ability, they began contacting service managers of car dealerships. Now, six years later, AirSept, their home-based company, is a family business, employing two sons and a daughter. They supply air-conditioning, cleaning, and odor treatments to fifteen thousand car dealerships nationwide.

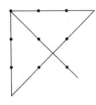

SIX SIGNS FOR SPOTTING OPPORTUNITY

1. Complaints and Problems. Usually we hate to hear people complain about their problems. In fact, we tend to tune out complaints and ignore problems whenever possible. Instead, you should turn up the volume, because within each complaint or problem you encounter lies an opportunity to help, an opportunity to give, that might spark an idea for how you could package your skills and assets into the livelihood you're seeking.

Ever hear working parents complaining about not being able to take their kids to *after-school activities?* Victoria Digby and Patricia Djokovich did. They created Kiddie Kab to chauffeur children to soccer games, ballet classes, and other such events.

Ever hear people complaining about trying to avoid *dog poop* on the sidewalk? Richard Scott did. So did Chris Crosson. But they took different routes to solving the same problem. Scott became a professional pooper scooper earning more than $50,000 a year as The Dog Butler, scooping up poop from his clients' yards. Crosson created Doggie Walk Bags, a pooper scooper in a capsule, which he dispenses through Doggie Walk Bag vending machines in parks and other recreation spots.

Ever hear pregnant women complaining about their choices of *maternity clothes?* Judy Schramm did. Pregnant herself, she and other mothers-to-be she knew often complained about not being able to find attractive formal wear, so she founded Judy's Maternity Rental, designing and renting flattering and colorful formal wear. Three years later, this business, which she runs from a showroom in her home, pays more than her former job as an international marketing manager and it allows her to be at home to raise her two children.

Ever hear people complaining about how much they hate *waiting in line?* Nick Montgomery and Greg Campbell did. They now earn their living waiting in line to get their clients' cars registered or inspected.

Ever hear people complaining about how much they hate all the work involved in *moving?* Marilyn Katleman did. So did William Rodriquez. Katleman started Inside Moves and does everything movers won't do when you're moving out or moving in. She cleans out the closets, hangs the pictures, puts out the towels, places the soap in the soap dish, and stocks the refrigerator with food. After retiring from the military, Rodriquez remembered how tedious he and his fellow navy personnel found it to keep track of their home inventory as they moved from location to location. So he put his personal computer to work and became a home inventory specialist, logging and updating the household belongings of military officers and other professionals.

Ever hear business owners complaining about *not getting paid* the money they're owed? Bill collector John Harrison did, all the

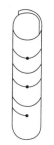

SOLUTION 2

Roll paper and trace around and around, connecting all the dots

SOLUTION 3

Fold paper until all dots line up and punch a hole through them

SOLUTION 4

Cut out dots, line them up, and draw a line through them

time. After he lost his job, however, he started getting calls from bill collectors himself and, having experienced the problem from both sides, decided to start teaching businesspeople the tricks of his trade. He wrote *Collection Techniques for Small Business*.

Ever hear people complaining that the video they want is *out of print*, sold out, or unavailable at their local video store? Barbara Lambert did. A retired art auctioneer, she and her husband, John, have become known as the video detectives. She turned their love for research and her background and contacts with collectors into A Million and One World-Wide Video. They will buy, sell, trade, rent, broker, and auction any video in the world.

Ever hear women in *high heels* complaining about their aching feet? Orthopedic surgeon Fred Swerdloff and his nurse-practitioner Rose Lewis heard such complaints every day and decided to provide a solution. They created a shoe with a heel that can change heights. By twisting off the heel and replacing it with another, the same Rose-Lee shoe can go from high to low for any occasion. It takes only twenty seconds.

Ever hear people complaining about how they wish they could get *revenge* on someone who did them wrong? Allen Pool did. And after leaving his job as an airline attendant, he decided he could help people do something about it. He started Revenge à la Carte, which helps his clients get revenge by having some fun with an ugly situation. He concocts and carries out harmless, but clever dirty tricks on wrongdoers.

These are just a few examples of more unusual opportunities born from complaints. So turn up the volume on complaints you hear just loud enough and long enough to ask yourself if you could help and, if so, would doing so be a means for creating your perfect work? And while you're at it, pay extra attention to problems you see people struggling with, too. That's what these folks did:

While doing residential designs, Robert Dobnick spent a lot of time in furniture stores where he noticed problems wholesalers were having getting *showrooms* built. Recognizing the need, he quickly got in on the ground floor of what became a booming field, providing full-service space planning and design for wholesale showrooms, including decorative fabrics, furniture, and accessories.

Artist Deborah Smith saw her fellow *novice artists* struggling along with her to get galleries to display their art. She decided she could help. With her business-oriented brother, she created Fine Art Tease, silk-screening images of her work and that of other local artists onto T-shirts and selling them through clothing stores. Each shirt comes with a brief biography of the artist and discusses his or her work.

Struggling inventor Scott McGregor got a winning idea from a failed cellular rental firm he started in the eighties. He observed that one of the cellular industry's biggest problems was an inability to get *instant readouts* of calls made from rented phones. McGregor thought the right computer program could help. This idea took him from living on food stamps to a thriving family business. He called on the aid of his computer whiz-kid son and set out to attract investors. The result was TRAC, Telemac Rental Accounting Cellular, a patented system McGregor now produces through his family business, Telemac.

After seven years of treatment for *infertility,* Beverly Sherid finally was able to have a baby, but she never forgot the pain and desperation of coping with the difficulty she had becoming a mother. She knew there were two and a half million other couples going through those same feelings, and she wanted to help. She decided to draw on her background in publishing and start a bimonthly newsletter summarizing the latest medical literature on fertility for patients and professionals in the field. It's called *The Parkway Fertility Report.*

Remember how Samantha Greenberg turned her problem with *carpal tunnel syndrome* into a business helping companies protect their employees? When Jennifer Brown developed a similar illness, she too wanted to help solve this problem. She and her husband created MouseMitts™, unique and colorful glovelike wrist protectors for computer professionals.

Like many others on her block, Marilyn Noonan's children often played in the street despite her begging and pleading with them not to. Along with the other parents, she worried about their

What People Most Hate Doing

Housecleaning
Paying bills
Writing letters
Shopping
Repairing things

USA Today

safety. Noonan decided to do something about it. She bought some orange safety cones and, using a Magic Marker, drew a picture of a cartoon cop on them to warn drivers of "Children at Play." Then she put them alongside the street. When it worked and cars slowed down, other parents wanted some too. Housewife Noonan ended up in business, as Noonan Designs. She produces the $10 cones, called Sidewalk Sergeant, and has sold over 25,000 of them through Toys " Я " Us stores and other chains.

Listen to complaints.
Notice problems people are having.

2. Trends. When you can connect what you want to do in your life to a rising trend, your journey can be a fortuitous one indeed. Before they became the status quo, the way things are were once a trend. And as the status quo gives way to change, today's trends will evolve into the way things will be. But in between that transition lie many opportunities.

A trend refers to any pattern of events or behaviors shared by growing numbers of people that creates new needs they are eager and willing to address. Trends hold the seeds of so many opportunities, in fact, that trend tracking has become a growing field. Forecasters like John Naisbitt, Faith Popcorn, and Joe Cappo and futurists like Alvin Toffler and Don Tapscott write and speak extensively on the trends they see emerging and their implications. Over a quarter of the businesses we've included in our book *Best Home Businesses for the 90s* have become successful routes to self-employment over the past few years because they're responding directly to trends that are emerging in our society. Here are just a few examples of how others have created unique and original livelihoods by recognizing and applying their talents, skills, and assets to an emerging trend:

Less Free Time. With two-thirds of people feeling that they have less free time, time is becoming one of our most valued commodities. In fact, many people are feeling so pressed for time that they'll gladly pay money to save some. The result is an unprecedented opportunity to earn a living doing things that people don't have time to do for themselves.

Trend-Driven Best Home Businesses

Calendar service

Cleaning services

Employee trainer

Errand service

Expert services broker

Facialist

Family child-care provider

Fitness trainer

Indoor environmental tester

In-home health care

Professional organizer

Mediator

Mystery shopper

Pet-sitting

Plant care giver

Professional practice consultant

Referral service

Reunion planner

Rubber stamp business

Security consultant

Special events planner

Specialized temporary agency

Wedding consultant

Wedding makeup artist

- As *Rent-a-Mom,* Robin Sherman provides most any household task for two-career couples and single-parent families who don't have the time to do it.
- Richard Egle creates healthy, homemade meals for a family to eat at home through his service, *Diet-to-Go.*
- Lynda Wright supports herself full-time *washing dogs* for her clients. She picks the dogs up, washes and grooms them, and brings them back all nice and clean.
- Marcia Foots has a *concierge* service in the lobby of three-dozen residential and office buildings to help tenants pick up dry cleaning, get theater tickets, and take their cars in for servicing.
- Knowing how stressed Wall Street executives can be and how pressed they are for time, psychologist Dr. Ursula Strauss created *Mobile Psychological Services* in Manhattan. She literally does therapy on the run. Working from a chauffeur-driven limo, she picks up her clients at their homes for a session on the way to work, provides therapy while clients eat during a lunch-hour ride or while they're being driven home from work. The limo has been customized and decorated to resemble any professional counselor's office, and it offers complete privacy. A soundproof partition assures that the limo driver cannot overhear sessions. Therapy is available for a full range of disorders including depression, stress and related physical symptoms, marital and family dysfunction, anxiety, and alcohol and substance abuse. Individual or small-group sessions are available.
- As leisure time shrinks, people turn to nostalgia and what Faith Popcorn calls small indulgences. Hence we see the rise of personalized items like Myla Fahn's handcrafted *one-of-a-kind wedding cake decorations.* For $525 Fahn will hand-paint the bride and groom's likenesses, including their faces and wedding attire, onto a generic cake-top couple.
- For busy single executives who don't have time to make friends, Kate and Dane Teague have created *Buddy Brokers,* providing subscribers to their computer database with the names of twenty-five other subscribers of the same sex who have similar interests and backgrounds.

Concern about the Environment. As our society has become increasingly manufacturing oriented, concerns about indoor and outdoor pollution, global warming, pesticides, and other effects of manmade chemicals has risen along with the recognition that we need to recycle natural resources if we don't want to lose them. Often addressing these concerns requires that we dramatically change the way we live and do business. This offers a wealth of opportunities for people who wish to use their skills, talents, and assets to help make us make these changes. You may recall, for example, that David and Dennis Singsank turned their experience in the food-packaging business into a company helping organic grain farmers market and distribute their crops. They are among a growing number of what *In Business* magazine calls Environmental Entrepreneurs. *In Business* publishes a directory of environmental entrepreneurs each year and the products and services they offer.

Among those *In Business* has featured are David Katz and Karen Van Epen. This husband-and-wife team created Ag Access, specializing in publishing catalogs and books featuring hard-to-find information on ecological agriculture. They also do consulting and market research. Here are some other examples of environmental entrepreneurs.

- Once people find out that Jim Vallareal and Steve Schluchter's shingles are recycled, they say that's all it takes to make the sale. Their company, *Treecycle,* recycles cedar shingles from damaged roofs.
- Architect-inventor David Hertz recycles not only shingles but trash of all kinds. He grinds it up and turns it into *synecrite,* a lightweight concrete from which he makes tiles, tabletops, flooring, and much more.
- Rebecca Cole is a recycling artist. She creates *miniature gardens* inside old objects of all kinds from laundry soap cans to old flour bins to cracked leather satchels.
- With the help of her parents, twelve-year-old Natalie Lederman makes *recycled jewelry* from aluminum soda pop cans. Her line of jewelry is called R-Wear!
- Jake Blehm raises and sells twenty varieties of "killer" bugs that help farmers cut back on pesticides.

- Cashing in on an interest in the interface between technology and the environment, Michael Creek publishes *Environmental Business Machines Catalog and Newsletter*. His motto is "The Bridge Between Walden Pond and Silicon Valley." He reviews products and does feature articles that cover "green" news.

Changing Family Patterns. With so many married women with children under age six working outside the home and the growing number of single working parents, many of the things stay-at-home moms once did must be done by someone else. We already mentioned how Victoria Digby and Patricia Djokovich founded Kiddie Kab and how Robin Sherman developed Rent-a-Mom. This trend is giving rise to other family-oriented services throughout the country. For example:

- Working parents, challenged to find affordable, high-quality child care can turn to CCARE and instantly access an *on-line database* of thousands of available child-care providers in forty-five states, which they can search to find someone who meets their particular needs. Educational psychologist Roger Billings founded and created this database service.
- Companies too are feeling the effects of a dual-career and single-parent workforce, and some are trying to develop programs that will help their working parents better juggle the strain of work and family responsibilities. Fran Sussner Rodgers recognized this trend early and founded *Work/Family Directions,* working as a consultant to help companies develop such programs.
- Many grandparents today live *miles from their grandchildren,* but Marion Forrest has developed a way to bring them a little closer. Using a photo and a patented process she has developed, Forrest creates lifelike dolls with the grandchild's face and can even customize the clothing if desired. Her company is called You Are a Living Doll.
- As *divorce* has become part of so many people's experience, we need ways to integrate it into our lives. Recognizing this need, Diane Sherman operates a gift basket service for

those who want to console or celebrate with friends and loved ones going through divorce.

- The National Center for Health Services reports that 23.5 percent of American brides are now *marrying younger men,* and for women thirty-five to forty-four years of age, that number jumps to 41 percent. Addressing this trend, Lois Banner, who has had a seven-year relationship with a younger man, has written a book about changing attitudes toward aging called *In Full Flower.* Vicar Houston has written *Loving a Younger Man,* and Doe Genry has started a dating service matching younger men with older women. The majority of her clients are men seeking older women to date.

So to find a way to use your talents and assets to achieve your desires, become a trend watcher. Read daily newspapers or weekly news magazines, looking for statistics about what people are doing compared with what they used to do. Did you know, for example, that:

- The number of temporary jobs has climbed 240 percent in the past ten years.
- After taking a dive during the early 1990s, trade show attendance is growing again, up 16 percent since last year.
- Advertising spending is also on the rise, growing according to industry forecasters more rapidly than at any time since 1988.
- The National Federation of Independent Businesses found these problems to be the greatest concerns of small businesses:
- Taxes: 25 percent
- Regulation/red tape: 23 percent
- Insurance costs: 11 percent
- Weak sales: 10 percent
- Competition from large companies: 8 percent
- Finding good workers: 7 percent
- Reversing a trend, the U.S. Department of Commerce reports that personal income in the 1990s is growing faster in rural than in metropolitan areas.

Our Choice for the Top Twelve Trends Creating Self-Employment Opportunities

Our research indicates these trends are opening, and will continue to open, many doors to opportunities for self employment.

Aging population

Corporate downsizing and outsourcing

Fear of violent crime

Home as locus of work and recreation

Interactive multimedia

Interest in health and fitness

Problems from environmental pollution

Rising levels of psychological stress

Shifting population from urban centers to remote locations

Shrinking leisure time

Single-parent families

Two-career couples

- While 46 percent of all large companies provide continuing health benefits to retiring employees, fewer than one in ten small employers, with under five hundred employees, provided health coverage to retirees in 1993.
- The Census Bureau claims the number of children who come home to an empty house after school has grown to five million. A third of these children are under the age of twelve.
- Interactive entertainment (arcade, video, and personal computer games) is an $8.8-billion business, making it more lucrative than the Hollywood movie industry, which brings in only $5.2 billion in revenue a year.

All these statistics appeared recently in newspapers or magazines. Each suggests a range of possible opportunities. Take note of such trends routinely and as you do, ask yourself, What needs or problems do these trends suggest? How could I help? Would doing that be a means to achieving my goals and desires?

Become a trend tracker

3. Special Needs. Another way to spot opportunities for matching your talents and assets to what's needed in the world is to look for people or organizations that have special needs. Look for who isn't already being served or for those who because of their special needs are not being served adequately. Here's a few examples of special needs others have found:

- New York city is filled with *immigrants* who have a tremendous drive to become middle class, but they're struggling to learn English and adjust to a new country. They want to succeed and are ready to become part of American culture but, as ex–food stamp administrator Arthur Schiff noticed, they can't digest our newspapers and magazines as they're written. Schiff saw this special need and decided to help. He publishes *City Family* magazine. His quarterly is distributed free in waiting rooms in public clinics and hospitals. Half the magazine is written in English and half in Spanish. His

Fastest-Growing Fields

Fastest-growing job markets suggest areas of fastest-growing needs. Consider these fields identified as fastest growing by the Department of Labor:

- Paralegal
- Medical assistant
- Physical therapist
- Physical therapist assistant
- Data-processing equipment repair
- Podiatrist
- Computer system analyst
- Employment interviewer
- Home health aide

Statistics Suggest Needs

You don't have to be a researcher or academician to see needs amidst the facts. On the following pages you'll see several examples of statistics we saw in popular media. Each suggests a range of opportunities to create a career.

Fifty-six percent of companies surveyed reported they needed to stamp out discriminatory attitudes, but only 10 percent have implemented educational programs to do so.

USA Today

One in every six couples in the U.S. is infertile.

CBS Television

Forty-eight million Americans are disabled.

The Susan Powter Show

An IBM survey found that half of all small-business executives don't know what the "information highway" is.

Home-Based Business News

Americans generate about 4.4 pounds of garbage a day—and that number is growing steadily.

New York Times

circulation has grown from 10,000 to 210,000 in just two years.

- According to Dr. William Wargo, most *doctoral students* do not get their degrees even though they have completed their coursework. The barrier is finishing their dissertation. Dr. Wargo calls these students ABDs (All But Dissertations) and finds they are among the brightest and most creative of Ph.D. candidates, but they have special needs that no one is helping them address. He began Dissertation Completion Consulting, offering a special program by phone, mail, or in person, to assist ABDs achieve their goal to obtain their doctoral degrees.

- Mike Miles started doing theatrical résumés and noticed that *aspiring actors and actresses* needed much more than someone to hand them a piece of paper summarizing their achievements. He found that although they are highly motivated, they have special needs no one was addressing. So he created Star Network, providing career counseling, graphic design, and other support services to performing artists.

- Christy Wachter noticed that many of the bands she most enjoyed listening to did not have albums available because they couldn't get a record contract. She recognized these *upstart rock bands* had a special need. They were faced with the chicken-or-the-egg situation: they couldn't get a record out because they didn't have a following, and they didn't have a following because they didn't have a record. So Wachter founded Racer Records, a small independent record label that "believes in choice, power, and rock-and-roll." Her goal is to bring the music she enjoys to the public by providing subscriptions to sampler albums of the artists she represents and then selling full albums of artists listeners want to hear more of.

- When veterinarian Valerie Nestrick was laid off from the clinic where she worked, although she hadn't thought about starting her own business, she was aware of a large group of pet owners who have special needs that weren't being addressed: people who cannot get their pets to a clinic. She decided that instead of looking for another job, she would become a mobile vet, traveling to her clients instead of their coming to her. She put a payment down on a twenty-four-foot mobile home and set up a mobile clinic. She offers a full range of services from checkups to vaccinations, minor surgery, dentistry, and euthanasia. Although she doesn't do major surgery in her traveling clinic, she does provide para-medic services transporting pets from their homes to emergency hospitals.

- Lisa Calmenson noticed that some *meeting planners* have a special need: they're trying to put on an event in some other location than where they're based, and coordinating the various services involved via long distance can become a headache—not to mention being fraught with disastrous surprises that may await them when they arrive. Calmenson decided to capitalize on her fifteen years of experience in the training and travel fields to create Destination Directors, which provides temporary on-site staffing services and airport meet-and-greet services for tours, meetings, conventions, seminars, trade shows, and special events.
- Artist Holly Christian noticed that commercial greeting cards rarely feature people from varied ethnic backgrounds, and yet when people receive a greeting card they like to feel that it was selected with them in mind. So she set out to fill this special need. She creates original greeting cards for all *ethnic groups.* Each card is suitable for framing and essentially a work of art.

Holly Christian, artist

Be on the alert for people and organizations with special needs that aren't being met.

4. *People Like You.* One easy way to find a special need you're ideally suited to meet is to think about what you have needed yourself and apply your talents, skills, and assets to meeting the needs of people like you. After all, we usually prefer to do business with people we feel comfortable with and can trust. Who better than someone who has had the same experiences and problems we have. So think about it: Who needs what you need? Who needs

A child's diet contains five to ten times more sodium than he or she needs.

New Age Journal

FINDING SPECIAL NEEDS

Special needs are everywhere. Finding them is a matter of clustering people and their experiences into groups based on common experiences, similarities, and differences. Here are examples of general clusters to consider exploring:

ADULTS
- Single
- Married without children
- Parents—mothers, fathers, empty nesters
- Single parents
- Female/male heads of household
- Two-career parents
- Housewives
- Gay singles/Gay couples
- Stepfamilies
- Grandparents
- Seniors—the young old/ the very old/the sick old/ the healthy old

BUSINESSES
- Industry
- Type of client or customer

- Size of business
- one person
- husband and wife
- family
- small corporation
- Fortune 500 company
- Type of remuneration needed
- Type of product or service offered
- Delivery system used

CHILDREN
- Babies
- Toddlers
- Preschool age
- Elementary-school age
- Teenagers
- College students

---

to know what you know or are willing to learn or do? How could you help them to get it? Many people have built their livelihood on making just such a connection.

- Wendy Perkins has become a "Temp" Expert. She held so many temporary jobs and knew the problems "*temps*" face so intimately that she decided to capitalize on her knowledge by sharing it with others like herself. She wrote the book *Temporarily Yours* and has gone on to do speaking, consulting, and training in this rapidly growing field.
- Dimitri Vazelakis felt left out of the birthing experience when his wife, Elsie, became pregnant with their son,

GEOGRAPHIC LOCATION
- Local
- State
- Regional
- National
- International

PHYSICAL AND MENTAL HEALTH
- Physically fit and health conscious
- Ill
- Terminally ill
- Disabled
- Recovering

INTERESTS TOO NUMEROUS TO LIST
- Aerobics . . . Zen
- Aviation . . . Zoology

RESIDENCE
- Single-family homes
- Condos
- Renters
- Vacation-home owners
- Mobile-home owners
- Do-it-yourselfers

SOCIAL CHARACTERISTICS
- Ethnic groups
- Savers/investors
- Downscale/upscale
- Immigrants
- Middle income/working class/low income
- Residence (see above)

Alexander. He found that although childbirth was a time of great joy and excitement, it was also a time of stress and anxiety. Both Dimitri and Elsie thought a little humor would help him and other fathers feel more a part of the experience and came up with the idea for The Labor Coach (TLC) Kit, which is filled with both humorous and practical items for the *father-to-be* who's helping his wife through delivery.

- Left-hander Brenda Green had long resented the many little inconveniences of having to adjust to a right-handed world. When she saw a shop for *left-handers* while on a trip, she decided to start one in her hometown. After all, she discovered, 9 percent of women and 13 percent of men are left-handed just like her.
- Of the more than eight million Americans who have a history of cancer, five million are living five years past their initial diagnosis. But Susan Nessim didn't know that when she

was stricken with cancer nearly two decades ago. What she discovered was that the cancer was easier to fight than living with the isolation and rejection she experienced after she recovered. So after overcoming this challenge, she decided to help others going through *cancer recovery*. She founded Cancervive, a nonprofit organization that helps survivors of cancer deal with the unique challenges they face after their treatment ends. Nessim holds group sessions for members and has written three books including *A Friend for Life*. She is creating a documentary on this topic as well and is writing a manual for teachers of children diagnosed with cancer.

- Dana Desselle, who had a Ford Bronco, wasn't happy with the service she was getting at the dealership. And she wasn't alone; lots of people feel frustrated with trying to find a reliable mechanic. But Desselle and her partner, Megan Carmichael, both of whom worked for a dental referral service, saw an opportunity. They created a referral service called FIX-A-CAR, based on the popular 1 (800) DENTIST concept, to address the needs of people who, like them, need help finding a good mechanic.

- When Phil and Jan Carey's son was diagnosed with diabetes, they had to find a way to handle many situations they'd never imagined facing. They were able to come up with useful solutions to their challenges, and so they decided to package what they'd learned into medical kits for diabetics. They now have fifteen other people working with them to create and supply the kits.

- Seventy percent of women are under five feet, five inches tall, but just try becoming a fashion model if you're five-five or under! Ann Lauren was, and everyone told her she could never be a model. She wasn't one to take "no" for an answer, though. She started her own modeling agency for "short" women like herself, USA Petites Productions, Inc.

- Approximately one in every twenty children in America will lose a parent to death before the age of fifteen, but when seventeen-year-old Hope Edelman lost her mother to breast cancer, she found no books written for young women on coping with their grief. Unaddressed, her grief never stopped. Ten years later, she decided to write the book she had wanted to read as a young woman without a mother. It's called *Motherless Daughters: A Legacy of Loss*.

- Twelve years of experience trying to be "a supermom" and a background in media and art education prepared Robyn Spizman to become a dynamic motivational speaker, writer, and media personality on the subject of parenting. She has authored over fifty-five educational and craft books, appears weekly on Atlanta's NBC WXIA's TV show *Noonday,* and lectures widely to parents on topics like how to creatively motivate your children, balance your family life, organize yourself, and use your fullest potential.

- An avid sportswoman, Marilyn Hamilton refused to give up her love for sports after an injury left her paralyzed. She tracked down people who could help her design a lightweight wheelchair that would enable her to continue enjoying outdoor sports. Her company, Quickie Designs, now produces a line of sports-oriented wheelchairs.

- Peter Baylies is a full-time stay-at-home dad. When he lost his computer job several years ago, he and his wife, a full-time teacher, decided they didn't want their son to be in day care all day long, so Baylies has been at home ever since. At first he couldn't find any other at-home dads, but he has since discovered there are two million dads at home and the number is increasing. Why, he asked, should they feel isolated and alone when there are so many other dads out there at home? With this thought in mind he created *At Home Dad,* a quarterly newsletter for men who have chosen fatherhood as a career. He publishes the newsletter from his home in North Andover, Massachusetts, and has over four hundred subscribers. Each subscriber receives the names, addresses, and E-mail IDs of one hundred other stay-at-home dads. Income from the newsletter currently augments the Baylies family budget by $4,000 a year.

- Singles often complain about not being able to meet compatible people to date. Garvin Mark was no exception. But being disabled, he found he had special needs that dating

> "If you build a dream, the dream builds you."
> *Marilyn Hamilton,*
> *Quickie Designs*

services were not addressing, and he thought other disabled individuals did too. So he started VSP Dating, a dating service designed for single people with physical, learning, or emotional disabilities, including illnesses.

- When Beth Howard was trying to become pregnant she had to have her blood taken twice a week. Trekking over to the doctor's office was a drag, and she often thought it would be nice if someone could come to her house to do it. Well, that's what she does now as a mobile phlebotomist. She takes her syringe on the road visiting homes and offices to draw blood for all varieties of blood work to test for everything from HIV to fertility.

- Writer's block is a writer's greatest fear, and it hit Julie Cameron in the prime of her career. Actually her block came at the time when she decided to clean up her life and write sober. What she learned from that painful growth experience has become the basis for her mission. Author of *The Artist's Way,* Cameron has become a creativity expert, helping artists and other people tap naturally into their spontaneous creativity.

5. New Technology. Every technological breakthrough ushers in a multiplicity of opportunities for those who see them and have the desire and resources to capitalize on them. In the previous chapter, we listed many types of businesses you can start with a personal computer. Twenty percent of those businesses didn't even exist until the personal computer or some other new home/office technology made it possible to perform such services. But now, new technologies or new applications for existing technologies are entering the marketplace at an accelerating rate. Here's an unusual and interesting example. Brad and Kitty Freeman are using their copy machine to imprint the pictures of an owner's horse on T-shirts. The technology that makes it possible for a couple to do this cost-effectively from their home didn't exist only a few years ago. You also met Elsie and Ted McConnell, who are using their experience in property management to provide a roof-leak-detection service. The device making the service possible had only recently been developed when they bought it. Here are several

> *30 Ways People Are Helping Others Like Them*
> *You Might Never Think Of*
>
> - Succeeding in the workplace after your hair's turned gray
> - Getting even with bill collectors
> - Preparing for the death of a mate
> - Recovering from debt
> - Claiming one's American Indian heritage
> - Negotiating fees with your lawyer
> - Raising nonviolent children
> - Keeping romance alive after thirty years of marriage
> - Helping your ADD child succeed in school
> - Dealing with the history of slavery in America
> - Handling jerks at the office
> - Improving your memory
> - Turning household chores into a workout
> - Beating the winter blues
> - Selling your home yourself
> - Putting your best foot forward while traveling abroad
> - Collecting child support from an ex-spouse who won't pay
> - Becoming the parent for your children's children
> - Attracting black men as a black woman
> - Profiting from NAFTA
> - Cutting the costs of your wedding
> - Recovering from an addiction
> - Keeping cool when you feel like a fool
> - Moving to the country
> - Surviving as a community-based retail store
> - Selling anything to anybody
> - Winning at the casino
> - Getting a job on-line
> - Recovering from bankruptcy
> - Avoiding bad investments

other examples of people who have seized opportunities created by new technology in order to pursue their goals for independence:

- While the technology to save lost computer data for large mainframe computers has existed for some time, only in the past few years has it been possible to retrieve data for personal computer owners when their files have been destroyed by power outages, storms, floods, and so forth. Now that it's possible, Scott Gaidano has started Drivesaver and comes to the rescue of desperate computer owners. Fielding from sixty to eighty calls per day, he says that in 90 percent of the cases, the data can be recovered.

- Much of today's new technology is produced in countries that speak a language other than English. Kenneth Mc-Kethan recognized this as an opportunity and is using his background as a translator to translate technical documents from all major Western and Asian languages into English. Although he planned to generate only enough work to keep himself busy, he began getting more business in additional foreign languages, so his company, Techni-Lingua, has grown to include twenty-four other independent translators who are native speakers of the language they translate.

- Former accountant Michelle Deziel had spent three years bouncing around on boats in bathing suits that never fit. When she read that a computer whiz had written a program to custom-design a bikini for his wife, Deziel decided to buy the rights to the software and with the help of her father, a computer manufacturer, she began designing custom-made swimming suits. She says of her suits, "We can hide what you don't like." And Florida-based Second Skin Swimwear obviously hit upon a need. She's selling a million dollars' worth of her $70 to $170 suits. She has expanded to three franchises in other locations and has licensed the software to twenty other shops nationwide.

- New technology creates unprecedented opportunities to get in on the ground floor of new industries. That is exactly what George Alistair Sanger has done in the fast-growing, opportunity-rich field of interactive media. Known as the Fat Man, Sanger, a musician with experience operating a mobile sound studio, had always loved video games, but he thought the sound tracks were limited. Through his college roommate's brother, who worked for a major video-game manufacturer, Sanger had the chance to write what turned out to be ten seconds of music for a cartridge machine. From that moment on he was hooked. Writing music for computer and multimedia products became his lifework, and he is now one of multimedia's first superstars. Whereas he was paid only $1,000 for his first project and it seemed that all his initial clients went out of business, he and his Team Fat of composers reportedly now get $10,000 plus royalties for doing the music track for computer games. He has a newsletter and bulletin board for his Fat Man Fan Club members and a Fat Man coloring book. Coming up, he may even have a record deal in the wings.

Note: You don't have to have technical expertise to capitalize on new technology. In fact, as Ann McIndoo did in starting her computer tutoring business, you can use your novice status to your advantage as you help others who know even less than you do to understand, buy, and become comfortable using technology. McIndoo's greatest asset in starting her business was not being a computer whiz. She wasn't. Her greatest asset was having only recently been a secretary just like her students, having to learn to use a strange and complex piece of equipment. And so it was with marketing consultant Michael Cahlin. It wasn't computer savvy that helped him develop a public-relations firm for small high-tech companies. It was his ability to communicate about that technology with reporters and producers who were as intimidated by the computer software his clients were creating as the audiences they would be addressing and many of the customers the software was designed for.

> *Be among the first to recognize the potential*
> *of new technologies.*

6. New Legislation, Regulations, and Policy Changes. We sometimes jokingly refer to any piece of significant new legislation as a Self-Employment Opportunity Act. All jokes aside, new laws do create opportunity because every new piece of legislation gen-

Needs Created by New Technology

Every time new technology is introduced not only can it be used to provide the purpose for which it was intended, it also creates the following ancillary needs for products and services:

- Writing documentation for using it
- Promoting it
- Selling it
- Consulting on selecting and installing it
- Teaching people to use it
- Publishing books, tapes, and videos on using it
- Maintaining and repairing it
- Developing accessories for it
- Discovering new applications for it
- Brokering used models

erates the need for a raft of new services. Consultants are needed to explain it and help people comply with it. Manuals need to be developed to create in-house policies for it. Training is needed for individuals and employees who must follow it. In some cases, independent inspectors may be needed to certify compliance. Sometimes arbitration and mediation is needed. Sometimes products, ancillary services, or accessories are needed: i.e., signs or posters may be required to be displayed, new ramps may need to be constructed.

Certainly it is the proliferation of local, state, and national legislation that has created red-tape consultants like David Kalb, whom you met in the last chapter. As you may recall, Kalb, whose company is Capital Services, has been helping his clients unsnarl the bureaucratic complexities of dozens of state agencies for the past nine years. Here are a few examples of others who have turned new legislation into an opportunity to serve:

- When governmental spending cuts led Rob White to be laid off from his job in the health field, his search for a new job began to seem fruitless, and as time passed he became increasingly despondent. A friend, sensing his desperation, was puzzled and pointed out to White that the very forces that had eliminated his job held seeds of opportunity for him to create a new job for himself. Doctors, feeling pressed to leave their solo practices and join HMOs and PPOs, are often at a loss as to how to proceed. With White's experience in the field, the friend pointed out, he could provide them with the information and direction they needed. It was true, and White has created an excellent and rewarding living for himself helping doctors locate and negotiate their way successfully into group practices.

- When sexual harassment in the workplace stormed into national awareness in the early nineties, Dorene Ludwig saw the opportunity to draw upon her experience and love of acting to address her long-felt concern about equal rights and women's issues. She developed a training seminar and manual to teach employees about the subtleties of sexual harassment, using role-playing scenes to help participants identify their thoughts and feelings on the issues involved. Having already done corporate communications training, she was well positioned to begin consulting and training on this subject in the workplace.

■ As a result of equal-opportunity laws, affirmative-action programs, and increased international trade, today's workplace is increasingly culturally diverse. Such diversity can result in misunderstandings and miscommunications as one culture's expectations collide with those of others. Thus we've seen a rise in cultural-diversity training programs nationwide to help employees better understand and appreciate cultural differences. Cross-cultural communications has become a specialty, for example, for image consultants like Dorothea Johnson, whose background and contacts in the diplomatic community have positioned her to consult with companies on issues of intercultural protocol and etiquette, and for Lewis Brown Griggs, who specializes in cultural-diversity training in the workplace and has cowritten the book *Valuing Diversity*.

"Nothing is really work unless you would rather be doing something else."
J. M. Barrie

Take note of new legislation, regulations, and policy changes.

You may have noticed that the people in many of the examples we've used have actually tapped into a combination of the criteria that can make an opportunity into a livelihood. They're tapping into special needs that arise from trends which they can capitalize on because of their own experience and background or they're using their own experiences to help others just like them deal with the complaints and problems posed by new legislation or new technology. We find such overlapping is often the case. The best opportunities often lie at the crossroads or the intersection of diverse or even unrelated phenomena. Use the following work sheet to help identify and explore possible combinations or intersections of opportunities open to you.

"The basic test of freedom is perhaps less in what we are free to do than in what we are free not to do."
Eric Hoffer

IDENTIFYING YOUR OPPORTUNITIES WORK SHEET

What opportunities are you best suited to connect with? Identify possible opportunities in each of the following categories. Then evaluate each of them in terms of: 1) Could you help? 2) On a scale of 1 to 10, how much would you want to? 3) On a scale of 1 to 10, how well would seizing such an opportunity match with achieving your goals? In what possible ways might you relate what you want to do to any of these opportunities?

1. Complaints and Problems. What do you hear people around you complaining about? What do people hate doing that you enjoy? Build a list of the complaints you hear and problems you see.

COMPLAINTS AND PROBLEMS	Could You Help? (Yes or No)	Do You Want To? (Scale of 1 to 10)	Match with Your Goals? (Scale of 1 to 10)

2. Trends. What trends have you observed that you identify with?

TRENDS	Could You Help? (Yes or No)	Do You Want To? (Scale of 1 to 10)	Match with Your Goals? (Scale of 1 to 10)

3. Special Needs. What special needs do others around you have? Who isn't being served? Who is unhappy with the way they are being served?

SPECIAL NEEDS	Could You Help? (Yes or No)	Do You Want To? (Scale of 1 to 10)	Match with Your Goals? (Scale of 1 to 10)

4. People Like You. What special needs have you had? What problems have you faced? Who else like you needs what you have needed? Who needs what you know, have learned, or could do?

PEOPLE LIKE ME	Could You Help? (Yes or No)	Do You Want To? (Scale of 1 to 10)	Match with Your Goals? (Scale of 1 to 10)

5. New Technology. What new technology are you aware of, have you used or have an interest in? How might you capitalize on its introduction to help others?

NEW TECHNOLOGY	Could You Help? (Yes or No)	Do You Want To? (Scale of 1 to 10)	Match with Your Goals? (Scale of 1 to 10)

6. *New Legislation, Regulations, and Policy Changes.* What legislation, regulations, or policy changes are affecting your field or a field of interest to you? How could you help others adapt to these changes?

LEGISLATION, REGULATIONS, POLICIES	Could You Help? (Yes or No)	Do You Want To? (Scale of 1 to 10)	Match with Your Goals? (Scale of 1 to 10)

Star (*) any of the above opportunities you could help with that you'd score at a seven (7) or above in both interest and compatibility with your goals. Then brainstorm ideas of possible ways you could relate what you want to do to any one or a combination of these opportunities. You can peruse **Appendix II, "An Alphabetical Directory of Self-Employment Careers,"** to stimulate your thinking. Star (*) the ideas that most appeal to you.

IDEAS

_____

_____

_____

_____

_____

_____

TEN

Packaging Your Desires with Opportunity

SPOTTING ONE or more appealing opportunities is the first step to connecting your desires to what people will pay for. The next step is identifying how to package your skills, talents, and assets to be responsive to those opportunities in a way that will also meet your personal desires and financial needs.

Finding a way to take advantage of opportunities while unwaveringly pursuing your own personal goals is probably the most elusive step in the entire process of finding your perfect work. But you may have noticed there is a common thread woven through the many diverse stories of all the people you've met throughout this book, even though you met them in the context of only one aspect of their story. It's this common thread that holds the secret to packaging what you can offer in a way that will match both your desires and what people will pay for.

It wasn't until we had studied literally thousands of stories like the ones you've read that we recognized this thread. Once we saw it, however, we realized it was present whenever people were succeeding and it was missing whenever people were struggling

I always say when you have the opportunity to do something but you don't have the courage, do it anyway. The courage will come.

Trick of the Eye

or failing. This pattern was there in all cases, whether the individuals had stumbled onto their opportunities, set out to create them, or gone looking for them. They had made a series of connections, usually unconsciously through chance or trial and error. Only rarely was this a conscious process. But it was definitely the thread we personally had been looking for in searching to find our own perfect work so many years ago. It was as if we were searching in the dark, though, because we didn't know what we were looking for. We just knew that somehow we had to find a way to support ourselves in living a better life. If we'd known there was a pattern to follow, we would have known where to look and could have circumvented years of wandering along dead-end paths.

"Where your talents and the world's needs cross, there lies your vocation."

Aristotle

We call the pattern we've identified Matrixing. And if you've completed the work sheets in each chapter up to this point, you've already done all the research you need to create a matrix that will support you along the path of your choice.

MATRIXING: THE THREAD THAT WEAVES WISHES INTO PRACTICAL REALITIES

All those who successfully support themselves on their own have found a way to matrix—that is, they've discovered where three elements you've already explored in depth during this and previous chapters intersect:

1. Personally Compelling Desires. The passion, mission, or other compelling personal desires strongly motivating you to pursue a path to work on your own and create a new life

2. Resources. The gifts, talents, skills, and assets you can call upon to actualize your desires and create the life you're seeking

3. Opportunities. The needs or desires in the world people will pay you to help them meet

By finding as many intersections between these elements as possible, you can create a *matrix,* or net, so to speak, that will literally support you pursuing what you're seeking in life. The key word here is *create.*

MATRIXING: A FORMULA FOR SUCCESS

○ *Desires.* Combine what's motivating you (your passion, mission, or other compelling personal goals that are driving you to create a new life).

○ *Resources.* Use your gifts (talents, skills) and assets (job and life experience, education and training, personal contacts, equipment, facilities, and other possessions).

○ *Opportunity.* Aim to meet specific needs in the world that people will pay for.

◉ *Means.* Work in a way that achieves your desires and supports you on the path of your choice.

We "create" the means to our livelihood from our resource-full-ness.

Matrixing is essentially about owning your resource-full-ness. As you've seen from these many pages of stories, we each have a unique set of resources to draw upon, both internal and external. Through the work sheets, you've been identifying yours. And you've read how others are using theirs. These resources are as unique as your fingerprints and your DNA. They are the sum total of all your experiences. Marshaling your resources and applying them to the opportunities around you can provide you with the means you've been seeking. Matrixing is a pattern, or a formula, for marshaling your resources to pursue any path. Written out as a formula, it looks like this:

MATRIXING FORMULA

Anyone who wishes to become self-employed can apply this formula to create the means to support his or her dreams. When this formula is applied to any existing effort, you can clearly see why it's working or why it isn't.

Let's look at two hypothetical examples, based on composites

"The price of having the freedom to live life your way is paid in creativity. Although some people will gladly tell you what to do, unless you create your own path, experimenting until you find your way, you'll never be truly free."

of common situations: one in which the person has matrixed successfully, the other in which the person has not.

Jack happened onto a health cream. It had wonderful properties, and those who used it saw immediate and dramatic results. Eager to free himself from the dead-end job writing computer codes that dominated most of his waking hours, he decided to give this opportunity everything he had. After all, health and beauty is a major trend that shows no sign of abating as Baby Boomers begin entering their fifties en masse.

Jack had no background, contacts, or experience in the health-and-beauty industry, but he was motivated. He invested all his savings in producing and packaging his health cream and set about getting it into department stores and health-food stores nationwide. He hit one brick wall after another, however. Buyers were not interested. He was a tiny fish trying to get into the big pond of the health-and-beauty industry, and he was swimming upstream. When he came to us, he had been trying to peddle his cream for three years and still wasn't getting even near the pond.

Judy also had a health-and-beauty product. She had stumbled onto it while working as a flight attendant who needed to cover the dark circles under her eyes. Like Jack, she had no background in the health-and-beauty field, but she took an entirely different approach than he. Instead of swimming upstream, she matrixed her resources into a means of support for herself and her daughter.

She studied to get licensed as a facialist and started seeing clients in her home. Most of her early clients were flight attendants she'd known through her job. Of course, she applied her product under the eyes of each client before their session ended. Soon she had word-of-mouth going for her among hundreds of airline employees who started clamoring for her product. She began selling it to them through the mail. Then she started writing a newsletter about health and beauty for her clients and anyone who expressed interest in her eye cream. She got many orders through the newsletter. She also started doing skin-care seminars for airline employees and eventually wrote a book about skin care. Although Judy's cream can't be found in any store, by drawing upon her resources she has created the means to a steady income based upon the opportunities of the health-and-beauty field. Were she to want to expand into retail stores, the track record of success and the national following she's built up over the past several years could open closed doors.

We can plot her matrix as follows:

Compelling Personal Desires. She wanted to stop traveling and get on a more normal schedule while retaining the freedom, flexibility, and income being a flight attendant provided to support herself and raise her daughter.

Resources. She drew upon her experience of trying to care for her skin as an airline employee, used the money she had to get licensed as a facialist, and built on her contacts with other flight attendants. She also drew upon things that come naturally to her. She has an outgoing personality and is eager to help others, so she created a personal service business. A good communicator, she publishes a newsletter, gives speeches and seminars, and is eager to help others. (Improver/Leader/Creator)

Opportunity. She recognized the value of the face cream and that, like her, other flight attendants need to give special care to their skin. Plus, she had the know-how and resources to provide her service.

Means. Working from home as a facialist under the company name Facialese, she sells her eye cream directly to clients, through a newsletter, and at seminars for flight attendants.

By building this matrix, Judy had woven a pattern for success. The path she chose capitalized upon her assets, and she was able to package her resources to meet the real needs of people like her. Now, let's go back to Jack's situation. Let's analyze his matrix and see where the holes are:

Compelling Personal Desires. Jack is clearly in touch with his desire. He wants to be his own boss doing more fulfilling work. Like Judy, he's chosen the path to capitalize on his assets. Obviously he's motivated at a seven (7) or above because he's still trying, three years later, long after a less-motivated person would have given up.

Resources. The only resource Jack has drawn upon so far is his savings. He is not drawing upon his natural abilities (Orga-

Judy's Matrix

DESIRES   RESOURCES

Good Income, No Travel

Contacts, Experienced Facialist

Eye Cream

OPPORTUNITY

Jack's Matrix

More Fulfilling Work as Own Boss

Financial Resources

Skin Cream

nizer/Problem Solver/Builder). In fact, in trying to sell his product to buyers (Leader/Builder/Improver), he's operating outside what he does naturally and it's no wonder he's feeling discouraged. Chances are his self-esteem is hurting as well.

Opportunity. The skin cream Jack acquired is certainly an opportunity. People who use it get results. But as yet, he has not found a way to package this resource to take advantage of the opportunity it provides. So far, it's an opportunity in idea only. As yet he has found no overlap to create a means for success.

You may be thinking Jack doesn't have the right resources and that Judy is far better positioned for success. Jack doesn't want to be a facialist, for example. He doesn't have friends who are flight attendants. How could he possibly be as successful as Judy? But that only appears to be the case because Judy has matrixed her resources, and the weak link in Jack's efforts lies in the fact that he has *not* marshaled his resources, and that leaves a big hole in his matrix. As you will see in a few minutes, if Jack were fully marshaling his resources he could be achieving a similar level of success—and you'd be thinking how ideally positioned he is for it.

While it would appear that Jack is better positioned to become a freelance programmer than to get involved in health and beauty, becoming a freelancer wouldn't accomplish his goal to find more fulfilling work. He may not have the interest in beauty or the built-in customers Judy has, but he nonetheless sees the potential in his cream and is motivated to pursue it. The fact that getting this face cream onto the market is so challenging is actually part of why he wants to do it. He welcomes doing something more challenging. But to be successful, he needs to do a better job of using the resources he has to actually make a connection between this opportunity and his desires.

He has many resources he has not yet bundled into his package:

1. He has excellent computer skills.
2. His personality is naturally suited to organizing, problem solving, and working with materials.

3. He spends many hours of his free time interacting on computer on-line services.
4. His wife and sister both go to facialists.

These resources position him nicely to sell his product on the Internet or by mail-order. He has the computer skills to do database marketing and the problem-solving skills to place small three-line classified ads making a variety of special offers in a variety of publications and tracking the responses until he finds the most compelling ad copy and the most cost-effective publications. He would be right at home doing a demographic analysis of those who respond in order to carve out a unique niche for himself from among an infinite range of possibilities: i.e., women over sixty-five, women who have just had cosmetic surgery, recently divorced women over fifty, professional women, men who go to manicurists, men who go to facialists, etc.

He can also experiment with selling his product via the Internet or through any online service on an Electronic Mall, since he's familiar with this world and network through health and news-groups and forums. And finally, since his product produces dramatic results once someone uses it, he can work through what we call gatekeepers, people who come into regular contact with his potential customers on a regular basis in the course of what they do. Facialists, for example, would be excellent gatekeepers for Jack, and through his contacts he already has access to at least two of them. What he needs to do is contact them and provide them with a sample of his product. When they like the results, they can become distributors. In fact, Jack should talk to Judy!

Judy would probably be as ill prepared to do complex demographic analysis as Jack would be giving a speech on skin care to a roomful of flight attendants. Both have resources, however, that they can more naturally marshal to reach their goals.

If you look back over the profiles in this and previous chapters, you'll notice how they all have done this kind of matrixing of their resources to connect their desires to real-life opportunities. But often it's only after the fact that these connections appear to be so obviously suited for each individual. Judy, for example, could just as easily have overlooked her resources as Jack did. She too could have tried to break into retail stores. She too could have met with one closed door after another. If you don't believe that the people who find successful connections might just as easily have overlooked them, remember Rob White. He was so close to his own situation that it wasn't until his friend pointed out the "obvious" connection that he realized he could use his past experience on the job to help doctors solve a real-life problem they would gladly pay to avoid.

Since building a matrix has primarily been, up until recently, an unconscious process, some people have been fortunate enough to fall into or stumble over theirs while others, like us, had to struggle and flail around to build ours. Since until now books and other materials have related to only one or perhaps two of the elements needed to build a matrix, for most people weaving these elements together has primarily been a process of trial and error. But now anyone can do a matrix analysis and see various options for constructing a successful livelihood. It's a matter of putting the information together, looking at the possibilities, and making a choice. Here are just a few examples that demonstrate retrospectively how people you've met earlier were able to find work of their own by matrixing.

HERE'S HOW THEY DID IT

GEORGE ALISTAIR SANGER, FAT MAN

Compelling Desires. Sanger had a passion for video games.
Resources. So he drew upon his quirky personality, his musical talent, his understanding of the complex technology of video games, and the marketing expertise he'd gained from previous businesses.
Opportunity. To participate in the meteoric growth of the multimedia home-entertainment industry.
Means. Sanger creates musical soundtracks for multimedia games.

BARBARA LAMBERT, ONE MILLION AND ONE VIDEOS

Compelling Desires. Lambert wanted to find work that involved less travel, and she loves doing research.
Resources. So she drew upon her sales experience as the first fe-

male auctioneer in Georgia and the background and the contacts she had made with art collectors from coast to coast.

Opportunity. To do something about the frequent complaints she'd heard from family and friends that videos they wanted to buy or rent weren't available from video stores

Means. Lambert has become a video detective. She tracks down, buys, rents, sells, brokers, or auctions any video anywhere in the world, all without leaving home.

DAVID KATZ, AGACCESS

Compelling Desire. A lifelong activist, Katz has a missionary zeal for ecological issues, and he wanted to create a livelihood finding environmental solutions without having to be dependent upon what he calls the "tin cup" of nonprofit grants and foundations.

Resources. So he called upon his experience working as a market gardener, foreman, and general manager for a large commercial farm and later doing organic farming himself.

Opportunity. To provide organic farmers with information he knows they need to respond to the growing demand from consumers for organically grown foodstuff. He knew the information was available but hard to find.

Means. Katz and his wife, Karen Van Epen, provide consulting, market research, catalogs, books, and videotapes for organic farmers.

ARTHUR SCHIFF, *FAMILY CITY* MAGAZINE

Compelling Desire. Schiff was disillusioned about the lack of information available to poor immigrants to help them achieve their dream to become middle-class citizens, and he's dedicated to changing America's attitude toward the poor from thinking of them as a burden to regarding them as a valued consumer market.

Resources. So he drew upon his experience as the former head of New York City's food stamp program and upon charitable friends who were willing to help finance his mission.

Opportunity. To help fill the void he'd noticed: there were no magazines or newspapers tailored to the reading and comprehension level or other special needs of poor immigrants. The result is they are not getting the information they need to achieve their dreams.

Means. With $40,000 from his friends, Schiff launched *Family City* magazine, which he publishes from a tiny office in his apartment. In 1993, *Library Journal* named *Family City* as one of the ten best new magazines, along with *Wired* and *Men's Journal.*

MIKE MILLIS, STAR NETWORK

Compelling Desire. Millis loves the theater and acting and has a passionate desire to help aspiring actors and actresses triumph over odds to achieve their dreams.

Resources. So he drew upon his ten years of experience performing with and conducting the business of small theater companies he helped to found and put his graphics-loaded PC to work.

Opportunity. Initially he started a résumé-writing service for performing artists but quickly realized that they had many other special needs if they were to succeed in entertainment.

Means. Millis's Star Network provides career counseling, résumés, and other support services to performing artists.

DAVID KALB, CAPITAL SERVICES

Compelling Desire. Kalb wanted to help people get through government bureaucracy.

Resources. So he drew on his past experience working for the state government, his educational background in public administration and government, and know-how he gained from growing up in an entrepreneurial family.

Opportunity. To do something about the thousands of letters he'd seen on his job from unhappy citizens who were frustrated by increasing levels of government regulation and bureaucracy.

Means. Kalb started Capital Services, a service to help cut red tape.

WARREN FAIDLEY, WEATHER PHOTOGRAPHER

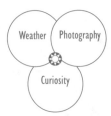

Compelling Desire. Faidley has had a lifelong fascination with the weather, and he wanted to earn a living doing what he enjoys most.

Resources. So he drew upon the skills he'd developed from his hobby, photography, and his job experiences and contacts as a journalist.

Opportunity. To take photos that no one else was daring enough to take of hurricanes, storms, tornadoes, and other weather events.

Means. Faidley has become the nation's only full-time professional weather photographer and refers to himself as an artistical weather historian.

THERESA POLLACK, PARTY ANIMAL

Compelling Desires. Pollack wanted the independence of working for herself with the two things she loves best: children and animals. She also has a personal mission: she wants to break down people's fear of reptiles.

Resources. So she used her experience as a preschool teacher and animal trainer and contacts she made through her husband's reptile store.

Opportunity. To provide unique educational party experiences for children. Parents are always looking for different and unique entertainment for their children's parties, and Pollack's program provides both entertainment and education.

Means. Pollack makes her living primarily on weekends. She brings her snakes, lizards, tarantulas, and a range of other reptilian creatures to children's parties and teaches the children about their habits and characteristics.

MATRIXING TO FIND YOUR PERFECT WORK

As you can see, the best livelihoods are at the crossroads where our own interests, desires, and resources meet up with real-life everyday needs of other people. Your best chance for creating the life you desire lies at the intersection where the widest possible variety of your own resources and desires overlap with the trends, problems, complaints, and hopes and dreams of others. Matrixing enables you to start identifying these intersections, these crossroads along your chosen path. Think of the elements of your matrix as pieces of a puzzle that you can move around to intersect in various ways. When you find the best match, the best fit, among your desires, your resources, and the needs of others, you will have found the winning combination for your perfect work.

When you matrix your desires and resources with the needs of others, you will have created a unique niche or specialty for yourself that will enable you to stand out from the crowd of temps, freelancers, and other contingent workers who are pouring into the workforce today. Whether you choose to do something like weather photographer Warren Faidley or party animal trainer Theresa Pollack, something that's so unique virtually no one else is doing anything like it, or whether you choose a career like word processing or bookkeeping that thousands of others are doing, when you matrix you can create a "designer" career for yourself, a career with your own label on it.

The choice that best mixes and matches the possibilities suggested by your particular desires, resources, and opportunities will best position you for success. You will have little true competition when you pursue that choice. The more of us who opt for a tailor-made livelihood, the more each of us will succeed. The less we will have to butt heads with each other, fighting and struggling to scratch out a living dividing up little pieces of the same pie. When we each bake our own pie, there will always be plenty to go around.

Use the work sheets that follow to matrix your own desires, resources, and opportunities into in a tailor-made independent career. As you use these work sheets, here's what to look for to find the perfect match.

"He may well win the race that runs by himself."

Benjamin Franklin

WHAT TO LOOK FOR

As you begin exploring the many possible ways your desires, resources, and opportunities could overlap, look for the following signs to guide you to the most natural choice:

Similarities. What do your desires and resources have in common with the opportunities around you? Look for the common ground, the shared experiences, problems, goals, dreams.

Sky Dayton, twenty-three, founder of Earthline Network, saw similarities between his longtime interest in coffeehouses and the Internet on-line communication network. To him they're one and the same thing: a place where people can go to communicate without getting intoxicated.

Coincidences. What unexpected or seemingly random events have occurred in your life that relate to your search? Has someone called complaining of the very problem you're thinking about addressing? Did you just happen to hear about someone else who's doing something similar to what you want to do? Did a friend mention a book you should read? Pay attention to these seemingly chance occurences.

Kevin Hughes was working in a medical unit when some friends entered him in a comedy competition. Although it was his first time on stage, once he got there he knew that was where he belonged.

Hunches. What hunches do you have about the relationship between what you want to do and what people need? Catch yourself saying things like "I bet . . ." "I wonder if . . ." "Why couldn't . . ." Don't dismiss such ruminations.

Luke Hwang provides a service that lets people gain access to the information highway through the Internet. He got the idea on the hunch that "technical types" like him needed better and quicker access.

Connections. What connections do you see between your desires and resources and what people need? How could one relate to another?

Alexis Lanni had a background in the computer industry, having managed a software company. Her husband was a musician. She saw a connection between her experience and the needs of musicians like her husband and started a worldwide referral service for professional and amateur musicians, which she markets on-line via computer.

Relationships. Whom do you know who is an example of the way your desires and resources could overlap? For example, have you ever said to yourself, "A guy I once worked with is starting a new business. I bet he needs . . ." or "Someone I read about in the paper is doing something I could do with a slightly different twist"?

Gloria Strickland was watching a daytime talk show when she saw a guest showing off pillow pattern designs. Having done needlepoint pillows as a hobby most of her life, her first thought was "I could do that!" She called the show, got the name of the guest, and called to find out how she could pursue her craft as a livelihood.

Wild Ideas. What are the wildest ideas you can imagine for linking your desires, resources, and opportunities? Give your imagination free rein. The seed for your most natural choice may lie in one of those "wild, crazy ideas."

Technical writer Sarah Stambler was a pilot user of a home-banking program. She had a wild idea, unheard of at the time: Why not help the bank market home banking via E-mail? She pitched the idea to the bank president. He bought it, and Stambler has gone on to become one of the first electronic marketers in the nation.

Memories and Reveries. What memories or reveries come to mind as you explore the possible connections between your desires, resources, and opportunities? Sometimes long-forgotten events or childhood memories, even dreams, will provide a glimpse of an otherwise overlooked natural choice.

The memory of how much Jim Haggart had loved to play with model trains swept over him while standing at a newsstand. The pleasant feeling was such a contrast to the way he felt on his job in mortgage banking that he could see how his love for model trains overlapped his other skills. He started building limited-edition HO-scale model railroad kits.

Forgotten Flights of Fancy. What were your old and long-forgotten wishes and fantasies? "Remember how we used to fantasize about . . ." Such old flights of fancy could hold the key to an idea of how to link your desires, resources, and opportunities.

Long ago Leroy LoPresti had dreamed about building his own airplanes. He decided do turn that fantasy into reality and created LoPresti Engineering, where he builds small-scale airplanes.

CREATING YOUR MATRIX

Opportunity is like a head of lettuce: fresh and crisp today, faded and wilted tomorrow.

Hart to Hart

If you have completed the work sheets in this and other chapters, you have already done the research you need to do to matrix your opportunities. This work sheet enables you to pull together all the work you've done in other chapters. By filling it out, you will discover where your desires, resources, and opportunities overlap so you can make the most natural choice. To create your matrix from the preparation you've already done, complete the following three steps. Examples are provided for each step.

STEP ONE: THREE SUMMARY CIRCLES WORK SHEET

Fill in the following circles by reviewing previous work sheets you've completed:

COMPELLING DESIRES CIRCLE

To complete this circle, review your conclusions from the:

- Pursuing Your Passion Work Sheet (page 137)
- Following a Mission Work Sheet (page 182)
- What Are You Doing This For? Work Sheet in Capitalizing on Your Assets (page 212)

YOUR COMPELLING DESIRES

PASSIONS: _____

_____

_____

MISSIONS: _____

_____

_____

OTHER DESIRES: _____

_____

_____

EXAMPLE: GLORIA J. COMPLETED HER CIRCLES AS FOLLOWS:

Compelling Desires. Gloria loves to travel. She grew up traveling throughout the world with her parents, who worked for a worldwide church mission. She also likes reading, writing, movies, and studying foreign cultures. She believes that we should all have more fun in our lives and that we need to have a better understanding and appreciation of other cultures. Also she has two small children and wants to spend more time at home with them.

COMPELLING DESIRES

PASSIONS: Travel, reading writing, movies, foreign cultures

MISSIONS: We should have more fun in life. We should know and appreciate other cultures.

OTHER DESIRES: Being home with my kids, time to read and watch movies.

RESOURCES CIRCLE

To complete this circle, review your conclusions from the:

- Gifts I Might Want to Harvest Work Sheet (page 118)
- Capitalizing on Your Assets Work Sheet (page 205)

YOUR RESOURCES

GIFTS: TALENTS AND SKILLS _____

_____

_____

_____

ASSETS: JOB AND LIFE EXPERIENCE, EDUCATION AND TRAINING,
CONTACTS, FACILITIES, TOOLS, EQUIPMENT, AND PERSONAL STYLE _____

_____

_____

_____

_____

_____

EXAMPLE: RESOURCES CIRCLE

Resources. Now Gloria works in the marketing department of a large Japanese-owned company. Her job responsibilities include publishing the in-house newsletter. She speaks some Japanese and is fluent in Spanish. She has a knack for understanding others' problems, is calm under pressure, and is often complimented on being able to put her finger on just about any resource someone is looking for. Her personal style is Organizer/Improver/Problem Solver.

RESOURCES

GIFTS: TALENTS AND SKILLS *Understand problems, calm under pressure, find resources easily, write well, speak Spanish and some Japanese.*

ASSETS: JOB AND LIFE EXPERIENCE, EDUCATION AND TRAINING, CONTACTS, FACILITIES, TOOLS, EQUIPMENT, AND PERSONAL STYLE

Contacts worldwide through church, organizer, improver, problem solver, volunteer work for church world food program; job in marketing department of large Japanese-owned company.

OPPORTUNITIES CIRCLE

To complete this circle, review your conclusions from the:

- Identifying Your Opportunities Work Sheet (page 268)
- Include in this circle the possible careers you've identified as Possible Self-Employment Careers That Come Naturally to You (page 222) based on working with the appendices.

YOUR OPPORTUNITIES

TRENDS, PROBLEMS, COMPLAINTS, SPECIAL NEEDS, PEOPLE LIKE ME, NEW TECHNOLOGY, LEGISLATION, CAREERS FROM APPENDIX II: _____

EXAMPLE: OPPORTUNITIES CIRCLE

Opportunities. In assessing opportunities related to her desires and resources, Gloria has noticed growing cultural conflicts in the workplace. She is aware of the increasing number of people entering retirement age who are ready and eager to travel. She also knows that with increasing international trade more companies will be transferring growing numbers of employees to live and work in other countries. She has known Japanese families who've had to take positions here and American families who have been transferred to Japan. Often they've both had a difficult time adjusting to living in a foreign country. For some time she has been thinking about starting a company to do cultural diversity training, but for some reason she hasn't actually pursued it. Looking in Appendix III under her Personal Style, she finds careers like abstracting, publishing, red-tape wrangler, referral service, relocation service, and tour operator.

OPPORTUNITIES

TRENDS, PROBLEMS, COMPLAINTS, SPECIAL NEEDS, PEOPLE LIKE ME, NEW TECHNOLOGY, LEGISLATION, CAREERS FROM APPENDIX II: _____

Growing conflicts between cultures in workplace, more people of retirement age who want to travel, more international companies, people being transferred into jobs in other countries. Careers: abstracting, publishing, red-tape wrangler, referral service, tour operator, relocation service.

STEP TWO: OVERLAPPING CIRCLES WORK SHEET

Look at your three Summary Circles and notice how the elements in them might overlap. Draw various circles, as Gloria has done in the example that follows, to explore possible ways your various desires, resources and opportunities could overlap. Your best livelihood lies at these intersections. Evaluate each possibility as to how well they match, as Gloria has done.

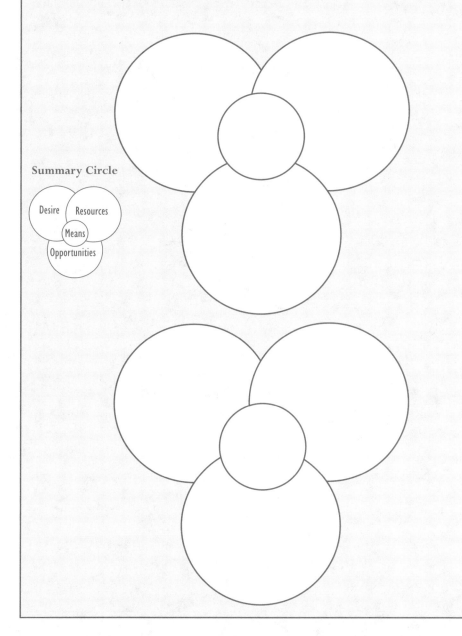

Summary Circle

Desire

Resources

Means

Opportunities

"While I was watching a herd of elephants, I realized that those animals were doing what they're supposed to be doing. They were free."

Deanie Kramer,
The Divorce
Resource

EXAMPLE: OVERLAPPING CIRCLES

Since Gloria has been thinking about doing cultural diversity training, she starts there and it does overlap in several ways, but not all:

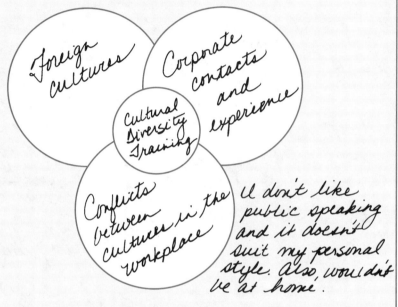

Next she considers publishing a travel newsletter. It, too, overlaps in a variety of ways, but not all:

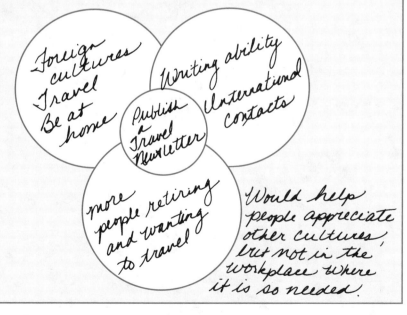

Being a tour operator is especially intriguing, but as she tests it out, it clearly isn't a good match:

Travel / Foreign cultures

International contacts

Tour Operator

more people wanting and needing to travel abroad

I could help people have more fun and I would appreciate other cultures, but I would have to be away from home too much.

A relocation service, however, seems to be a most natural match:

Travel / Reading / Be at home

Corporate contacts

Problem solving abilities

Relocation Service

International contacts

more people working for international companies

GLORIA'S CHOICE

Gloria decides to combine her corporate contacts and experience with her world-wide church contacts to start a relocation service helping employees and their families get established in foreign countries. Her slogan will be "Feeling at Home Working Away from Home." She plans to draw on her writing skills by publishing booklets on living in various cultures and a quarterly newsletter for the families she helps relocate. The newsletter will include abstracts of tours and recreational and resort facilities in these countries so her clients can learn to enjoy relaxing as well as working in their new culture. Although she will be able to run her business almost entirely from home, she can also work in periodic travel to locations she wishes to research in person.

STEP THREE: MATRIXING FORMULA **WORK SHEET**

Test your choice of possible ideal livelihoods using this Matrixing Formula, as Gloria has done in the example that follows:

I want to (The passion, mission, or other compelling desire that's motivating you to find work of your own): _____

_____

_____

so I will draw on my (Gifts, talents, skills, assets like background, experience, contacts, or personality traits): _____

_____

_____

to (The needs you see that you could meet): _____

_____

by (What product or service you could offer to meet those needs using your talents, assets, etc.): _____

EXAMPLE: MATRIXING FORMULA

Here's how Gloria uses the matrixing formula to describe her ideal livelihood:

I want to (The passion, mission, or other compelling desire that's motivating you to find work of your own): *help people understand and enjoy living and working in foreign cultures, and still spend most of my time at home.*

so I will draw on my (Gifts, talents, skills, assets like background, experience, contacts, or personality traits): *writing and problem-solving skills and my corporate and international church contacts.*

to (The needs you see that you could meet): *help employers and their families transferring to foreign countries.*

by (What product or service you could offer to meet those needs using your talents, assets, etc.): *creating an international relocation service, specializing in Japanese and Spanish-speaking countries.*

MORE MATRIXING EXAMPLES

You may want to study the following additional examples of how others have matrixed their desires and resources and keep experimenting to create your own "designer-label" career. Or you can skip on to page 304 to begin exploring the viability of the choices you're considering.

GARY NAKAMURA, ALL-ART SERVICES, INC.

Compelling Desire. Nakamura is an artist but realized once he graduated from college that, as romantic as the idea of being a starving artist might be, he was hungry.

Resources. So he took a job working for an art-transport business, which went out of business.

Opportunity. He got so many calls from past clients who needed art services that were no longer available

Means. that he decided to go out on his own doing logistics for traveling art exhibitions and managing art collections for corporations. He moves and tracks their art in transit and installs it once it arrives.

One of Nakamura's clients is a dinosaur exhibit that's traveling in forty-five forty-foot sea containers. Another is the City of Vienna's North American traveling exhibition on the Music of Vienna.

TOM REITER, TRIAL PRESENTATION TECHNOLOGIES

Compelling Desire. When Reiter's acting career stalled, he learned new skills in computer programming and database management, but when multimedia burst onto the scene, he had the chance to bring drama back into his life in a new and unexpected way.

Resources. He combined his experiences in drama with his training and experience in programming and database management.

Opportunity. Reiter seized a chance to bring multimedia presentations into the courtroom.

Means. Working from his home, Reiter has become a Techno-Guru, enabling lawyers to show juries a wide array of multimedia presentations like computer-animated reenactments of crime scenes.

Reiter installed the multimedia technology for the O.J. Simpson trial.

LINDA FELLINGTON-JONES, TTOUCH

Compelling Desire. Fellington-Jones loves animals.

Resources. So she used her experience as a horse trainer and her training as a Feldenkrais body-work practitioner.

Opportunity. Fellington-Jones saw that she could apply cutting-edge techniques being used with people with ill and stressed-out pets and animals. As animals have become increasingly significant members of our families, people are willing to spend more time and money providing for their pets' well-being.

Means. Fellington-Jones has created her own special method of animal body work called Tellington Touch, or TTouch, to heal physical and emotional problems of animals. In addition to working with animals herself, she also teaches others her methods through books, videos, and audios.

Tellington-Jones's patients have included an overly aggressive lynx and a balding cockatoo.

DAVID HERTZ, SYNDESE

Compelling Desire. Hertz wants to prove trash can be put to creative, functional uses.

Resources. So he uses his background and training as an architect and his passion and remarkable talents for creating innovative solutions.

Opportunity. Hertz recognized people's growing concern for the environment and our dwindling natural resources.

Means. Hertz designs innovative, ecologically responsible buildings and uses recycled materials like the lightweight concrete he's created from trash.

Trash and other recycled material Hertz has incorporated into attractive, custom-designed decorative items for his clients' decor include pencils, glass, golf tees, nuts and bolts, and used eyeglasses.

DIANE KELLY, PET BEREAVEMENT

Compelling Desire. Kelly is an animal lover. She has two dogs, two cats, and a husband who's a veterinarian.

Resources. She's had a private psychotherapy practice for ten years.

Opportunity. Kelly noticed that many of her clients had a special, but often overlooked, need for help in dealing with the grief of losing a pet.

Means. She now specializes in offering pet bereavement counseling.

DIANE SHALET, NOVELIST

Compelling Desire. Shalet had a difficult time dealing with the death of her husband. Books she found on grief didn't help, so she began writing a journal and signed up for a writing class she had long been wanting to take. Classmates loved her stories and encouraged her to turn them into a novel.

Resources. So after winning a prize for the unfinished manuscript, she called upon her experience as a veteran actress in both L.A. and New York to help develop her characters.

Opportunity. Drawing upon her own experiences as a widow, she began acting out her story ideas creating a mini–stage setting complete with props in her home and using her improvisational and comedic abilities to see if they were realistic and compelling. Then she'd sit down to write.

Means. Her first novel, *Grief in a Sunny Climate*, deals with a grieving widow with both compassion and humor. It has received critical praise.

ROBERT MAURER, WRITING COACH

Compelling Desire. Maurer has a passion for the theater.

Resources. So he used his background, experience, and training as a psychologist

Opportunity. When a friend asked him to give a lecture at a university on the psychological underpinnings of the thriller, he realized that good writers are good psychologists.

Means. Now he counsels drama and dance companies in the U.S. and England and works with writers to develop characters that ring true and engage audiences.

MARCEY HAMM, HAMM MUSIC

Compelling Desire. Hamm was sitting on top of the world having achieved great success as a designer of nuclear reactors, but she was miserable. After writing down the unsatisfying aspects of her career, she made a list of the three things that were most important to her: mathematics, music, and computers. Suddenly the whole room lit up, and she knew what she would be doing.

Resources. She had trained in classical music as a child and completed degrees in electronics and computer science.

Opportunity. Hamm left her prestigious job as a software engineer after a holistic healing cured the chronic neck and back pain she'd had following an automobile accident.

Means. Hamm pursues her three loves as a composer of what's been called healing music. She publishes New Age computer-generated music to help reduce stress and speed healing.

When Hamm composes in the home-based studio she built herself, she goes into an altered state and doesn't actually hear the music until she plays it back after she's finished. "It's like it's in my cells," she says. "I compose the music with my physical body, but I don't remember a minute of it."

CYNTHIA BUTCHER, CYNTHIA'S CLEAN TEAM

Compelling Desire. Butcher was cleaning the carpet one day, when the fumes made her dizzy. She realized she didn't like the way she felt after using chemical cleansers.

Opportunity. She figured other people might not like them either.

Resources. So she used her experience and contacts from having been active for years in a local organic food cooperative.

Means. Butcher started an environmentally sensitive cleaning service.

Butcher uses no commercial soaps, only nontoxic homemade and biodegradable products.

OSCAR VARGAS, PIÑATA PARTY

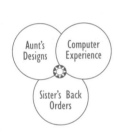

Compelling Desire. Vargas had always wanted to run his own business.

Resources. His background was working in electronics and the computer industry.

Opportunity. Vargas realized his sister always had a backlog of orders from family and friends in her hobby of making piñatas. So using his aunt's secret piñata party designs

Means. he began creating piñatas that blend the traditional piñata with modern technology.

BOB DOUMOUCHEL, FOGGY BOTTOM PUBLICATIONS

Compelling Desire. Doumouchel wanted to move to the Bahamas with his Bahamian wife.

Resources. He had worked for many years with a variety of government agencies and had published a directory of governmental resources.

Opportunity. A company wanted to acquire his publication and have him do an annual update.

Means. Publishing the almanac annually became the route to achieving his desire. He and his wife now live in Nassau where he lives and works at home two blocks from the beach.

ANITA GREEN, NINI DESIGNS

Compelling Desire. Green loves to sew.

Resources. She lives in the Pacific Northwest

Opportunity. This area is a center for ski buffs and outdoor enthusiasts who want trendy, customized outerwear for their outdoor lifestyle and who are also environmentally conscious.

Means. So she started a business designing and repairing expensive outdoor clothing and equipment.

JAN DAVIDSON, DAVIDSON & ASSOCIATES

Compelling Desire. Since age thirteen Jan Davidson knew she wanted to teach.

Resources. She was a mother of three and had been teaching for twelve years when

Opportunity. personal computers hit the market and Davidson had a vision. Why not use the computer to teach kids math?

Means. Using her Apple computer, she began publishing educational software for her students, using engaging activities and entertaining games to motivate users to learn. Her vision has grown into a 60-million-dollar education software company.

Davidson has developed and published over twenty-five award-winning software titles, including the best-selling MathBlaster series.

DON SILVERS, KITCHENS BY DESIGN

Compelling Desire. Silvers wanted to design kitchens that a chef could use.

Resources. Silvers was a chef.

Opportunity. He was asked to arrange to have the kitchen where he worked redesigned only to find that the designers didn't know how to design a kitchen to cook in.

Means. So he put down his spatula and picked up a drafting pen, going back to school to learn how to design kitchens that not only look good but also are also geared to the needs of cooking.

Among Silvers' specialties are separate sinks for preparation and cleanup, ample counter space, and lots of room for appliances. When he completes a new kitchen, he helps the owner celebrate by catering a dinner party for eight to twelve guests.

Sarah and Paul
Edwards

PAUL AND SARAH'S MATRIX

Compelling Personal Desires. Initially, we wanted to create a healthier lifestyle, be at home for our son, and work with each other. Once we'd done that, we found our mission: to help others do it too.

Resources. Sarah: Uses her background as a teacher and psychotherapist along with her experience speaking, writing, and training for the federal government, creating and running a mental-health treatment center, doing corporate training in communications and presentation skills, and working from home in private psychotherapy practice.

Paul: Drew upon his education in sociology and law and his experience running political campaigns, practicing law, running a nonprofit organization, doing media training, and teaching presentation skills to candidates and executives along with what he learned about working from home.

Opportunity. We saw that people needed help to make the transition from a time when jobs were plentiful to a time of downsizing and outsourcing that makes it possible and sometimes imperative for us to create work of our own using personal computers and other office technology that enable those who want to to work from virtually anywhere.

Means. We provide information, resources, and support through all possible media (books, radio, television, on-line, speaking, audiotapes, and videotapes) for making it on your own working from home or elsewhere.

For more examples of how to see a pattern emerge from your overlapping circles, read through the profiles in **Appendix I** (pages 343–64) and see how six people were able to find their perfect work.

GENERATING
YOUR OWN LIVELIHOOD

At this point, you may have a very clear idea of what you want to do and how you will earn a living doing it; now you're wondering how to make sure you'll succeed. Or you may still see a variety of possibilities and feel uncertain as to which one to pursue. We urge that you not try pursuing several choices at once. This is a common trap too many people fall into. Trying to develop a variety of sources of income dissipates the time, energy, and money you have to build the connection that will actually produce a steady, reliable income for you. No one activity will get the full investment of time, energy, and money it requires and deserves. And to complicate matters further, not only are your energies split, but your image or identity with the public and potential client sources is split as well. People may become confused about what you're doing and will most likely take your efforts less seriously. You can expand into additional means later, if you wish, but get one livelihood well under way before trying to build another.

Income is always preceded by achieving some type of outcome for someone else.

So just what is involved in making sure the choice you make is something that you can truly make a livelihood at that will enable you to achieve your desires? In his book *What Color Is Your Parachute?* Richard Bolles says that self-employment is like being on a continual job search. But that's true only if you have yet to successfully connect your desires and resources to something people are ready and willing to pay for. Once you find such a connection, if you invest sufficiently in developing that connection, the time will come when your efforts will take on a life of their own. Then you will not be searching for work. Opportunities will be coming to you. Bolles long ago reached this point in his own career. He is highly sought after and many people who are looking for jobs eagerly await each new edition of his book. That type of eagerness is exactly the kind of reaction your own perfect work can ultimately generate for you in its own way. But being able to generate the livelihood of your choice from your perfect work is a four-phase process and a steady, reliable income is the result of the final phase. Understanding this four-phase process can help you both clarify your choice and know how to make it work most successfully.

THE FOUR PHASES TO GENERATING
YOUR OWN LIVELIHOOD

Fill yourself with the inspiration that comes from embracing your dream. Use the energy that inspiration provides you to make a connection with an outcome you can begin to help others achieve. Keep drawing upon the dream until the results you get for them brings back the energy you've invested multiplied.

Phase 1: Casting Forth. Once you decide what you think your perfect work might be, you must start casting forth what you want to offer, letting people you think need it know about it and testing out if there really is a connection between your desires and meeting the needs of those you intend to serve. This phase can feel a lot like looking for a job, but often it's actually easier to get small pieces of work than it is to land a full-time job doing what you want to do at the full salary you're seeking. You should be able to start making a connection with people or companies that need you in less time than it would take you to find a well-paying job doing the kind of work you want to do. But only if you invest the time and effort to continue casting forth will you actually make a connection that does meet other people's needs.

Phase 2: Connecting. As you continue casting forth what you have to offer and responding to what you discover, you'll learn how you can best connect your interests to what people need and will pay for. As long as you have yet to make such a connection, though, earning an income will be difficult. If you find yourself struggling once you get under way, realize that it's this connection you're seeking and continue to use the overlapping matrixing circles to further define how you can connect what you desire and what you have to offer with what people actually need. For some people, like Oscar Vargas in starting Piñata Party, the connection is in place right from the beginning: his sister had back orders waiting for him, so he never felt as if he was looking for a job. He had work to do right from the get go. For others, like Gregg Warren in starting Worry Free, the connection comes immediately upon announcing what you will offer. He had 5,000 responses in five months to the ad he placed in the newspaper. For still others, like Jonathan Storm in starting Earthtunes, making the needed connection takes longer. Storm is still seeking avenues for linking what he does to something a sufficient number of people will eagerly pay for, but his connection has been growing stronger every year.

Phase 3: Feeding the Connection. Usually simply making a connection will not be enough to generate the steady income you seek. Up until this phase, what you're doing is a lot like fishing. You cast your net, you connect. But once you connect, it's no longer like fishing because only rarely can you simply reel in nets full of fish. Instead, you actually have to start feeding the connection you've made by investing time, energy, and money in becoming known and trusted by those who need what you're offering, doing a good job for them, getting results for them, and building a reputation for your work.

How long you will need to feed the connection before your career supports you through a life of its own is directly related to the level of effort that will be involved for you to launch the path you've chosen: i.e., how many people are eager and waiting for what you're offering, how closely the work you've chosen matches doing things that come naturally to you instead of your having to acquire new abilities, and how well positioned you are to tap into the needs people have instead of having to build a relationship and reputation from scratch among key contacts and clients. If the career you've chosen falls in the Serendipity quadrant of the Viability Grid, for example, the feeding phase will be shorter than if your choice falls in the Long Haul quadrant.

But even if you start out with a backlog like Oscar Vargas's Piñata Party, you will need to satisfy your clients and build your connection to them so they will want to return to you and you can attract still others. In other words, once you connect, you haven't necessarily got the job. You're on probation, so to speak.

Phase 4: The Quickening. This is the stage we're all seeking. It's the point at which you've invested sufficient energy, time, and money into your connection so that the word is out and begins to spread about what you do. At this point your work will take on a life of its own. It may even grow beyond what you can handle, and you will have to decide whether you simply want to create a good income for yourself or if you want to start employing or contracting out with others to help you respond to the momentum you've created. Many people choose to limit their work to what they personally can do; they're not interested in building a business, having employees and turning over the work to other people

"My desires are like seeds left in the ground; they wait for the right season and then spontaneously manifest into beautiful flowers and mighty trees, into enchanted gardens and majestic forests."

The Vedas

whom they must supervise or oversee. Others are happy to let their enterprise grow beyond themselves in response to the demand they've created.

You can see from this process that to find your perfect work and create a livelihood for yourself from it, you can't simply be looking for a way to make some money. You must have an *outcome* that you're working to achieve *for your clients,* some result they need or desire; when you can achieve that outcome for them consistently, then you can consistently have an *income* for yourself. And at that point, you are no longer looking for work, you are working. You are doing what you do, which includes continuing to feed your connection. If you stop giving, you will stop getting. If you stop initiating and reaching out, if you stop serving and achieving outcomes for your clients or customers, eventually, even if you once achieved a momentum that had a life of its own, that momentum will die and the income will stop coming back to you.

FIRST YOU HAVE AN OUTCOME, THEN YOU HAVE AN INCOME

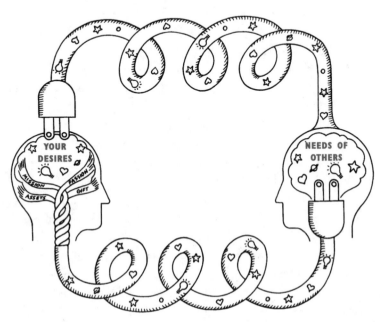

As you continue connecting your unique combination of gifts, passions, missions, and assets in ways that meet the needs of others, the time, energy, and money you invest in serving their needs will begin returning to you a rich array of rewards, both personal and financial, that will enable you to live the life you desire.

The following individuals have made such a connection. They are meeting their own needs by meeting the needs of others. Here's how they did it.

Les Clark was a *bodyguard* for a CEO, but he was *bored* and wanted to do something more interesting, so he drew on his skills as a bodyguard and his *military training* as an *Emergency Medical Technician* to do what he enjoys most, *photography*. He has created a career for himself *accompanying photographers on dangerous, remote shoots.*

While on an African safari vacation, paralegal Deanie Kramer saw herds of wild animals running *free* and realized that she felt like a caged animal on her job. So she quit and drew on her *paralegal training* to meet the needs of *people who can't afford a lawyer*. She processes *legal paperwork* for divorce, separation, guardianships, and other family-law issues and teaches people how to obtain legal services.

While working in a major accounting firm, Luis Barajas realized that he was misapplying his talent and decided to use his *master's degree in business administration* and his credentials as a *registered investment adviser* to teach *barrio residents* and business owners *how to invest* rather than simply make ends meet. He quit his job and opened a *financial consulting* office in the neighborhood where he grew up.

On a lark, Gregg Warren wanted to pursue a *"crazy"idea*. As a *Buddhist*, he believes that one of the best ways to get rid of *worries* is to toss them out the window of an airplane. So he put his *pilot's license* and his *philosophy* to work offering to take over people's worries that they've written out on paper, burn the paper, and *toss the ashes out of an airplane* over the tiny town of Carefree, Arizona. Surprisingly, within months, he'd handled 5,000 such requests at $5 each. His company is *Worry Free*, and he's planning a Worry Free book and Worry Free seminars.

Shortly after Richard Jurmain was laid off from his *engineer-*

ing job, he and his wife were watching a television show about *teenagers learning the responsibilities of being parents* by carrying around a sack of flour as a make-believe baby. His wife had an idea. She said, "Richard, why don't you come up with something that cries?" Richard took up the challenge and the next day set about using his skills in *math, physics, and computer science* to create a simulated crying-baby doll. He created *The Baby Think It Over Doll,* which weighs from seven to ten pounds and has a microprocessor inside its head that automatically causes it to cry loudly every two to four hours twenty-four hours a day. The crying will stop only after the baby has been held for ten to thirty-five minutes. The computer chip records how long the "baby" cried before being picked up and how roughly it was handled. Jurmain sells the dolls, which cost $200 each, to schools, teachers, counselors, and doctors.

Jon Gindick wanted to *write novels and screenplays* and he needed to support himself in the meantime. So he applied his *writing skills* and his *experience writing advertising copy* to his lifelong love, playing the harmonica. In 1977 he spent $2,000 to self-publish a *how-to book* on playing the harmonica. That idea has grown into a six-figure income. Now he sells harmonica-related instructional books, audios, and videotapes through his mail-order catalog Cross Harp Press. Gindick's book, Country and Blues Harmonica for the Musically Hopeless (Klutz Press) comes packaged in a red net with a harmonica. He's made his living from the harmonica for more than ten years now, and he's written two novels and three screenplays along the way. His newest book is Harmonica America. "Just about everything I'm good at I am able to bring to bear in my projects. I found the key for my success: if others won't do it for you, you have to do it yourself, but you have to take the leap."

Insurance broker Chris Clark *loves horses and horse racing.* He's combined his passion with his profession. He is one of a handful of insurance brokers who issue *insurance policies* for *thoroughbred horses* and the only one who conducts his business daily at the racetrack. He writes *equine mortality insurance* for about three hundred owners and workers' compensation for about four hundred trainers.

So, think about your outcome. What results will your efforts produce for those you serve? The clearer and more needed that outcome is, the easier producing a steady, reliable income will be.

THE OUTCOME OF MY WORK

Review the outcomes listed here of others you've met in this and previous chapters and summarize the outcome of your work for the choice(s) you're considering.

OUTCOMES

Teach people to play the harmonica

Protect photographers

Assure art arrives safely

Make trash functional

Heal with music

Help legal nurse consultants get more business

Clean houses safely

Provide annual updates of government resources

Teach kids math via computer

Design kitchens for gourmet cooks

Disperse people's worries

Get multimedia into the courtroom

Help doctors join group practices

Solve computer problems for new computer users

Preserve wedding memories

Make travel abroad hassle-free and fun

Teach kids the realities of parenthood

Design bathing suits that camouflage flaws

Keep law libraries up to date

Help employees better appreciate cultural diversity

Attract more customers for malls

Improve customer service

Capture the music of nature

Restore historic homes

Improve teenagers' self-esteem

Aid ill travelers

Collect court-ordered child support

Recover funds for burned investors

Help clients stand up to the IRS

Teach minority business owners about investing

Complete legal paperwork for divorce and separation

My Outcome: Choice #1 _____

_____

_____

My Outcome: Choice #2 _____

_____

_____

My Outcome: Choice #3 _____

_____

_____

MAKING YOUR FINAL CHOICE AND PACKAGING IT FOR SUCCESS

Once you understand the four phases involved in generating an income from your chosen work, you can see how important your own motivation and investment will be to your ultimate success. When we talk with people who thought they wanted to be self-employed but never pursued doing so, for example, they tell us such things as:

> *"I got pregnant and ended up taking a job."*
> *"I needed the money, so I took a job."*
> *"My spouse got sick, so I just kept my job."*
> *"I got this offer I couldn't refuse and stayed on my job."*

"Has anything ever held someone back from doing what he or *she really* wants to do?"

"As soon as I started talking about doing travel consulting, people started wanting my help. I didn't even have time to get my cards printed."

Obviously if remaining employed is what these people really wanted to do, such conclusions are fine, but usually that's not what has happened. Usually what has happened is that they have yet to find a sufficiently compelling connection between their deepest desires and what others will pay for. So either they're not sufficiently motivated to keep casting, connecting, and feeding the connection long enough for it to develop a life of its own that will support them, or the demand for the products or services they're offering is not strong enough yet to support them. You'll want to make sure the work you choose to do won't lead you to either such dead end.

TESTING FOR VIABILITY

To make a final choice you can feel confident about committing your full energies to, test the choices you're still considering for viability by listing your top three contenders on the following work sheet and rating them on a scale of 1 to 10 for each of the questions regarding the following three criteria:

1. Motivation. How motivated are you to do this?

(Evaluate your answer to each question on a scale of 1 to 10, one being not at all, 10 being very strongly or very much. Then total your score for Motivation.)

___ Do you feel drawn to this activity? If you got busy doing other things, if a crisis developed, would your attention be riveted back on this activity or would you probably let it drop? If you got a great job offer, would you turn it down to do this or would you willingly take the job?

___ When you become successful at this activity, it will consume your days. Will that please you? How much Magic does the thought of doing this hold for you? Check off the words that describe the way this activity makes you feel on the "That Magic Feeling!" list along the side of this page.

___ How compatible is this pursuit with your destination? Review your dream at the conclusion of **Chapter 2, "The Destination."** How directly does this activity take you there? Is it a straight line? A detour? A long and winding road?

___ **Total Your Score for Motivation**

2. Demand. How much in demand is what you're thinking of offering?

(Evaluate your answer to each question on a scale of 1 to 10—10 being high; 1 being low. Then total your score for Demand.)

___ Are there people asking for what you intend to offer?
___ Do you already know these people?
___ Do they know you?
___ When you tell people who need what you will offer about it, are they eager to get involved?
___ Do they immediately understand what you're offering and seem interested and excited to know more about it?
___ Are you comfortable explaining what you're offering?
___ Can you describe it simply and clearly?
___ **Total Your Score for Demand**

3. Ease. How naturally will pursuing this come to you?

(Evaluate your answer to each question on a scale of 1 to 10 and total your score for Ease.)

___ Does it draw upon your gifts, talents, and skills? Can you do it well?
___ Does it suit your personality? Are you at ease doing what's involved?
___ Does doing it feed your self-esteem?
___ Does it feed your confidence?
___ **Total Your Score for Ease**

That Magic Feeling!

The following words are often used to describe the magic feeling your work should provide. Check off how the work you're considering makes you feel. The more the better.

Amped
Charmed
Charged
Delighted
Driven
Electric
Dynamic
Exhilarated
Fired up
Flowing
Glowing
In harmony
Hot
Irresistible
Joyful
Magnetic
On fire
Peaceful
Pulsating
Pumped
Sizzling
Wondrous
Whole
Zapped

Unless you're up for a Long Haul, you will want to choose work that scores as high as possible in the upper-right-hand quadrant of the Viability Grid, as shown here:

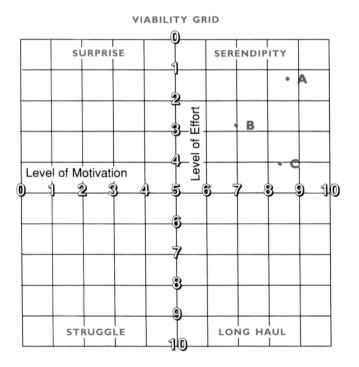

VIABILITY GRID

For example, Oscar Vargas's Piñata Party (A) scores very high in the upper-right-hand corner both because he is highly motivated and because there is an ample existing demand. Gregg Warren's Worry Free scores (B) almost as high, but he had to cast forth through advertising to find out just what the demand was. Marcy Hamm (C) also scores in the upper-right-hand corner, because while she had to work at building demand for her healing music, her motivation is high and her personal gifts, passion, and mission so closely match her work.

To plot your Level of Motivation for each option you're considering, divide the Motivation Total by (3) three. To plot the Level of Effort, add your scores for Demand and Ease and use the chart to the right of the Viability Grid to find your level of effort. Place a mark where the two scores intersect, as illustrated above, for each of the options you're still considering and compare the results. If your top contender isn't in the top quadrants, you may want to consider repackaging your options until you find one that scores as high as possible in the Serendipity quadrant.

VIABILITY GRID

FINDING YOUR LEVEL OF EFFORT

Total Points for Demand and Ease	Level of Effort
101–110	0
91–100	1
81–90	2
71–80	3
61–70	4
51–60	5
41–50	6
31–40	7
21–30	8
11–20	9
10	10

Plot your top three choices on this grid.

Repackaging and Multipackaging

If you haven't found an activity that places you squarely in the Serendipity quadrant of the Viability Grid, there is a wealth of ways you can repackage what you'd like to do to make it more viable. For example, Susan Palowski wanted to start a calendar service that would enable clients like the media, meeting planners, and charitable organizations to know about the scheduled upcoming events in the Boston area. She knew there was a need for such a service, because so many people require this information to make planning and scheduling decisions. So she began trying to provide a printed monthly calendar of events to her clients. Unfortunately, sending the material out in a printed calendar was too expensive to be viable, and her business was about to go under when she had the inspiration to repackage it as a fax-back service.

As pressXpress, she now offers what she calls "Boston's most complete event resource by fax." Individuals, nonprofit companies, businesses, and the media subscribe to her service for a yearly rate. When they first join, they receive her one hundred–page calendar of events in printed form via the mail. Then every week subscribers receive a PXP Weekly Update by fax that reviews the current week's events and announces the new events she's added since the week before, projecting up to a year ahead.

By repackaging her idea from a print product to a fax service, she was able to make the connection she needed. The business clicked in place and is taking on a life of its own. We had a similar experience. When we decided we wanted to provide information, resources, and support to people who wanted to work on their own from home, we planned to offer weekend seminars. But too many people starting out on their own found it difficult to pay for a seminar at the price we needed to charge to make them viable. One of our mentors, consultant Howard Shenson, suggested that a book would be a better medium for our message, and indeed, he was right. We wrote *Working from Home* in 1985 and it's now in its fourth edition, having sold over a quarter of a million copies.

Although we now have six books, making a living on the royalties from one book can be quite a challenge, so we began packaging our information in multiple forms. We started the Working from Home Forum on CompuServe Information Service in 1983 and over half a million messages later, we are able to assist hundreds of self-employed people every day via the Forum. We started our radio show, *Working from Home,* on Business Radio in 1987 and our TV show, *Working from Home with Paul & Sarah Edwards,* began airing on the Home and Garden Cable Network in 1994. Although we give many speeches and seminars on self-employment at conferences and other sponsored events, paid public seminars like the ones we first planned to give are still not the best way to package our information.

We call this process of offering your product or service in various formats *multipackaging.* And you may have noticed that many of the people you've met throughout this book are multipackaging. Sometimes it's necessary for viability, other times it's simply a handy way to expand and grow. You may recall that Susan Loewenberg is multipackaging her radio theater broadcasts in the form of a tape library. Jon Gindick is selling his information on how to play a harmonica in books and on audiotapes and videotapes. Gregg Warren plans to expand Worry Free into a book and seminar. In addition to treating her own patients, Linda Fellington-Jones is teaching her TTouch method of doing body work with animals to others through books, videos, and audios. As AgAccess, David Katz and Karen Van Epen provide information to organic farmers through consulting, catalogs, books, and videotapes. Each medium has its strengths and limitations, and each calls upon us to use different aspects of our personalities. If you have yet to find a viable package for your favorite idea, review the many choices you have for packaging it to achieve your goals and experiment with developing the various avenues best suited to you.

CHOOSING THE BEST WAY TO PACKAGE
WHAT YOU HAVE TO OFFER

MEDIUM	STRENGTHS	LIMITATIONS	RELEVANT PERSONAL STYLES
PROVIDE SERVICES	Generally lower marketing cost	Limit of 1,000-2,000 billable hours a year	All personal styles
DEVELOP A PRODUCT	You control the process and can enjoy the entire profit.	Difficulties of distribution, capital required for inventory and risk	Creator, Leader, Problem Solver, Builder
PROVIDE CONSULTING	Varied work at good to excellent rates	Work can be solitary and you may yearn for control.	Depends on the type of consulting—see Appendix II
PUBLISH A NEWSLETTER	Work can be done anywhere with minimal face-to-face contact with people.	Building up circulation and profitability can take time.	Leader, Improver, Builder
WRITE A BOOK	A book builds credibility for consulting, speaking, and other income-producing work. A successful book provides almost passive income.	Writing a good book requires much time and discipline. Few books are commercially successful. Those that are successful often must be continually updated and promoted.	Creator, Improver, Problem Solver, Leader
CONDUCT SEMINARS	Potential earnings can be good for stimulating work that helps people.	More difficult than average product to sell and may require extensive travel	All personal styles
PRODUCE AUDIOTAPES	Easier and less costly to produce than other media and has a high perceived value relative to the cost of production.	Fewer people listens to tapes than read books. Distribution can be a challenge.	Leader, Creator, Improver
PRODUCE VIDEOTAPES	Visual information makes the most powerful communication. Decreasing cost to produce desktop video	Distribution can be a challenge and result in selling the videos yourself using advertising and direct mail.	Leader, Improver, Creator
PRODUCE CD-ROM	Growing market; medium allows for a high level of creative expression	More difficult and expensive to produce than other media	Builder, Organizer, Leader
GET A RADIO OR TV SHOW	Possible to reach large numbers of people	Getting paid to perform is difficult and purchasing "brokered" time is expensive.	Leader, Creator, Improver

MEDIUM	STRENGTHS	LIMITATIONS	RELEVANT PERSONAL STYLES
DEVELOP SELF-STUDY MATERIALS	Adds value to seminars or may be sold separately; can be produced inexpensively using desktop publishing	Effective distribution	Problem Solver, Creator, Improver, Organizer
TEACH OTHER PEOPLE TO DO WHAT YOU DO	Multiplies your impact and ability to profit from your time and work.	Quality of your work may be diluted and people may learn your system and become your competitor	Improver, Leader, Builder
BE AN INFORMATION PROVIDER ON-LINE	Low costs and may produce income in a growing medium	Not as well accepted as other media by the public	Improver, Problem Solver, Leader
SELL BY MAIL ORDER	Highly flexible business not dependent on selling your time	Finding profitable products with effective promotion at the right price is a challenge most people who try mail order don't master	Problem Solver, Leader, Creator, Builder
PROVIDE SERVICE BY PHONE	Personal medium allowing individual attention to people that can be done from anywhere	You must figure out how to get clients; this can require costly advertising	Improver, Leader, Problem Solver
FAX YOUR PRODUCT OR SERVICE	Much lower cost than traditional publishing with most businesses able to receive what you do	Like newsletter publishing, it may take time to build circulation.	Leader, Improver, Creator, Problem Solver
BROKER SERVICES	Needed service appreciated by clients on both ends	Primarily selling by telephone and follow-up contacts	Leader, Improver, Problem Solver, Organizer

MULTIPACKAGING

PROFILE: KEN BROWN, CALLIGRAPHY FOR EVERYONE

Ken Brown is a self-taught professional calligrapher. He first discovered hand lettering in 1961 while a student in architectural design. From an introductory class in Gothic and Roman alphabets grew an instant love that Brown pursued as an all-consuming hobby while working full-time.

But Brown had no idea he could earn a living from calligraphy or that there was a field of professional calligraphers, until people

Ken Brown,
calligrapher

┌─ **WORK SHEET** ─────────────────────────────────┐

EXPLORING OPTIONS FOR PACKAGING YOUR OUTCOME

Consider ideas for how you might accomplish your outcome through one or more of these various media and weigh the viability of each:

Offer your services in person. _____

_____

Develop a product. _____

_____

Consult with others. _____

_____

Write a newsletter. _____

_____

Write a book or series of books. _____

_____

Conduct seminars. _____

_____

Produce audiotapes. _____

_____

Provide videotapes of what you do. _____

_____

Have a radio or television program on what you do. _____

_____

Develop self-study materials. _____

_____

Put what you do on CD-ROM. _____

_____

Teach others to do what you do. _____

_____

Serve others on-line. _____

_____

Sell what you offer by mail order. _____

_____

Provide your service via telephone. _____

_____

Fax your product or service. _____

_____

_____

started asking him to do artwork for them. It was seven years before he had his first client and ten years before he met anyone else who shared his interest. But in 1970 he had sold 8,000 pieces of his reproductions and launched an international business.

He sells his work through a mail-order catalog, at shows, and by commission. He has over fourteen million reproductions of his designs in print. But that is just the beginning. He has built his business by sharing his love of calligraphy in many forms. He has a newsletter for calligraphers called *BrownLines*. He has developed a calligraphy kit with all the necessary supplies, samples, and instructions for getting started in calligraphy. He has a videotape that teaches calligraphy, and he demonstrates the art of calligraphy on his thirteen-week PBS television series *Calligraphy for Everyone*. He has written three books for calligraphy enthusiasts, has developed many products for beginning devotees, and, of course, he conducts workshops and classes all across the country for those who want to learn in person.

And by the way, he got a B– on his writing assignment in his first, and only, class! He's living proof of what he teaches: you can learn calligraphy even if your handwriting is horrible!

We urge you to keep exploring options until you find a viable connection: something you are truly excited about that will provide you with the life you want to lead—something that feels as natural to you as the herd of elephants Deanie Kramer of The Divorce Connection saw running free on the plains of Africa. There are such means for pursuing your dreams. And you owe it to yourself and all those who can benefit from it to find that means. Hopefully it has already become clear to you, but if not, you've done the research and you have structures and criteria to continue exploring until you find what you're looking for.

RESOURCES

BOOKS
Trend Tracking. Gerald Celente with Tom Milton. New York: Warner, 1991.

The Popcorn Report. Faith Popcorn. New York: Doubleday Currency, 1991.

MegaTrends 2000: Ten New Directions for the 1990's. John Naisbitt. New York: Morrow, 1990.

TREND REPORTS

American Demographics. American Demographics, Inc., 127 W. State Street, Ithaca, NY 14850. (607) 273-6343. Monthly magazine. $69/year.

John Naisbitt's Trend Letter. The Global Network, 101 30th St. NW, Suite 130, Washington, DC 20007; (202) 337-5960. Biweekly newsletter. $195/year.

Research Alert. EPM Communications, Inc., 48 East 18th Street, Brooklyn, NY 11226; (718) 469-9330. 24 issues/year newsletter. $345/year.

Beginning the Journey

MOST BOOKS END WITH A CONCLUSION. Not this book. This
book ends with a beginning. You are about to begin your journey.
Having completed the process of envisioning where you want to
go in life and begun exploring and evaluating your choices for the
path that will take you there, you can now look forward to executing your decisions and beginning your journey. And begin is
what you must do. From this day forward, you will need to take
action every day, one or more steps, be they big or small, along the
path you've chosen.

As you proceed down your path, you will not only be creating a new career, you will be creating a new life. You will be building a new foundation for meeting all your basic needs. Your
survival, your security, your social support system, your self-esteem, and your self-fulfillment will all hang in the balance as you
make the transition from the life you've known to the life you're
seeking to create. You may feel tempted at times to turn back, hungry for the familiarity of life as it has been. Do not be fooled by
this sense of insecurity. It doesn't mean you must turn back. It

means you must go on. It means you must find new ways to achieve the security you knew before.

Be happy that you are beginning your journey at a fortuitous time. There is a wealth of resources available to provide you with the information and support you need and an army of fellow so-journers traveling elbow to elbow with you along their own paths. Here are some guidelines for tapping into these resources as you begin to execute your decisions and get under way.

WHERE ARE YOU NOW?

At what point are you in the process of creating your own work? Check off the stages you have completed.

___ **Envisioning.** I know my destination. I know where I want to go.

___ **Exploring.** I've explored my desires and resources and chosen my path.

___ **Evaluating.** I've noticed and weighed the opportunities around me and have found a means for earning a living along my path.

___ **Executing.** I am taking the steps I need to take to get my journey under way.

Begin today talking about what you're doing. Now that you're poised to begin, you must do so. You must take at least the smallest of beginning steps toward your new life. If you don't begin now, if you delay, if you hesitate, you will most likely begin to feel a creeping sense of depression. You will begin to feel drained and weary. But even the smallest action steps will energize you. With each step you take, no matter how small, you will feel your confidence and enthusiasm building and, as you proceed, your path will unfold with increasing clarity.

While few people give much credence to what someone is "going to do someday," as soon as you start talking about a journey you've actually undertaken, even if you're just beginning, you'll be amazed at how people will start coming forward with ideas and suggestions. So don't say, "I'm thinking about, possibly, maybe, do-ing . . ." or "Someday I'm going to . . ." Say, "I want to tell you what I'm doing. I'm . . ." And you'll find that you will start getting a wealth of reactions that hold clues as to what your next steps should be. You must weigh these reactions and suggestions, of course, but many will be helpful and fruitful. Discard those that aren't and follow through on those that could be. In many ways, launching your journey will be like following a trail of clues. Someone may suggest a book, for example. Someone else may provide a name to call. Someone may urge you to take a course or join a particular organization. Each of these suggestions may lead to other new clues. By reading the book, you may pick up an idea to pursue. By calling the name you were given, you may discover an opportunity to present your services to someone who needs them. And so forth.

Start talking and taking action. That's how you'll actually carry out the process of casting forth, connecting, and feeding your ideas and plans.

"None of us can change our yesterdays, but all of us can change our tomorrows."

President Bill Clinton

Read everything you can get your hands on that will provide you with the information you need at each step of the way. Go down to the bookstore or to the library and head for the career and business sections. Look for the books you've seen in the resource lists at the end of each section of this book and in other books you've read. Thumb through these books. Pick up those that seem to provide the information you're seeking in order to take your next steps. Review as many books as you can. Read them all, if need be. If you're not seeing anything helpful to your plans in one source, move on to others that are.

Take courses on becoming self-employed. Many community colleges, trade schools, and adult-education centers offer courses or extended programs on becoming self-employed or starting a business. Such a course may even be available for the particular kind of work you want to do. If not, however, an overview course can be equally useful. Some sources of such courses are listed among the resources at the end of the section.

Ask for help. After you have read and attended courses on getting started, you will be well prepared to start asking for help. Avoid the temptation to start asking for help before you have done the reading and taken the courses that will enable you to ask the right questions of the right people. Generally people are eager and willing to help if you ask them questions they can respond to. For example, you will probably not get a particularly helpful response if you ask a colleague a question like "I want to become a wedding consultant. Where do I start?" You will get a much better response to a question like "I was reading that wedding consulting can be seasonal in nature. Have you found that to be true for you? How have you handled that? I want to create a steady flow of income."

"Ask, and it shall be given you; Seek, and ye shall find; Knock, and it shall be opened unto you."

Matthew 7:7

Professional and trade associations can be excellent sources of information and contacts. *Best Home Businesses for the 90s* lists professional and trade associations for many of the businesses it profiles. Gale's *Encyclopedia of Associations,* which you'll find on the resource list at the end of this chapter, includes information on just about every trade and professional association in existence. National associations may have written materials, such as a newsletter or magazine, that could help you get started in their field. They may have national and regional conferences you can attend and local chapters you can become involved in. It may be worth your while to join the association to get these materials and begin meeting people. However, DO NOT call a national association and ask how you can get started working independently in their field, expecting that they will provide you with all the details. That is not what associations do; they are there to serve their members. So call to find out what services they offer, what their membership requirements are, and how you could join or otherwise take advantage of their services. If they do not have any services open to you, at the very least, you can ask them for the name of one or more contacts in your area with whom you could talk about their field.

Keep following the clues. As you talk, read, attend courses, and ask questions, notice coincidences and opportunities. Notice the people you run into, the people who call you, the ideas you have, the urges you get to call someone, the impulses you have to go to a particular event or do something specific. Each such coincidence, each such impulse could hold the clues to your next step. This is in fact how your path will probably unfold before you. There may not be any blazing breakthrough—no flash of blinding

"Be a light unto yourself."

Buddha

light that will lay it all out for you in minute detail, although that does occasionally happen. It's more likely that you will pick up one clue here, another there. Don't let these seemingly minute opportunities fly by. Grab them and follow up on them immediately. You'll be surprised that as you move forward, one step at a time, even if you can't see clearly very far down the road, as you proceed, a little more of the road ahead of you will come into view.

One thing is for sure, though: If you don't proceed, if you wait for something to happen, nothing will happen. Remember you must cast forth, connect, and feed your ideas and intentions before they will quicken with a life of their own. Think of yourself as riding a bicycle. As long as you stand by looking at the bike or just sit on it, you won't go anywhere. You have to start pedaling and keep pedaling until the momentum of your effort takes over and starts carrying you along under its own power.

Will your journey be easy? It may be. It may be easier than you ever imagined. Will it be difficult? It may be. It may be more difficult than you ever imagined. But if you have chosen your path well, it will be filled with such magic that whatever effort is required will be worth it, because you'll know you're on the road to your dreams. If you must stop for a while, that's okay. Do so. If you must take a detour, that's okay. Do so. But never forget where you're going. And never give up the journey. Along the road that's filled with the magic of your dreams, as long as you continue walking forward in the direction you want to go, anything is possible, anything can happen.

RESOURCES

BOOKS

The Best Home-Based Franchises. Gregory Matusky and The Phillip Lief Group. New York: Doubleday, 1992.

Best Home Businesses for the 90s. Paul and Sarah Edwards. New York: Tarcher/Putnam, 1994.

Bookkeeping on Your Home-Based PC. Linda Stern. Blue Ridge Summit, Pa.: Windcrest/McGraw-Hill, 1993.

Career Shifting. William A. Charland, Jr. Holbrook, Mass.: Bob Adams, Inc., 1993.

The Complete Handbook for the Entrepreneur. Gary Brenner, MBA, JD; Joel Ewan, MBA; and Henry Chuster, Ph.D., CPA. Englewood Cliffs, N.J.: Prentice-Hall, 1990.

The Complete Work-at-Home Companion. Herman Holtz. Rocklin, Calif.: Prima Pub Communications, 1990.

Computer Consulting on Your Home-Based PC. Herman Holtz. Blue Ridge Summit, Pa.: Windcrest/McGraw-Hill, 1994.

Creative Cash: How to Sell Crafts, Needlework, Designs and Know-How. Barbara Brabec. Huntington Beach, Calif.: Aames-Allen Publishing, 1986.

Encyclopedia of Associations. Detroit: Gale Research Company. Published annually.

Government Assistance Almanac: The Guide to All Federal Financial and Other Domestic Programs. J. Robert Dumouchel. Detroit: Omnigraphics. Annual.

Growing a Business. Paul Hawken. New York: Simon & Schuster, 1987.

Health Services Businesses on Your Home-Based PC. Rick Benzel. Blue Ridge Summit, Pa.: Windcrest/McGraw-Hill, 1993.

Home Inc.: The Canadian Home-Based Business Guide. Douglas A. Gray and Diana Lynn. Toronto: McGraw-Hill Ryerson, 1989.

Homemade Business. Donna Partow. Colorado Springs, Co.: Focus on the Family, 1992.

Homemade Money. Barbara Brabec. White Hall, Va.: Betterway Publications, 1994.

Information for Sale. John Everett and Elizabeth P. Crowe. Blue Ridge Summit, Pa.: Windcrest/McGraw-Hill, 1994.

Info-Power II. Matthew Lesko. Detroit: Visible Ink Press, 1994.

Legal and Paralegal Services on Your Home-Based PC. Katherine Sheehy Hussey and Rick Benzel. Blue Ridge Summit, Pa.: Windcrest/McGraw-Hill, 1994.

Mailing List Services on Your Home-Based PC. Linda Rohrbach. Blue Ridge Summit, Pa.: Windcrest/McGraw-Hill, 1994.

Making It on Your Own. Sarah and Paul Edwards. New York: Tarcher/Putnam, 1991.

Making Money with Your Computer at Home. Paul and Sarah Edwards. New York: Tarcher/Putnam, 1993.

Making Money Sharing Your Shareware. Steven C. Hudgik. Blue Ridge Summit, Pa.: Windcrest/McGraw-Hill, 1994.

Operating a Desktop Video Service on Your Home-Based PC. Harvey Summers. Blue Ridge Summit, Pa.: Windcrest/McGraw-Hill, 1994.

Running a One-Person Business. Claude Whitmyer, Salli Rasberry, and Michael Phillips. Berkeley, Calif.: Ten Speed Press, 1989.

Self-Made in America. John McCormack with David R. Legge. Reading, Mass.: Addison-Wesley, 1990.

Succeeding in Business. Jane Applegate. New York: Plume, 1992.

A Whack on the Side of the Head—How to Unlock Your Mind for Innovation. Roger von Oech. New York: Warner, 1988.

Working from Home: **Everything You Need to Know to Live and Work Under the Same Roof.** Paul and Sarah Edwards. New York: Tarcher/Putnam, 1994.

Working Solo. Terri Lonier. New Paltz, N.Y.: Portico Press, 1994.

Working Solo Sourcebook. Terri Lonier. New Paltz, N.Y.: Portico Press, 1995.

PERIODICALS

Entrepreneur. 2392 Morse Ave., Irvine, CA 92714. *Entrepreneur* also periodically publishes Entrepreneur Magazine's Guide to Home-Based Business.

Head Office at Home: The Canadian Magazine for People Who Work at Home. Abasco Communications, Ltd., 145 Royal Crest Court, Unit 2, Markham, ON L3R 924.

Home-Based Business News, 0424 SW Pendleton St., Portland OR 97201.

Home Inc. Home Incorporated, 824 East Baltimore St., Baltimore, MD 21202.

Home Office Computing. Scholastic, Inc., 730 Broadway, New York, NY 10003.

In Business. Magna Publications, Inc., 2718 Dryden Dr., Madison, WI 53704. Focuses on environmentally oriented businesses.

Small Business Opportunities. Harris Publications, 1115 Broadway, New York, NY 10010.

The Whole Work Catalog. The New Careers Center, P.O. Box 2193, Boulder, CO 80306.

COURSES

Hire Yourself and Work from Home. Eight-week course developed by Sarah and Paul Edwards. Home Business Services, 1540 Race, Denver, CO 80206; (303) 320-9675. Offered by licensed colleges in cities across the United States.

The Learning Annex offers evening seminars in five major metropolitan areas on a variety of specific independent careers: Los Angeles (310) 478-6677; New York (212) 570-6500; San Francisco (415) 788-5500; San Diego (619) 544-9700; and Toronto (416) 964-0011.

GOVERNMENT AND COMMUNITY RESOURCES

Small Business Administration. The Small Business Administration offers a variety of services that, although primarily focused on larger small businesses, can also benefit home-based businesses. These include:

Advice and technical assistance through Small Business Centers operated by universities and chambers of commerce, the Service Corps of Retired Executives (SCORE), and Small Business Information Centers in major cities. To contact the Small Business Administration for the locations of these services in your area, look in your telephone directory under U.S. Government for your local SBA office or call the Small Business Answer Desk at (800) 8-ASK-SBA ([800] 827-5722).

Publications. To determine current publications and prices, write for order forms 115A and 115B, Small Business Administration, P.O. Box 15434, Ft. Worth, TX 76119.

Microloans processed by local nonprofit organizations.

SBA Online is available using your modem by phoning (800) 859-INFO for 2400 baud access; (800) 697-INFO for 9600. Some parts of this service are free, some are not.

Department of Defense. The Department of Defense has a Small Business Innovation Grant program. To get information, call the Defense Technical Information Center at (800) 225-3842.

Internal Revenue Service. New Business Tax Kit. Available in local IRS offices or phone (800) 424-3676 for further information.

State and Local Sources. Most parts of the United States and Canada provide some assistance to small business. These include:

State and provincial economic development agencies

Local Colleges

Public Libraries

Chambers of Commerce

RADIO AND TELEVISION

Working from Home with Paul and Sarah Edwards. On the Home and Garden Cable Network and with a satellite dish on Galaxy 1; Transponder 20.

Working from Home Show. Hosted by Paul and Sarah Edwards (Sundays at 10 P.M. Eastern, 7 P.M. Pacific time) on Business Radio and with a satellite dish on Digital: Satcom C-5, Transponder 15 and Analog: Satcom C-5, Transponder 3.

SOFTWARE

B-Tools. Star Software Systems, 363 Van Ness Way, Torrance, CA 90501; (310) 533-1190.

BizPlan Builder, Jian Tools for Sales, Inc. 127 Second Street, Los Altos, CA 94022; (800) 346-5426; (415) 941-9191.

IdeaFisher. Idea Fisher System, Inc., 2222 Martin Street, Ste. 110, Irvine, CA 92715; (800)289-4332, (714)474-8111.

Success, Inc. Dynamic Pathways, 180 Newport Center Drive, Ste. 180, Newport Beach, CA 92660; (714) 720-8462.

Tim Berry's Business Plan Toolkit. Palo Alto Software, Inc., 144 E. 14th Street, Eugene, OR 94301; (800)229-7526, (503)683-6162.

MARKETING TOOLS

The Business Generator. Here's How, P.O. Box 5091 Santa Monica, CA 90409. Includes Paul and Sarah Edwards's book **Getting Business to Come to You,** a seventy-five-minute videotape *Top of the Mind Marketing,* and *The Marketing Partner,* a sixty-four-page workbook and guide for developing and following through on marketing that comes naturally for you and the type of work you've chosen to do.

OnLine Services. The Working from Home Forum, CompuServe Information Service. On-line address: GO WORK. Twenty-four-hour support, bulletin boards, libraries, special-interest groups, and a quarterly newsletter. HOC Online, America Online and Microsoft Network. Keyword: GO HOC. WorldWide Web Online address: WWW. homeworks.com.

NATIONAL HOME BUSINESS ASSOCIATIONS

American Association of Home-Based Businesses
P.O. Box 10023
Rockville, MD 20849.

Home Office Association of America
909 Third Avenue, Suite 990
New York, NY 10022.
(212) 980-4622

Independent Business Alliance
111 John Street, Suite 2320
New York, NY 10038.
(212) 513-1446

National Home Office Association
1828 L Street, NW, Ste. 402
Washington, DC 20036.
(800) 664-6462

Small Office Home Office Association
1767 Business Center Drive
Reston, VA 22090.
(703) 438-3060

Personal Style Survey
Doing What Comes Naturally

YOU DON'T HAVE TO BE a classic "entrepreneurial type" to succeed in a career as a self-employed individual. One out of five of those who are successfully self-employed will go on to employ others, some becoming large corporations like Microsoft and Apple Computer, but most self-employed people continue to do what they love to do and do it themselves without hiring a staff. Either way, we've found that the most successful self-employed individuals do things that come naturally to them that they enjoy doing.

This Appendix used in conjunction with the directories of self-employment careers that follow in Appendices II and III will enable you to identify the kind of independent work you can do most comfortably and naturally. Using these Appendices will be particularly useful if you are having trouble deciding what type of independent work you want to do, because you don't see any options, you see too many options, or you are having a hard time deciding among seemingly equal options. It's also useful in helping to identify ideas for work you could do to pursue profitably your gifts, passions, mission, and assets.

Finding those things that come most naturally to you is a three-step process: you'll begin by discovering your natural style, then you'll identify career choices open to you, and finally you'll narrow your choices down so you can make the most natural choice.

STEP ONE: DISCOVERING YOUR NATURAL STYLE

Just as for many decades nearly everyone was expected to find a job, today most of us may need to figure out how we could support ourselves on our own if need be. Fortunately, we have seen ample proof that there are self-employment careers to match virtually anyone's personal style. By discovering the activities that come most naturally to you, you can match what you're best suited to do with what various self-employment careers call for. And to help you do this, we've worked with psychologist Dr. Jessica Schairer to develop a survey that will enable you to identify your personal style.

Dr. Schairer specializes in the psychological issues of self-employment and has worked and studied with the eminent vocational counselor John Crystal, whose pioneering ideas underlie the work of Richard Bolles, author of *What Color Is Your Parachute?* Working with Dr. Schairer, we've been able to build upon this rich history and create a new tool specifically designed for exploring self-employment opportunities.

To find your personal style, start by taking the Doing What Comes Naturally survey that follows. Rank the choices under each statement on the survey in order of your preference with six (6) being the most descriptive of your preferences and one (1) being the least descriptive of your preferences. *Remember, pick the aspect you like best and would most enjoy doing as number six (6).*

RATE EACH SET OF ANSWERS FROM 1 TO 6 LIKE THIS:
   6: I like this option the best.
   5: I like this option a lot.
   4: This option is okay.
   3: I like this option somewhat.
   2: I like this option very little.
   1: I like this option the least.

As you rank the options, focus on what you most enjoy and what you do best. You may be surprised by your answers. On this survey, take Joseph Campbell's advice: "Follow your bliss." It's very important to pick a self-employment career that you can really enjoy doing, because to succeed you're going to have to spend a lot of time at it—and you'll be much more likely to do what it takes if you experience it as fun!

Remember, the best type of work for you on your own will be that which builds your self-esteem, feeds your confidence, keeps you motivated, suits your temperament, calls upon your talents and skills, provides you with enjoyment, holds your interest, and energizes and fulfills you. This survey is designed to help you identify which self-employment careers might do these things for you.

Sample: 1. I Feel Best About Myself When:

<u>1.</u> ■: I'm challenging my physical abilities.
<u>6.</u> ●: I know that someone appreciates what I've created.
<u>5.</u> ◆: I'm figuring out what needs to be done.
<u>3.</u> ▲: I'm mobilizing people and activities to achieve a goal.
<u>4.</u> ♥: I know that what I'm doing is improving the lives of others.
<u>2.</u> ✳: I get things operating smoothly and accurately.
This person likes "●" best and "■" least.

START YOUR SURVEY HERE

Remember, give the statement that describes what you like to do best a 6, the next best a 5, down to a 1 for the statement that describe what you like to do least.

1. I Feel Best About Myself When:

<u>1</u> ■: I'm challenging my physical abilities.
<u>6</u> ●: I know that someone appreciates what I've created.
<u>5</u> ◆: I'm figuring out what needs to be done.
<u>2</u> ▲: I'm mobilizing people and activities to achieve a goal.
<u>3</u> ♥: I know that what I'm doing is improving the lives of others.
<u>4</u> ✳: I get things operating smoothly and accurately.

2. I Grow More Confident When I:

<u>5</u> ▲: Overcome obstacles.
<u>3</u> ◆: Make sense out of analyzing and investigating complexities.
<u>4</u> ♥: Put others at ease and let them know that I understand their situation.
<u>2</u> ✳: Know that others find what I do invaluable.
<u>6</u> ●: Can see my ideas and concepts actually taking form.
<u>1</u> ■: Get things to work properly.

3. I Am Nearly Always Eager To:

<u>4</u> ●: Create something new.
<u>3</u> ✳: Get things in order.
<u>6</u> ▲: Take charge.
<u>1</u> ■: Roll up my sleeves, dig in, and get something done.

_5_ ◆: Solve a problem.

_2_ ♥: Help out.

4. I FEEL MOST AT EASE AND NATURAL:

_4_ ♥: Sitting and talking intimately with others.

_6_ ▲: On center stage, in the spotlight, in front of a crowd.

_2_ ◆: Working quietly with information and facts in my study.

_5_ ●: Working on my own with materials or ideas.

_3_ ✳: Completing projects accurately as specified.

_1_ ■: Out of doors or in a workshop working with plants, animals, or my hands.

5. I CONSIDER MYSELF:

_3_ ◆: Intelligent and informed.

_1_ ■: Practical and down-to-earth.

_2_ ●: Imaginative, creative, and innovative.

_5_ ♥: Kind and supportive.

_4_ ✳: Conscientious and reliable.

_6_ ▲: Ambitious and competitive.

6. I MOST ENJOY:

_2_ ✳: Following through on what needs to be done.

_5_ ●: Exploring new possibilities and creating new realities.

_6_ ▲: Leading the way.

_1_ ■: Working with machines and tools.

_3_ ◆: Finding the answers.

_4_ ♥: Teaching, informing, and transforming.

7. I GET SO INVOLVED THAT TIME JUST FLIES BY WHEN I'M:

_1_ ■: Fixing, building, planting, repairing, or tinkering.

_2_ ✳: Computing, calculating, working with numbers and figures, sorting and arranging.

_5_ ▲: Performing, directing, persuading, or pursuing a goal.

_4_ ◆: Gathering and analyzing information and data.

_6_ ●: Fantasizing, creating, imagining, and exploring ideas and possibilities.

_3_ ♥: Interacting with other people to make things better.

8. I FEEL MOST ALERT AND ENERGIZED WHEN:

_6_ ▲: I'm on the spot and under pressure.

_5_ ◆: Faced with a seemingly impossible problem.

<u>3</u> ♥: When someone needs me to help him or her through a crisis.
<u>1</u> ✳: There's a mess that needs straightening out or correcting.
<u>4</u> ●: A new idea or concept pops into my mind.
<u>2</u> ■: I can see things taking shape.

WHAT'S YOUR STYLE?
Total your scores for each symbol:

<u>9</u> ■: Builder   <u>21</u> ✳: Organizer   – <u>42</u> ▲: Leader
<u>28</u> ◆: Problem Solver – <u>38</u> ●: Creator   <u>28</u> ♥: Improver

Circle your three highest scores and enter the three highest styles here, highest score first:

Leader   _Creator_   _____

This is your personal style. Now that you've scored your survey, read about your top three personal styles on the following pages to help identify the kind of work that comes naturally to you.

BUILDER

You have mechanical and athletic skills. You prefer to work with tools, objects, machines, plants, and animals. Outdoor environments give you special pleasure.

You are a hands-on person and take great pride in doing your work well. You've got good coordination, in sports and at work. You learn best through action: by moving around and handling things. You can look at a diagram or blueprint of a project and easily understand how it will look when it's built in three-dimensional space.

You are more interested in doing what you do than you are in talking about it or in relating to your customers or clients. You prefer action to introspection. Primarily you want to get your work done well and show results.

Strengths. People tend to perceive you as trained and possessing skills that make your products or services worth paying for. People like your naturalness and common sense. You are practical, good at mechanical and technical skills and, as a result, one of your greatest assets can be building a reputation for a job well done.

Your creativity often lies in your ability to invent practical solutions to technical problems. Freedom, self-control, and self-determination are among your highest values. You look for a business that lets you be your own boss.

Weaknesses. You may be quiet and reserved, so for your business to thrive, you must pay attention to making sure your work is noticed. You may fade into the woodwork, but you must make sure your products and services aren't overlooked. You can also be hardheaded and dogmatic at times, so you need to remember to listen and account for the needs and desires of your customers and clients and patiently show them how your way will work for them.

Businesses Suited to Your Personal Style. Self-employed Builders often work as contractors in construction trades, engineers, architects, repairers, makers of handcrafted items, farmers, gardeners, and landscapers. You'll find many other businesses suited to Builders in **Appendix III**. It's best, however, to focus on the Builder careers that also use two of your other high-scoring personal styles.

ORGANIZER

You like to work with data, numbers, files, and details and to follow through on instructions. You have a memory for details. You may find you have an affinity for working with computers. You're in your natural element using word processors and spreadsheets.

You are a precise, dependable, and accurate worker. You take great pride in doing a thorough job. You are good at following through on what your clients direct you to do, and you are most comfortable when they tell you specifically what they want and need done. You are at your best organizing information, data, and things. You enjoy bringing order out of chaos.

Your greatest area of interest and expertise is often the business of business: personal financial and business management. You value productivity, economic success, and financial security for yourself, your business, and your clients.

Strengths. You're invested in making sure your work comes out right, so people tend to view you as a dependable, hard worker who produces a lot. You are neat, practical, courteous, and polite. Your cautious and conservative approach is reassuring. People like your loyalty and reliability. As a result, satisfied customers see your contribution as invaluable and well worth the price.

Weaknesses. You're not particularly imaginative and innovative, and you don't like the unpredictable. You can also be "penny-wise, but pound-foolish." So it's important for you to proceed ahead toward your goals. Initiate what you consider to be the best risks after analyzing the cost-benefit ratios involved. Avoid getting bound up in "analysis paralysis" about if and what to do. Take deliberate action.

Businesses Suited to Your Personal Style. Self-employed Organizers often work as computer programmers, bookkeepers, medical billers, transcribers, proofreaders, professional organizers, and red-tape wranglers. You'll find many other businesses suited to Organizers in Appendix III. It's best, however, to focus on the Organizer careers that also use two of your other high-scoring personal styles.

LEADER

You like to work with groups of people, influencing, persuading, performing, leading, and managing. You enjoy interacting with other people.

You are a goal-driven self-starter. You have a strong sense of what needs to be done, and you are ready to do it. You're eager for the chance to convince and persuade others. You like the challenge of running your own business, calling the shots, and coordinating everything to achieve the goals at hand.

Strengths. Temperamentally, you fit the profile of the classic entrepreneur. You're energetic, gregarious, enthusiastic, self-confident, ambitious, and a communicator. Freedom to achieve your ambitions is important to you. You are self-reliant and have a take-charge attitude. People perceive you as a dynamic leader and look to you for direction. You are a strong competitor and enjoy leading your team to victory.

Your greatest creativity often lies in your ability to influence others in business or public affairs. You may find you love the business of business and easily develop an expertise in sales, marketing, and finance.

Weaknesses. You may overlook others' feelings in your pursuit of objective results. Some people may be intimidated by your drive and perceive you as pushy, domineering, and overly competitive. As a result, you may feel unappreciated and "lonely at the top." Taking time to listen and stand in others' shoes will make you even more effective as a leader. Otherwise, you may become too involved in the pleasure of amassing money and power for their own sake and lose sight of why you wanted them in the first place.

Businesses Suited to Your Personal Style. Self-employed Leaders often work as lawyers, entertainers, real estate brokers, investment bankers, public-relations specialists, corporate trainers, management consultants, family day-care providers, newsletter publishers, television and film producers and directors, tour operators, urban planners, pilots, and private investigators. You'll find many other businesses suited to Leaders in Appendix III. It's best, however, to focus on the Leader careers that also use two of your other high-scoring personal styles.

IMPROVER

You like to work with people, usually one-on-one, teaching, informing, enlightening, healing, helping, and developing.

You're a natural with people, warm and sociable. You love to help others change and grow. You're friendly, sincere, generous, and devoted. You're eager to reach out and be of service.

Strengths. People tend to feel comfortable and at ease with you immediately.

They perceive you as understanding, caring, patient, capable, and influential. They trust you and appreciate your communication skills. People perceive you as a good leader, with a collaborative rather than a competitive style.

You may be surprised to find you can develop an effective "soft-sell" sales style to communicate who you are and what you do to potential clients and customers.

Your greatest creativity often lies in your interpersonal assessment and problem-solving skills. You express your highest values when you are helping others in difficulty or contributing to human welfare in some way.

Weaknesses. Your desire to serve and help others may cause you to overwork and undercharge. You may be tempted to give away many of your services. You must be sure to appreciate your value and charge what you're worth. Not wanting to impose, you may wait for people to contact you instead of taking the initiative in helping them decide to use your services. This may lead to you feel unappreciated and frustrated that you are unable to reach many of those you are capable of helping.

Businesses Suited to Your Personal Style. Self-employed Improvers often work as teachers, physicians, nurses, psychotherapists, desktop publishers, child care providers, historians, mediators, and political campaign managers. You'll find many other businesses suited to Improvers in Appendix III. It's best, however, to focus on the Improver careers that also use two of your other high-scoring personal styles.

CREATOR

You are artistic, innovative, intuitive, unstructured, imaginative, and creative.

You are artistic and creative in your work. You like doing what you do in an imaginative, original way. You become so involved in creating your work that it's easy to forget the business side of business: marketing, selling, and keeping track of finances.

You like to work independently, letting inspiration flow, and then you enjoy watching the reactions and pleasure your work brings others once you're finished.

Strengths. You have a courageous, expressive, energetic spirit. People perceive you as talented and interesting. You're idealistic, imaginative, verbal, witty, and never dull or close minded. You think big and are one-of-a-kind, so your work stands out in a crowd and is not easily forgotten. Your originality gives you an advantage in creating a unique niche for your business.

You may have special gifts in music and art, or a flair for writing or foreign languages. You may find it easy to visualize things three-dimensionally and enjoy designing craftwork or models.

You are independent, strong willed, and self-directed. Others may perceive you marching to the beat of a different drum as you create your own style of dress, behavior, and general attitude, but your deep sense of self-confidence carries you forward. You know your own mind and inner feelings, and you act accordingly.

Weaknesses. You tend to be introverted. Sometimes it's hard for you to draw attention to yourself. You prefer that your creations get the attention, and it's important to make sure they do.

You also become easily bored and restless, so it's important for you to structure your business so that there's a balance between new and interesting activities and following up on those you've begun.

You may appear disorganized or temperamental. Therefore, you need to cultivate a serious business image while maintaining your freedom and flexibility.

Businesses Suited to Your Personal Style. Self-employed Creators often work as architects, artists, entertainers, actors, writers, dancers, graphic designers, makeup artists, model makers, musicians and composers, photographers, puppeteers, journalists, dance therapists, play therapists, TV camera operators, and film editors.

Creators are most likely to choose a career based on their passion—their love for their art or some form of creative expression. You'll find many other businesses suited to Creators in Appendix III. It's best, however, to focus on the Creator careers that also use two of your other high-scoring personal styles.

PROBLEM SOLVER

You like to observe, learn, investigate, analyze, evaluate, and solve problems. You like to explore patterns, categories, and relationships. You easily group and order data and then like to analyze, interpret, and make predictions. You enjoy puzzles and playing to win games of strategy. You like using computers.

Your greatest areas of interest and expertise are often in math and science. Usually you intuitively understand how mechanical things work. If you don't, you are naturally drawn to doing the research and experimentation necessary to find out what you didn't know.

You are inventive and highly motivated to make theoretical or technical contributions to your field.

You take a scientific approach to your work. In your business, your goal is to investigate your clients' needs, gather and analyze as much information as possible, research the facts, and bring back a perfect, customized solution.

Strengths. You research your work thoroughly and logically and have an inquisitive and open mind. People respect your intelligence and analytical approach. Sometimes you're considered brilliant.

You're ambitious and your commitment to getting to the bottom of a problem makes you a valued resource. Your expertise is definitely a public-relations asset.

Weaknesses. Sometimes it's difficult for you to communicate in ways that are simple enough for others who know less about your work to understand. What you say about your work may be too complex and complicated, overly detailed and technical. So you will want to learn to describe the benefits your problem-solving approach provides in a clear and simple way.

Businesses Suited to Your Personal Style. Self-employed Problem Solvers often work as engineers, inventors, surgeons, chiropractors, pediatricians, psychiatrists, educational therapists, ethnographers, art critics, horticulturists, pilots, specialty management consultants, statisticians, stock market analysts, taxi drivers, videographers, and technical writers.

You'll find many other businesses suited to Problem Solvers in **Appendix III**. It's best, however, to focus on the Problem Solver careers that also use two of your other high-scoring personal styles.

STEP TWO: IDENTIFYING YOUR NATURAL CHOICES

Now that you're familiar with your top three natural styles, look at the "Directory of Self-Employment Careers" in **Appendix III** (p. 419) to identify various careers that other people are pursuing independently that best suit your style. Use a pen or Magic Marker to highlight all the businesses that utilize your three top-scoring styles in order.

If, at this point, you don't feel you have generated enough options, reverse the order of your second- and third-ranked styles. Some personality styles are more unique and, as a result, lend themselves to fewer self-employment career choices. For example, if you are an Improver/Organizer/Builder, you will not find any options listed, so just turn to the careers listed under Improver/Builder/Organizer. If you want to consider still other options, look for the careers that use your second-highest score, followed by your first and third scores in any combination. Highlight these choices in a different color. If your third and fourth style scores are within three points of each other, you can consider careers that use your fourth personal style as well.

You will probably be surprised at how many independent careers you're suited for. It could be a dozen or over a hundred. Many will probably have no appeal to you, so now that you've highlighted all the options you want to consider, it's time to make your first cut. After skimming through the lists, record any career that you would like to explore further on the Self-Employment Careers to Explore work sheet on pages 344 and 345.

Once you've identified the careers you would like to explore further, look them up in **Appendix II, "An Alphabetical Directory of Self-Employment Careers,"** where you will find more information about whether these careers match your desires, resources, and circumstances. There you will find such things, for example, as whether they require an advanced degree or license, whether they can be done from home, whether they involve a significant capital investment, and whether they are family friendly. After reviewing this information, you may wish to eliminate certain choices. You may also want to read the Profiles that follow to see how others have done this to find their perfect work.

If you do not know what a particular career is, **Appendix II** will also tell you whether you can read more about it in *Best Home Businesses for the 90s* or *Making Money with Your Computer at Home*. You may be surprised to find out what some of these careers actually involve! You may find that you would really enjoy being an event planner, for example, but until you read about it, you didn't know there was such a career.

When you have identified several careers you'd like to consider further, transfer them to the appropriate work sheets in **Part II, "The Path."**

PROFILES: IDENTIFYING YOUR NATURAL CHOICES

PROFILES: PETE, PROBLEM SOLVER/BUILDER/LEADER

Pete, a forty-two-year-old mechanical engineer, was laid off six months ago by the aerospace firm he had worked for since he graduated from college twenty years ago. He has been unable to find a job commensurate with his experience and skills, so he's seriously considering becoming his own boss. At the aerospace firm, he supervised a team of five engineers. He has extensive experience using and programming computers. So he's been thinking about doing something similar to what he'd been doing. After reading chapters 2 through 6, however, he's not so sure.

He's always been an audio buff and an ardent Sierra Club member. Since college, he's spent his vacations wilderness hiking and rock climbing with his family, bringing back breathtaking photos. If possible he'd like to do some kind of work that ties in these interests. Right now his son is a sophomore in college, and his daughter is in high-school. So a few years from now, after his daughter gets in college, he and his wife would actually like to relocate to an area nearer the wilderness he and his family love, where his wife can still teach.

So with these goals in mind, he discovers his personal style is Problem Solver/Builder/Leader and, looking at the "Directory of Self-Employment Careers by Personal Style" in **Appendix III** under Problem Solver/Builder/Leader, he finds approximately sixty self-employment possibilities.

SELF-EMPLOYMENT CAREERS TO EXPLORE WORK SHEET

GROUP ONE:
CAREERS OF INTEREST THAT MATCH YOUR THREE TOP STYLES IN RANK ORDER

I was trying very hard not to be what I most wanted to be, which is a pretty limiting way to live.

Michael Douglas,
actor

1. _____

2. _____

3. _____

_____   _____

I'm not the tie-wearing type. I like to be outside on the roof in the wind. Anything that can break, I can fix. Everything's hands-on, it's almost like I'm an artist when I apply my craft.

Roof vent
installer

_____   _____

_____   _____

_____   _____

GROUP TWO (OPTIONAL):
CAREERS OF INTEREST THAT MATCH YOUR SECOND HIGHEST STYLE FOLLOWED BY YOUR OTHER TWO TOP STYLES

My God-given gift is to organize people and lead.

Community
organizer

2. _____

1. _____

3. _____

If we did all the things we are capable of, we would astound ourselves.

Thomas Edison

_____   _____

_____   _____

_____   _____

GROUP THREE (OPTIONAL):
CAREERS THAT MATCH YOUR THIRD HIGHEST STYLE
FOLLOWED BY YOUR OTHER TOP STYLES

3. _____

1. _____

2. _____

_____   _____

_____   _____

_____   _____

_____   _____

To be nobody but yourself in a world which is doing its best, day and night, to make you like everybody else is to fight the hardest battle which any human being can fight....but never give up fighting.

e. e. cummings

An oak tree is a nut that stood its ground.

GROUP FOUR (OPTIONAL):
CAREERS THAT MATCH YOUR FIRST HIGHEST SCORING
STYLE FOLLOWED BY YOUR SECOND AND FOURTH
HIGHEST STYLES

1. _____

2. _____

4. _____

_____   _____

_____   _____

_____   _____

I don't believe in circumstance. The people who get on in this world are people who look for the circumstances they want, and if they don't find them, they make them.

George Bernard Shaw

Skimming the list, his eye jumps to the obvious things he's been thinking about: *technical writing, computer consulting,* and *management consulting.* All these draw on his past experience doing computer consulting and technical writing as part of his previous job. But they don't tap into the other things he's interested in. Other careers like running a *mailing list service* or doing *data backup* or *conversion* he can quickly eliminate because, although they fit his Personal Style Profile, he doesn't find them to be sufficiently challenging to be interesting to him. There are a number of possibilities, though, that do sound intriguing enough to explore further. He is especially interested in combining his technical skills and his passion for the outdoors, but he feels he needs to consider indoor options, too. So his first-cut list looks like this:

FIRST-CUT CAREERS

- Scientific computer programming
- Expert brokering
- Information brokering
- Database marketing services
- Environmental services

- Forest service trail contractor
- Pilot
- Audio/video engineering and production
- Drafting service
- Engineering

- Indoor environmental tester
- Environmental planner
- Scientific software developer
- Energy management consultant

He's not familiar with what database marketing is and doesn't know just what an indoor environmental tester does, so he decides to find out more about them by turning to **Appendix II.** There he discovers both these businesses appear in *Best Home Businesses for the 90s* or *Making Money with Your Computer at Home,* so he decides to read more about them. He determines that database marketing could be done from a remote location but doesn't involve his passions for the outdoors, so he scratches it off along with drafting services, scientific computer programming, and information brokering as being too confining. He transfers the rest to his list of possibilities in **Chapter 4, "Pursuing a Passion."**

BEN, BUILDER/ORGANIZER/PROBLEM SOLVER

Ben is a twenty-three-year-old unemployed single man living with his mother and his dog. He loves surfing and racing his motorcycle. After dropping out of high school, he worked on construction crews as a day laborer until he enlisted in the Army, where he was trained as a tank driver. He left the service with an honorable discharge after serving four years. Since returning home, he found the construction industry too slow to work regularly as a day laborer. At his mother's urging to "just get a regular job, any job," he went to work at McDonald's. The crowds of people made him uncomfortable, however, so he quit. That's when he started to wonder if there was some way he could be his own boss like several construction workers he knows.

After reading **Chapter 2**, he realized that he has several specific goals: he doesn't want to be cooped up in an office somewhere; he really wants to work outdoors with his hands; and he wants to be able to take his dog with him to work. Equally important, though, is earning enough money on a steady basis to get his own place and buy a pickup truck, which he probably couldn't do if he waited around for day work. So with these goals in mind, he discovers his personal style is Builder/Problem Solver/Organizer, and looks in **Appendix III**, where he finds only eight self-employed careers that fit his profile:

- Auto battery reconditioning service
- Construction cost estimator
- Construction inspector
- Garage door service
- Home inspector
- Laser technician
- Sign maker
- Solar energy systems designer

To increase his choices, he looks at opportunities that use his skills in a different order: Builder/Organizer/Problem Solver. This yields an additional twenty-four options to consider:

- Construction contractor, home renovation
- Drafting service
- Electrocardiograph technician
- Electroplating service
- Home security systems installation
- Swimming pool installer
- Inventory control services for businesses
- Inventory household effects
- Pattern maker
- Photo search service
- Plant care
- Furniture restorer
- Garden care
- Garden care, rototilling service
- Heavy equipment owner and operator
- Plant caregiver
- Postmark service
- Rare recordings and videos search service
- Security systems installer
- Telephone repair service
- Van and R.V. customizing
- Video data service
- Video clipping service

Ben is amazed that there were so many things on this initial list that he can do! Some of them, like the things that have to do with video, are of no interest to him at all. After crossing out everything he didn't like, his first-cut list looks like this:

FIRST-CUT CAREERS

- Auto battery reconditioning service
- Garage door service
- Construction contractor, home renovation
- Electrocardiograph technician
- Garden care
- Garden care, rototilling service
- Heavy equipment owner and operator
- Home security systems installation
- Plant caregiver
- Security systems installer
- Telephone repair service
- Van and R.V. customizing
- Furniture restorer
- Swimming pool installer

Looking over this list, though, raises some questions Ben needed to explore further:

- Does he know anyone who is doing any of these things? He talked to his friends in the construction trades. They knew some telephone installers and pool installers. He talked to them, too, to find out how business was, how they got started in the business, and how they like it.
- Could he use his veteran's benefits to get training in any of the areas that interested him? He called the Veterans' Administration to find out.
- What about motorcycle customizing? It wasn't on the list, but he knew a guy who was doing it. He called him to find out if he was earning a decent living.
- What was an electrocardiograph technician? Did you have to have a high-school degree? A college degree? He checked that in **Appendix II** and found he would need a degree and a license. Ben said, "No, thanks!"
- Garage door service? What was that about? He put in his mom's garage door opener. No big deal. He called some garage door services listed in the yellow pages and found out a lot of people don't have a clue about how to install garage doors or openers.
- Heavy equipment operator? Sounded great, but how could he afford to buy, or even rent, equipment? He would have to work for someone else.

So he narrows his list down appropriately and transfers it to the list of possibilities in **Chapter 7, "Capitalizing on Your Assets."**

CAROL, CREATOR/LEADER/IMPROVER

Carol is a single thirty-year-old woman. She feels dissatisfied with her job as an account executive for a Fortune-500 personal products manufacturer, even though she is doing well there. Customers and colleagues often comment on how her comprehensive and highly effective sales presentations are also humorous and entertaining. She, however, is increasingly unhappy with what she perceives as corporate inflexibility and a looming glass ceiling. She often wonders if she was right to be persuaded by her father to get an M.B.A. Her dream in high school and college was to be an actress, and she'd excelled in school drama productions. Her father, a successful businessman himself, had insisted that a career in business would be much more practical. Financially, of course, he was right. She has earned an excellent salary and doesn't want to give up the lifestyle it provides.

After reading chapters 2 through 4, Carol is convinced she has to make a change. She feels stultified by the confines of her job. She wants greater independence, more creative control, and, frankly, more fun in her work than corporate life offers her. Also since childhood, she's always been complimented on her sense of humor and her ability to entertain. An aunt once told her she could have made Scrooge laugh. So she's concluded that she shouldn't let this gift go to waste any longer and is committed to finding a way to use it without having to give up a good income.

First she looks in **Appendix II** for entertainment-oriented careers. There are many, from being an actor or comedian to entertaining at children's parties, but she's really not interested in starting over in the entertainment field. Getting her income up to the level she's used to would take too long, if it were feasible at all. She looks in **Appendix III** for careers related to her personal style, Creator-Leader-Improver, and finds over 150 careers that use her particular strengths. Besides actor, comedian, and other kinds of entertainers, she finds the following possibilities that also use her business training and experience:

- Business plan writer
- Desktop publishing service
- Public-relations specialist
- Résumé-writing service
- Advertising agency
- Arts critic
- Motivational lecturer
- Professional speaker
- Radio talk show host
- Speechwriter
- Writer

She quickly eliminates desktop publishing, résumé writing, and business plan writing because they don't draw sufficiently on her sense of humor. She also eliminates arts critic and public-relations specialist because they wouldn't give her a chance to perform. So after her first cut, she has five careers to transfer to her final list in **Chapter 4, "Harvesting a Gift."**

OLIVIA, ORGANIZER/IMPROVER/PROBLEM SOLVER

Olivia is a twenty-seven-year-old financial analyst with seven years' experience. She is being laid off due to the merger of her bank with another. She'll receive one week of severance pay for each year she's worked, plus two weeks' notice, so she has a nine-week cushion to find out what she'll do. She has an Associate of Arts degree in business from the local junior college, with computer and bookkeeping skills and describes her current job as "one step above a bookkeeper. I keep track of where the money goes." So she could look for another job, but she knows that due to mergers and layoffs in the banking industry, there are few positions open.

She's not that interested in finding another job, anyway. Divorced and without child support, she and her three-year-old daughter live with her mother in a rented apartment. Her mother has been taking care of her daughter while Olivia's been working, but Olivia would rather spend more time with her daughter. She wants to start a home-based business and her mother, who's also interested in increasing her income, will support and participate in any home-based business Olivia creates.

So with this goal in mind, she discovers that her personality style is Organizer/Improver/Problem Solver and, looking in **Appendix III**, she finds nine possibilities:

- Abstracting and indexing service
- Educational record-keeping service
- Proofreading services
- Property tax reduction service
- Publisher of catalogs
- Real estate abstract searcher
- Red-tape wrangler
- Transcript digesting service
- Government bid notification service

To increase her options, Olivia also looks at the careers that use the components of her personality style in a different order: Organizer/Problem Solver/Improver. This yields seven more possibilities:

- Book indexing service
- Medical claims assistance professional
- Consolidation services: freight odd-lot
- Moving consultant
- Polygraph technician

Olivia knows she's much more interested in dealing with numbers than with words or word processing, so out of these sixteen possibilities, she selects eight for her first-cut short list by eliminating all the careers that primarily deal with words, like book indexing, abstracting, proofreading, or transcript digesting. Since she wants to use her banking and financial expertise, if possible, she also discards careers in the medical field, like medical claims or polygraph technician. This leaves:

FIRST-CUT CAREERS

- Government bid notification service
- Property tax reduction service
- Consolidation services: freight odd-lot
- Red-tape wrangler
- Moving consultant
- Real estate abstract searcher

Olivia's next step is to investigate what these fields are. What are "consolidation ser-vices"? She finds out this involves consolidating odd-lots of merchandise into large enough quantities to sell at a profit. This doesn't appeal to her, so she crosses that off her list.

What's a "red-tape wrangler"? This is a term we've coined to describe services that help individuals or companies deal with massive bureaucracies. For instance, Olivia real-ized that she could help people deal with their banks to negotiate a loan or obtain more favorable interest rates or special services the general public may not be aware of. Prop-erty tax reduction services and real estate abstract searchers also fall into the category of red-tape wrangler. Property tax reduction services search tax assessor records and put together and present the case that their clients' property taxes should be lowered. Their fee is usually a percentage of the client's tax savings. Real estate abstract searchers perform similar functions and also research titles. Olivia realizes she knows a lot about these areas already, so she transfers these three businesses along with government bid notification service to her list of possible careers to consider in **Chapter 7, "Capital-izing on Your Assets."**

LAURA AND LYLE, LEADER/ORGANIZER/IMPROVER AND LEADER/IMPROVER/BUILDER

Laura and Lyle are a fifty-year-old married couple, both self-employed real estate agents. Neither has closed a sale in the past year. They are living on their savings. They own five houses, three of which are rented out and covering their costs. They live in the fourth, and the fifth is empty. Their four children are all grown and on their own. They feel a need to do something different and to do it now, but they can't agree on what to do.

After reading **Chapter 2**, they agree that finding a way to work together is very important to them, as is continuing to be their own boss. They want to get their in-come back up, but they don't need to make as much money as they were in the prime real estate market. Besides, retirement is on the horizon. Laura also is adamant that's she's ready for a change! She says, "I don't want to broker anything anymore! I'm sick and tired of it." Lyle's tired of real estate, too. Their minds are wide open to new op-portunities.

So they're overjoyed when, after discovering their personal styles (Leader/Orga-nizer/Improver and Leader/Improver/Builder) and looking at **Appendix II**, they find ap-proximately 422 self-employment possibilities! This enormous range gives them plenty of ideas to explore.

Laura looks at the fifty-three careers listed under Leader/Organizer/Improver:

- Art show promoter
- Auto brokering, new
- Auto brokering, used
- Auto brokering, vintage
- Broker autos, new and used
- Broker autos, vintage
- Broker bail bond
- Broker boat

- Broker bulk food
- Broker consultant
- Broker expert witness
- Broker furniture
- Broker government surplus
- Broker import/export
- Broker international food
- Broker livestock
- Broker motorcycle
- Broker printing
- Broker real estate
- Broker recycling
- Income tax service
- Motorcycle broker
- Printing broker
- Real estate broker
- Real estate sales

- RVs and vans broker
- Show organizer, antique cars
- Broker restaurant food
- Broker salvage
- Broker scrap
- Broker secondhand and vintage clothing
- Broker solar equipment
- Broker training
- Broker vacation home
- Broker venture capital
- Broker wedding gowns
- Conference planner
- Consultant broker
- Escrow temporary agency
- Estate sale coordinator

- Event planner, children's parties
- Event planner, fund-raisers
- Event planner, spouse programs
- Expert broker
- Exposition manager
- Free classified advertising newspaper
- Show organizer, art shows
- Travel agency
- Used computer broker
- Wedding gown rental/brokering
- Yacht broker
- Yellow page brokering

Lyle looks at the fifty-seven careers listed under Leader/Improver/Builder:

- Agent, sports
- Antique locating service
- Apartment finders
- Association management service
- Bed-and-breakfast inn
- Body makeup artist
- Claims adjuster
- Cleaning service
- Consultant, corporate benefits
- Corporate trainer
- Counselor, alcohol, drug, and substance abuse
- Day-care provider
- Employee training

- Executive director services
- Financial consulting
- Financial planning
- Food service management
- Hauling service
- Home security analysis service
- Home security patrol service
- Housing consultant
- Human relations counselor
- Human resources consultant
- Instructor, sports

- Landscape contractor
- Management training
- Marksmanship instructor
- Needlepoint supplies sales
- Newsletter copywriting
- Newsletter publisher
- Payroll preparation service
- Personal shopper
- Personnel consulting
- Pets identification service
- Purchasing agent service
- Real estate agent
- Repossession service
- Security consultant

- Selling odd lots
- Shopping services
- Specialty consultant:
  Executive recruiting
  Materials
  management
  Outplacement
  Personnel/human
  resources

- Purchasing
- Retirement planning
- Time management
- Specialty employment
  agency
- Temporary help
  service
- Tour operator

- Trainer:
  Corporate
  Disabled
  Driving
  Employee
  Umpire/referee

They are astonished to find that the only career they have in common on their two lists is real estate! So, now they narrow their lists down and figure out some other way to complement each other's strengths. Even though Laura's personality is ideally suited to brokering, she crosses off all types of brokering, which leaves her with a much shortened first cut:

FIRST-CUT CAREERS

- Art show promoter
- Conference planner
- Event planner, children's
  parties
- Event planner, fund-
  raisers

- Event planner, spouse
  programs
- Exposition manager
- Free classified
  advertising newspaper

- Show organizer, antique
  cars
- Show organizer, art
  shows
- Travel agency

Lyle looks at the careers listed under Leader/Improver/Builder and eliminates the ones he finds uninteresting or unlikely. Even though he loves sports, he doesn't want to start a career as a sports agent at age fifty and doing something like apartment finders is too much like real estate. As for body makeup artist, it sounds like fun, but as far as he's concerned it would be more suited for a prank to surprise his wife than a career. He also rejects anything that needs additional schooling or licensing because he wants to move laterally from what he's been doing not "retrain." This leaves him, too, with a much shortened first cut:

FIRST-CUT CAREERS

- Antique locating service
- Association management service
- Bed-and-breakfast inn
- Newsletter publisher
- Home security analysis service
- Home security patrol service
- Newsletter copywriting
- Security consultant
- Tour operator
- Executive director services

Laura and Lyle can now transfer these lists to their possibilities on the work sheets in **Chapter 7, "Capitalizing on Your Assets."**

IRIS, IMPROVER/LEADER/ORGANIZER

Iris is a thirty-eight-year-old married mother and homemaker. Her husband is an accountant bringing home a comfortable income. With the last of three children under twelve starting private school, she wants to help contribute to the family income, especially to their college fund. Before her children were born, she was a child services caseworker and put in long hours for low pay to help abused and neglected children and their families. Now that her youngest son is in preschool, she wants to do something again to help foster the well-being of children, but she also wants to be with her own children while they are growing up. She already volunteers as a tutor at her children's schools but feels her skills are underutilized there.

After reading **Chapter 2,** she knows she wants both to do something that really makes a difference and to work from home so she can have the flexibility to continue to coach her daughter's soccer team and take care of her four-year-old after preschool. After reading **Part II,** she realizes her mission is (and always was) improving the lives of as many children as possible.

Her self-employment personal style is Improver/Leader/Organizer. Looking in **Appendix III,** she finds fifty-nine possibilities:

- Addiction counselor
- Baby-sitting/au-pair/nanny agency
- Baby-sitting/au-pair/nanny referral service
- Bartender
- Birth parents search service
- Camp consultant
- Chartering service, airplanes
- Charter bus service
- Charter yacht service
- Computer trainer
- Day-care, children
- Deed investigator
- Dental practice management consulting
- Director, casting
- Director, motion picture
- Educational therapist
- Employment agency
- Escort service
- Etiquette consultant

- Export agent
- Exporter
- Family child care provider
- Fire safety consultant
- Foster parent
- Fund-raiser
- Home schooling consultant
- Home schooling grader
- Horse trainer
- Importer
- In-home health care
- Law library management
- Law office management consultant
- Lawyers' aide/freelance paralegal

- Library management, law
- Litigation support
- Math tutor
- New Age crafts: astrology
- New Age crafts: numerology
- Nurse consultant
- Packaging and shipping service
- Paralegal
- Paralegal services
- Party planning
- Personal services broker
- Psychotherapist: hypnotherapist
- Recreational therapist

- Retirement counseling
- Scout, professional sports
- Security escort service
- Specialty consultant, fund-raising
- Specialty consultant, health care
- Trainer, computer
- Travel consultant/guide/packager
- Tutoring, academic
- Tutoring, Achievement Tests
- Tutoring, home
- Weight loss instruction
- Wig dresser

At first, Iris crosses off all the items that do not relate to her mission of helping children. But some of the non-child-oriented careers, like importer and party planner, sound interesting. She wonders if maybe there is a way to tie these in with her mission, so she puts them back on the list. She's not interested in learning about law, so she crosses off law library management, law office management consultant, lawyers' aide/freelance paralegal, litigation support, and paralegal services. Other careers such as bartender, motion picture director, chartering services, New Age crafts, or wig dresser seem too far from her mission, conflict with her desire to work from home, require too much additional training, or are of no personal interest.

This leaves her with a first-cut short list of eighteen self-employment careers related to her mission:

FIRST-CUT CAREERS

- Addiction counselor
- Baby-sitting/au-pair/nanny agency
- Baby-sitting/au-pair/nanny referral service
- Birth parents search service
- Camp consultant

- Day care, children
- Family child care provider
- Foster parent
- Fund-raiser
- Home schooling consultant
- Home schooling grader
- Home tutor

- Importer
- Math tutor
- Party planning
- Specialty consultant, fund-raising
- Tutoring, academic
- Tutoring, Achievement Tests

She adds them to her list of final possibilities in **Chapter 6, "Pursuing a Mission."**

As you can see, most people will find a wide array of independent careers they are naturally suited to. The next step is to make a natural choice from among these options.

STEP THREE: MAKING THE NATURAL CHOICE

The secret to finding the means to support your dreams lies in matching what you most want to do and the resources you have to do it successfully with opportunities to provide what people need and will pay for. In **Part III, "The Means,"** we introduce a process we've developed for finding such a match called matrixing. Choosing from among the careers you've identified in **Appendices II and III** or building a career around doing something similar to one of these careers has three definite advantages for helping you matrix successfully.

1. Other people have already found there to be a demand for this type of work or it wouldn't be included in the appendices. So although there may not necessarily be a need in your community, these careers at least have a proven track record of meeting some existing needs.

2. The fact that each of these careers involves types of activities that you enjoy doing makes it easier to motivate yourself and to keep working toward your goals.

3. Each also involves activities that call upon a variety of the things you do most naturally. This means your self-confidence will be higher and your learning curve is apt to be shorter than would be the case with other businesses less suited to your personal style.

So as you proceed to read **Part III** and complete the exercises there, be sure to include the possibilities you've identified here among the opportunities you include and test out in building your matrix.

Remember, though, while these careers are ones other people have already succeeded in following on their own, there may be other independent careers not included in the Appendices that are even better suited to you. In reading and doing the exercises in Part III, you may even have excellent ideas that no one has thought of yet that meet needs you recognize because of your particular experiences, contacts, and background.

So, if you have such ideas, don't discard them. Use what you've learned about what comes naturally to you to build on your ideas in ways that draw upon your personal styles.

If you're curious as to how the individuals just profiled can matrix their interests and resources and make their natural choice, after you've read **Part III** and learned how to matrix, read the following profiles. These profiles may also be helpful to you if you're struggling with how to matrix your various options.

PROFILES: PUTTING IT ALL TOGETHER TO FIND YOUR PERFECT WORK

PETER, PURSUING HIS PASSION

Peter, the forty-two-year-old engineer who spends his free time hiking, rock climbing, and taking wilderness photos, has matrixed his desires and resources with the various possibilities from his first cut as shown on the following pages:

Peter's Natural Choice: Wilderness Adventure Video Memories. In searching for the intersections where what he wants, his resources, and the possibilities for careers that come most naturally to him cross, Peter finds one livelihood clearly stands out as his first choice: audio/video engineering and production. It's a natural for him because it combines his engineering skills with his interest in audio and photography. With his computer skills, desktop video editing and postproduction will be easy for him to learn. Working with his computer at home, he can create and edit his own video productions.

As he explores possibilities of how this work could overlap with his love for the outdoors, his thoughts return repeatedly to memories of the many evenings his family has enjoyed re-viewing the videos and photo albums from their wilderness trips. Then he had an idea! He will specialize in creating souvenir or promotional still photographs

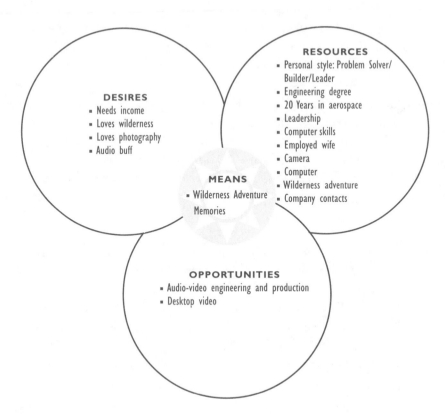

DESIRES
- Needs income
- Loves wilderness
- Loves photography
- Audio buff

RESOURCES
- Personal style: Problem Solver/ Builder/Leader
- Engineering degree
- 20 Years in aerospace
- Leadership
- Computer skills
- Employed wife
- Camera
- Computer
- Wilderness adventure
- Company contacts

MEANS
- Wilderness Adventure Memories

OPPORTUNITIES
- Audio-video engineering and production
- Desktop video

or video records of adventure tours. This is a natural choice because he can use his contacts from his past wilderness adventures to get started. His target customers will be wilderness adventure companies who want to enhance their customers' wilderness experiences by providing a video or still souvenir record of their personal trips and/or want one such record for promotional purposes.

Because his wife has a steady job, they can cut their living expenses initially while he builds his business. And his wife can go on trips with him during her vacations and summer breaks, just as she's done for the past twenty years. Then perhaps when his daughter goes off to college, they will move closer to one of the wilderness areas where he will be working.

BEN, CAPITALIZING ON HIS ASSETS

Here's how Ben, the twenty-three-year-old returning from the Army, has matrixed his desires and resources with the various possibilities from his first cut:

Ben's Natural Choice: Open Sesame Garage Door Service. In searching for the intersections where what he wants, his resources, and the possibilities for careers that come most naturally to him cross, Ben remembers how easily he installed the garage door for his mother and how pleased she had been to have it installed. As he imagines doing this for others, he feels excited. A garage door service—installing and repairing garage doors and garage door openers—requires very little capital investment, and he already knows how to do it. He can attract initial customers through a yellow page listing and contacts he already has with contractors. Later as he acquires confidence and experience, he imagines he'll be able to help his customers with other home-repair jobs too. It's a nat-

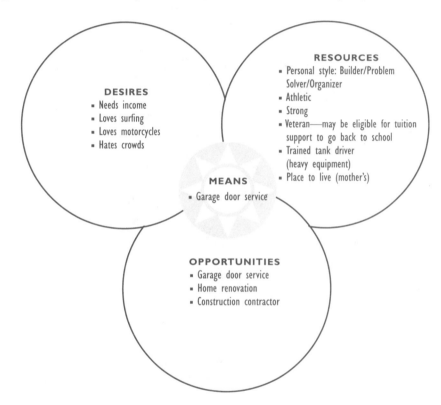

DESIRES
- Needs income
- Loves surfing
- Loves motorcycles
- Hates crowds

RESOURCES
- Personal style: Builder/Problem Solver/Organizer
- Athletic
- Strong
- Veteran—may be eligible for tuition support to go back to school
- Trained tank driver (heavy equipment)
- Place to live (mother's)

MEANS
- Garage door service

OPPORTUNITIES
- Garage door service
- Home renovation
- Construction contractor

ural for him. Customers will appreciate his solid craftsmanship and attention to detail. He will find that working with customers one-on-one is okay; it's just crowds of them he doesn't like. As his business continues to grow, he may decide to get his construction contractor's license, going to contractors' licensing school with the help of his veteran's benefits. And of course, his dog can ride along in the pickup with him to his work sites!

CAROL, HARVESTING A GIFT

In order to harvest her gift, a great sense of humor, Carol, the frustrated Fortune-500 account executive, has matrixed her desires and resources with the various possibilities from her first cut as follows:

Carol's Natural Choice: Making Money Fun Workshops and Seminars for Small-Business Owners. As Carol looked at where her desires, resources, and opportunities might overlap, a perfect match that puts it all together came to her in a flash. She can combine her knowledge and expertise in the business world with her irresistible sense of humor by developing and offering seminars that teach small-business owners about how to make making money fun. She decides to start testing her idea while she's still employed and building it into a full-time business, as she becomes better known as an expert in her field. Her reputation grows quickly, however, because everyone in her seminars has so much fun learning things that will make them more money.

To help the process along, she plans to write a book on solid business advice for

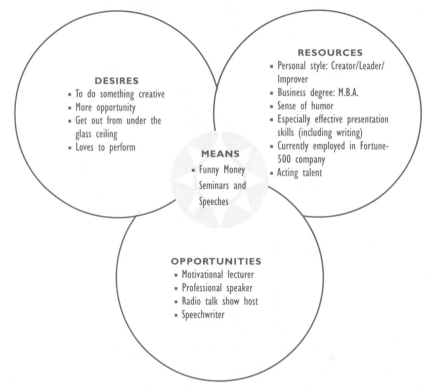

DESIRES
- To do something creative
- More opportunity
- Get out from under the glass ceiling
- Loves to perform

RESOURCES
- Personal style: Creator/Leader/Improver
- Business degree: M.B.A.
- Sense of humor
- Especially effective presentation skills (including writing)
- Currently employed in Fortune-500 company
- Acting talent

MEANS
- Funny Money Seminars and Speeches

OPPORTUNITIES
- Motivational lecturer
- Professional speaker
- Radio talk show host
- Speechwriter

women, featuring the humorous axioms that express her unique point of view. This provides her with access to publicity as an expert interviewed on local radio and television programs. Talk show hosts love her because she's so funny. Someday she might even have her own show.

OLIVIA, CAPITALIZING ON HER ASSETS

Olivia, the twenty-seven-year-old single mother and financial analyst who had just lost her job and wants to start a home business, has matrixed her desires and resources with the various possibilities from her first cut as follows:

Olivia's Natural Choice: Red-Tape Wrangler. Remembering how frustrated bank customers were with the complexity of various financial transactions, Olivia decides to combine her experience working in the banking industry with her natural proclivity to help people navigate the system she knows so well. She starts a red-tape reduction service to help small-business owners and consumers cut through financial red tape. She can use some of her severance pay to buy a computer and printer for her home office. And she can use her contacts in the banking industry as gatekeepers who can refer clients to her who are in need of help untangling their financial red tape.

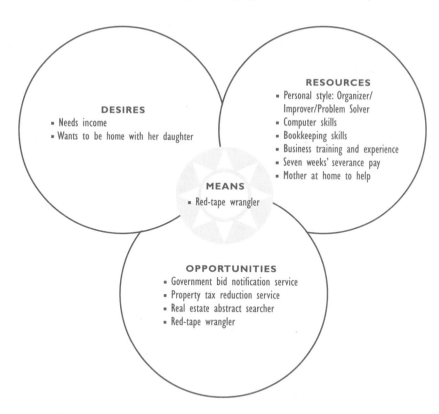

DESIRES
- Needs income
- Wants to be home with her daughter

RESOURCES
- Personal style: Organizer/ Improver/Problem Solver
- Computer skills
- Bookkeeping skills
- Business training and experience
- Seven weeks' severance pay
- Mother at home to help

MEANS
- Red-tape wrangler

OPPORTUNITIES
- Government bid notification service
- Property tax reduction service
- Real estate abstract searcher
- Red-tape wrangler

This is a natural choice for Olivia because she can run this business from home. Her clients will value her organizational skill and problem-solving ability, which she can use to find solutions to their problems and implement them quickly. Since Improver is the second aspect of her personal style, she will enjoy being supportive to clients, who will probably be quite frustrated by the time they get to her.

LAURA AND LYLE, CAPITALIZING ON THEIR ASSETS

Laura and Lyle have matrixed their collective desires and resources with the various possibilities from their first cuts as below.

Lyle and Laura's Natural Choice: a Bed-and-Breakfast Inn. Looking at the pattern of common interests their matrix suggests, Laura and Lyle began to shape an idea of how they would meet their needs and use many of their talents and skills. Lyle's personal style is ideally suited to the bed-and-breakfast inn business. By making this choice, he'll even get to shop for antiques to furnish the inn—a hobby he would love an excuse to engage in more often. Laura's personal style, especially her organizing skills, make her well suited to act as a concierge for their guests, helping them plan the details of their stay for maximum enjoyment, as well as to take care of the myriad details involved in a smoothly operating inn. And, surprisingly, Lyle and Laura remember that many years ago before their children were born they had stayed at a bed-and-breakfast and fantasized jokingly about running one of their own someday.

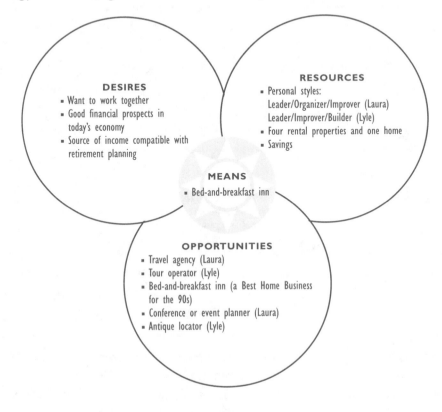

DESIRES
- Want to work together
- Good financial prospects in today's economy
- Source of income compatible with retirement planning

RESOURCES
- Personal styles:
  Leader/Organizer/Improver (Laura)
  Leader/Improver/Builder (Lyle)
- Four rental properties and one home
- Savings

MEANS
- Bed-and-breakfast inn

OPPORTUNITIES
- Travel agency (Laura)
- Tour operator (Lyle)
- Bed-and-breakfast inn (a Best Home Business for the 90s)
- Conference or event planner (Laura)
- Antique locator (Lyle)

Their next step is to investigate whether any of their existing properties could be converted into a profitable bed-and-breakfast. Are any in a suitable location? Are any big enough? Can they get a zoning variance, or will they have to acquire a new property? Lyle's building skills will come in handy if remodeling is needed to add enough rooms for their inn to be profitable.

After investigation, they decide to move now to the community where they planned to retire and establish their bed-and-breakfast inn there. They decide to sell their empty rental property in order to finance their new acquisition. Their prior experience in real estate and their status as licensed real estate agents will enable them to find and buy property of good value in an ideal location.

IRIS, EARNING A LIVING FROM A MISSION

Iris, the mother of three who wants to return to work improving the welfare of children, has matrixed her desires and resources with the various possibilities from her first cut as on page 364.

Iris's Natural Choice: Quality Child-Care Registry. In looking over where her interests, resources, and opportunities overlap, Iris sees several possibilities, but one is clearly a better fit. She *is* an excellent tutor as a volunteer, but she doesn't really want to go into the tutoring business. While she has no doubt she could provide high-quality day care or foster care in her home, she feels that would only help a few children. She wants to do something that will make a difference for lots of children. She knows there is a pressing need for good-quality child care. Only one in five children is cared for by a licensed provider. Far too many are receiving poor care. By coincidence a friend was complaining about how disappointed she was with her child care just that past week. Iris was reminded of how frequently she hears friends complaining about finding good care. And she's aware of the latest studies showing that the most expensive day care isn't always the best.

So she decides to start a high-quality child-care registry, a day-care referral service, listing only those day-care settings that meet her high standards as a child-welfare professional. It's a natural for her. By running the registry, she can pursue her mission by helping parents find good-quality, affordable day care. Her background in child welfare uniquely qualifies her to assess day-care settings, which she can visit while her children are in school and still be home when they need her. And she can enlist her husband's help in setting up the financial side of her business.

Iris also notices that people with her personal style do well at fund-raising. Even though she has planned many successful fund-raisers for her children's schools and teams, she's never thought of this as a skill she could base a career on. Also fund-raising uses a lot of the same skills as party planning, something else she finds interesting. Peo-

DESIRES
- Passion: loves children
- Mission: to help children
- To work from home
- To spend time with own children

RESOURCES
- Personal style: Improver/Leader/ Organizer
- Social work training and experience
- Experience as a mother
- Employed husband
- Contacts in business field through husband
- Husband's business expertise as CPA
- Fund-raising experience
- Gives wonderful parties
- Sees NEED for high-quality day care

MEANS
- Referral service

OPPORTUNITIES
- Baby-sitting referral service
- Day care, children
- Fund-raiser
- Party planner

ple are always complimenting her on her wonderful parties, but she'd never thought of this as a marketable talent.

Now she has an idea of how to build on these skills to further pursue her mission. She can use her fund-raising abilities and social connections with her husband's business associates to start a "day-care scholarship fund." The fund will provide "scholarships" for high-quality day care for children whose mothers are working to get off welfare. The scholarship fund-raisers will serve the dual purpose of helping needy children and publicizing her registry.

CONCLUSION

As you can see, you can use the **Doing What Comes Naturally** survey and the **Directories of Self-Employment Careers to create** "designer" businesses custommade to match your personality, gifts, missions, passions, and assets with concrete opportunities that will meet genuine customer needs.

So work with the ideas you've gained here as you matrix your own possibilities in **Part III.** Let your creative juices flow and let yourself be free to imagine a self-employed career that includes everything you want for a genuinely fulfilling life.

An Alphabetical Directory of Self-Employment Careers

PEOPLE ARE SUCCESSFULLY working in literally hundreds of independent careers. This directory lists over 1,600 independent careers you can review to generate ideas for finding your perfect work. In this appendix, each career has been evaluated in terms of a number of criteria you can use to determine if it matches your goals, resources, and lifestyle.

EXPLANATIONS OF COLUMNS

CAREER OR BUSINESS
This column lists the self-employment career or business alphabetically. In many instances specialties of a career are also listed. This column enables you to look up specific careers by name and allows you to peruse the list for careers of interest to you.

PERSONAL STYLE
These columns tell you what personal qualities each career draws most heavily upon. Once you've taken the Doing What Comes Naturally survey in **Appendix I**, you can identify to what extent any career you look up would match with your personal style.

To find a list of the specific careers that do match your personal style, see **Appendix III.**

Degree Requirements

This column lets you know if a specialized academic degree or formal certification is required in order to pursue a particular career. A degree requirement is indicated when a specialized degree or a course leading to formal certification is required for the career or business.

License Requirements

This column indicates whether any specialized formal license is required to pursue a particular career. While any kind of business activity requires a city or county business license, some occupations and professions require special licenses. State governments are the usual source of occupational and professional licenses.

If fewer than half of the fifty states require a license, certification, or registration, we use the symbol □; if more than half of the states have a requirement, we use the symbol ◨; and if all states impose a requirement, as is the case for attorneys and doctors, we use the symbol ■. At the end of **Appendix II** are listed the primary agencies in each state and province that you can contact to determine what the requirements are for businesses or careers that interest you.

In some cases, the federal government and sometimes municipalities may also require an occupational and professional license; for example, providing investment advice and making and dealing in firearms require federal licenses. When a license or registration is needed from a federal agency, that is indicated with the word FED. Another exception is that in states that do not license private detectives, some local governments require registering with a police or sheriff's department.

Occupational and professional licenses are different from and in addition to business licenses required of all businesses. They differ in that business licenses are solely revenue sources for city or county governments. Occupational and professional licenses involve some element of regulation of entry into a field in order to protect the public. Failing to get an occupational or professional license is often treated as a criminal offense. So, even for occupations and businesses not listed as requiring special licenses, it's a good idea to check.

Greater than Average Capital Required

This column indicates when the capital required to get into this career on an independent basis is greater than average. Where the amount of money needed for start-up is greater than what we found to be the average (about $7,500 for a medium-cost start-up) for businesses profiled in *Best Home Businesses for the 90s,* we indicated that the business required more than average capital.

CAREERS FREQUENTLY PURSUED AT HOME

This column indicates independent careers that are frequently followed at home. While many of the other businesses listed can also be conducted at home, we have indicated those where a large proportion of people in a business do operate at home.

SITE REQUIREMENTS—LAND OR COMMERCIAL BUILDING

This column indicates whether land or a commercial building is needed to pursue this career independently. We have indicated where a business cannot be operated from home and has specific building or land needs. The capital required for such businesses will consequently be higher.

FAMILY FRIENDLY

A "family-friendly" business is one that usually can be run successfully by parents with children at home or in school, provide the parents with flexible hours, and create a minimum of intrusion into family life or danger from machines or materials.

BOOK RESOURCES

This column lets you know if additional information is available in more depth about a career in any of our other books:

B = *Best Home Businesses for the 90s.* Second edition, Paul and Sarah Edwards (New York: Tarcher/Putnam, 1994).

M = *Making Money with Your Computer at Home.* Paul and Sarah Edwards (New York: Tarcher/Putnam, 1993).

MH = McGraw-Hill Computer Entrepreneur Entrepreneurial PC Series, which includes:

Bookkeeping on Your Home-Based PC. Linda Stern (Blue Ridge Summit, Pa.: Windcrest/McGraw-Hill, 1993).

Computer Consulting on Your Home-Based PC. Herman Holtz (Blue Ridge Summit, Pa.: Windcrest/McGraw-Hill, 1994).

Health Services Businesses on Your Home-Based PC. Rick Benzel (Blue Ridge Summit, Pa.: Windcrest/McGraw-Hill, 1993).

Information for Sale. John H. Everett and Elizabeth P. Crowe (Blue Ridge Summit, Pa; Windcrest/McGraw-Hill, 1994).

Legal and Paralegal Services on Your Home-Based PC. Katherine Sheehy Hussey and Rick Benzel (Blue Ridge Summit, Pa.: Windcrest/McGraw-Hill, 1994).

Mailing List Services on Your Home-Based PC. Linda Rohrbach (Blue Ridge Summit, Pa.: Windcrest/McGraw-Hill, 1994).

Making Money Selling Your Shareware. Steven C. Hudgik (Blue Ridge Summit, Pa.: Windcrest/McGraw-Hill, 1994).

Operating a Desktop Video Service on Your Home-Based PC. Harvey Summers (Blue Ridge Summit, Pa.: Windcrest/McGraw-Hill, 1994).

Start Your Own Computer Repair, Maintenance, and Training Business. Linda Rohrbach (Blue Ridge Summit, Pa.: Windcrest/McGraw-Hill, 1995).

CAREER OR BUSINESS	PERSONAL STYLE 1	2	3	DEGREE REQUIRED	LICENSE REQUIREMENT	AVERAGE CAPITAL REQUIRED	DONE AT HOME	LAND OR COMMERCIAL BUILDING REQUIRED	FAMILY FRIENDLY	BOOK RESOURCES
ABSTRACTING SERVICE	ORG	IMP	PRO				◧		✓	B,M
ACCIDENT INVESTIGATOR	LEA	IMP	PRO							
ACCIDENT INVESTIGATOR	LEA	PRO	BUI							
ACCOUNTANT, CPA	LEA	IMP	ORG	✓	■		◧		✓	
	ORG	LEA	IMP	✓	■		◧		✓	
ACCOUNTANT, PUBLIC	LEA	IMP	ORG	✓	◧		◧		✓	
	ORG	LEA	IMP	✓	◧		◧		✓	
ACOUSTICS ENGINEER	BUI	LEA	IMP	✓	□					
ACTING/DRAMA COACH	IMP	CRE	LEA							
	CRE	IMP	LEA							
ACTOR	CRE	LEA	IMP							
ACUPRESSURIST	PRO	IMP	BUI				◧			
ACUPUNCTURIST	PRO	IMP	LEA	✓	◧		◧			
ADDICTION/SUBSTANCE ABUSE COUNSELOR	IMP	LEA	ORG	✓	□			■		
ADMINISTRATIVE SERVICES CONSULTANT	LEA	IMP	ORG							
ADOPTION ADVOCATE	IMP	LEA	CRE						✓	
ADVERTISING/AGENCY	CRE	LEA	IMP				◧			B
	LEA	IMP	PRO				◧			
ADVERTISING/BROKER	LEA	IMP	PRO				◧			
ADVERTISING/SALES	LEA	IMP	PRO				◧		✓	
AEROBICS CLASSES	IMP	BUI	LEA			✓		■		
AFFIXING COMPANY LOGOS TO BASEBALL CAPS	BUI	ORG	LEA				◧		✓	
AGROLOGIST	PRO	BUI	IMP	✓						
AGRONOMIST	PRO	BUI	IMP	✓						
AIRCRAFT MECHANIC	BUI	LEA	PRO					■		
	BUI	PRO	LEA					■		
ALARM SERVICE	LEA	BUI	IMP	□			◧			
ANIMAL BREEDER/BIRDS, EXOTIC	BUI	LEA	IMP	□			◧		✓	
	PRO	BUI	LEA	□			◧		✓	
ANIMAL BREEDER/CATS	BUI	LEA	IMP				◧		✓	
	PRO	BUI	LEA				◧		✓	
ANIMAL BREEDER/CATTLE	BUI	LEA	IMP					■	✓	
	PRO	BUI	LEA					■	✓	
ANIMAL BREEDER/CHICKENS	BUI	LEA	IMP					■	✓	
	PRO	BUI	LEA					■	✓	
ANIMAL BREEDER/DOGS	BUI	LEA	IMP				◧		✓	
	PRO	BUI	LEA				◧		✓	

BUI=Builder, CRE=Creator, IMP=Improver, LEA=Leader, ORG=Organizer, PRO=Problem Solver, ■=Always, ◧=Usually, □=Some

CAREER OR BUSINESS	PERSONAL STYLE 1	2	3	DEGREE REQUIRED	LICENSE REQUIREMENT	AVERAGE CAPITAL REQUIRED	DONE AT HOME	LAND OR COMMERCIAL BUILDING REQUIRED	FAMILY FRIENDLY	BOOK RESOURCES
ANIMAL BREEDER/FISH FARMER	BUI	LEA	IMP	□				■	✓	
	PRO	BUI	LEA	□				■	✓	
ANIMAL BREEDER/FUR BEARING	BUI	LEA	IMP	□	✓			■	✓	
	PRO	BUI	LEA	□	✓			■	✓	
ANIMAL BREEDER/GAME BIRDS	BUI	LEA	PRO	□	✓			■	✓	
ANIMAL BREEDER/GAME FISH	BUI	LEA	PRO	□	✓			■	✓	
ANIMAL BREEDER/HORSES	BUI	LEA	IMP		✓			■	✓	
	PRO	BUI	LEA		✓			■	✓	
ANIMAL BREEDER/LLAMAS	BUI	LEA	IMP		✓			■	✓	
	PRO	BUI	LEA		✓			■	✓	
ANIMAL BREEDER/SHEEP	BUI	LEA	IMP		✓			■	✓	
	PRO	BUI	IMP		✓			■	✓	
ANIMAL BREEDER/WILD ANIMALS	BUI	LEA	IMP	□	✓			■	✓	
	PRO	BUI	IMP	□	✓			■	✓	
ANIMAL BREEDER/WORMS	BUI	LEA	PRO				▮		✓	
ANIMAL SHOW JUDGE/BIRDS	PRO	LEA	IMP						✓	
ANIMAL SHOW JUDGE/CATS	PRO	LEA	IMP						✓	
ANIMAL SHOW JUDGE/DOGS	PRO	LEA	IMP						✓	
ANIMAL SHOW JUDGE/FISH, TROPICAL AND EXOTIC	PRO	LEA	IMP						✓	
ANIMAL SHOW JUDGE/HORSES	PRO	LEA	IMP						✓	
ANIMAL TRAINER/GUARD DOG	BUI	LEA	IMP					■	✓	
ANIMAL TRAINER/HORSES	BUI	LEA	IMP					■	✓	
ANIMAL TRAINER/OBEDIENCE	BUI	LEA	IMP					■	✓	
ANSWERING SERVICE	ORG	IMP	LEA				▮			
ANTHROPOLOGIST	PRO	BUI	LEA	✓						
ANTIQUE/DEALER	LEA	BUI	CRE					■	✓	
ANTIQUE/REPAIR	BUI	PRO	IMP				▮		✓	
ANTIQUE/LOCATING SERVICE	LEA	IMP	BUI				▮		✓	
ANTIQUE/REFINISHING	BUI	PRO	IMP				▮		✓	
ANTIQUE/RESTORATION	BUI	PRO	IMP				▮		✓	B
APARTMENT FINDERS	LEA	IMP	BUI				▮		✓	
APPLIANCE/REFINISHING	BUI	PRO	LEA						✓	
APPLIANCE/REPAIR	BUI	PRO	LEA						✓	
APPRAISER/ART	PRO	CRE	IMP	□					✓	
APPRAISER/AUTOMOBILE DAMAGE	LEA	BUI	IMP	□						
APPRAISER/GEMSTONES	PRO	CRE	IMP	□		▮			✓	
APPRAISER/INSURANCE	PRO	BUI	LEA	▮						

BUI=Builder, CRE=Creator, IMP=Improver, LEA=Leader, ORG=Organizer, PRO=Problem Solver, ■=Always, ▮=Usually, □=Some

CAREER OR BUSINESS	PERSONAL STYLE 1	2	3	DEGREE REQUIRED	LICENSE REQUIREMENT	AVERAGE CAPITAL REQUIRED	DONE AT HOME	LAND OR COMMERCIAL BUILDING REQUIRED	FAMILY FRIENDLY	BOOK RESOURCES
APPRAISER/JEWELRY	PRO	CRE	IMP		□		◨		✓	
APPRAISER/PERSONAL COLLECTIONS	BUI	PRO	IMP		□				✓	
APPRAISER/PRECIOUS METALS	BUI	PRO	IMP		□				✓	
APPRAISER/REAL ESTATE	IMP	ORG	LEA		◨					B
AQUACULTURIST (FISH GROWER)	BUI	LEA	PRO		□			■		
ARBITRATOR	IMP	LEA	CRE							
ARBORIST	ORG	BUI	IMP		□				✓	
ARCHAEOLOGIST	PRO	BUI	LEA	✓						
ARCHITECT	CRE	PRO	LEA	✓	■		◨			
ARCHITECTURAL/SALVAGE	CRE	PRO	BUI			✓				
ARCHITECTURAL/DESIGNER	CRE	PRO	BUI	✓	□		◨		✓	
ARCHITECTURAL/MODEL MAKER	CRE	PRO	BUI				◨		✓	
ARCHIVIST	CRE	LEA	IMP							
ART/CONSERVATIONIST	LEA	IMP	PRO							
ART/CORPORATE ART CONSULTANT	IMP	LEA	CRE							
	CRE	LEA	IMP				◨		✓	
ART/CRITIC	PRO	LEA	IMP				◨		✓	
ART/DEALER	IMP	LEA	CRE				◨		✓	
ART/GALLERY OWNER	IMP	LEA	CRE					■		
ART/HISTORIAN	CRE	LEA	IMP	✓			◨		✓	
	IMP	LEA	PRO	✓			◨		✓	
ART/INSTRUCTOR	CRE	IMP	LEA	✓						
ART/REPAIRS	IMP	BUI	ORG				◨		✓	
ART/SHOW PROMOTER	LEA	ORG	CRE			✓	◨			
	LEA	ORG	IMP			✓	◨			
	LEA	ORG	PRO			✓	◨			
ART/THERAPIST	LEA	IMP	PRO	✓	□		◨		✓	
ARTIFICIAL INSEMINATOR OF ANIMALS	BUI	LEA	IMP		□		◨		✓	
	PRO	BUI	LEA							
ARTIFICIAL INTELLIGENCE CONSULTANT	PRO	BUI	LEA				◨		✓	
ARTIST/AIRBRUSH	CRE	LEA	IMP				◨		✓	
ARTIST/CARICATURE	CRE	LEA	IMP				◨		✓	
ARTIST/CARTOONIST	CRE	LEA	IMP				◨		✓	
ARTIST/COMPUTER	CRE	PRO	LEA				◨		✓	
	CRE	IMP	LEA				◨		✓	
ARTIST/COURTROOM	CRE	IMP	LEA							
ARTIST/HOME PORTRAITS	CRE	IMP	LEA				◨			

BUI=Builder, CRE=Creator, IMP=Improver, LEA=Leader, ORG=Organizer, PRO=Problem Solver, ■=Always, ◨=Usually, □=Some

CAREER OR BUSINESS	Personal Style 1	2	3	Degree Required	License Requirement	Average Capital Required	Done at Home	Land or Commercial Building Required	Family Friendly	Book Resources
ARTIST/NEEDLEWORK	CRE	IMP	ORG				◧		✓	
ARTIST/NEON	CRE	IMP	PRO				◧		✓	
ARTIST/STAINED GLASS	CRE	IMP	LEA				◧		✓	
ARTIST/TEXTILE	CRE	IMP	LEA				◧		✓	
ARTIST/WILDLIFE	CRE	IMP	LEA				◧		✓	
ASBESTOS ABATEMENT SERVICES	PRO	BUI	LEA	□						MH
ASSAYER	BUI	ORG	PRO	□						
ASSET PLANNING CONSULTANT	LEA	IMP	ORG	◧				◧		
ASSOCIATION MANAGEMENT SERVICE	LEA	IMP	BUI				◧			B,M
ASTROLOGER	IMP	LEA	ORG							M
ATHLETE, PROFESSIONAL	BUI	LEA	ORG	□						
ATHLETIC CLOTHING DESIGNER	CRE	IMP	LEA				◧		✓	
ATHLETIC EQUIPMENT REPAIR	CRE	LEA	BUI				◧		✓	
ATHLETIC RACE/MEET ORGANIZER/PROMOTER	LEA	IMP	CRE			✓				
ATTORNEY	LEA	IMP	CRE	■						
AUCTIONEER	CRE	LEA	IMP	□						
AUDIO/VIDEO/DUPLICATION	BUI	ORG	LEA				◧		✓	
AUDIO/VIDEO/EDITING	CRE	LEA	IMP				◧		✓	
AUDIO/VIDEO/ENGINEERING	PRO	LEA	BUI							
AUDIO/VIDEO/PRODUCTION	PRO	LEA	BUI				◧			
AUDIO/VIDEO/REPAIRER	BUI	IMP	LEA							
AUDIOLOGIST	PRO	IMP	BUI	✓	■					
AUDIOTEXT (900) PROVIDER	LEA	CRE	IMP			✓	◧		✓	
AUDITING MORTGAGES	PRO	ORG	IMP							B
AUDITING AND EXPENSE REDUCTION SERVICE	PRO	ORG	CRE				◧		✓	B
	PRO	LEA	ORG				◧		✓	B
AUTO/BATTERY RECONDITIONING SERVICE	BUI	PRO	ORG					■		
AUTO/BODY CUSTOMIZER	BUI	LEA	IMP							
AUTO/BODY PAINTING	CRE	BUI	LEA			✓		■		
AUTO/BODY RESTORER	BUI	LEA	IMP							
AUTO/BROKER	LEA	ORG	IMP				◧			
	BUI	LEA	IMP				◧			
AUTO/DETAILING	BUI	ORG	LEA							
AUTO/DRIVING INSTRUCTOR	LEA	IMP	ORG							
AUTO/GLASS INSTALLER	BUI	ORG	LEA							
AUTO/GLASS TINTING	BUI	LEA	ORG					■		
AUTO/MECHANIC	BUI	IMP	LEA	□						

BUI=Builder, CRE=Creator, IMP=Improver, LEA=Leader, ORG=Organizer, PRO=Problem Solver, ■=Always, ◧=Usually, □=Some

CAREER OR BUSINESS	PERSONAL STYLE 1	2	3	DEGREE REQUIRED	LICENSE REQUIREMENT	AVERAGE CAPITAL REQUIRED	DONE AT HOME	LAND OR COMMERCIAL BUILDING REQUIRED	FAMILY FRIENDLY	BOOK RESOURCES
	BUI	PRO	IMP	□						
AUTO/SECURITY INSTALLER	BUI	LEA	IMP					■		
AUTO/TEST DRIVER	BUI	IMP	LEA							
AUTO/UPHOLSTERY CLEANING	BUI	LEA	IMP							
BABY-SITTING/AU-PAIR/NANNY/AGENCY	IMP	LEA	ORG				◧			
BABY-SITTING/AU-PAIR/NANNY/REFERRAL SERVICE	IMP	LEA	ORG				◧			
BADGE AND BUTTON-MAKER	BUI	LEA	ORG				◧		✓	
BAIL BOND AGENT	LEA	BUI	PRO	□	✓					
BAIT DEALER	BUI	LEA	IMP	□					✓	
BAKER	BUI	CRE	LEA							
BALLOON DECORATOR	CRE	LEA	IMP				◧		✓	
BANDLEADER/CONDUCTOR	CRE	LEA	IMP							
BARBER	CRE	IMP	ORG	✓	◧					
BARTENDER	IMP	LEA	ORG	□						
BARTERING SERVICE	ORG	LEA	IMP							
BASEMENT/FINISHING	BUI	PRO	LEA							
BASEMENT/WATERPROOFING	BUI	PRO	LEA							
BEAUTICIAN/HAIRSTYLISTS	LEA	IMP	PRO	✓	■		◧			
	CRE	IMP	PRO	✓	■		◧			
	IMP	LEA	CRE	✓	■		◧			B
BEAUTY SUPPLIES/HOME DELIVERY	ORG	IMP	LEA							
BED-AND-BREAKFAST INN	LEA	IMP	BUI			✓	◧		✓	
BEEKEEPER	BUI	LEA	PRO	□			◧	■	✓	
BEER MICROBREWER	BUI	PRO	LEA			✓				
BICYCLE/CUSTOM CONSTRUCTION	BUI	PRO	IMP				◧		✓	
BICYCLE/REPAIRER	BUI	IMP	ORG				◧		✓	
BILL-PAYING SERVICE	ORG	LEA	BUI				◧		✓	
BILLING AND INVOICING SERVICE	ORG	LEA	BUI				◧		✓	B,M
BIRTH PARENTS SEARCH SERVICE	PRO	LEA	IMP	□			◧		✓	
BLACKSMITH	BUI	PRO	LEA							
BLASTER	BUI	PRO	LEA	□						
BLUEPRINT SERVICE	BUI	ORG	IMP	□			◧		✓	
BOAT/BROKER	LEA	ORG	IMP				◧			
BOAT/CLEANING	BUI	LEA	ORG							
BOAT/INSTRUCTOR	IMP	BUI	LEA							
BOAT/MAINTENANCE	BUI	LEA	IMP							
BOAT/NAVIGATIONAL INSTRUCTOR	PRO	ORG	BUI							

BUI=Builder, CRE=Creator, IMP=Improver, LEA=Leader, ORG=Organizer, PRO=Problem Solver, ■=Always, ◧=Usually, □=Some

CAREER OR BUSINESS	PERSONAL STYLE 1	2	3	DEGREE REQUIRED	LICENSE REQUIREMENT	AVERAGE CAPITAL REQUIRED	DONE AT HOME	LAND OR COMMERCIAL BUILDING REQUIRED	FAMILY FRIENDLY	BOOK RESOURCES
BOAT/REPAIR	BUI	LEA	IMP							
BOATBUILDER	BUI	LEA	PRO							
BODY MAKEUP ARTIST	LEA	IMP	BUI		□					
BODYGUARD	LEA	IMP	ORG							
BOILER INSTALLER/REPAIRER	BUI	PRO	ORG		□					
BOOK/INDEXING SERVICE	ORG	PRO	IMP				▮		✓	
BOOK/PACKAGER	LEA	CRE	PRO				▮			
BOOKBINDER	BUI	LEA	IMP				▮			
BOOKING AGENCY/ENTERTAINERS	IMP	LEA	CRE				▮			
BOOKING AGENCY/MODELS	IMP	LEA	CRE				▮			
BOOKKEEPING SERVICE	ORG	LEA	BUI				▮		✓	B,M,MH
	ORG	LEA	IMP				▮		✓	B,M,MH
	ORG	BUI	LEA				▮		✓	B,M,MH
	ORG	IMP	LEA				▮		✓	B,M,MH
BOUQUET DELIVERY SERVICE	LEA	BUI	IMP							
BRAILLE TYPIST	ORG	IMP	BUI				▮		✓	
BREAKFAST-IN-BED SERVICE	LEA	BUI	IMP							
BRICKLAYER/BRICK AND TILE	BUI	IMP	LEA							
BRIDAL/CONSULTING	CRE	LEA	IMP							B
BRIDAL/GOWNS	BUI	LEA	IMP				▮			
BRIDAL/MAKEUP SERVICE	CRE	LEA	BUI							B
BROKER/BAIL BONDS	LEA	ORG	IMP		□					
BROKER/BEADS	ORG	BUI	LEA				▮		✓	
BROKER/BULK FOOD	LEA	ORG	IMP				▮			
BROKER/CEMETERY REAL ESTATE	LEA	ORG	IMP		□		▮			
BROKER/EXOTIC BEADS	BUI	LEA	CRE				▮			
BROKER/EXPERT WITNESS	LEA	ORG	IMP				▮			
BROKER/FURNITURE	LEA	ORG	IMP				▮			
BROKER/GOVERNMENT SURPLUS	LEA	ORG	IMP		□		▮			
BROKER/IMPORT/EXPORT	LEA	ORG	IMP				▮			
BROKER/INTERNATIONAL FOOD	LEA	ORG	IMP				▮			
BROKER/LIVESTOCK	LEA	ORG	IMP		□		▮			
BROKER/LOAN	LEA	IMP	CRE							
BROKER/MANUFACTURED HOMES	LEA	ORG	IMP		□		▮			
BROKER/MONEY	LEA	ORG	IMP		□	✓				
BROKER/MORTGAGE	PRO	ORG	LEA		□		▮			
BROKER/MOTORCYCLE	LEA	ORG	IMP				▮			

BUI=Builder, CRE=Creator, IMP=Improver, LEA=Leader, ORG=Organizer, PRO=Problem Solver, ■=Always, ▮=Usually, □=Some

CAREER OR BUSINESS	PERSONAL STYLE 1	2	3	DEGREE REQUIRED	LICENSE REQUIREMENT	AVERAGE CAPITAL REQUIRED	DONE AT HOME	LAND OR COMMERCIAL BUILDING REQUIRED	FAMILY FRIENDLY	BOOK RESOURCES
BROKER/RECYCLING	LEA	ORG	IMP				◧			
BROKER/RESTAURANT FOOD	LEA	ORG	IMP				◧			
BROKER/RV'S AND VANS	LEA	ORG	IMP		□					
BROKER/SALVAGE	LEA	ORG	IMP				◧			
BROKER/SCRAP	LEA	ORG	IMP				◧			
BROKER/SECONDHAND PRODUCTS	BUI	PRO	LEA						✓	
BROKER/SOLAR EQUIPMENT	LEA	ORG	IMP				◧			
BROKER/VACATION HOMES	LEA	ORG	IMP		■		◧			
BROKER/VENTURE CAPITAL	LEA	ORG	IMP		□		◧			
BROKER/VINTAGE AUTOS	LEA	ORG	IMP				◧			
BROKER/VINTAGE CLOTHING	LEA	ORG	IMP				◧			
BRONZE WORK	BUI	PRO	IMP							
BUDGET ANALYST	ORG	PRO	LEA				◧		✓	
BUILDING INSPECTION SERVICE	BUI	ORG	LEA	□						
BUILDING MOVING/DEMOLITION CONTRACTOR	BUI	LEA	PRO	□	✓					
BUILDING RESTORATION AND PRESERVATION	BUI	ORG	PRO	□						
BUSINESS BROKER	LEA	IMP	ORG							B
BUSINESS CARD SALES/PHOTO-/HOLOGRAPHIC/POP-UPS	LEA	IMP	CRE							
BUSINESS INTELLIGENCE CONSULTANT	PRO	CRE	LEA				◧			B
BUSINESS NETWORK ORGANIZER	LEA	IMP	BUI							B,M
BUSINESS PLAN WRITER	PRO	CRE	LEA				◧		✓	B,M
CABINET MAKER/WOODWORKER	BUI	PRO	IMP	□			◧		✓	B
CAKE DECORATING	CRE	BUI	LEA				◧		✓	B
CALENDAR SERVICE	ORG	IMP	LEA				◧		✓	
CALLIGRAPHY	CRE	BUI	ORG				◧		✓	
CAMERA REPAIR	BUI	ORG	LEA				◧		✓	B
CAMP CONSULTANT	IMP	LEA	ORG				◧		✓	
CAMP DIRECTOR	LEA	IMP	PRO						✓	
CAMPING AND SAFARI LEADER	BUI	LEA	IMP							
CANING REPAIR	ORG	BUI	IMP				◧		✓	
CANTOR	CRE	IMP	LEA	✓						
CAR POOL SERVICE	ORG	LEA	IMP							
CAREER COUNSELING	IMP	PRO	LEA	□						
CARPENTER	BUI	LEA	PRO	□						
	BUI	PRO	LEA	□						
CARPET/SCULPTOR	CRE	IMP	LEA							
CARPET/WEAVER	BUI	ORG	IMP							

BUI=Builder, CRE=Creator, IMP=Improver, LEA=Leader, ORG=Organizer, PRO=Problem Solver, ■=Always, ◧=Usually, □=Some

CAREER OR BUSINESS	PERSONAL STYLE 1	2	3	DEGREE REQUIRED	LICENSE REQUIREMENT	AVERAGE CAPITAL REQUIRED	DONE AT HOME	LAND OR COMMERCIAL BUILDING REQUIRED	FAMILY FRIENDLY	BOOK RESOURCES
CARPETS AND RUGS/CLEANING	BUI	LEA	ORG							
	BUI	LEA	PRO							
CARPETS AND RUGS/LAYING	BUI	LEA	PRO							
CARTOONIST	CRE	LEA	IMP				◧		✓	
CASTING DIRECTOR	IMP	LEA	CRE							
CATERER	CRE	ORG	IMP				◧			
CATERING/BOX LUNCH CREATOR	CRE	ORG	IMP				◧			
CATERING/CUSTOM WEDDING CAKE CREATOR	CRE	ORG	IMP				◧			B
CATERING/FILM LOCATION	CRE	ORG	IMP			✓				
CEILING REPAIR	BUI	LEA	PRO							
CERAMIC DESIGNER	CRE	BUI	PRO				◧		✓	
CERTIFICATE AND AWARD CREATOR/COMPUTER GENERATED	CRE	BUI	ORG				◧			
CERTIFICATE AND AWARD CREATOR/HAND LETTERED	CRE	BUI	ORG				◧			
CHAIN SAW OPERATOR	BUI	LEA	IMP							
CHARTERING SERVICE/AIRPLANES	IMP	LEA	ORG							
CHARTERING SERVICE/YACHTS	IMP	LEA	ORG							
CHAUFFEUR	BUI	LEA	IMP							
	BUI	LEA	ORG							
CHEF/PERSONAL	LEA	IMP	CRE							
CHILD CARE PROVIDER/DAY CARE	IMP	LEA	ORG		□		◧		✓	B
CHILDBIRTH INSTRUCTOR	IMP	LEA	BUI							
CHILDREN'S BOOKS ILLUSTRATOR	CRE	LEA	IMP				◧		✓	
CHILDREN'S BOOKS WRITER	CRE	LEA	IMP				◧		✓	
CHILDREN'S COSTUME CREATOR	BUI	CRE	IMP				◧		✓	
	IMP	LEA	PRO							
CHILDREN'S TELEVISION PRODUCER	LEA	IMP	CRE							
CHILDREN'S THEATER DIRECTOR	IMP	LEA	PRO							
	LEA	IMP	CRE							
CHIMNEY SWEEP	BUI	LEA	ORG		□					B
CHIROPRACTOR	PRO	IMP	BUI	✓	■					
CHORAL DIRECTOR	CRE	LEA	IMP							
CHOREOGRAPHER	CRE	LEA	IMP							
CHRISTMAS TREE DECORATOR	CRE	BUI	IMP						✓	
CHRISTMAS TREE ORNAMENT CREATOR	CRE	IMP	LEA				◧		✓	
CLAIMS ADJUSTER	LEA	IMP	BUI							
CLEANING SERVICE/RV'S AND VANS	BUI	ORG	LEA							
CLEANING SERVICES/AIRDUCTS	BUI	LEA	ORG							B

BUI=Builder, CRE=Creator, IMP=Improver, LEA=Leader, ORG=Organizer, PRO=Problem Solver, ■=Always, ◧=Usually, □=Some

CAREER OR BUSINESS	PERSONAL STYLE			DEGREE REQUIRED	LICENSE REQUIREMENT	AVERAGE CAPITAL REQUIRED	DONE AT HOME	LAND OR COMMERCIAL BUILDING REQUIRED	FAMILY FRIENDLY	BOOK RESOURCES
	1	2	3							
CLEANING SERVICES/AQUARIUMS	BUI	LEA	ORG							
CLEANING SERVICES/AUTOS	BUI	LEA	ORG							B
CLEANING SERVICES/BASEMENT	BUI	LEA	ORG							
CLEANING SERVICES/CARPET	BUI	LEA	ORG							B
CLEANING SERVICES/CEILINGS	BUI	LEA	ORG							B
CLEANING SERVICES/CESSPOOL	BUI	LEA	ORG	□						B
CLEANING SERVICES/COMMERCIAL OR INSTITUTIONAL	LEA	IMP	BUI							B
CLEANING SERVICES/FLOORS	BUI	LEA	ORG							B
CLEANING SERVICES/FURNITURE	BUI	LEA	ORG							
CLEANING SERVICES/GUTTERS	BUI	LEA	ORG							
CLEANING SERVICES/HOME RESTORATION SERVICE	BUI	ORG	LEA							B
CLEANING SERVICES/HOT TUB/JACUZZI	BUI	LEA	ORG							
CLEANING SERVICES/POOL	BUI	LEA	ORG							B
CLEANING SERVICES/POWER WASHING	BUI	LEA	ORG							B
CLEANING SERVICES/SHIPS	BUI	LEA	ORG							
CLEANING SERVICES/SIGNS	BUI	ORG	LEA							
CLEANING SERVICES/TILE	BUI	LEA	ORG							
CLEANING SERVICES/WINDOW BLINDS	BUI	LEA	ORG							B
CLEANING SERVICES/WINDOWS	BUI	LEA	ORG							B
CLIP ART SERVICE	CRE	IMP	ORG				◧			M
	PRO	ORG	IMP				◧			
CLOSET/CONSTRUCTION	BUI	ORG	LEA							
CLOSET/DESIGN	PRO	CRE	IMP				◧		✓	M
CLOSET/ORGANIZING	PRO	ORG	IMP							
CLOTHING ALTERATIONS	BUI	PRO	LEA				◧		✓	
CLOTHING DESIGNER/ATHLETIC	CRE	IMP	BUI				◧		✓	
CLOTHING DESIGNER/CHILDREN'S	CRE	IMP	BUI				◧		✓	
CLOTHING DESIGNER	CRE	IMP	BUI				◧		✓	
CLOWN FOR PARTIES, PROMOTIONS	LEA	CRE	ORG						✓	
COIN-OPERATED EQUIP MAINTNCE/LAUNDRIES/DRY CLNRS	BUI	IMP	LEA					■		
COIN-OPERATED EQUIPMENT MAINTENANCE/TV	BUI	IMP	LEA					■		
COLLECTIBLES DEALER/ANTIQUES	BUI	LEA	ORG				◧		✓	
COLLECTIBLES DEALER/AUTOGRAPHS	BUI	LEA	ORG				◧		✓	
COLLECTIBLES DEALER/BUTTERFLIES	BUI	LEA	ORG				◧		✓	
COLLECTIBLES DEALER/COMIC BOOKS	BUI	LEA	ORG				◧		✓	
COLLECTIBLES DEALER/GEMSTONES/ROCKS	BUI	LEA	ORG				◧		✓	
COLLECTIBLES DEALER/MINIATURE CARS	BUI	LEA	ORG				◧		✓	

BUI=Builder, CRE=Creator, IMP=Improver, LEA=Leader, ORG=Organizer, PRO=Problem Solver, ■=Always, ◧=Usually, □=Some

CAREER OR BUSINESS	PERSONAL STYLE 1	2	3	DEGREE REQUIRED	LICENSE REQUIREMENT	AVERAGE CAPITAL REQUIRED	DONE AT HOME	LAND OR COMMERCIAL BUILDING REQUIRED	FAMILY FRIENDLY	BOOK RESOURCES
COLLECTIBLES DEALER/RARE BOOKS	BUI	LEA	ORG				▣		✓	
COLLECTIBLES DEALER/RARE COINS	BUI	LEA	ORG				▣		✓	
COLLECTIBLES DEALER/SPORTS CARDS	BUI	LEA	ORG				▣		✓	
COLLECTIBLES DEALER/STAMPS	BUI	LEA	ORG	□			▣		✓	
COLLECTION AGENCY	LEA	IMP	CRE	□			▣			B
	ORG	IMP	BUI	□			▣			B
COLLEGE/COUNSELING SERVICE	IMP	PRO	LEA	□			▣			
COLOR CONSULTING	CRE	LEA	IMP				▣			
COMEDIAN	CRE	LEA	IMP							
COMMODITIES TRADER	LEA	PRO	ORG							
COMMNICATNS CONTRACTOR/HM SECURITY SYSTEM INSTAL	LEA	PRO	BUI	□						
COMPANION/PERSONAL	IMP	LEA	BUI							
COMPOSER	CRE	IMP	LEA				▣		✓	
COMPUTER/BULLETIN BOARD SERVICE	PRO	IMP	LEA				▣			B,M
	PRO	IMP	ORG				▣			B,M
COMPUTER/SALES AND SERVICE	LEA	BUI	PRO						M	
COMPUTER/ACCESSORIES, CUSTOMIZED	CRE	IMP	BUI			✓	▣			
COMPUTER/ANIMATION	CRE	PRO	LEA			✓	▣		✓	
COMPUTER/ARTIST	CRE	PRO	LEA				▣		✓	
COMPUTER/BULLETIN BOARDS SERVICE	PRO	BUI	ORG				▣			B,M
COMPUTER/CD-ROM MASTERING	BUI	ORG	LEA				▣			
COMPUTER/CONSULTANT	PRO	BUI	LEA				▣		✓	B,M,MH
COMPUTER/DATA RECOVERY	PRO	BUI	ORG							
COMPUTER/DEBUGGING	PRO	BUI	ORG				▣			
COMPUTER/DISK DUPLICATING SERVICE	BUI	ORG	LEA				▣		✓	B, M
COMPUTER/DISK FORMATTING	BUI	ORG	LEA				▣		✓	B, M
COMPUTER/GRAPHICS	CRE	PRO	LEA				▣		✓	
COMPUTER/PROGRAMMER-BUSINESS	ORG	PRO	BUI				▣			B,M
COMPUTER/PROGRAMMER-SCIENTIFIC	PRO	BUI	LEA				▣			B,M
COMPUTER/REPAIR AND MAINTENANCE	BUI	LEA	PRO							B,M,MH
COMPUTER/ROOM INSTALLATION	BUI	LEA	PRO							
COMPUTER/SCANNING SERVICE	ORG	BUI	PRO				▣		✓	M
COMPUTER/SECURITY CONSULTANT	PRO	BUI	LEA							
COMPUTER/SHAREWARE DEVELOPER	PRO	CRE	LEA				▣		✓	
COMPUTER/SPECIAL EFFECTS	CRE	IMP	BUI				▣		✓	MH
COMPUTER/TECHNICAL SUPPORT SERVICE	IMP	PRO	CRE							
COMPUTER/TRAINER	IMP	LEA	ORG							B,M

BUI=Builder, CRE=Creator, IMP=Improver, LEA=Leader, ORG=Organizer, PRO=Problem Solver, ■■=Always, ■□=Usually, □=Some

CAREER OR BUSINESS	PERSONAL STYLE 1	2	3	DEGREE REQUIRED	LICENSE REQUIREMENT	AVERAGE CAPITAL REQUIRED	DONE AT HOME	LAND OR COMMERCIAL BUILDING REQUIRED	FAMILY FRIENDLY	BOOK RESOURCES
COMPUTER/TUTOR	IMP	LEA	ORG							B,M
COMPUTER BACKUP SERVICE	LEA	PRO	IMP				▮			M
COMPUTER-AIDED DESIGN SERVICE	BUI	ORG	PRO				▮			M
	BUI	PRO	LEA				▮			M
	CRE	PRO	IMP				▮			M
	PRO	BUI	LEA				▮			M
	PRO	BUI	ORG				▮			M
CONCIERGE SERVICES	IMP	PRO	CRE							
CONCRETE FENCE BUILDER	BUI	LEA	PRO							
CONCRETE SCULPTOR	BUI	LEA	IMP				▮		✓	
CONDOMINIUM MANAGER	LEA	IMP	ORG							
CONFERENCE PLANNER	LEA	IMP	CRE							
	LEA	ORG	IMP							
CONSOLIDATION SERVICES/FREIGHT	ORG	PRO	IMP							
CONSOLIDATION SERVICES/ODD-LOT	ORG	PRO	IMP							
CONSTRUCTION CONTRACTOR/AIR-CONDITIONING	BUI	LEA	PRO		□					
CONSTRUCTION CONTRACTOR/CONCRETE	BUI	LEA	PRO		□					
CONSTRUCTION CONTRACTOR/DRYWALL	LEA	PRO	BUI		□					
CONSTRUCTION CONTRACTOR/EARTHWORK/PAVING	LEA	PRO	BUI		□					
CONSTRUCTION CONTRACTOR/FIRE PROTECTION SYSTEMS	LEA	PRO	BUI		□					
CONSTRUCTION CONTRACTOR/GENERAL	LEA	PRO	BUI		□					
CONSTRUCTION CONTRACTOR/GREENHOUSES	LEA	PRO	BUI		□					
CONSTRUCTION CONTRACTOR/HOME RENOVATION	BUI	ORG	PRO		□					
CONSTRUCTION CONTRACTOR/HOMES	LEA	PRO	BUI		□					
CONSTRUCTION CONTRACTOR/SMART HOUSE SYSTEMS	LEA	PRO	BUI		□					
CONSTRUCTION CONTRACTOR/STUCCO/MASONRY	BUI	LEA	PRO		□					
CONSTRUCTION CONTRACTOR/SWIMMING POOLS	LEA	PRO	BUI		□					
CONSTRUCTION COST ESTIMATOR	BUI	PRO	ORG							M
CONSTRUCTION INSPECTOR	BUI	LEA	ORG		□					
	BUI	PRO	ORG		□					
CONSULTANT/BROKER	LEA	ORG	IMP				▮		✓	B, M
CONSULTANT/CORPORATE BENEFITS	LEA	IMP	BUI							
CONSULTANT/SAFETY	LEA	IMP	PRO						✓	
CONSULTANT/SATELLITE COMMUNICATIONS	PRO	BUI	CRE							
CONSULTANT/TALENT	IMP	LEA	CRE						✓	
CONTEST ORGANIZER	LEA	CRE	ORG				▮		✓	
COOKBOOK RECIPE TESTER	BUI	IMP	LEA				▮		✓	

BUI=Builder, CRE=Creator, IMP=Improver, LEA=Leader, ORG=Organizer, PRO=Problem Solver, ■=Always, ▮=Usually, □=Some

CAREER OR BUSINESS	PERSONAL STYLE 1	2	3	DEGREE REQUIRED	LICENSE REQUIREMENT	AVERAGE CAPITAL REQUIRED	DONE AT HOME	LAND OR COMMERCIAL BUILDING REQUIRED	FAMILY FRIENDLY	BOOK RESOURCES
COOKING TEACHER	IMP	LEA	CRE							
COPYWRITER/ADVERTISING	CRE	IMP	PRO				▯		✓	B,M
COPYWRITER/BOOK COVER	CRE	IMP	PRO				▯		✓	
COPYWRITER/CORPORATE	CRE	IMP	PRO				▯		✓	
COPYWRITER/NEWSPAPER	CRE	IMP	PRO				▯		✓	
COPYWRITER/TECHNICAL	PRO	BUI	IMP				▯		✓	
COSMETOLOGIST	IMP	LEA	CRE	✓	■					
COSTUME DESIGNER	BUI	CRE	IMP				▯		✓	
COSTUME MAKER	BUI	CRE	IMP				▯		✓	
	BUI	LEA	IMP				▯		✓	
COSTUME RENTAL	BUI	LEA	IMP							
COUNSELOR/ALCOHOL, DRUG AND SUBSTANCE ABUSE	LEA	IMP	BUI	✓	□					
COUPON NEWSPAPER PUBLISHING	LEA	IMP	ORG							M
COURT REPORTER	BUI	ORG	IMP		□					B,M,MH
CRAFTS/CANDLE MAKER	BUI	LEA	ORG				▯		✓	
CRAFTS/CHRISTMAS TREE ORNAMENTS AND WREATHS	CRE	IMP	LEA				▯			
CRAFTS/DOLL HOUSES	CRE	BUI	LEA				▯		✓	
CRAFTS/DRIED FLOWER ARRANGEMENTS CREATOR	ORG	BUI	LEA				▯		✓	
CRAFTS/INSTRUCTOR	BUI	LEA	IMP							
CRAFTS/JEWELRY	BUI	LEA	ORG				▯		✓	
CRAFTS/KITE MAKER	BUI	CRE	PRO				▯		✓	
CRAFTS/KNITWEAR	BUI	ORG	LEA				▯		✓	
CRAFTS/PET TOY CREATOR	CRE	BUI	IMP				▯		✓	
CRAFTS/PRINTMAKER	CRE	LEA	IMP				▯		✓	
CRAFTS/QUILTS	BUI	LEA	ORG				▯		✓	
CRAFTS/RUGS	BUI	LEA	ORG				▯		✓	
CRAFTS/STUFFED TOYS	ORG	BUI	IMP				▯		✓	
	ORG	BUI	LEA				▯		✓	
CRAFTS/TOYS	ORG	BUI	IMP				▯		✓	
	ORG	BUI	LEA							
CRAFTS/WOOL SPINNING AND DYEING	BUI	ORG	LEA							
CRAFTS/WORKSHOP ORGANIZER	CRE	LEA	IMP							
CREATIVITY CONSULTANT	CRE	LEA	IMP							M
CRITIC/ART	CRE	LEA	IMP				▯		✓	
CRITIC/BOOKS	CRE	LEA	IMP				▯		✓	
CRITIC/FASHION	CRE	LEA	IMP							
CRITIC/MOVIES	CRE	LEA	IMP							

BUI=Builder, CRE=Creator, IMP=Improver, LEA=Leader, ORG=Organizer, PRO=Problem Solver, ■=Always, ▯=Usually, □=Some

CAREER OR BUSINESS	PERSONAL STYLE 1	2	3	DEGREE REQUIRED	LICENSE REQUIREMENT	AVERAGE CAPITAL REQUIRED	DONE AT HOME	LAND OR COMMERCIAL BUILDING REQUIRED	FAMILY FRIENDLY	BOOK RESOURCES
CRITIC/TV	CRE	LEA	IMP				◧		✓	
CROP DUSTER	BUI	PRO	LEA							
CROSS-CULTURAL TRAINING CONSULTANT	PRO	BUI	LEA							
CURATOR	PRO	BUI	IMP							
CUSTOMER SERVICE CONSULTANT	BUI	ORG	LEA							
DANCE INSTRUCTOR	CRE	IMP	LEA							
DANCE THERAPIST	CRE	IMP	PRO	✓						
DANCER	CRE	LEA	BUI							
DANCING/INSTRUCTOR	CRE	IMP	LEA							
DATA/CONVERTING SERVICE	PRO	BUI	ORG				◧		✓	
DATA/ENTRY OVERLOAD	ORG	IMP	LEA				◧		✓	
DATA/PROCESSING SERVICE	ORG	PRO	BUI							
DATABASE CONSULTANT	PRO	LEA	ORG				◧		✓	
DATABASE ENTRY AND MAINTENANCE	ORG	IMP	LEA				◧		✓	
DATABASE MARKETING SERVICE	LEA	PRO	CRE							M
DATING SERVICE	IMP	LEA	CRE							
DAY CARE/ADULTS	IMP	LEA	ORG		☐					
DEBT NEGOTIATION SERVICE	LEA	IMP	PRO				◧		✓	B
DEBUGGING SOFTWARE	PRO	BUI	CRE				◧		✓	
DEED INVESTIGATOR	IMP	LEA	ORG							
DELIVERY SERVICE	LEA	BUI	IMP							
	ORG	LEA	IMP							
DELIVERY SERVICES/CANDY	LEA	BUI	IMP							
DELIVERY SERVICES/FIREWOOD	LEA	BUI	IMP							
DELIVERY SERVICES/FLOWERS	LEA	BUI	IMP							
DELIVERY SERVICES/GROCERIES	LEA	BUI	IMP							
DELIVERY SERVICES/MEALS	ORG	LEA	IMP							
DELIVERY SERVICES/PARCELS	LEA	BUI	IMP							
DEMOLITION SPECIALIST	BUI	LEA	IMP		☐					
DENTAL HYGIENIST	IMP	CRE	PRO	✓	■					
DENTAL PRACTICE MANAGEMENT CONSULTING	IMP	LEA	ORG							
DENTAL TECHNICIAN/DENTURIST	BUI	ORG	PRO		☐					
DENTIST	PRO	IMP	BUI	✓	■	✓				
DESIGNER/INDUSTRIAL	CRE	LEA	IMP							
DESIGNER/LIGHTING	CRE	LEA	IMP							
DESIGNER/RESIDENTIAL	CRE	LEA	IMP		☐					
DESIGNER/TEXTILE	CRE	LEA	IMP				◧		✓	

BUI=Builder, CRE=Creator, IMP=Improver, LEA=Leader, ORG=Organizer, PRO=Problem Solver, ■=Always, ◧=Usually, ☐=Some

CAREER OR BUSINESS	PERSONAL STYLE 1	2	3	DEGREE REQUIRED	LICENSE REQUIREMENT	AVERAGE CAPITAL REQUIRED	DONE AT HOME	LAND OR COMMERCIAL BUILDING REQUIRED	FAMILY FRIENDLY	BOOK RESOURCES
DESIGNER/TOOL	CRE	LEA	IMP							
DESKTOP PUBLISHING SERVICE	BUI	PRO	IMP				▮		✓	B,M
	CRE	LEA	IMP				▮		✓	B,M
	IMP	PRO	CRE				▮		✓	
DESKTOP VIDEO/ANIMATION	CRE	PRO	LEA			✓	▮		✓	B,M,MH
DESKTOP VIDEO/SPECIAL EFFECTS	CRE	IMP	BUI			✓	▮		✓	B,M,MH
DESKTOP VIDEO SERVICES	CRE	BUI	LEA			✓	▮		✓	B,M,MH
DETECTIVE	PRO	BUI	IMP		▮▮					B
DIET COUNSELING	IMP	PRO	LEA				▮▮		✓	M
DIETITIAN	IMP	PRO	LEA	✓	□					
	IMP	LEA	PRO	✓	□					
DIRECT MAILING CONSULTANT	IMP	LEA	CRE							
DIRECT MARKETING CONSULTANT	IMP	LEA	CRE							
DIRECTOR/CASTING	IMP	LEA	ORG							
DIRECTOR/MOTION PICTURE	IMP	LEA	ORG							
DIRECTOR/PHOTOGRAPHY	CRE	LEA	IMP							
DIRECTOR/THEATER	CRE	LEA	IMP							
DIRECTOR/TV	IMP	LEA	CRE							
DIRECTOR/VIDEO	IMP	LEA	CRE							
DISASTER RECOVERY CONSULTANT	LEA	BUI	IMP							
DISASTER/EMERGENCY PREPAREDNESS	LEA	BUI	IMP							
DISK COPYING SERVICE	BUI	ORG	LEA				▮		✓	M
DISK FORMATTING SERVICE	BUI	ORG	LEA				▮		✓	
DISK JOCKEY SERVICE	CRE	IMP	LEA							B
DISPATCHER/TAXI	LEA	IMP	ORG							
DOG GROOMING	BUI	IMP	LEA							
DOG HANDLER	BUI	LEA	IMP		□					
DOLL/CLOTHING MAKING	BUI	IMP	LEA				▮		✓	
DOLL/HOUSE BUILDING	CRE	BUI	ORG				▮		✓	
DOLL/REPAIR	ORG	BUI	LEA				▮		✓	
DRAFTING SERVICE	BUI	ORG	PRO				▮		✓	M
	BUI	PRO	LEA				▮		✓	M
	PRO	BUI	LEA				▮		✓	M
	PRO	BUI	ORG				▮		✓	M
DRAMA COACH	CRE	IMP	LEA							
DRESSMAKING	BUI	IMP	LEA				▮		✓	
DRIVER/AUTO TEST	BUI	IMP	LEA							

BUI=Builder, CRE=Creator, IMP=Improver, LEA=Leader, ORG=Organizer, PRO=Problem Solver, ■■=Always, ▮=Usually, □=Some

CAREER OR BUSINESS	PERSONAL STYLE			DEGREE REQUIRED	LICENSE REQUIREMENT	AVERAGE CAPITAL REQUIRED	DONE AT HOME	LAND OR COMMERCIAL BUILDING REQUIRED	FAMILY FRIENDLY	BOOK RESOURCES
	1	2	3							
	BUI	LEA	PRO							
DRIVER/BOTTLED WATER DELIVERY	LEA	BUI	IMP							
DRIVER/BREAKFAST DELIVERY	LEA	BUI	IMP							
DRIVER/BUS	BUI	LEA	IMP							
DRIVER/CARRIAGE	BUI	LEA	IMP							
DRIVER/CHAUFFEUR	BUI	LEA	IMP							
	BUI	LEA	ORG							
DRIVER/CHILDREN'S TAXI SERVICE	BUI	LEA	IMP							
DRIVER/COFFEE DELIVERY	LEA	BUI	IMP							
DRIVER/COURIER SERVICE	ORG	LEA	IMP							
DRIVER/DELIVERY ROUTE	LEA	BUI	IMP							
	ORG	LEA	IMP							
DRIVER/DUMP TRUCK	BUI	PRO	LEA							
DRIVER/GROCERY DELIVERIES	LEA	BUI	IMP							
DRIVER/HANDICAPPED TRANSPORTATION	BUI	LEA	IMP							
DRIVER/INDEPENDENT TRUCKER	BUI	IMP	LEA							
DRIVER/PET TAXI SERVICE	BUI	LEA	IMP							
DRIVER/TAXI	PRO	BUI	LEA							
DRIVER/TRACTOR-TRAILER TRUCK	BUI	PRO	LEA							
DRIVING/INSTRUCTOR	IMP	LEA	BUI							
DRIVING SCHOOL OPERATOR	LEA	IMP	ORG							
DRUG AND ALCOHOL COUNSELOR	LEA	IMP	BUI	✓	□					
DUDE RANCH WRANGLER	LEA	IMP	ORG							
DUPLICATING SERVICE/AUDIOTAPES	BUI	ORG	LEA				◧		✓	B
DUPLICATING SERVICE/COMPUTER MEDIA	BUI	ORG	LEA				◧		✓	B, M
DUPLICATING SERVICE/SLIDES/OVERHEADS	BUI	ORG	LEA				◧		✓	B
DUPLICATING SERVICE/VIDEOTAPES	BUI	ORG	LEA				◧		✓	B
ECOLOGY CONSULTANT	PRO	BUI	IMP				◧			
ECONOMICS RESEARCH	PRO	CRE	IMP				◧		✓	
EDITOR/BOOKS	CRE	LEA	IMP							
EDITOR/FILM	CRE	LEA	IMP							
EDUCATION/CONSULTANT	IMP	ORG	LEA							
EDUCATIONAL/THERAPIST	PRO	LEA	IMP	✓	□					
EDUCATIONAL/RECORD-KEEPING SERVICE	ORG	IMP	PRO							
EDUCATIONAL/THERAPIST	IMP	LEA	ORG	✓	□					
ELDER CARE/ADULT DAY CARE	IMP	PRO	LEA		□	✓				
ELECTRICAL ENGINEER	PRO	BUI	LEA	✓	□					

BUI=Builder, CRE=Creator, IMP=Improver, LEA=Leader, ORG=Organizer, PRO=Problem Solver, ■=Always, ◧=Usually, □=Some

CAREER OR BUSINESS	PERSONAL STYLE 1	2	3	DEGREE REQUIRED	LICENSE REQUIREMENT	AVERAGE CAPITAL REQUIRED	DONE AT HOME	LAND OR COMMERCIAL BUILDING REQUIRED	FAMILY FRIENDLY	BOOK RESOURCES
ELECTRICIAN/ELECTRICAL CONTRACTOR	BUI	LEA	PRO		□					
	BUI	PRO	LEA		□					
ELECTROCARDIOGRAPH TECHNICIAN	BUI	ORG	PRO							
ELECTROLOGIST/ELECTRIC HAIR REMOVAL	ORG	BUI	LEA	✓	◧					
ELECTRONIC MARKETER	PRO	CRE	LEA				◧		✓	
ELECTROPLATING SERVICE	BUI	ORG	PRO			✓		■		
ELEVATOR CONTRACTOR	BUI	LEA	PRO		□					
EMBROIDERY	ORG	IMP	BUI				◧		✓	
EMERGENCY MEDICAL TECHNICIAN	PRO	BUI	IMP	✓	◧					
EMPLOYEE TRAINER	LEA	IMP	BUI							B
	LEA	IMP	CRE							B
	LEA	IMP	PRO							B
EMPLOYMENT AGENCY	IMP	LEA	ORG		□			□		
EMPLOYMENT APPLICATION CHECKING	ORG	LEA	IMP		□		◧		✓	
ENAMELING REPAIR	BUI	LEA	PRO							
ENERGY CONSERVATION CONSULTANT	BUI	LEA	IMP							
ENERGY CONSULTING/ALTERNATIVE	BUI	LEA	IMP				◧		✓	
ENERGY MANAGEMENT CONSULTANT	PRO	BUI	LEA							
ENGINEER/ACOUSTICS	PRO	BUI	LEA	✓	□					
ENGINEER/BROADCAST	PRO	LEA	BUI	✓	□					
ENGINEER/CERAMIC DESIGN	PRO	BUI	LEA	✓	□					
ENGINEER/CHEMICAL RESEARCH	PRO	BUI	LEA	✓	□					
ENGINEER/COMMUNICATIONS	PRO	BUI	LEA	✓	□					
ENGINEER/COMPUTER	PRO	BUI	LEA	✓	□					
ENGINEER/ELECTRICAL AND ELECTRONIC	PRO	BUI	LEA	✓	□					
ENGINEER/INDUSTRIAL	LEA	PRO	BUI	✓	□					
	PRO	LEA	BUI	✓	□					
ENGINEER/NUCLEAR	PRO	BUI	LEA	✓	□					
ENGINEER/RECORDING	PRO	LEA	BUI	✓	□					
ENGINEER/STRESS TESTING	PRO	LEA	BUI	✓	□					
ENGINEER/TEST	PRO	LEA	BUI	✓	□					
ENGINEER	BUI	LEA	IMP	✓	□					
	BUI	LEA	IMP				◧		✓	
	BUI	ORG	LEA				◧		✓	
ENTERTAINER/AMUSEMENT PARK	CRE	LEA	IMP							
ENTERTAINER/BELLY DANCER	CRE	LEA	IMP							
ENTERTAINER/CHARACTER IMPERSONATOR	LEA	IMP	CRE							

BUI=Builder, CRE=Creator, IMP=Improver, LEA=Leader, ORG=Organizer, PRO=Problem Solver, ■=Always, ◧=Usually, □=Some

CAREER OR BUSINESS	PERSONAL STYLE 1	2	3	DEGREE REQUIRED	LICENSE REQUIREMENT	AVERAGE CAPITAL REQUIRED	DONE AT HOME	LAND OR COMMERCIAL BUILDING REQUIRED	FAMILY FRIENDLY	BOOK RESOURCES
ENTERTAINER/COMEDIAN	CRE	IMP	LEA							
ENTERTAINER/CRUISE SHIP	LEA	IMP	CRE							
ENTERTAINER/DANCER	CRE	LEA	IMP							
ENTERTAINER/GLASSBLOWER	CRE	LEA	IMP							
ENTERTAINER/HOSPITAL	LEA	IMP	CRE							
ENTERTAINER/IMPERSONATOR	LEA	IMP	CRE							
ENTERTAINER/MAGICIAN	CRE	LEA	PRO							
ENTERTAINER/MIME	CRE	LEA	PRO							
ENTERTAINER/MUSICIAN	CRE	LEA	IMP							
ENTERTAINER/NURSING HOME	LEA	IMP	CRE							
ENTERTAINER/PUPPETEER	CRE	LEA	PRO							
ENTERTAINER/SINGER	CRE	LEA	IMP							
ENTERTAINER/STORYTELLER	LEA	IMP	CRE							
ENTERTAINER/VENTRILOQUIST	CRE	LEA	IMP							
ENVIRONMENTAL PLANNER	PRO	BUI	LEA				▮▯			
ENVIRONMENTAL SERVICES/HAZARDOUS WASTE REMOVAL	PRO	BUI	LEA		▯	✓				
ENVIRNMNTL SERVICES/INDOOR ENVIRNMNTL TESTER	BUI	LEA	IMP		▯					
ENVIRONMENTAL SERVICES/POLLUTION CONTROL	BUI	LEA	IMP							
ENVIRONMENTAL SERVICES/RECYCLING	BUI	LEA	IMP		▯					
ENVIRNMNTL SERVICES/WASTE MNGMNT CONSULTANT	BUI	LEA	IMP		▯					
EQUIPMENT EVALUATION AND SELECTION CONSULTANT	LEA	IMP	BUI							
ERRAND SERVICE	IMP	BUI	ORG							B
ESCORT SERVICE	IMP	LEA	ORG							
ESCROW TEMPORARY AGENCY	LEA	ORG	IMP				▮▯		✓	
ESTATE SALE COORDINATOR	LEA	ORG	IMP							
ESTATE-PLANNING SERVICE	LEA	IMP	PRO		▯					
ETHNOGRAPHER	PRO	BUI	LEA	✓						
ETIQUETTE CONSULTANT	IMP	LEA	ORG				▮▯		✓	B
EVENT CLEARINGHOUSE	IMP	PRO	ORG							
EVENT PLANNER/ART SHOWS	LEA	ORG	CRE							B,M
EVENT PLANNER/CHILDREN'S PARTIES	LEA	ORG	IMP						✓	B,M
EVENT PLANNER/CONFERENCES	LEA	ORG	PRO							B,M
EVENT PLANNER/CONVENTIONS	LEA	ORG	PRO							B,M
EVENT PLANNER/FUND-RAISERS	LEA	ORG	IMP		▯					B,M
EVENT PLANNER/SPORTS EVENTS	LEA	ORG	BUI							B,M
EVENT PLANNER/SPOUSE PROGRAMS	LEA	ORG	IMP							B,M
EVENT PLANNER/TRADE SHOWS	LEA	ORG	PRO							B,M

BUI=Builder, CRE=Creator, IMP=Improver, LEA=Leader, ORG=Organizer, PRO=Problem Solver, ▮▮=Always, ▮▯=Usually, ▯=Some

CAREER OR BUSINESS	PERSONAL STYLE			DEGREE REQUIRED	LICENSE REQUIREMENT	AVERAGE CAPITAL REQUIRED	DONE AT HOME	LAND OR COMMERCIAL BUILDING REQUIRED	FAMILY FRIENDLY	BOOK RESOURCES
	1	2	3							
EXCAVATION SERVICE	BUI	LEA	IMP		□					
EXECUTIVE DIRECTOR SERVICES	LEA	IMP	BUI							
	LEA	IMP	CRE							B
EXECUTIVE RECRUITER	IMP	BUI	LEA		□		▮			B
EXERCISE AND PHYSICAL FITNESS INSTRUCTION	IMP	LEA	BUI							B
EXPENSE REDUCTION SERVICE	PRO	ORG	LEA							B
EXPERT BROKER	LEA	ORG	IMP				▮			B,M
EXPERT LOCATION SERVICE	PRO	LEA	ORG				▮			
EXPERT WITNESS IN YOUR SPECIALTY	PRO	LEA	IMP							
EXPLORER	PRO	LEA	BUI			✓				
EXPORT AGENT	IMP	LEA	ORG							B
EXPORTER	IMP	LEA	ORG							
EXPOSITION MANAGER	LEA	ORG	IMP							
EXTERMINATOR	BUI	LEA	IMP		□					
EYESIGHT TRAINER	PRO	IMP	BUI		□					
FABRIC DESIGNER	CRE	LEA	ORG				▮		✓	
FACIALIST/SKIN CARE SPECIALIST	IMP	CRE	ORG	✓	□					B
	IMP	LEA	CRE	✓	□					B
FAMILY CHILD-CARE PROVIDER	IMP	LEA	ORG		□		▮		✓	B
FAMILY HISTORIAN	LEA	IMP	ORG				▮		✓	
FARMER	BUI	PRO	IMP			✓		■	✓	
FASHION/CONSULTANT	LEA	CRE	IMP				▮		✓	
FASHION/ILLUSTRATOR	CRE	LEA	PRO				▮		✓	
FASHION/MERCHANDISING CONSULTANT	CRE	LEA	IMP							
FASHION/COORDINATOR	LEA	CRE	IMP							
FASHION/CRITIC	CRE	LEA	IMP							
FASHION/DESIGNER	CRE	LEA	PRO				▮		✓	
FASHION/EDITOR	CRE	LEA	IMP				▮		✓	
FASHION/WRITER	CRE	LEA	IMP				▮		✓	
FASHION MERCHANDISING/CONSULTANT	LEA	IMP	CRE							
FAX-ON-DEMAND SERVICE	LEA	IMP	CRE				▮		✓	M
FENCE CONSTRUCTION	BUI	LEA	PRO		□					
FILM PRODUCER	LEA	IMP	CRE							
FILM-PROCESSING SERVICE	BUI	LEA	IMP							
FINANCIAL CONSULTANT	LEA	IMP	BUI		FED		▮		✓	
FINANCIAL INFORMATION SERVICE	PRO	LEA	CRE		FED		▮		✓	M
FINANCIAL PLANNER	LEA	IMP	BUI		FED		▮		✓	

BUI=Builder, CRE=Creator, IMP=Improver, LEA=Leader, ORG=Organizer, PRO=Problem Solver, ■=Always, ▮=Usually, □=Some

CAREER OR BUSINESS	PERSONAL STYLE 1	2	3	DEGREE REQUIRED	LICENSE REQUIREMENT	AVERAGE CAPITAL REQUIRED	DONE AT HOME	LAND OR COMMERCIAL BUILDING REQUIRED	FAMILY FRIENDLY	BOOK RESOURCES
FINDOLOGIST	PRO	IMP	ORG				▣		✓	
	BUI	LEA	PRO		□					
	IMP	LEA	ORG		□					
FIRE SAFETY CONSULTANT	ORG	LEA	IMP		□					
FIREWOOD DELIVERY AND STACKING	LEA	BUI	IMP							
FIREWORKS DISPLAY	LEA	IMP	PRO		□					
FIREWORKS DISPLAY PRODUCER	BUI	LEA	PRO		□					
FISHERMAN, COMMERCIAL	BUI	LEA	PRO		□	✓				
FISHING AND HUNTING INFORMATION	BUI	LEA	IMP				▣		✓	
FITNESS INSTRUCTOR	IMP	LEA	BUI							
FITNESS TRAINER	IMP	BUI	LEA		□					B
FLIGHT INSTRUCTOR	BUI	LEA	IMP	✓						
FLOWER DELIVERY SERVICE, WEEKLY	ORG	LEA	IMP							
FLOWER-ARRANGING SERVICE	ORG	BUI	LEA							
FLYING/INSTRUCTOR	IMP	BUI	LEA							
	LEA	BUI	IMP							
FOCUS GROUP RESEARCH	IMP	PRO	CRE							
FOLEY ARTIST (SOUND EFFECTS CREATOR)	BUI	CRE	LEA							
FOOD/CRAFTING	PRO	IMP	BUI						✓	
FOOD/MAIL ORDER SALES	BUI	LEA	IMP							
FOOD/ROADSIDE FRUIT STAND	BUI	ORG	LEA							
FOOD/SERVICE MANAGEMENT	LEA	IMP	BUI							
FOOD/SPECIAL DIET DELIVERY	ORG	LEA	IMP							
FOOD/SPECIALTY JAMS AND PRESERVES	PRO	IMP	BUI							
FOOD/STYLIST	PRO	IMP	BUI							
FOREIGN CORRESPONDENT	LEA	CRE	IMP							
FORENSIC RECONSTRUCTION SPECIALIST	PRO	BUI	ORG							
FOREST SERVICE TRAIL CONTRACTOR	PRO	BUI	LEA							
FORESTER	BUI	PRO	IMP							
FORM DESIGNING	BUI	ORG	IMP				▣		✓	B
FOSTER PARENT	IMP	LEA	ORG				▣		✓	
FOUNTAIN PEN REPAIR	BUI	LEA	PRO				▣		✓	
FRAMER/PICTURES, MIRRORS	ORG	BUI	LEA							
FRANCHISE BROKER/DEALER	LEA	ORG	IMP		□		▣			
FRANCHISING CONSULTANT	LEA	IMP	CRE							
FREE CLASSIFIED ADVERTISING NEWSPAPER	LEA	ORG	IMP							
FREIGHT TRAFFIC CONSULTANT	ORG	PRO	BUI							

BUI=Builder, CRE=Creator, IMP=Improver, LEA=Leader, ORG=Organizer, PRO=Problem Solver, ■■=Always, ▣=Usually, □=Some

CAREER OR BUSINESS	PERSONAL STYLE 1	2	3	DEGREE REQUIRED	LICENSE REQUIREMENT	AVERAGE CAPITAL REQUIRED	DONE AT HOME	LAND OR COMMERCIAL BUILDING REQUIRED	FAMILY FRIENDLY	BOOK RESOURCES
FUND-RAISER, PROFESSIONAL	LEA	IMP	CRE	□						
	IMP	LEA	ORG	□						
FUNERAL DIRECTOR	LEA	IMP	BUI	▮	✓					
FUR TRAPPER	BUI	LEA	IMP	□						
FURNACE INSTALLER AND REPAIRER	BUI	LEA	PRO	□						
FURNITURE/REFINISHER	IMP	BUI	LEA				▮		✓	
FURNITURE/RENTAL CONSULTANT	IMP	LEA	BUI							
FURNITURE/REPRODUCER	PRO	IMP	LEA				▮		✓	
FURNITURE/CLEANER	BUI	LEA	IMP							
FURNITURE/CUSTOM MADE	PRO	IMP	LEA				▮		✓	
FURNITURE/DESIGNER	CRE	LEA	IMP				▮		✓	
	BUI	ORG	LEA				▮		✓	
FURNITURE/RESTORER	BUI	ORG	IMP				▮		✓	
FURNITURE/STRIPPER	IMP	BUI	LEA				▮		✓	
GAME BIRD PROPAGATOR	BUI	LEA	PRO		■			■	✓	
GAME DESIGNER/COMPUTER	CRE	PRO	LEA				▮		✓	
GAME DESIGNER/EDUCATIONAL	CRE	PRO	IMP				▮		✓	
GARAGE DOOR SERVICE	BUI	PRO	LEA							
GARDEN CARE	BUI	ORG	PRO							
GARDEN CARE/ROTOTILLING SERVICE	BUI	ORG	PRO							
GEM AND DIAMOND CUTTER	BUI	ORG	LEA							
GEMOLOGIST	BUI	LEA	PRO							
GEMSTONE DEALER	BUI	LEA	IMP				▮			
GENEALOGY RESEARCH SERVICE	LEA	IMP	ORG				▮		✓	
GENERATING SALES LEADS	LEA	IMP	CRE				▮			
GEOLOGIST	PRO	BUI	LEA	✓	□		▮			
GHOSTWRITING SERVICE	CRE	IMP	PRO				▮		✓	
GIFT/BASKET SERVICE	CRE	BUI	IMP				▮			B
GIFT/BUYING SERVICE	LEA	IMP	ORG				▮			B
GIFT/WRAPPING SERVICE	BUI	ORG	LEA				▮			
GLASS/CREATOR	BUI	ORG	IMP				▮		✓	
GLASS/STAINED	BUI	LEA	CRE				▮		✓	
	PRO	IMP	CRE				▮		✓	
GLASS/ETCHING	BUI	LEA	PRO	□			▮		✓	
GLASS/REPAIR	BUI	IMP	LEA	□						
GLAZIER	ORG	BUI	LEA	□						
	BUI	IMP	LEA	□						

BUI=Builder, CRE=Creator, IMP=Improver, LEA=Leader, ORG=Organizer, PRO=Problem Solver, ■=Always, ▮=Usually, □=Some

CAREER OR BUSINESS	PERSONAL STYLE 1	2	3	DEGREE REQUIRED	LICENSE REQUIREMENT	AVERAGE CAPITAL REQUIRED	DONE AT HOME	LAND OR COMMERCIAL BUILDING REQUIRED	FAMILY FRIENDLY	BOOK RESOURCES
GOLDSMITH	BUI	LEA	ORG				◧		✓	
GOLF COACH	IMP	BUI	LEA							
GOLF-HANDICAPPING SERVICE	BUI	PRO	IMP				◧			
GOURMET COOKING SCHOOL	BUI	LEA	IMP							
GOVERNMENT/BID NOTIFICATION SERVICE	ORG	IMP	PRO				◧		✓	
GOVERNMENT/FORM-FILLING SERVICE	ORG	IMP	LEA				◧		✓	
GOVERNMENT/PROCUREMENT CONSULTANT	LEA	ORG	PRO				◧		✓	
GOVERNMENT ADMINISTRATION CONSULTANT	LEA	IMP	ORG							
	LEA	IMP	CRE							
GRANT WRITER	CRE	IMP	PRO				◧		✓	B
	PRO	BUI	IMP				◧		✓	B
GRAPHIC DESIGNER	CRE	LEA	IMP				◧		✓	
GRAPHOLOGIST	CRE	ORG	IMP				◧		✓	
GREETING CARD/ARTIST/DESIGNER	CRE	LEA	IMP				◧		✓	
GREETING CARD/WRITER	CRE	LEA	IMP				◧		✓	
GROWER/BONSAI	BUI	CRE	LEA				◧		✓	
GROWER/CHRISTMAS TREE	BUI	LEA	PRO					■	✓	
GROWER/FRUIT TREE	BUI	LEA	PRO					■	✓	
GROWER/NURSERY	BUI	LEA	PRO		□		◧		✓	
GROWER/ORCHID	BUI	LEA	PRO				◧		✓	
GROWER, SPECIALTY FOODS/EDIBLE FLOWERS	BUI	LEA	PRO				◧		✓	B
GROWER, SPECIALTY FOODS/GINSENG	BUI	LEA	PRO		□		◧		✓	B
GROWER, SPECIALTY FOODS/HERBS	BUI	LEA	PRO				◧		✓	B
GROWER, SPECIALTY FOODS/MUSHROOM	BUI	LEA	PRO				◧		✓	B
GROWER, SPECIALTY FOODS/SPROUTS	BUI	LEA	PRO				◧		✓	B
GUIDE/ALPINE	BUI	LEA	PRO		□					
GUIDE/HUNTING AND FISHING	BUI	LEA	IMP		□					
GUIDE/RIVER RAFTING	BUI	LEA	IMP		□					
GUN REPAIR	BUI	LEA	IMP		FED					
GUNSMITH	BUI	LEA	IMP		FED					
GYMNASTICS INSTRUCTOR	IMP	BUI	LEA							
HAIR COLORIST	CRE	BUI	PRO	✓	■					
HAIR JEWELRY DESIGNER	BUI	LEA	CRE				◧		✓	
HAIR JEWELRY MAKER	BUI	LEA	ORG				◧		✓	
HAIRSTYLIST	CRE	IMP	BUI	✓	■					
	IMP	LEA	BUI	✓	■					
HAND LETTERING	CRE	BUI	ORG				◧		✓	

BUI=Builder, CRE=Creator, IMP=Improver, LEA=Leader, ORG=Organizer, PRO=Problem Solver, ■=Always, ◧=Usually, □=Some

CAREER OR BUSINESS	PERSONAL STYLE 1	2	3	DEGREE REQUIRED	LICENSE REQUIREMENT	AVERAGE CAPITAL REQUIRED	DONE AT HOME	LAND OR COMMERCIAL BUILDING REQUIRED	FAMILY FRIENDLY	BOOK RESOURCES
HANDICRAFT/MAKING	BUI	LEA	IMP				▣		✓	
HANDICRAFT/MANUFACTURE	BUI	LEA	ORG				▣		✓	
HANDWRITING ANALYST	CRE	ORG	IMP				▣		✓	
HANDYMAN SERVICE	BUI	LEA	PRO							
HARPSICHORD MAKER	BUI	LEA	PRO				▣		✓	
HAULING SERVICE	LEA	IMP	BUI							B
HEALTH CARE CONSULTANT	BUI	PRO	ORG				▣		✓	
HEALTH ENHANCEMENT PRODUCT SALES	LEA	IMP	CRE				▣		✓	
HEATING AND AIR-CONDITIONING CONTRACTOR	BUI	LEA	PRO		■					
HEAVY EQUIPMENT OWNER AND OPERATOR	BUI	LEA	ORG		□	✓				
	BUI	ORG	PRO		□	✓				
HELICOPTER PILOT	BUI	PRO	IMP	✓	■	✓				
HERB GROWER	PRO	BUI	ORG				▣		✓	
HISTORIAN/ART	IMP	LEA	PRO	✓			▣		✓	
HISTORIAN/FAMILY	IMP	LEA	PRO				▣		✓	
HISTORIAN/HOUSE	IMP	LEA	PRO				▣		✓	
HISTORIAN/ORGANIZATIONAL	IMP	LEA	PRO				▣		✓	
HISTORIAN/PERSONAL	IMP	LEA	PRO				▣		✓	
HOME/ECONOMIST	IMP	LEA	CRE	✓			▣		✓	
HOME/HEALTH AIDE	IMP	PRO	LEA		■					
HOME/HISTORIAN	IMP	LEA	PRO				▣		✓	
HOME/INSPECTOR	BUI	LEA	ORG		□					B
	BUI	PRO	ORG		□					B
	CRE	IMP	LEA		□					B
HOME/REPAIR SERVICES	BUI	ORG	PRO							
HOME/SCHOOLING CONSULTANT	IMP	LEA	ORG				▣		✓	
HOME/SCHOOLING GRADER	IMP	LEA	ORG				▣		✓	
HOME/SECURITY ANALYSIS SERVICE	LEA	IMP	BUI							
HOME/SECURITY PATROL SERVICE	LEA	IMP	BUI							
HOME/TUTOR	IMP	LEA	ORG				▣		✓	B
HOME HEALTH AIDE	IMP	CRE	ORG		□					
HOMEOPATH	PRO	LEA	IMP		□					
HORSE EXERCISER	BUI	LEA	CRE							
HORSE TRAINER	IMP	LEA	ORG							
HORSEBACK-RIDING INSTRUCTION	CRE	LEA	BUI			✓				
HORTICULTURIST	PRO	BUI	IMP		□					
HOT-AIR BALLOONIST	BUI	LEA	PRO			✓				

BUI=Builder, CRE=Creator, IMP=Improver, LEA=Leader, ORG=Organizer, PRO=Problem Solver, ■=Always, ▣=Usually, □=Some

CAREER OR BUSINESS	PERSONAL STYLE 1	2	3	DEGREE REQUIRED	LICENSE REQUIREMENT	AVERAGE CAPITAL REQUIRED	DONE AT HOME	LAND OR COMMERCIAL BUILDING REQUIRED	FAMILY FRIENDLY	BOOK RESOURCES
HOTEL MARKETING/CONSULTANT	LEA	IMP	ORG							
HOUSE/MOVER	BUI	IMP	LEA		□					
HOUSE/PAINTER	BUI	IMP	LEA		□					
HOUSE/PORTRAIT PAINTING	CRE	IMP	LEA				◪		✓	
HOUSE-SITTER	BUI	ORG	IMP							
HOUSING CONSULTANT	LEA	IMP	BUI				◪			
HUMAN RELATIONS COUNSELOR	LEA	IMP	BUI							
HUMAN REPRODUCTION CONSULTANT	IMP	PRO	CRE				◪			
HUMAN RESOURCES CONSULTANT	LEA	IMP	BUI							
HUMORIST	CRE	IMP	LEA				◪		✓	
HUNTER EDUCATION INSTRUCTOR	BUI	LEA	IMP		□					
HUNTING GUIDE	BUI	LEA	IMP		□					
HYPNOTHERAPIST	BUI	LEA	ORG	✓	□				✓	
	BUI	LEA	CRE							
ICE CARVER	BUI	LEA	PRO							
ICE-SKATING/COACH	IMP	BUI	LEA							
ILLUSTRATOR/CATALOGS	CRE	LEA	IMP				◪		✓	
ILLUSTRATOR/CHILDREN'S BOOKS	CRE	LEA	IMP				◪		✓	
ILLUSTRATOR/FASHION	CRE	LEA	IMP				◪		✓	
	CRE	LEA	IMP				◪		✓	
ILLUSTRATOR/MEDICAL	CRE	LEA	IMP				◪		✓	
	CRE	PRO	LEA				◪		✓	
ILLUSTRATOR/TECHNICAL	CRE	PRO	LEA				◪		✓	
IMAGE CONSULTANT	CRE	LEA	PRO							B
	IMP	CRE	LEA							B
IMPERSONATOR	CRE	LEA	IMP							
IMPORTER	IMP	LEA	ORG							
IN-HOME HEALTH CARE	IMP	LEA	BUI		□		◪			
	IMP	LEA	ORG		□		◪			
IN-STORE PROMOTIONS SERVICE	LEA	IMP	ORG							
INCOME TAX SERVICE	LEA	ORG	IMP		□		◪			
INDEXING SERVICE	ORG	PRO	IMP				◪		✓	B
INDOOR ENVIRONMENTAL TESTER	PRO	BUI	IMP							B
	PRO	BUI	LEA							
INFORMATION BROKER	PRO	LEA	CRE		□		◪		✓	B,M,MH
	PRO	ORG	BUI		□		◪		✓	B,M,MH
INFORMATION TECHNOLOGY AND SYSTEMS CONSULTANT	LEA	PRO	IMP							

BUI=Builder, CRE=Creator, IMP=Improver, LEA=Leader, ORG=Organizer, PRO=Problem Solver, ■=Always, ◪=Usually, □=Some

CAREER OR BUSINESS	PERSONAL STYLE 1	2	3	DEGREE REQUIRED	LICENSE REQUIREMENT	AVERAGE CAPITAL REQUIRED	DONE AT HOME	LAND OR COMMERCIAL BUILDING REQUIRED	FAMILY FRIENDLY	BOOK RESOURCES
INSECT BREEDER/BUTTERFLIES	BUI	LEA	IMP						✓	
INSECT BREEDER/EARTHWORMS	BUI	LEA	IMP				◐		✓	
INSECT BREEDER/FISH BAIT	BUI	LEA	IMP						✓	
INSECT BREEDER/LADYBUGS	BUI	LEA	IMP						✓	
INSTALLER/AIR-CONDITIONING	BUI	LEA	PRO		□					
INSTALLER/CAR STEREOS	BUI	LEA	IMP							
INSTALLER/DRYWALL	BUI	PRO	LEA							
INSTALLER/ELECTRIC FANS	BUI	IMP	LEA		□					
INSTALLER/FLOORING	BUI	LEA	IMP		□					
INSTALLER/FURNITURE GLASS	BUI	ORG	IMP		□					
INSTALLER/MILK EQUIPMENT	BUI	PRO	IMP		□					
INSTALLER/MUSEUM	BUI	IMP	ORG							
INSTALLER/PUMP	BUI	LEA	IMP		□					
INSTALLER/SATELLITE DISH	BUI	IMP	ORG		□					
INSTALLER/SECURITY SYSTEMS	BUI	IMP	ORG		□					
INSTALLER/SEWAGE SYSTEM	BUI	LEA	IMP		□					
INSTALLER/SKYLIGHTS	BUI	IMP	LEA		□					
INSTALLER/STAINED GLASS	BUI	PRO	LEA		□					
INSTALLER/SWIMMING POOL	BUI	ORG	PRO		□					
INSTALLER/TELEPHONE	BUI	PRO	LEA		□					
INSTALLER/TILE	BUI	IMP	LEA		□					
INSTALLER/TV/RADIO	BUI	PRO	LEA		□					
INSTALLER/WATER PURIFIERS AND SOFTENERS	BUI	ORG	IMP		□					
INSTALLER/WINDOW	BUI	PRO	LEA		□					
INSTALLER/WOOD STOVE	BUI	LEA	PRO		□					
INSTRUCTIONAL DESIGNER	PRO	IMP	CRE				◐		✓	
INSTRUCTOR/GUIDE DOGS FOR THE BLIND	BUI	LEA	IMP		□		◐		✓	
INSULATION AND ACOUSTICAL CONTRACTOR	LEA	PRO	BUI		□					
INSURANCE ADJUSTER	LEA	IMP	ORG		□					
	IMP	LEA	PRO		□					
INSURANCE AGENT	LEA	IMP	ORG		■				✓	
INSURANCE BROKER	LEA	IMP	ORG		□				✓	
INSURANCE CONSULTANT	LEA	IMP	ORG		□				✓	
INSURANCE INSPECTION AND AUDITS	LEA	IMP	ORG							
INSURANCE PARAMEDICAL EXAMINER	PRO	IMP	BUI							
INSURANCE SOLICITOR	LEA	IMP	ORG		□					
INSURANCE THIRD PARTY ADMINISTRATOR	LEA	IMP	ORG		□					

BUI=Builder, CRE=Creator, IMP=Improver, LEA=Leader, ORG=Organizer, PRO=Problem Solver, ■■=Always, ◐=Usually, □=Some

CAREER OR BUSINESS	PERSONAL STYLE 1	2	3	DEGREE REQUIRED	LICENSE REQUIREMENT	AVERAGE CAPITAL REQUIRED	DONE AT HOME	LAND OR COMMERCIAL BUILDING REQUIRED	FAMILY FRIENDLY	BOOK RESOURCES
INTERIOR DECORATOR	CRE	LEA	IMP							B
INTERIOR DESIGNER	CRE	LEA	IMP	✓	□					
INTERNATIONAL OPERATIONS CONSULTANT	IMP	PRO	CRE							
INTERPRETER/SIGN LANGUAGE	IMP	ORG	LEA							
INTERPRETING SERVICE/LANGUAGES	LEA	IMP	CRE							
INTERVIEW COACH	CRE	IMP	LEA							
INTERVIEWER—PRINT, RADIO, OR TV	CRE	IMP	LEA							
INVENTOR	PRO	BUI	CRE				◧		✓	
INVENTORY CONTROL SERVICES FOR BUSINESSES	BUI	ORG	PRO							M
INVENTORY HOUSEHOLD EFFECTS	BUI	ORG	PRO							
INVESTIGATOR, PRIVATE	LEA	IMP	PRO		◧					
INVESTMENT/ADVISOR REFERRAL SERVICE	IMP	PRO	LEA		FED					
INVESTMENT/BANKER	LEA	IMP	ORG		FED					
INVESTMENT/COUNSELOR	PRO	IMP	LEA		FED					
IRRIGATION SYSTEM/CONSULTANT	PRO	BUI	LEA							
JANITORIAL SERVICE	BUI	LEA	IMP							B
JEWELRY/APPRAISAL	BUI	PRO	IMP				◧		✓	
JEWELRY/DESIGN	BUI	LEA	CRE				◧		✓	
JEWELRY/MAKING	BUI	LEA	CRE				◧		✓	
JEWELRY/REPAIR	BUI	LEA	CRE				◧		✓	
JOB PLACEMENT AND REFERRAL SERVICE	PRO	LEA	IMP	✓	□		◧			
JOURNALIST	CRE	IMP	LEA	✓			◧		✓	
KAYAK BUILDER	BUI	LEA	PRO							
KAYAK INSTRUCTOR	BUI	LEA	IMP							
KEY SERVICE	BUI	ORG	LEA							
KITCHEN/DESIGN	CRE	PRO	LEA				◧		✓	
KITCHEN/REMODELING	BUI	LEA	PRO		□					
KITE DEALER	BUI	LEA	PRO							
KITE MAKER	BUI	LEA	PRO				◧		✓	
KNITTING/BY AUTOMATED MACHINE	BUI	ORG	LEA				◧		✓	
KNITTING/INSTRUCTION	ORG	BUI	LEA							
KNITTING/SELLING SUPPLIES	LEA	IMP	CRE				◧		✓	
KNITWEAR CREATOR	BUI	CRE	PRO				◧		✓	
LABOR CONTRACTOR	LEA	IMP	PRO		□					
LAND SURVEYOR	PRO	LEA	CRE		■					
LANDSCAPE ARCHITECT	CRE	PRO	BUI	✓	◧		◧			
LANDSCAPE CONTRACTOR	LEA	IMP	BUI		□					

BUI=Builder, CRE=Creator, IMP=Improver, LEA=Leader, ORG=Organizer, PRO=Problem Solver, ■=Always, ◧=Usually, □=Some

CAREER OR BUSINESS	PERSONAL STYLE 1	2	3	DEGREE REQUIRED	LICENSE REQUIREMENT	AVERAGE CAPITAL REQUIRED	DONE AT HOME	LAND OR COMMERCIAL BUILDING REQUIRED	FAMILY FRIENDLY	BOOK RESOURCES
LANDSCAPE DESIGNER	CRE	PRO	BUI							
LANDSCAPE GARDENER	BUI	LEA	ORG							
LANDSCAPING SERVICE	BUI	PRO	IMP							
LANGUAGE INSTRUCTION	CRE	LEA	IMP							
LASER CARTRIDGE MANUFACTURING	BUI	ORG	LEA							
LASER LIGHT SHOW PRODUCER	BUI	PRO	CRE							
LASER TECHNICIAN	BUI	PRO	ORG							
LAUNDRY SERVICES	BUI	LEA	PRO							
LAW/OFFICE MANAGEMENT CONSULTANT	IMP	LEA	ORG							
LAWN & YARD CARE, MWNG, RKNG, MLCHNG, SNOW RMVL	BUI	LEA	PRO							
LAWN CARE SERVICE	BUI	LEA	PRO							
LEAK DETECTION SERVICE	BUI	LEA	PRO							B
LEATHER WORKER	BUI	IMP	LEA						✓	
LECTURER/PUBLIC SPEAKING/INFORMATIONAL	PRO	LEA	IMP							
LECTURER/PUBLIC SPEAKING/MOTIVATIONAL	CRE	LEA	IMP							
LEGAL SECRETARIAL SERVICES	ORG	IMP	LEA							
LEGAL TRANSCRIPTION SERVICE	ORG	IMP	LEA				▮		✓	M,MH
LEGAL VIDEO SERVICES	LEA	IMP	CRE							
LETTER WRITER	CRE	IMP	LEA				▮		✓	
LIBRARY MANAGER/FILM	IMP	CRE	PRO	□						
LIBRARY MANAGER/LAW	IMP	LEA	ORG	□						
LIBRARY MANAGER/TAPE	IMP	CRE	PRO	□						
LIBRETTIST	CRE	IMP	LEA						✓	
LIGHTING CONSULTANT	BUI	LEA	PRO							
LIGHTING DESIGNER	BUI	PRO	CRE							
LIMOUSINE SERVICE	BUI	LEA	IMP							
LINGERIE SALES	LEA	IMP	CRE						✓	
LIQUIDATED GOODS BROKER	LEA	ORG	BUI							
LITERARY AGENT	LEA	IMP	CRE				▮		✓	
LITIGATION SUPPORT	IMP	LEA	ORG							
LIVESTOCK AGENT	BUI	LEA	PRO		□					
LIVESTOCK AUCTION OPERATOR	LEA	BUI	PRO		□					
LIVESTOCK AUCTIONEER	CRE	LEA	IMP		□					
LIVESTOCK BUYER/BROKER/DEALER	BUI	LEA	PRO		□					
LIVESTOCK HAULER	BUI	IMP	PRO		□					
LIVESTOCK RANCHER	BUI	IMP	PRO		□					
LOAN/PACKAGER	LEA	IMP	CRE							

BUI=Builder, CRE=Creator, IMP=Improver, LEA=Leader, ORG=Organizer, PRO=Problem Solver, ▮=Always, ▮=Usually, □=Some

CAREER OR BUSINESS	PERSONAL STYLE 1	2	3	DEGREE REQUIRED	LICENSE REQUIREMENT	AVERAGE CAPITAL REQUIRED	DONE AT HOME	LAND OR COMMERCIAL BUILDING REQUIRED	FAMILY FRIENDLY	BOOK RESOURCES
LOBBYIST	LEA	CRE	BUI		□					
LOCKSMITHING	BUI	LEA	ORG							
LOST PET LOCATION SERVICE/(PET DETECTIVE)	LEA	IMP	PRO							
LUGGAGE REPAIRER	BUI	IMP	LEA							
LUNCH TRUCK SERVICE	LEA	BUI	IMP			✓				
LYRICIST	CRE	IMP	LEA						✓	
MACHINIST	BUI	PRO	LEA							
MAGICIAN	CRE	LEA	IMP						✓	
MAIL ORDER BUSINESS	LEA	CRE	BUI						✓	B
MAILING LIST BROKER	PRO	ORG	BUI						✓	B,MH
MAILING LIST SERVICE	PRO	ORG	BUI							B,M,MH
MAILING LIST SERVICES/BULK MAILING	PRO	ORG	BUI							B,M,MH
MAILING LIST SERVICES/COMPILATION AND RENTAL	PRO	ORG	BUI							B,M,MH
MAILING LIST SERVICES/MAINTENANCE	PRO	ORG	BUI				◨		✓	B,M,MH
MAILING SERVICE/FULFILLMENT SERVICE	PRO	ORG	BUI							
MAILING SERVICE/HANDWRITTEN ADDRESSING	PRO	ORG	BUI				◨		✓	
MAILING SERVICE/PRESORTING	PRO	ORG	BUI							
MAKEUP ARTIST/CONSULTANT	CRE	LEA	BUI		□					
MANAGEMENT CONSULTANT	PRO	LEA	BUI						✓	B
MANAGEMENT TRAINING	LEA	IMP	BUI							B
MANTEL REPAIR	IMP	BUI	LEA							
MANUFACTURER'S AGENT/REPRESENTATIVE	LEA	IMP	CRE							B
MANUFACTURING SPECIALTY PRODUCTS/BIRDHOUSES	BUI	LEA	IMP						✓	
MANUFCTURNG SPECIALTY PRDUCTS/CUSTOM PARTY FAVORS	ORG	BUI	LEA							
MANUFACTURING SPECIALTY PRODUCTS/DOGHOUSES	BUI	LEA	IMP						✓	
MANUFCTURNG SPECIALTY PRDUCTS/NAPKIN IMPRINTING	BUI	LEA	IMP						✓	
MANUFCTURNG SPECIALTY PRDUCTS/PERSONALIZED ITEMS	BUI	LEA	IMP							
MANUFACTURING SPECIALTY PRODUCTS/SOUVENIRS	BUI	LEA	IMP						✓	
MANUSCRIPT EDITING	CRE	LEA	IMP				◨		✓	
MARKET MAPPING SERVICE	CRE	PRO	IMP							M
MARKETING CONSULTANT	LEA	IMP	CRE				◨		✓	
MARKETING RESEARCH	PRO	IMP	ORG							
MARKSMANSHIP INSTRUCTOR	LEA	IMP	BUI							
MARRIAGE AND FAMILY COUNSELOR/THERAPIST	IMP	LEA	PRO	✓	◼					
MARRIAGE BROKER	IMP	PRO	CRE						✓	
MARTIAL ARTS INSTRUCTOR	IMP	LEA	BUI							
MASSAGE INSTRUCTOR	BUI	LEA	IMP		□					

BUI=Builder, CRE=Creator, IMP=Improver, LEA=Leader, ORG=Organizer, PRO=Problem Solver, ◼=Always, ◨=Usually, □=Some

CAREER OR BUSINESS	PERSONAL STYLE 1	2	3	DEGREE REQUIRED	LICENSE REQUIREMENT	AVERAGE CAPITAL REQUIRED	DONE AT HOME	LAND OR COMMERCIAL BUILDING REQUIRED	FAMILY FRIENDLY	BOOK RESOURCES
MASSAGE THERAPIST	BUI	LEA	IMP		□					
MATCHMAKER	IMP	PRO	CRE						✓	
MATERIALS MANAGEMENT CONSULTANT	LEA	IMP	BUI							
MATH TUTOR	IMP	LEA	PRO						✓	B
MEDIATOR/MARITAL	IMP	PRO	CRE		□					B
MEDIATOR	IMP	PRO	CRE							B,MH
MEDICAL RECORDS REVIEW	ORG	IMP	LEA							
MEDICAL TRANSCRIPTION SERVICE	PRO	ORG	IMP				◧		✓	B,M,MH
	ORG	BUI	PRO				◧		✓	B,M,MH
MEDICAL BILLING SERVICE	ORG	IMP	BUI				◧		✓	B,M,MH
MEDICAL CLAIMS ASSISTANCE	ORG	PRO	IMP				◧		✓	B,MH
MEDICAL CLAIMS PROCESSING SERVICE	ORG	IMP	BUI							B,MH
MEDICAL ILLUSTRATOR	CRE	PRO	LEA				◧		✓	
MEDICAL PHYSICIST	PRO	BUI	IMP	✓	□					
MEETING PLANNER	CRE	LEA	IMP							B
MESSENGER SERVICE	ORG	LEA	IMP							
MICROBIOLOGIST	PRO	BUI	IMP	✓	□					
MIDWIFE	IMP	PRO	BUI	✓	◧					
MILK GRADER/SAMPLER/HAULER	BUI	PRO	IMP		◧					
MILLINER/HAT MAKER	CRE	LEA	IMP							
MINE BLASTER	BUI	PRO	LEA		□					
MINIATURE ITEMS FOR COLLECTORS	CRE	BUI	LEA						✓	
	CRE	BUI	ORG						✓	
MINIATURE SET CONSTRUCTOR	CRE	BUI	LEA						✓	
MIRROR/CUSTOM DESIGN AND INSTALLATION	BUI	ORG	LEA		□					
MOBILE/BARBECUE CLEANER	BUI	LEA	IMP							
MOBILE/BEAUTICIAN	IMP	LEA	CRE	✓	■					
MOBILE/CAR WASH	BUI	ORG	LEA							
MOBILE/COMMUNICATIONS SERVICE	BUI	PRO	LEA							
MOBILE/HAIRSTYLIST	IMP	LEA	BUI	✓	■					
MOBILE/LUNCH WAGON	ORG	LEA	IMP		□					
MOBILE/MANICURIST	LEA	IMP	ORG	✓	◧					
MOBILE/MASSAGE	BUI	LEA	IMP		□					
MOBILE/MECHANIC	BUI	PRO	IMP		□					
MOBILE/NOTARY	ORG	IMP	LEA		□					
MOBILE/OIL CHANGE SERVICE	BUI	IMP	LEA		□					
MOBILE/PARAMEDIC	LEA	IMP	PRO	✓	■					

BUI=Builder, CRE=Creator, IMP=Improver, LEA=Leader, ORG=Organizer, PRO=Problem Solver, ■=Always, ◧=Usually, □=Some

CAREER OR BUSINESS	PERSONAL STYLE 1	2	3	DEGREE REQUIRED	LICENSE REQUIREMENT	AVERAGE CAPITAL REQUIRED	DONE AT HOME	LAND OR COMMERCIAL BUILDING REQUIRED	FAMILY FRIENDLY	BOOK RESOURCES
MOBILE/PET GROOMING	BUI	ORG	IMP							
MOBILE/PHLEBOTOMISTS	PRO	IMP	BUI	✓	□					
MOBILE/TUNEUP	BUI	IMP	LEA		□					
MOBILE/VEHICLE DETAILER	BUI	ORG	LEA							
MOBILE/WINDOW SCREEN REPAIR	BUI	IMP	LEA							
MOBILE HOME PARK OPERATOR	LEA	BUI	IMP		□					
MOBILE POWER WASHING SERVICE	BUI	ORG	LEA							B
MODEL MAKING	CRE	BUI	PRO						✓	
MODELING AGENCY	LEA	CRE	IMP							
MONITORING TV, RADIO	ORG	BUI	IMP							
MONOGRAMMING	ORG	BUI	IMP						✓	
MOTORCYCLE BROKER	LEA	ORG	IMP		□					
MOTORCYCLE REPAIR	BUI	PRO	LEA		□					
MOVIE LOCATION SCOUT	BUI	PRO	CRE							
MOVING CONSULTANT	ORG	PRO	IMP						✓	
MULTIMEDIA PRODUCER	LEA	ORG	PRO							B,M
MURALS	CRE	LEA	IMP							
MUSEUM EXHIBIT DESIGNER	CRE	BUI	IMP							
MUSIC/ARRANGING AND COMPOSITION	CRE	IMP	LEA							
MUSIC/CONDUCTOR	CRE	IMP	ORG							
MUSIC/COPYIST	ORG	BUI	IMP						✓	
MUSIC/LIBRARIAN	IMP	BUI	LEA		□					
MUSIC/TEACHER	CRE	LEA	IMP						✓	
MUSIC/THERAPIST	LEA	IMP	PRO	✓	□					
MUSIC TOUR COORDINATOR	LEA	IMP	CRE							
MUSICAL ACCOMPANIST	CRE	IMP	PRO							
MUSICAL INSTRUMENT MAKER	BUI	IMP	ORG				◧		✓	
MUSICAL INSTRUMENT REPAIR	BUI	IMP	ORG							
MUSICIAN	CRE	IMP	PRO							
MYSTERY SHOPPER	LEA	IMP	ORG		□					B
NAME CREATION CONSULTANT	LEA	IMP	CRE							
NAPRAPATH	PRO	IMP	BUI	✓	□					
NATUROPATH	PRO	IMP	BUI	✓	□					
NAVIGATIONAL INSTRUCTOR	IMP	BUI	PRO							
NEEDLEWORK ARTIST	CRE	IMP	LEA						✓	
NEEDLEPOINT INSTRUCTOR	IMP	BUI	LEA						✓	
NEEDLEPOINT SUPPLIES SALES	LEA	IMP	BUI							

BUI=Builder, CRE=Creator, IMP=Improver, LEA=Leader, ORG=Organizer, PRO=Problem Solver, ■=Always, ◧=Usually, □=Some

CAREER OR BUSINESS	PERSONAL STYLE 1	2	3	DEGREE REQUIRED	LICENSE REQUIREMENT	AVERAGE CAPITAL REQUIRED	DONE AT HOME	LAND OR COMMERCIAL BUILDING REQUIRED	FAMILY FRIENDLY	BOOK RESOURCES
NEON ARTIST	CRE	IMP	LEA							
NEON SIGN SERVICER	BUI	IMP	LEA							
NETWORKING/CLASSES	LEA	IMP	PRO							
NETWORKING/ORGANIZATION	LEA	IMP	ORG							
NEW AGE CRAFTS/ASTROLOGY	IMP	LEA	ORG							M
NEW AGE CRAFTS/CHANNELING	CRE	IMP	LEA							
NEW AGE CRAFTS/FOLK HEALER	IMP	LEA	PRO							
NEW AGE CRAFTS/NUMEROLOGY	IMP	LEA	ORG							
NEW AGE CRAFTS/PSYCHIC READING	CRE	LEA	ORG							
NEWSLETTER COPYWRITING	LEA	IMP	BUI						✓	
NEWSLETTER PUBLISHER	LEA	IMP	BUI				◧		✓	B,M
NOTARY SERVICE	ORG	IMP	LEA		□				✓	
NUCLEAR IMAGING TECHNOLOGIST	BUI	PRO	IMP							
NURSE/LICENSED PRACTICAL	IMP	LEA	ORG	✓	■					
NURSE PRACTITIONER	PRO	IMP	CRE	✓	◧					
NURSE/PSYCHIATRIC	PRO	IMP	CRE	✓	□					
NURSE/REGISTERED	PRO	IMP	BUI	✓	■					
NURSERY OF RARE AND UNUSUAL PLANTS	BUI	CRE	LEA					■		
NURSES' REGISTRY	IMP	LEA	PRO						✓	
NUTRITION COUNSELOR	IMP	PRO	LEA		□				✓	
NUTRITIONIST	IMP	PRO	LEA	✓	□					
OCCUPATIONAL THERAPIST	IMP	BUI	LEA	✓	◧					
OCCUPATIONAL THERAPIST	LEA	IMP	PRO	✓	◧					
OFFICE AUTOMATION CONSULTANT	BUI	PRO	LEA						✓	
OFFICE LUNCH SERVICE	CRE	ORG	IMP							
OFFICE SUPPORT SERVICES	ORG	IMP	LEA				◧			B
OPHTHALMOLOGIST	PRO	IMP	BUI	✓	■					
OPTICIAN	BUI	ORG	LEA		□					
	IMP	BUI	LEA		□					
OPTOMETRIST	PRO	IMP	BUI	✓	■					
ORDER FULFILLMENT SERVICE	ORG	BUI	IMP						✓	
ORGAN TRANSPLANT COORDINATOR	PRO	BUI	IMP							
ORGANIZATIONAL DEVELOPMENT CONSULTANT	LEA	IMP	PRO						✓	
ORIENTAL RUG REPAIRER	BUI	IMP	LEA						✓	
ORTHODONTIST	PRO	BUI	IMP	✓	■					
ORTHOTIST	BUI	IMP	LEA							
OSTEOPATHIC PHYSICIAN	PRO	IMP	BUI	✓	■					

BUI=Builder, CRE=Creator, IMP=Improver, LEA=Leader, ORG=Organizer, PRO=Problem Solver, ■=Always, ◧=Usually, □=Some

CAREER OR BUSINESS	PERSONAL STYLE 1	2	3	DEGREE REQUIRED	LICENSE REQUIREMENT	AVERAGE CAPITAL REQUIRED	DONE AT HOME	LAND OR COMMERCIAL BUILDING REQUIRED	FAMILY FRIENDLY	BOOK RESOURCES
OUT-OF-TOWN BUSINESS SERVICE	ORG	IMP	LEA							
OUTPLACEMENT CONSULTANT	LEA	IMP	BUI							
PACKAGE DESIGN AND DEVELOPMENT	CRE	LEA	PRO						✓	
PACKAGING AND SHIPPING SERVICE	BUI	LEA	PRO							
	IMP	LEA	ORG							
PACKAGING MACHINERY CONSULTANT	IMP	ORG	PRO							
PACKAGING PRINTING CONSULTANT	CRE	LEA	PRO							
PACKAGING STRUCTURAL DESIGN CONSULTANT	IMP	ORG	PRO							
PAGING SERVICE	ORG	IMP	LEA							
PAINTER/FINE ART	CRE	IMP	PRO				▌▐		✓	
PAINTER/HAND-PAINTED ITEMS	CRE	BUI	LEA							
PAINTER/HOUSE	BUI	IMP	LEA							
PAINTER/JEWELRY	ORG	LEA	BUI							
PAINTER/SIGN	BUI	LEA	PRO						✓	
PAINTING RESTORER	CRE	IMP	BUI						✓	
PAPERHANGER	BUI	IMP	LEA							
	BUI	ORG	LEA							
PARALEGAL	IMP	LEA	CRE						✓	MH
	PRO	IMP	ORG							
PARENT GUIDANCE INSTRUCTION	BUI	PRO	LEA							
PARKING CONSULTANT	BUI	PRO	LEA							
PARKING LOT MAINTENANCE	BUI	LEA	IMP			✓				
PARTY/ENTERTAINMENT	CRE	ORG	IMP							
PARTY/PLANNING	IMP	LEA	ORG							
PARTY/PRODUCTION	IMP	LEA	PRO							
PARTY SALES/CANDLE	LEA	IMP	CRE							
PARTY SALES/CLOTHING	LEA	IMP	CRE							
PARTY SALES/COOKWARE	LEA	IMP	CRE							
PARTY SALES/HOUSEWARES	LEA	IMP	CRE							
PARTY SALES/JEWELRY	LEA	IMP	CRE							
PARTY SALES/LINGERIE	LEA	IMP	CRE							
PARTY SALES/MAKEUP	LEA	IMP	CRE							
PASTORAL COUNSELOR	IMP	CRE	PRO	✓	☐					
PATIO CONSTRUCTION	BUI	LEA	IMP							
PATTERN MAKER	BUI	PRO	LEA						✓	
PAYROLL PREPARATION SERVICE	LEA	IMP	BUI						✓	M
PEDIATRICIAN	PRO	IMP	LEA	✓	■					

BUI=Builder, CRE=Creator, IMP=Improver, LEA=Leader, ORG=Organizer, PRO=Problem Solver, ■=Always, ▌▐=Usually, ☐=Some

CAREER OR BUSINESS	PERSONAL STYLE 1	2	3	DEGREE REQUIRED	LICENSE REQUIREMENT	AVERAGE CAPITAL REQUIRED	DONE AT HOME	LAND OR COMMERCIAL BUILDING REQUIRED	FAMILY FRIENDLY	BOOK RESOURCES
PERSONAL BUSINESS MANAGER	CRE	LEA	ORG							
PERSONAL SERVICES BROKER	IMP	LEA	ORG						✓	
PERSONAL SHOPPER	LEA	IMP	BUI							
PERSONNEL CONSULTING	LEA	IMP	BUI							
PERSONNEL/HUMAN RESOURCES CONSULTANT	LEA	IMP	BUI							
PEST CONTROL SERVICE	BUI	LEA	IMP		□					
PET IDENTIFICATION SERVICE	LEA	IMP	BUI							
PET PORTRAITS	CRE	IMP	LEA							
PET SERVICES/ANIMAL REMOVER	IMP	LEA	BUI							
PET SERVICES/AQUARIUM CLEANING SERVICE	BUI	LEA	IMP							
PET SERVICES/BLACKSMITH/HORSESHOEING SERVICE	BUI	PRO	LEA							
PET SERVICES/BOARDING: DOGS, HORSES, ETC.	BUI	ORG	IMP							
PET SERVICES/GROOMER	PRO	ORG	IMP							
PET TAXI SERVICE	BUI	ORG	IMP							
PET TOYS CREATOR	CRE	BUI	PRO						✓	
PET TRAINING	BUI	LEA	IMP							
PET WALKER	BUI	ORG	IMP							
PET-SITTER	BUI	ORG	IMP							
PET-SITTING FOR UNUSUAL ANIMALS	BUI	ORG	IMP							
PETTING ZOO OPERATOR	BUI	LEA	IMP							
PHARMACIST	PRO	LEA	IMP	✓	■					
PHLEBOTOMIST	PRO	IMP	BUI		□					
PHOTO SEARCH SERVICE	BUI	ORG	PRO						✓	
PHOTO SERVICES	LEA	BUI	IMP							
PHOTOGRAPHER/AERIAL	BUI	LEA	CRE							
PHOTOGRAPHER/MOVIES, VIDEO	CRE	LEA	IMP							
PHOTOGRAPHER/REAL ESTATE	CRE	IMP	LEA							
PHOTOGRAPHER/UNIQUE LOCAL LANDMARKS	CRE	LEA	IMP							
PHOTOGRAPHER/WEDDING	CRE	LEA	IMP							
PHOTOGRAPHER'S REPRESENTATIVE	LEA	IMP	CRE							
PHOTOGRAPHY/BLOWUP SERVICE	LEA	BUI	IMP							
PHOTOGRAPHY/COLOR CORRCTN, RETOUCHNG, RESTRNG	BUI	LEA	ORG							
PHOTOJOURNALIST	CRE	LEA	ORG							
PHYSICAL DISTRIBUTION AND LOGISTICS CONSULTANT	LEA	BUI	IMP							
PHYSICAL THERAPIST	IMP	PRO	LEA	✓	■					
PHYSICIAN	PRO	IMP	BUI	✓	■					
PHYSICIAN'S ASSISTANT	PRO	IMP	CRE	✓	■					

BUI=Builder, CRE=Creator, IMP=Improver, LEA=Leader, ORG=Organizer, PRO=Problem Solver, ■=Always, ◧=Usually, □=Some

CAREER OR BUSINESS	PERSONAL STYLE 1	2	3	DEGREE REQUIRED	LICENSE REQUIREMENT	AVERAGE CAPITAL REQUIRED	DONE AT HOME	LAND OR COMMERCIAL BUILDING REQUIRED	FAMILY FRIENDLY	BOOK RESOURCES
PIANIST	CRE	IMP	PRO							
PIANO TEACHER	CRE	LEA	IMP				◨		✓	
PIANO TUNER	BUI	IMP	ORG							
PICTURE FRAMER	BUI	ORG	LEA						✓	
PILOT/AIRPLANE	PRO	BUI	LEA	✓	FED					
PILOT/AIRPLANE, COMMERCIAL	BUI	PRO	LEA	✓	FED					
PILOT/INSTRUCTOR	IMP	BUI	LEA							
PILOT/MARINE	LEA	BUI	IMP	✓	☐					
PLANT/PROPAGATOR	BUI	PRO	IMP						✓	
PLANT/BREEDER	PRO	BUI	IMP						✓	
PLANT/CARE	BUI	ORG	PRO							
PLANT/DOCTOR	PRO	BUI	IMP							
PLANT/INTERIOR PLANT DESIGN	BUI	PRO	IMP							
PLANT/RENT-A-PLANT SERVICE	BUI	LEA	IMP							
PLASTERER	BUI	LEA	IMP		☐					
PLASTICS/LAMINATING	BUI	LEA	IMP						✓	
PLASTICS/RECYCLING	ORG	BUI	LEA							
PLAY/THERAPIST	CRE	LEA	IMP	✓	☐					
PLAYGROUND EQUIPMENT ERECTOR	BUI	ORG	LEA							
PLAYWRIGHT	CRE	IMP	LEA				◨		✓	
PLUMBER	BUI	LEA	PRO		☐					
PODIATRIST	IMP	PRO	BUI	✓	■					
POET	CRE	LEA	IMP				◨		✓	
POLITICAL CAMPAIGN CONSULTANT	IMP	LEA	PRO							
POLLING AND SURVEYING	ORG	IMP	LEA							
POLLUTION CONTROL ENGINEER	PRO	LEA	BUI	✓	☐					
POLYGRAPH EXAMINER	ORG	PRO	IMP		◨					
POOL-CLEANING SERVICE	BUI	LEA	IMP							
PORTRAIT ARTIST	CRE	LEA	IMP						✓	
POSTMARK SERVICE	BUI	ORG	PRO						✓	
POTTER	CRE	BUI	PRO						✓	
POULTRY FARMER	BUI	IMP	LEA					■		
POWER WASH SERVICES	BUI	LEA	IMP							
PRESENTATION GRAPHICS SPECIALIST	CRE	PRO	LEA							
PRESENTATION SUPPORT	BUI	CRE	PRO							
PRICING AND ESTIMATING CONSULTANT	PRO	ORG	LEA							
PRINTER/QUICK	BUI	PRO	LEA							

BUI=Builder, CRE=Creator, IMP=Improver, LEA=Leader, ORG=Organizer, PRO=Problem Solver, ■=Always, ◨=Usually, ☐=Some

CAREER OR BUSINESS	PERSONAL STYLE 1	2	3	DEGREE REQUIRED	LICENSE REQUIREMENT	AVERAGE CAPITAL REQUIRED	DONE AT HOME	LAND OR COMMERCIAL BUILDING REQUIRED	FAMILY FRIENDLY	BOOK RESOURCES
PRINTING BROKER	LEA	ORG	IMP				◨			
PRINTMAKER	CRE	LEA	IMP						✓	
PRIVATE INVESTIGATOR	LEA	IMP	PRO	◨						B
PROCESS SERVER	LEA	IMP	ORG							
PRODUCER/DOCUMENTARIES	LEA	IMP	CRE							
PRODUCER/FILM	LEA	IMP	CRE							
PRODUCER/LASER LIGHT SHOW	LEA	IMP	PRO							
PRODUCER/RADIO BROADCAST	IMP	LEA	PRO							
PRODUCER/THEATER	LEA	IMP	CRE							
PRODUCER/TV BROADCAST	IMP	LEA	PRO							
PRODUCER/VIDEO	LEA	IMP	CRE							
PRODUCT DEMONSTRATOR	LEA	IMP	CRE							
PROFESSIONAL ORGANIZER	ORG	BUI	IMP							B
PROFESSIONAL PRACTICE CONSULTANT/MEDICAL/DENTAL	LEA	IMP	ORG							B
PROMOTIONS/IN-STORE	LEA	IMP	CRE							
PROOFREADER	ORG	IMP	PRO				◨		✓	B,MH
PROPERTY MANAGEMENT SERVICE/CONDOMINIUMS	LEA	IMP	PRO		☐					
PROPERTY TAX REDUCTION SERVICE	ORG	IMP	PRO							
PROPOSAL AND GRANT WRITER	PRO	BUI	IMP						✓	B,M
PROSTHETIST	BUI	IMP	LEA		☐					
PROSTHODONTIST	PRO	BUI	IMP	✓	■					
PSYCHIATRIST	PRO	IMP	CRE	✓	■					
PSYCHOLOGIST/CLINICAL	IMP	PRO	CRE	✓	■					
PSYCHOLOGIST/EDUCATIONAL	PRO	LEA	IMP	✓	■					
PSYCHOLOGIST/FORENSIC	LEA	PRO	CRE	✓	■					
PSYCHOLOGIST/INDUSTRIAL-ORGANIZATIONAL	IMP	LEA	PRO	✓	■					
PSYCHOTHERAPIST/HYPNOTHERAPIST	IMP	LEA	ORG	✓	☐					
PSYCHOTHERAPIST/MARRIAGE AND FAMILY COUNSELOR	IMP	PRO	CRE	✓	◨					
PSYCHOTHERAPIST/PASTORAL COUNSELOR	IMP	CRE	PRO	✓	☐					
PSYCHOTHERAPIST/SOCIAL WORKER	IMP	LEA	CRE	✓	☐					
PUBLIC OPINION/ANALYSIS	PRO	IMP	CRE						✓	
PUBLIC OPINION/POLLING AND SURVEYS	PRO	IMP	CRE							
PUBLIC RELATIONS SPECIALIST	LEA	CRE	IMP				◨		✓	B,M
PUBLICITY SERVICE	LEA	CRE	IMP				◨		✓	
PUBLISHER/BOOKS	LEA	PRO	CRE						✓	
PUBLISHER/CATALOGS	LEA	PRO	CRE						✓	
PUBLISHER/DIRECTORIES	LEA	PRO	CRE						✓	

BUI=Builder, CRE=Creator, IMP=Improver, LEA=Leader, ORG=Organizer, PRO=Problem Solver, ■=Always, ◨=Usually, ☐=Some

CAREER OR BUSINESS	PERSONAL STYLE 1	2	3	DEGREE REQUIRED	LICENSE REQUIREMENT	AVERAGE CAPITAL REQUIRED	DONE AT HOME	LAND OR COMMERCIAL BUILDING REQUIRED	FAMILY FRIENDLY	BOOK RESOURCES
PUBLISHER/GUIDES	LEA	PRO	CRE						✓	
PUBLISHER/NEWSLETTER	LEA	PRO	CRE						✓	
PUBLISHER/SMALL LOTS	LEA	PRO	CRE						✓	
PUBLISHING RIGHTS NEGOTIATOR	LEA	IMP	PRO						✓	
PUPPETEER	CRE	LEA	PRO							
PURCHASING AGENT SERVICE	LEA	IMP	CRE							
PURCHASING CONSULTANT	LEA	IMP	CRE							
PUSHCART VENDOR/STREET AND MALL	BUI	ORG	LEA							
QUILT MAKER	BUI	CRE	ORG				◧		✓	
RACE CAR DRIVER	BUI	LEA	PRO							
RADIO TALK SHOW HOST	CRE	LEA	IMP							
RADIO TIME SALES REPRESENTATIVE	LEA	BUI	IMP							
RADIOLOGIST	PRO	BUI	IMP	✓	■					
RADON MEASUREMENT AND MITIGATION	BUI	LEA	IMP		□					
RARE RECORDINGS AND VIDEOS SEARCH SERVICE	BUI	ORG	PRO						✓	
READING SERVICE	IMP	CRE	LEA							
REAL ESTATE/ABSTRACT SEARCHER	ORG	IMP	PRO							
REAL ESTATE/AGENT	LEA	IMP	BUI		■					
REAL ESTATE/AUCTIONEER	CRE	LEA	IMP		□					
REAL ESTATE/BROCHURE SERVICE	CRE	LEA	IMP						✓	M
REAL ESTATE/BROKER	LEA	ORG	IMP		■		◧			
	LEA	ORG	IMP		■					
REAL ESTATE/PHOTOGRAPHER	CRE	IMP	LEA							
REAL ESTATE/SALES	LEA	ORG	IMP		■					
RECORD-SEARCHING SERVICE	ORG	IMP	BUI						✓	
RECORDING ENGINEER	BUI	LEA	IMP							
RECORDING STUDIO OPERATOR	BUI	LEA	IMP							
RECORD-KEEPING SERVICE	ORG	IMP	BUI						✓	
RECREATIONAL THERAPIST	IMP	LEA	ORG	✓	□					
RED-TAPE WRANGLER	ORG	IMP	PRO							
REFERRAL SERVICE/BED-AND-BREAKFAST INNS	IMP	PRO	ORG						✓	
REFERRAL SERVICE/CHILD CARE	IMP	PRO	LEA						✓	
REFERRAL SERVICE/DENTAL	IMP	PRO	LEA						✓	
REFERRAL SERVICE/HOUSING SWAP SERVICE	IMP	PRO	LEA						✓	
REFERRAL SERVICE/MEDICAL	IMP	PRO	LEA							
REFERRAL SERVICE/PHYSICIAN	IMP	PRO	LEA						✓	
REFERRAL SERVICE/ROOMMATES	IMP	PRO	LEA							

BUI=Builder, CRE=Creator, IMP=Improver, LEA=Leader, ORG=Organizer, PRO=Problem Solver, ■=Always, ◧=Usually, □=Some

CAREER OR BUSINESS	PERSONAL STYLE			DEGREE REQUIRED	LICENSE REQUIREMENT	AVERAGE CAPITAL REQUIRED	DONE AT HOME	LAND OR COMMERCIAL BUILDING REQUIRED	FAMILY FRIENDLY	BOOK RESOURCES
	1	2	3							
REFERRAL SERVICE/SECOND MEDICAL OPINION	IMP	PRO	LEA						✓	
REFERRAL SERVICE/TRADESPEOPLE	IMP	PRO	BUI							
REFLEXOLOGY THERAPIST	BUI	LEA	IMP		☐					
REHABILITATION COUNSELOR	IMP	BUI	LEA		☐					
RELOCATION CONSULTING	LEA	BUI	IMP						✓	
REMINDER SERVICE	ORG	IMP	LEA						✓	
RENTAL SERVICES/BOOKS/TAPES	IMP	ORG	CRE							
RENTAL SERVICES/OFFICE EQUIPMENT	IMP	LEA	BUI							
RENTAL SERVICES/PICTURES	IMP	LEA	CRE							
RENTAL SERVICES/ROBOTS	BUI	PRO	LEA							
REPAIR/RV'S AND VANS	BUI	IMP	CRE		☐					
REPAIR SERVICE/GENERAL	BUI	LEA	IMP							B
REPAIR SERVICES/AIRCRAFT	BUI	LEA	PRO							
REPAIR SERVICES/APPLIANCES	BUI	LEA	IMP							
REPAIR SERVICES/ART OBJECTS	IMP	BUI	ORG							
REPAIR SERVICES/BICYCLES	BUI	LEA	PRO							
REPAIR SERVICES/BOATS	BUI	LEA	PRO							
REPAIR SERVICES/CAMERAS	BUI	LEA	PRO							
REPAIR SERVICES/CANE CHAIRS	ORG	BUI	IMP							
REPAIR SERVICES/CONCRETE	BUI	LEA	IMP							
REPAIR SERVICES/FARM EQUIPMENT	BUI	LEA	IMP							
REPAIR SERVICES/FINE CHINA	IMP	BUI	ORG							
REPAIR SERVICES/GUN	BUI	LEA	PRO							
REPAIR SERVICES/HEATING, AIR-COND, AND REFRIG	BUI	LEA	ORG		☐					
REPAIR SERVICES/ICE SKATES	BUI	LEA	IMP							
REPAIR SERVICES/LAMPSHADES	IMP	BUI	ORG							
REPAIR SERVICES/LAWN MOWER	BUI	LEA	PRO							
REPAIR SERVICES/MICROWAVE OVENS	BUI	LEA	IMP							
REPAIR SERVICES/MOBILE HOMES	BUI	LEA	PRO							
REPAIR SERVICES/MOTORCYCLE	BUI	LEA	IMP							
REPAIR SERVICES/MUSICAL INSTRUMENTS	BUI	IMP	ORG							
REPAIR SERVICES/NECKLACE RESTRINGING	IMP	BUI	ORG							
REPAIR SERVICES/PHOTOCOPIER	BUI	LEA	IMP							
REPAIR SERVICES/RUG	BUI	LEA	IMP							
REPAIR SERVICES/SAILS	ORG	BUI	IMP							
REPAIR SERVICES/SEWING MACHINES	BUI	LEA	PRO							
REPAIR SERVICES/SHAVERS	BUI	LEA	IMP							

BUI=Builder, CRE=Creator, IMP=Improver, LEA=Leader, ORG=Organizer, PRO=Problem Solver, ■=Always, ▣=Usually, ☐=Some

CAREER OR BUSINESS	PERSONAL STYLE 1	2	3	DEGREE REQUIRED	LICENSE REQUIREMENT	AVERAGE CAPITAL REQUIRED	DONE AT HOME	LAND OR COMMERCIAL BUILDING REQUIRED	FAMILY FRIENDLY	BOOK RESOURCES
REPAIR SERVICES/SHOES	BUI	LEA	IMP							
REPAIR SERVICES/SNOW BLOWERS	BUI	LEA	PRO							
REPAIR SERVICES/SPORTS EQUIPMENT	BUI	LEA	IMP							
REPAIR SERVICES/STATUARY	IMP	BUI	ORG							
REPAIR SERVICES/SWIMMING POOLS	BUI	LEA	IMP							
REPAIR SERVICES/TELEPHONE	BUI	ORG	IMP							
REPAIR SERVICES/TOOLS	BUI	LEA	IMP							
REPAIR SERVICES/TV/RADIO	BUI	LEA	IMP		□					
REPAIR SERVICES/UMBRELLAS	ORG	BUI	IMP							
REPAIR SERVICES/VACUUM CLEANER	BUI	LEA	PRO							
REPAIR SERVICES/VCR	BUI	LEA	PRO							
REPAIR SERVICES/VENDING MACHINES	BUI	ORG	LEA							
REPAIR SERVICES/VINTAGE BOOKS	IMP	BUI	ORG							
REPAIR SERVICES/WATCHES	BUI	LEA	PRO							
REPAIR SERVICES/WINDOW SCREENS	ORG	BUI	IMP							
REPORTER	CRE	IMP	LEA							
REPOSSESSION SERVICE	LEA	IMP	BUI		□					
REPTILE FARMER	BUI	PRO	LEA						✓	
RESEARCH ANALYSIS	IMP	LEA	BUI						✓	
RESEARCH AND DEVELOPMENT CONSULTANT	IMP	LEA	BUI							
RESEARCH SERVICE	IMP	LEA	BUI						✓	
RESPIRATORY THERAPIST	IMP	PRO	BUI	▮▯						
RESTAURANT CONSULTANT	BUI	PRO	LEA						✓	
RESTORATION SERVICES/ANTIQUES	IMP	BUI	ORG						✓	
RESTORATION SERVICES/AUTO	IMP	BUI	ORG						✓	
RESTORATION SERVICES/FLOORING	IMP	BUI	ORG						✓	
RESTORATION SERVICES/FURNITURE	BUI	CRE	PRO						✓	
RESTORATION SERVICES/MUSICAL INSTRUMENTS	BUI	CRE	PRO							
RESTORATION SERVICES/PAPER AND PRINTS	CRE	PRO	IMP						✓	
RESTORATION SERVICES/PHOTOGRAPHS	BUI	CRE	PRO						✓	
RESTORATION SERVICES/VINTAGE AUTO	BUI	CRE	PRO						✓	
RÉSUMÉ WRITING/PORTFOLIO PREPARATION SERVICE	CRE	LEA	IMP				▮▯			B
RESURFACER/DRIVEWAY/PARKING LOT	BUI	LEA	ORG							
RESURFACER/TENNIS COURT	BUI	LEA	ORG							
RETAIL CLOTHING BUYER	LEA	IMP	CRE							
RETIREMENT COUNSELING	IMP	LEA	ORG							
RETIREMENT PLANNING CONSULTANT	LEA	IMP	BUI						✓	

BUI=Builder, CRE=Creator, IMP=Improver, LEA=Leader, ORG=Organizer, PRO=Problem Solver, ▮=Always, ▮▯=Usually, □=Some

CAREER OR BUSINESS	PERSONAL STYLE 1	2	3	DEGREE REQUIRED	LICENSE REQUIREMENT	AVERAGE CAPITAL REQUIRED	DONE AT HOME	LAND OR COMMERCIAL BUILDING REQUIRED	FAMILY FRIENDLY	BOOK RESOURCES
REUNION PLANNER	CRE	LEA	IMP							B
	CRE	LEA	ORG							B
REUPHOLSTERER	BUI	ORG	IMP							
REWEAVER	BUI	ORG	IMP				▮▌		✓	
RISK MANAGEMENT CONSULTANT	PRO	ORG	LEA							
RODEO PERFORMER	BUI	LEA	IMP							
ROMANCE NOVELIST	CRE	LEA	IMP						✓	
ROOF INSPECTOR	BUI	LEA	ORG							
ROOFER	BUI	LEA	ORG		□					
ROTOTILLING SERVICE	BUI	ORG	LEA							
ROWING/INSTRUCTOR	BUI	LEA	IMP							
RUBBER STAMP BUSINESS	BUI	IMP	ORG						✓	B
RUG MAKER	BUI	ORG	LEA							
RUG REPAIRER	BUI	LEA	IMP							
RV'S AND VANS/CUSTOMIZING	BUI	ORG	PRO						✓	
SADDLE MAKER	BUI	IMP	LEA						✓	
SAFETY/CLOTHING DEVELOPER	PRO	IMP	BUI						✓	
SAFETY/ENGINEER	PRO	IMP	BUI	✓						
SAFETY/EQUIPMENT DEVELOPER	PRO	IMP	BUI							
SAILING INSTRUCTOR	BUI	PRO	LEA							
SALES REPRESENTATIVE	LEA	BUI	IMP							
SALES TRAINER	LEA	CRE	IMP							
SANDBLASTER	BUI	LEA	PRO							
SANDWICH SNACK ROUTE	LEA	BUI	IMP							
SCHOLARSHIP MATCHING	LEA	IMP	CRE						✓	
SCOPIST	ORG	BUI	PRO							B,M,MH
SCOUT/PROFESSIONAL SPORTS	IMP	LEA	ORG							
SCREENWRITER	CRE	LEA	PRO						✓	
SCRIPT PREPARATION SERVICE	ORG	IMP	LEA						✓	
SCRIPT READER	CRE	LEA	IMP						✓	
SCRIPTWRITER	CRE	LEA	IMP						✓	
SCUBA DIVING/INSTRUCTOR	IMP	LEA	BUI							
	BUI	LEA	PRO							
SCULPTOR	CRE	LEA	BUI						✓	
SECRETARIAL SERVICES	ORG	IMP	LEA							
SECURITIES/BROKER	LEA	IMP	CRE		▮/F					
SECURITIES AGENT	LEA	IMP	CRE		□/F					

BUI=Builder, CRE=Creator, IMP=Improver, LEA=Leader, ORG=Organizer, PRO=Problem Solver, ▮=Always, ▮▌=Usually, □=Some

CAREER OR BUSINESS	PERSONAL STYLE 1	2	3	DEGREE REQUIRED	LICENSE REQUIREMENT	AVERAGE CAPITAL REQUIRED	DONE AT HOME	LAND OR COMMERCIAL BUILDING REQUIRED	FAMILY FRIENDLY	BOOK RESOURCES
SECURITIES INVESTMENT ADVISER	LEA	IMP	CRE		□/F					
SECURITY CONSULTANT	LEA	IMP	BUI		□				✓	B
SECURITY ESCORT SERVICE	LEA	IMP	ORG		□					
SECURITY SERVICE	BUI	LEA	ORG		□					
SELF-DEFENSE INSTRUCTOR	IMP	LEA	BUI							
SELLING/CLOSEOUT AND SURPLUS	LEA	IMP	BUI							
SELLING/OLD CURRENCY AND STOCK	LEA	IMP	CRE							
SEMINAR/LEADER	LEA	IMP	CRE							
	LEA	IMP	PRO							
SEMINAR/PRODUCER	LEA	IMP	CRE							
SEMINAR/PROMOTER	LEA	IMP	CRE							
SEPTIC TANK PUMPING/INSTALLING	BUI	LEA	PRO		□					
SET DECORATOR	CRE	LEA	IMP							
SET DESIGNER	CRE	LEA	IMP							
	CRE	PRO	LEA							
SEWING AND TAILORING/BRIDAL GOWNS AND VEILS	BUI	LEA	IMP							
SEWING AND TAILORING/CLOTHING	BUI	LEA	IMP						✓	
SEWING AND TAILORING/CLOTHING ALTERATIONS	BUI	PRO	LEA							
SEWING AND TAILORING/COSTUMES	BUI	LEA	IMP						✓	
SEWING AND TAILORING/CUSTOM PATCHES	ORG	BUI	LEA						✓	
SEWING AND TAILORING/DOLL CLOTHING	BUI	ORG	LEA						✓	
SEWING AND TAILORING/DRAPERIES	ORG	BUI	IMP						✓	
SEWING AND TAILORING/INSTRUCTOR	LEA	BUI	IMP							
SEWING AND TAILORING/SLIPCOVERS	ORG	BUI	IMP						✓	
SEWING MACHINE REPAIR	BUI	LEA	IMP							
SHARPENING SERVICES/KNIVES/SAWS/LAWN MOWERS	BUI	ORG	LEA							
SHEEP RANCHER	BUI	LEA	IMP							
SHEEP SHEARING	BUI	IMP	LEA							
SHEET-METAL WORKER	BUI	LEA	PRO							
SHELLFISH FISHER/GROWER	BUI	LEA	PRO		□	✓				
SHIPWRIGHT	BUI	LEA	IMP							
SHOE POLISHING SERVICE	BUI	ORG	IMP							
SHOE REPAIRER	BUI	IMP	LEA							
SHOEMAKER, CUSTOM	BUI	PRO	LEA							
SHOOTING PRESERVE OPERATOR	BUI	LEA	IMP		□	✓		■		
SHOW ORGANIZER/PROMOTER/ANTIQUE CARS	LEA	ORG	IMP							
SHOW ORGANIZER/PROMOTER/ART SHOWS	LEA	IMP	CRE							

BUI=Builder, CRE=Creator, IMP=Improver, LEA=Leader, ORG=Organizer, PRO=Problem Solver, ■=Always, ▣=Usually, □=Some

CAREER OR BUSINESS	PERSONAL STYLE 1	2	3	DEGREE REQUIRED	LICENSE REQUIREMENT	AVERAGE CAPITAL REQUIRED	DONE AT HOME	LAND OR COMMERCIAL BUILDING REQUIRED	FAMILY FRIENDLY	BOOK RESOURCES
SHOW ORGANIZER/PROMOTER/TRADE SHOWS	LEA	IMP	CRE							
SIGHTSEEING/GUIDE	LEA	IMP	ORG	□						
SIGHTSEEING GUIDE SERVICE	PRO	IMP	ORG	□						
SIGN CONTRACTOR	BUI	PRO	ORG	□						
SIGN LANGUAGE/INSTRUCTOR	LEA	IMP	CRE							
SIGN LANGUAGE/INTERPRETER	IMP	ORG	LEA							
SIGN MAKER	BUI	PRO	ORG						✓	B,M
SIGN PAINTING AND STENCILER	IMP	ORG	CRE						✓	
SILVERSMITH	BUI	IMP	ORG						✓	
SINGER	CRE	LEA	IMP							
SINGING TELEGRAM SERVICE	CRE	LEA	IMP							
SKI MAKER, CUSTOM	BUI	PRO	IMP						✓	
SKIP TRACING/MISSING PERSONS	BUI	ORG	LEA	□			▮▮			M
SKYLIGHT INSTALLATION	BUI	PRO	LEA							
SMALL AND START-UP BUSINESS CONSULTANT	LEA	IMP	PRO						✓	
SMALL-BUSINESS CONVENIENCE SERVICES	IMP	ORG	LEA							
SNOW REMOVAL	BUI	LEA	PRO							
SOCIAL SECURITY CLAIMANT REPRESENTATIVE	IMP	LEA	PRO							MH
SOCIAL WORKER/PSYCHIATRIC	IMP	LEA	CRE	✓	▮▮					
SOFTWARE/LOCATION SERVICE	PRO	ORG	IMP				▮▮		✓	M
SOFTWARE PUBLISHER	LEA	IMP	BUI				▮▮			M
SOFTWARE WRITER/DEVELOPER, BUSINESS	ORG	PRO	BUI				▮▮		✓	
SOFTWARE WRITER/DEVELOPER, GAME	CRE	PRO	BUI				▮▮		✓	
SOFTWARE WRITER/DEVELOPER, SCIENTIFIC	PRO	BUI	LEA				▮▮		✓	
SOIL CONSERVATIONIST	PRO	BUI	LEA							
SOIL-TESTING SERVICE	BUI	PRO	IMP	□						
SOLAR ENERGY CONTRACTOR	BUI	PRO	ORG	□					✓	
SONGWRITER/SPECIAL OCCASIONS	CRE	IMP	LEA				▮▮		✓	
SOUND MIXER	BUI	ORG	IMP						✓	
SOUND STUDIO	BUI	PRO	LEA			✓			✓	
SOUND TECHNICIAN	BUI	LEA	PRO							
SOUVENIR AND NOVELTY MAKER	BUI	LEA	IMP							
SPACE PLANNING	ORG	IMP	LEA							
SPEAKER, PROFESSIONAL/CONTENT EXPERT	LEA	IMP	ORG							
SPEAKER, PROFESSIONAL/HUMOROUS	CRE	IMP	LEA							
SPEAKER, PROFESSIONAL/KEYNOTE	LEA	IMP	CRE							
SPEAKER, PROFESSIONAL/MASTER OF CEREMONIES	LEA	IMP	CRE							

BUI=Builder, CRE=Creator, IMP=Improver, LEA=Leader, ORG=Organizer, PRO=Problem Solver, ■=Always, ▮▮=Usually, □=Some

CAREER OR BUSINESS	PERSONAL STYLE 1	2	3	DEGREE REQUIRED	LICENSE REQUIREMENT	AVERAGE CAPITAL REQUIRED	DONE AT HOME	LAND OR COMMERCIAL BUILDING REQUIRED	FAMILY FRIENDLY	BOOK RESOURCES
SPEAKER, PROFESSIONAL/MOTIVATIONAL	LEA	IMP	CRE							
SPEAKERS' BUREAU	ORG	IMP	LEA							
SPECIAL-EFFECTS TECHNICIAN	BUI	PRO	LEA							
SPECIALTY INFORMATION PROVIDER	IMP	CRE	PRO						✓	
	PRO	CRE	LEA						✓	
SPEECH COACH	CRE	IMP	LEA				▨			
SPEECH INSTRUCTOR	IMP	CRE	PRO							
SPEECH PATHOLOGIST	IMP	CRE	PRO	✓	▨					
SPEECHWRITER	CRE	LEA	IMP							
SPORTS/AGENT	LEA	IMP	BUI		□		▨			
SPORTS/INSTRUCTOR	LEA	IMP	BUI							
SPORTS EQUIPMENT REPAIRER	ORG	BUI	IMP							
SPORTS EVENTS ORGANIZER	LEA	IMP	BUI							
SPORTS LEAGUE STATISTICS	PRO	BUI	LEA						✓	M
SQUARE DANCE CALLER	CRE	LEA	IMP							
SQUARE DANCE INSTRUCTOR	BUI	IMP	LEA							
STAGE MANAGER	CRE	BUI	IMP							
STATISTICIAN	PRO	BUI	LEA	✓					✓	
STATUE REPAIR	BUI	CRE	LEA							
STOCK MARKET ANALYSIS	PRO	LEA	IMP		▨				✓	
STOCK PORTFOLIO MANAGEMENT	PRO	LEA	IMP		▨/F				✓	
STOCKBROKER	LEA	IMP	CRE		▨/F				✓	
STONE CARVER	BUI	CRE	LEA							
STONEMASON	BUI	IMP	LEA							
STORYTELLER	LEA	IMP	CRE							
STRUCTURAL ENGINEER	PRO	BUI	IMP	✓	□					
STUCCO MASON	BUI	LEA	PRO							
STUFFED-ANIMAL VENDOR	BUI	ORG	LEA							
STUNT PERFORMER	IMP	ORG	LEA							
SURGEON	PRO	BUI	CRE	✓	■					
SURVIVAL SPECIALIST	LEA	IMP	BUI							
SWIMMING POOL/SPA MAINTENANCE SERVICE	BUI	LEA	ORG							
TAILOR/ALTERATION	BUI	PRO	LEA						✓	
TAILOR/CUSTOM	BUI	LEA	IMP						✓	
TALENT/AGENT	LEA	IMP	CRE				▨			
TALENT/COORDINATOR	IMP	LEA	CRE							
TALENT/SCOUT	IMP	LEA	CRE							

BUI=Builder, CRE=Creator, IMP=Improver, LEA=Leader, ORG=Organizer, PRO=Problem Solver, ■=Always, ▨=Usually, □=Some

CAREER OR BUSINESS	PERSONAL STYLE 1	2	3	DEGREE REQUIRED	LICENSE REQUIREMENT	AVERAGE CAPITAL REQUIRED	DONE AT HOME	LAND OR COMMERCIAL BUILDING REQUIRED	FAMILY FRIENDLY	BOOK RESOURCES
TAPE-DUPLICATING SERVICE	BUI	ORG	LEA						✓	B
TATTOO ARTIST	CRE	LEA	ORG		☐					
TAX PREPARER/CONSULTANT	ORG	LEA	IMP		☐				✓	B
TAXI DRIVER	PRO	BUI	LEA		☐					
TAXIDERMIST	PRO	BUI	IMP		☐					
TEACHER/ADULT EDUCATION	LEA	IMP	PRO	✓						
TEAM-BUILDING CONSULTANT	PRO	LEA	IMP							
TELECOMMUNICATIONS CONSULTANT	PRO	BUI	LEA							
TELEMARKETING CONSULTANT	LEA	IMP	CRE							
TELEPHONE ANSWERING SERVICE	ORG	IMP	LEA							
TELEPHONE REPAIR SERVICE	BUI	ORG	PRO							
TELEPHONE SALES	LEA	IMP	ORG						✓	
TEMPORARY HELP AGENCY	LEA	IMP	BUI		☐					B
TENNIS/COACH	IMP	BUI	LEA					■		
TENNIS/INSTRUCTOR	IMP	BUI	LEA							
TENNIS COURT/MAINTENANCE	BUI	LEA	ORG							
TENNIS COURT/DESIGN	CRE	PRO	BUI							
TENNIS RACQUET RESTRINGING SERVICE	BUI	ORG	LEA							
TERRACE DESIGN AND REPAIR	BUI	CRE	PRO							
TEXTILE DESIGN	CRE	BUI	LEA						✓	
THERAPIST/ART	LEA	IMP	PRO	✓	☐					
THERAPIST/DANCE	CRE	IMP	PRO	✓	☐					
THERAPIST/MUSIC	LEA	IMP	PRO	✓	☐					
THERAPIST/PLAY	CRE	LEA	IMP	✓	☐					
TICKET AGENT	ORG	IMP	LEA							
TICKET BROKER	LEA	IMP	CRE							
TIME MANAGEMENT CONSULTANT	LEA	IMP	BUI							
TOOL REPAIRER	BUI	IMP	LEA							
TOUR OPERATOR/BICYCLE	BUI	LEA	IMP		☐					
TOUR OPERATOR/CHARTER-FISHING TOURS	BUI	LEA	IMP		☐					
TOUR OPERATOR/FISHING GUIDE	BUI	LEA	IMP		☐					
TOUR OPERATOR/FOOD	LEA	IMP	BUI		☐					
TOUR OPERATOR/GOLF	BUI	LEA	IMP		☐					
TOUR OPERATOR/MOUNTAIN-CLIMBING GUIDE	BUI	LEA	IMP		☐					
TOUR OPERATOR/MUSIC	LEA	IMP	CRE		☐					
TOUR OPERATOR/NATURE TOURS	BUI	LEA	IMP		☐					
TOUR OPERATOR/OUTLET SHOPPING MALLS	LEA	IMP	ORG		☐					

BUI=Builder, CRE=Creator, IMP=Improver, LEA=Leader, ORG=Organizer, PRO=Problem Solver, ■=Always, ▣=Usually, ☐=Some

CAREER OR BUSINESS	PERSONAL STYLE 1	2	3	DEGREE REQUIRED	LICENSE REQUIREMENT	AVERAGE CAPITAL REQUIRED	DONE AT HOME	LAND OR COMMERCIAL BUILDING REQUIRED	FAMILY FRIENDLY	BOOK RESOURCES
TOUR OPERATOR/RIVER RAFTING	BUI	LEA	IMP		□					
TOUR OPERATOR/SHOPPING TOUR	LEA	IMP	ORG		□					
TOUR OPERATOR	LEA	IMP	ORG		□					
TOW TRUCK OPERATOR	BUI	LEA	IMP							
TOYMAKER	BUI	LEA	ORG						✓	
TRADE ASSOCIATION OPERATOR	LEA	IMP	ORG							
TRADE SHOW EXHIBIT BUILDER	BUI	PRO	LEA							
TRAFFIC AND TRANSPORTATION CONSULTANT	LEA	IMP	BUI							
TRAINER/COMPUTER	IMP	LEA	ORG							
TRAINER/DISABLED	LEA	IMP	BUI							
TRAINER/DRIVING	LEA	IMP	BUI							
TRAINER/EMPLOYEE	LEA	IMP	BUI							
TRAINER/SALES	LEA	IMP	CRE							
TRAINING/BROKER	LEA	ORG	IMP				▉			
TRAINING BROKER	LEA	PRO	IMP						✓	
TRANSCRIBING/COURT REPORTER NOTES	ORG	IMP	LEA							B,M,MH
TRANSCRIBING/RADIO AND TV PROGRAMS	ORG	IMP	LEA							
TRANSCRIPT DIGESTING	PRO	IMP	ORG						✓	B,M
TRANSLATION SERVICE	BUI	LEA	IMP						✓	
TRAVEL/GUIDE	LEA	IMP	ORG		□					
TRAVEL AGENT	LEA	ORG	IMP		□					
TRAVEL CONSULTANT/GUIDE/PACKAGER	IMP	LEA	ORG		□				✓	B
TRAVELOGUE CREATOR	CRE	IMP	LEA						✓	
TREE PLANTING	BUI	LEA	ORG							
TREE PRUNING	BUI	ORG	LEA							
TREE REMOVAL	BUI	LEA	IMP							
TREE SURGEON/INJECTOR	BUI	LEA	PRO		□					
TROPHY/ENGRAVING	BUI	LEA	PRO							
TROPHY/MAKING	BUI	LEA	PRO							
TROPICAL FISH CARE	BUI	LEA	PRO							
TUGBOAT OPERATOR	BUI	LEA	PRO							
TUTORING/ACADEMIC/ACHIEVEMENT TESTS	IMP	LEA	ORG						✓	B
TV CAMERA OPERATOR	CRE	LEA	IMP							
TV DIRECTOR	IMP	LEA	CRE							
TV PRODUCER	IMP	LEA	PRO							
TYPEFACE DESIGNER	CRE	LEA	IMP						✓	
TYPESETTING	ORG	BUI	LEA						✓	

BUI=Builder, CRE=Creator, IMP=Improver, LEA=Leader, ORG=Organizer, PRO=Problem Solver, ■=Always, ▉=Usually, □=Some

CAREER OR BUSINESS	PERSONAL STYLE 1	2	3	DEGREE REQUIRED	LICENSE REQUIREMENT	AVERAGE CAPITAL REQUIRED	DONE AT HOME	LAND OR COMMERCIAL BUILDING REQUIRED	FAMILY FRIENDLY	BOOK RESOURCES
UMPIRE/REFEREE	LEA	IMP	BUI							
UNDERGROUND STORAGE TANK SERVICES	PRO	BUI	LEA		□					
UNION GRIEVANCE MEDIATOR	LEA	PRO	BUI							
UPHOLSTERY/CLEANER	BUI	IMP	LEA							
UPHOLSTERY/INSTALLATION AND REPAIR	BUI	ORG	IMP							
URBAN PLANNER	LEA	IMP	PRO	✓	□				✓	
USED-COMPUTER BROKER	LEA	ORG	IMP						✓	M
VAN AND RV CUSTOMIZING	BUI	ORG	PRO							
VENDING MACHINE/OPERATION	IMP	BUI	ORG							
VENDING MACHINE/REPAIR	BUI	ORG	LEA							
VENTRILOQUIST	CRE	LEA	IMP							
VETERINARIAN	PRO	BUI	IMP	✓	■					
VIDEO/DATA SERVICE	BUI	ORG	PRO						✓	
VIDEO/EDITING	CRE	PRO	BUI						✓	
VIDEO/PRODUCTION	LEA	IMP	CRE							
VIDEO/TRANSFER SERVICE	BUI	ORG	LEA						✓	
VIDEO BIOGRAPHER	CRE	IMP	BUI						✓	
VIDEO CLIPPING SERVICE	BUI	ORG	PRO						✓	
VIDEOGRAPHY/EDUCATIONAL	PRO	IMP	CRE							
VIDEOGRAPHY/INSURANCE DOCUMENTATION	PRO	IMP	CRE							
VIDEOGRAPHY/LITIGATION DOCUMENTATION	PRO	IMP	CRE							
VIDEOGRAPHY/PERSONAL EVENTS	PRO	IMP	CRE							
VIDEOGRAPHY/SPECIAL EVENTS	PRO	IMP	CRE							
VIDEOGRAPHY/YEARBOOKS	PRO	IMP	CRE							
VINYL REPAIRING SERVICE	BUI	LEA	IMP							
VISITING SERVICE FOR SHUT-INS	IMP	ORG	PRO							
VOICE/COACH	CRE	IMP	LEA				▮▯		✓	
VOICE INSTRUCTOR	PRO	LEA	BUI							
VOICE STRESS ANALYST	ORG	PRO	IMP		□					
VOICE-OVER ARTIST (LOOPING)	CRE	LEA	IMP							
WAKEUP SERVICE	ORG	IMP	LEA						✓	
WALL-COVERING TEXTURER	CRE	IMP	BUI							
WALLPAPER HANGER	BUI	IMP	LEA							
WARDROBE CONSULTING	CRE	LEA	IMP						✓	
WARDROBE COORDINATOR	BUI	LEA	IMP							
WAREHOUSE ARRNGMNTS AND MNGMNT CONSULTANT	BUI	IMP	LEA							
WASHING AND LAUNDRY SERVICES	BUI	ORG	IMP							

BUI=Builder, CRE=Creator, IMP=Improver, LEA=Leader, ORG=Organizer, PRO=Problem Solver, ■=Always, ▮▯=Usually, □=Some

CAREER OR BUSINESS	PERSONAL STYLE 1	2	3	DEGREE REQUIRED	LICENSE REQUIREMENT	AVERAGE CAPITAL REQUIRED	DONE AT HOME	LAND OR COMMERCIAL BUILDING REQUIRED	FAMILY FRIENDLY	BOOK RESOURCES
WATER SOFTENER SERVICE AND INSTALLER	BUI	ORG	LEA		□					
WEAVER	BUI	ORG	LEA				▮		✓	
WEDDING CONSULTANT	CRE	LEA	IMP							B
WEDDING GOWN RENTAL/BROKERING	LEA	ORG	IMP							
WEDDING GOWN BROKER	LEA	ORG	IMP				▮			
WEDDING MAKEUP ARTIST	IMP	LEA	CRE		□					B
WEDDING PHOTOGRAPHER	PRO	IMP	CRE							
WEDDING PLANNING	CRE	LEA	IMP							
WEIGHT LOSS INSTRUCTION	IMP	LEA	ORG							
WELDING AND SOLDERING	BUI	LEA	PRO		□					
WELL DRILLER	BUI	PRO	LEA		□					
WIG AND HAIRPIECE MAKER	IMP	BUI	LEA		□				✓	
WIG DRESSER	IMP	LEA	ORG							
WINDOW DRESSER	BUI	CRE	ORG							
WINDOW SIGN PAINTER	BUI	ORG	IMP							
WINDOW-WASHING SERVICE	BUI	LEA	IMP							B
WINE MAKER	BUI	PRO	LEA							
WOODWORKER	BUI	PRO	LEA							
WORD-PROCESSING/OFFICE SUPPORT	ORG	IMP	LEA				▮		✓	B,M
WRECKING AND DEMOLITION SERVICE	BUI	LEA	CRE		□					
WRITER/CHILDREN'S BOOKS	CRE	LEA	IMP				▮		✓	
WRITER/COMEDY	CRE	LEA	IMP				▮		✓	
WRITER/COMPANY NEWSLETTERS	CRE	LEA	IMP				▮		✓	
WRITER/COMPUTER DOCUMENTATION	PRO	BUI	IMP				▮		✓	
WRITER/FICTION	CRE	LEA	IMP				▮		✓	
WRITER/FOREIGN CORRESPONDENT	CRE	LEA	IMP				▮		✓	
WRITER/GHOST	CRE	LEA	IMP				▮		✓	
WRITER/GREETING CARDS	CRE	LEA	IMP				▮		✓	
WRITER/MANUALS	CRE	IMP	PRO				▮		✓	B,M
WRITER/MEMOIRS	CRE	LEA	IMP				▮		✓	
WRITER/NONFICTION	CRE	LEA	IMP				▮		✓	
WRITER/PLAYWRIGHT	CRE	LEA	IMP				▮		✓	
WRITER/PROPOSAL AND GRANT	PRO	CRE	IMP				▮		✓	
WRITER/ROMANCE	CRE	LEA	IMP				▮		✓	
WRITER/SCREENWRITER	CRE	LEA	IMP				▮		✓	
WRITER/SCRIPTWRITER	CRE	LEA	IMP				▮		✓	
WRITER/TECHNICAL	PRO	BUI	IMP				▮		✓	B,M

BUI=Builder, CRE=Creator, IMP=Improver, LEA=Leader, ORG=Organizer, PRO=Problem Solver, ■=Always, ▮=Usually, □=Some

CAREER OR BUSINESS	PERSONAL STYLE 1	2	3	DEGREE REQUIRED	LICENSE REQUIREMENT	AVERAGE CAPITAL REQUIRED	DONE AT HOME	LAND OR COMMERCIAL BUILDING REQUIRED	FAMILY FRIENDLY	BOOK RESOURCES
WRITER/TEXTBOOKS	PRO	BUI	IMP				◧		✓	
WRITER/TRADE PUBLICATIONS	PRO	BUI	IMP				◧		✓	
X-RAY TECHNICIAN	PRO	BUI	IMP		☐					
YACHT/BROKER	LEA	ORG	IMP							
YELLOW PAGE/BROKER	LEA	ORG	IMP							
YELLOW PAGE/CONSULTANT	LEA	IMP	CRE							
YOGA INSTRUCTOR	IMP	LEA	BUI							
ZIPPER REPAIR	BUI	ORG	IMP							

BUI=Builder, CRE=Creator, IMP=Improver, LEA=Leader, ORG=Organizer, PRO=Problem Solver, ■=Always, ◧=Usually, ☐=Some

WHERE TO INQUIRE ABOUT PROFESSIONAL AND OCCUPATIONAL LICENSES*

ALASKA
Division of Occupational
   Licensing
P.O. Box 110806
Juneau, AK 99811-0806

CALIFORNIA
Department of Consumer
   Affairs
400 R Street, Suite 3000
Sacramento, CA 95814-
   6200

COLORADO
Department of Regulatory
   Agencies
Division of Registration
1560 Broadway, Suite
   1300
Denver, CO 80202

CONNECTICUT
Department of Consumer
   Protection
Bureau of Licensing and
   Regulation
165 Capitol Ave
Hartford, CT 06106

DISTRICT OF
   COLUMBIA
Department of Consumer
   and Regulatory Affairs
Occupational and
   Professional Licensing
   Administration
614 H Street, N.W.
Washington, DC 20001

FLORIDA
Department of Business
   and Professional
   Regulation
1940 N. Monroe Street
Tallahassee, FL 32399-
   0797

GEORGIA
Georgia State Examining
   Boards
Office of Secretary of
   State
166 Pryor Street, S.W.
Atlanta, GA 30303

HAWAII
Department of Commerce
   and Consumer Affairs
P.O. Box 3469
Honolulu, HI 96801

IDAHO
Bureau of Occupational
   Licenses
1109 Main Street
Owyhee Plaza, Suite 220
Boise, ID 83702-5642

ILLINOIS
Department of
   Professional Regulation
320 W. Washington, 3d
   Floor
Springfield, IL 62786

INDIANA
Professional Licensing
   Agency
1021 Government Center
   North
100 N. Senate Ave
Indianapolis, IN 46204

*States not listed lack a centralized office that handles licensing. In these states, contact must be made with individual licensing agencies.

IOWA
Professional Licensing and
    Regulations Division
1918 S.E. Hulsizer Ave
Ankeny, IA 50021

KENTUCKY
Division of Occupations
    and Professions
P.O. Box 456
Frankfort, KY 40602-
    0456

LOUISIANA
Office of Licensing and
    Regulation
Department of Health and
    Human Resources
P.O. Box 3767
Baton Rouge, LA 70821

MAINE
Division of Licensing and
    Enforcement
State House Station 35
Augusta, ME 04333

MARYLAND
Department of Licensing
    and Regulation
Division of Occupational
    and Professional
    Licensing
501 St. Paul Place, 15th
    Floor
Baltimore, MD 21202-
    2272

MASSACHUSETTS
Executive Office of
    Consumer Affairs
Leverett Saltonstall
    Building
100 Cambridge Street,
    Room 1520
Boston, MA 02202

MICHIGAN
Bureau of Occupation and
    Professional Regulation
Department of Commerce
P.O. Box 30018
Lansing, MI 48909

MINNESOTA
Department of Commerce
Enforcement and
    Licensing
133 E. 7th Street
St. Paul, MN 55101

MISSISSIPPI
Secretary of State
State of Mississippi
401 Mississippi Street
Jackson, MS 39215

MISSOURI
Licensing Activities
Division of Professional
    Registration
P.O. Box 135
Jefferson City, MO 65102

MONTANA
Professional and
    Occupational Licensing
    Bureau
111 North Jackson
P.O. Box 200513
Helena, MT 59620-0513

NEBRASKA
Bureau of Examining
    Boards
301 Centennial Mall South
Box 95007
Lincoln, NE 68509

NEW HAMPSHIRE
Secretary of State
State of New Hampshire
State House; Room 204
Concord, NH 03301

NEW JERSEY
Division of Consumer
    Affairs
Department of Law and
    Public Safety
124 Halsey Street
P.O. Box 45027
Newark, NJ 07201

NEW MEXICO
Regulation and Licensing
    Department
P.O. Box 25101
725 Michael's Drive
Santa Fe, NM 87504

NEW YORK
New York State Education
   Department
Cultural Education
   Center, Room 3029
Albany, NY 12230

NORTH DAKOTA
Secretary of State
State of North Dakota
600 E. Boulevard Ave
State Capitol, 1st Floor
Bismarck, ND 58505-
   0500

PENNSYLVANIA
Bureau of Professional and
   Occupational Affairs
Department of State
618 Transportation and
   Safety Building
Harrisburg, PA 17120

RHODE ISLAND
Division of Professional
   Regulation
Department of Health
3 Capitol Hill, Cannon
   Building
Providence, RI 02908-
   5097

SOUTH CAROLINA
Department of Labor
Licensing and Regulations
P.O. Box 11329
Columbia, SC 29211

SOUTH DAKOTA
Professional and
   Occupational Licensing
Department of Commerce
910 East Sioux Ave
Pierre, SD 57501

TENNESSEE
Department of Commerce
   and Insurance
Division of Regulatory
   Boards
500 James Robertson
   Pkwy.
2d Floor
Nashville, TN 37243-0572

TEXAS
Department of Licensing
   and Regulation
P.O. Box 12157
Capitol Station
Austin, TX 78711

UTAH
Division of Occupational
   and Professional
   Licensing
P.O. Box 45805
Heber M. Wells Building
Salt Lake City, UT 84145-
   0805

VERMONT
Office of Professional
   Regulation
Office of the Secretary of
   State
109 State Street
Montpelier, VT 05609-
   1106

VIRGINIA
Department of
   Professional and
   Occupational
   Regulation
3600 W. Broad Street
Richmond, VA 23230

WASHINGTON
Department of Licensing
Highway-Licenses Building
PB-01
Olympia, WA 98504-8001

WISCONSIN
Department of Regulation
   and Licensing
P.O. Box 8935
Madison, WI 53708

CANADA

ALBERTA
Professions and
    Occupations Bureau
5th Floor, Kensington
    Place
Edmonton, AB T5J 358

BRITISH COLUMBIA
Legislation Policy,
    Planning and
    Legislation
Ministry of Health
    RBB5-2
1515 Blanchard Street
Victoria, BC V8W 3C8

MANITOBA
Ministry of Health
Legislative Building,
    Room 308
Winnipeg, MB R3C
    OV8

NEW BRUNSWICK
Department of Health and
    Community Services
Carleton Place, P.O. Box
    5100
Fredericton, NB E3B
    5G8

NEWFOUNDLAND
Department of Health
Confederation Building
P.O. Box 8700
West Block
St. Johns, NF A1B 4J6

NOVA SCOTIA
Department of Health
1690 Hollis Street
Joseph Howe Building
P.O. Box 488
Halifax, NS B3J 2R8

ONTARIO
Professional Relations
    Branch
Ministry of Health
7 Overlea Boulevard, 1st
    Floor
Toronto, ON M4H 1A8

PRINCE EDWARD
    ISLAND
Department of Health and
    Social Services
P.O. Box 2000
Charlottetown, PE CIA 7N8

QUEBEC
Office des Professions du
    Quebec
Complex-Place Jacques
    Cartier
320 rue Saint-Joseph est,
    1er étage
Quebec, PQ G1K 8G5

SASKATCHEWAN
Department of Health
TIC. Douglas Building
3475 Albert Street
Regina, SK S4S 6X6

APPENDIX ▮▮▮

Directory of Self-Employment Careers by Personal Style

FIRST	SECOND	THIRD	CAREER OR BUSINESS
BUILDER	CREATOR	IMPROVER	CHILDREN'S COSTUME CREATOR
			COSTUME DESIGNER
			COSTUME MAKER
BUILDER	CREATOR	LEADER	BAKER
			FOLEY ARTIST (SOUND EFFECTS CREATOR)
			GROWER/BONSAI
			NURSERY OF RARE AND UNUSUAL PLANTS
			STATUE REPAIR
			STONE CARVER
BUILDER	CREATOR	ORGANIZER	QUILT MAKER
			WINDOW DRESSER
BUILDER	CREATOR	PROBLEM SOLVER	CRAFTS/KITE MAKER
			KNITWEAR CREATOR
			PRESENTATION SUPPORT
			RESTORATION SERVICES/FURNITURE
			RESTORATION SERVICES/MUSICAL INSTRUMENTS
			RESTORATION SERVICES/PHOTOGRAPHS
			RESTORATION SERVICES/VINTAGE AUTO
			TERRACE DESIGN AND REPAIR
BUILDER	IMPROVER	LEADER	INSTALLER/SKYLIGHTS

FIRST	SECOND	THIRD	CAREER OR BUSINESS
BUILDER	IMPROVER	CREATOR	REPAIR/RV'S AND VANS
BUILDER	IMPROVER	LEADER	AUDIO/VIDEO/REPAIRER
BUILDER	IMPROVER	LEADER	INSTALLER/ELECTRIC FANS
			AUTO/MECHANIC
			AUTO/TEST DRIVER
			BRICKLAYER/BRICK AND TILE
			COIN-OPERATED EQUIP MAINTNCE/LAUNDRIES/DRY CLEANERS
			COIN-OPERATED EQUIPMENT MAINTENANCE/TV
			COIN-OPERATED EQUIPMENT MAINTENANCE
			COOKBOOK RECIPE TESTER
			DOG GROOMING
			DOLL/CLOTHING MAKING
			DRESSMAKING
			DRIVER/AUTO TEST
			DRIVER/INDEPENDENT TRUCKER
			GLASS/REPAIR
			GLAZIER
			HOUSE/MOVER
			HOUSE/PAINTER
			INSTALLER/TILE
			LEATHER WORKER
			LUGGAGE REPAIRER
			MESSENGER SERVICE
			MOBILE/OIL CHANGE SERVICE
			MOBILE/TUNEUP
			MOBILE/WINDOW SCREEN REPAIR
			NEON SIGN SERVICER
			ORIENTAL RUG REPAIRER
			ORTHOTIST
			PAINTER/HOUSE
			PAPERHANGER
			POULTRY FARMER
			PROSTHETIST
			SADDLE MAKER
			SHEEP SHEARING
			SHOE REPAIRER
			SQUARE DANCE INSTRUCTOR
			STONEMASON
			TOOL REPAIRER
			UPHOLSTERY/CLEANER
			WALLPAPER HANGER
BUILDER	IMPROVER	LEADER	WAREHOUSE ARRANGEMENTS AND MANAGEMENT CONSULTANT

FIRST	SECOND	THIRD	CAREER OR BUSINESS
BUILDER	IMPROVER	ORGANIZER	BICYCLE/REPAIRER
			INSTALLER/MUSEUM
			INSTALLER/SATELLITE DISH
			INSTALLER/SECURITY SYSTEMS
			MUSICAL INSTRUMENT MAKER
			MUSICAL INSTRUMENT REPAIR
			PIANO TUNER
			REPAIR SERVICES/MUSICAL INSTRUMENTS
			RUBBER STAMP BUSINESS
			SILVERSMITH
BUILDER	IMPROVER	PROBLEM SOLVER	LIVESTOCK HAULER
			LIVESTOCK RANCHER
BUILDER	LEADER	CREATOR	BROKER/EXOTIC BEADS
			GLASS/STAINED, CREATOR
			HAIR JEWELRY DESIGNER
			HORSE EXERCISER
			ICE CARVER
			JEWELRY/DESIGN
			JEWELRY/MAKING
			JEWELRY/REPAIR
			PHOTOGRAPHER/AERIAL
			WRECKING AND DEMOLITION SERVICE
BUILDER	LEADER	IMPROVER	PARKING LOT MAINTENANCE
			ACOUSTICS ENGINEER
			ANIMAL BREEDER/BIRDS, EXOTIC
			ANIMAL BREEDER/CATS
			ANIMAL BREEDER/CATTLE
			ANIMAL BREEDER/CHICKENS
			ANIMAL BREEDER/DOGS
			ANIMAL BREEDER/FISH FARMER
			ANIMAL BREEDER/FUR BEARING
			ANIMAL BREEDER/HORSES
			ANIMAL BREEDER/LLAMAS
			ANIMAL BREEDER/SHEEP
			ANIMAL BREEDER/WILD ANIMALS
			ANIMAL TRAINER/GUARD DOG
			ANIMAL TRAINER/HORSES
			ANIMAL TRAINER/OBEDIENCE
			ARTIFICIAL INSEMINATOR OF ANIMALS
			AUTO/BODY CUSTOMIZER
			AUTO/BODY RESTORER
			AUTO/BROKER

FIRST	SECOND	THIRD	CAREER OR BUSINESS
BUILDER	LEADER	IMPROVER	AUTO/SECURITY INSTALLER
			AUTO/UPHOLSTERY CLEANING
			BAIT DEALER
			BOAT/MAINTENANCE
			BOAT/REPAIR
			BOOKBINDER
			BRIDAL/GOWNS
			CAMPING AND SAFARI LEADER
			CHAIN SAW OPERATOR
			CHAUFFEUR
			CONCRETE SCULPTOR
			COSTUME MAKER
			COSTUME RENTAL
			CRAFTS/INSTRUCTOR
			DEMOLITION SPECIALIST
			DOG HANDLER
			DRIVER/BUS
			DRIVER/CARRIAGE
			DRIVER/CHAUFFEUR
			DRIVER/CHILDREN'S TAXI SERVICE
			DRIVER/HANDICAPPED TRANSPORTATION
			DRIVER/PET TAXI SERVICE
			ENERGY CONSERVATION CONSULTANT
			ENERGY CONSULTING/ALTERNATIVE
			ENGINEER
			ENGRAVER
			ENVIRONMENTAL SERVICES/INDOOR ENVIRONMENTAL TESTER
			ENVIRONMENTAL SERVICES/POLLUTION CONTROL
			ENVIRONMENTAL SERVICES/RECYCLING
			ENVIRONMENTAL SERVICES/WASTE MANAGEMENT CONSULTANT
			EXCAVATION SERVICE
			EXTERMINATOR
			FILM-PROCESSING SERVICE
			FISHING AND HUNTING INFORMATION
			FLIGHT INSTRUCTOR
			FOOD/MAIL ORDER SALES
			FUR TRAPPER
			FURNITURE/CLEANER
			GEMSTONE DEALER
			GOURMET COOKING SCHOOL
			GUIDE/HUNTING AND FISHING
			GUIDE/RIVER RAFTING

FIRST	SECOND	THIRD	CAREER OR BUSINESS
BUILDER	LEADER	IMPROVER	GUN REPAIR
			GUNSMITH
			HANDICRAFT/MAKING
			HUNTER EDUCATION INSTRUCTOR
			HUNTING GUIDE
			INSECT BREEDER/BUTTERFLIES
			INSECT BREEDER/EARTHWORMS
			INSECT BREEDER/FISH BAIT
			INSECT BREEDER/LADYBUGS
			INSTALLER/CAR STEREOS
			INSTALLER/FLOORING
			INSTALLER/PUMP
			INSTALLER/SEWAGE SYSTEM
			INSTRUCTOR/GUIDE DOGS FOR THE BLIND
			JANITORIAL SERVICE
			KAYAK INSTRUCTOR
			LIMOUSINE SERVICE
			MANUFACTURING SPECIALTY PRODUCTS/BIRDHOUSES
			MANUFACTURING SPECIALTY PRODUCTS/DOGHOUSES
			MANUFACTURING SPECIALTY PRODUCTS/NAPKIN IMPRINTING
			MANUFACTURING SPECIALTY PRODUCTS/PERSONALIZED ITEMS
			MANUFACTURING SPECIALTY PRODUCTS/SOUVENIRS
			MASSAGE INSTRUCTOR
			MASSAGE THERAPIST
			MOBILE/BARBECUE CLEANER
			MOBILE/MASSAGE
			PATIO CONSTRUCTION
			PEST CONTROL SERVICE
			PET SERVICES/AQUARIUM CLEANING SERVICE
			PET TRAINING
			PETTING ZOO OPERATOR
			PLANT/RENT-A-PLANT SERVICE
			PLASTERER
			PLASTICS/LAMINATING
			POOL CLEANING SERVICE
			POWER WASH SERVICES
			RADON MEASUREMENT AND MITIGATION
			RECORDING ENGINEER
			RECORDING STUDIO OPERATOR
			REFLEXOLOGY THERAPIST
			REPAIR SERVICE/GENERAL
			REPAIR SERVICES/APPLIANCES

FIRST	SECOND	THIRD	CAREER OR BUSINESS
BUILDER	LEADER	IMPROVERR	REPAIR SERVICES/CONCRETE
			REPAIR SERVICES/FARM EQUIPMENT
			REPAIR SERVICES/ICE SKATES
			REPAIR SERVICES/MICROWAVE OVENS
			REPAIR SERVICES/MOTORCYCLE
			REPAIR SERVICES/PHOTOCOPIER
			REPAIR SERVICES/RUG
			REPAIR SERVICES/SHAVERS
			REPAIR SERVICES/SHOES
			REPAIR SERVICES/SPORTS EQUIPMENT
			REPAIR SERVICES/SWIMMING POOLS
			REPAIR SERVICES/TOOLS
			REPAIR SERVICES/TV/RADIO
			RODEO PERFORMER
			ROWING/INSTRUCTOR
			RUG REPAIRER
			SEWING AND TAILORING/BRIDAL GOWNS AND VEILS
			SEWING AND TAILORING/CLOTHING
			SEWING AND TAILORING/COSTUMES
			SEWING MACHINE REPAIR
			SHEEP RANCHER
			SHIPWRIGHT
			SHOOTING PRESERVE OPERATOR
			SOUVENIR AND NOVELTY MAKER
			TAILOR/CUSTOM
			TOUR OPERATOR/BICYCLE
			TOUR OPERATOR/CHARTER FISHING TOURS
			TOUR OPERATOR/FISHING GUIDE
			TOUR OPERATOR/GOLF
			TOUR OPERATOR/MOUNTAIN-CLIMBING GUIDE
			TOUR OPERATOR/NATURE TOURS
			TOUR OPERATOR/RIVER RAFTING
			TOW TRUCK OPERATOR
			TRANSLATION SERVICE
			TREE REMOVAL
			VINYL REPAIRING SERVICE
			WARDROBE COORDINATOR
			WINDOW-WASHING SERVICE
BUILDER	LEADER	ORGANIZER	ATHLETE, PROFESSIONAL
			AUTO/GLASS TINTING
			BADGE AND BUTTON MAKER
			BOAT/CLEANING

FIRST	SECOND	THIRD	CAREER OR BUSINESS
BUILDER	LEADER	ORGANIZER	CARPETS AND RUGS/CLEANING
			CHAUFFEUR
			CHIMNEY SWEEP
			CLEANING SERVICES/AIRDUCTS
			CLEANING SERVICES/AQUARIUMS
			CLEANING SERVICES/AUTOS
			CLEANING SERVICES/BASEMENT
			CLEANING SERVICES/CARPET
			CLEANING SERVICES/CEILINGS
			CLEANING SERVICES/CESSPOOL
			CLEANING SERVICES/FLOORS
			CLEANING SERVICES/FURNITURE
			CLEANING SERVICES/GUTTERS
			CLEANING SERVICES/HOT TUB/JACUZZI
			CLEANING SERVICES/POOL
			CLEANING SERVICES/POWER WASHING
			CLEANING SERVICES/SHIPS
			CLEANING SERVICES/TILE
			CLEANING SERVICES/WINDOW BLINDS
			CLEANING SERVICES/WINDOWS
			COLLECTIBLES DEALER/ANTIQUES
			COLLECTIBLES DEALER/AUTOGRAPHS
			COLLECTIBLES DEALER/BUTTERFLIES
			COLLECTIBLES DEALER/COMIC BOOKS
			COLLECTIBLES DEALER/GEMSTONES/ROCKS
			COLLECTIBLES DEALER/MINIATURE CARS
			COLLECTIBLES DEALER/RARE BOOKS
			COLLECTIBLES DEALER/RARE COINS
			COLLECTIBLES DEALER/SPORTS CARDS
			COLLECTIBLES DEALER/STAMPS
			CONSTRUCTION INSPECTOR
			CRAFTS/CANDLE MAKER
			CRAFTS/JEWELRY
			CRAFTS/QUILTS
			CRAFTS/RUGS
			DRIVER/CHAUFFEUR
			GOLDSMITH
			HAIR JEWELRY MAKER
			HANDICRAFT/MANUFACTURE
			HEAVY EQUIPMENT OWNER AND OPERATOR
			HOME/INSPECTOR
			HYPNOTHERAPIST

FIRST	SECOND	THIRD	CAREER OR BUSINESS
BUILDER	LEADER	ORGANIZER	LANDSCAPE GARDENER
			LOCKSMITHING
			PHOTOGRAPHY/COLOR CORRECTION, RETOUCHING, RESTORING
			REPAIR SERVICES/HEATING, AIR-COND AND REFRIGERATION
			RESURFACER/DRIVEWAY/PARKING LOT
			RESURFACER/TENNIS COURT
			ROOF INSPECTOR
			ROOFER
			SECURITY SERVICE
			SWIMMING POOL/SPA MAINTENANCE SERVICE
			TENNIS COURT/MAINTENANCE
			TOYMAKER
			TREE PLANTING
BUILDER	LEADER	PROBLEM SOLVER	AIRCRAFT MECHANIC
			ANIMAL BREEDER/GAME BIRDS
			ANIMAL BREEDER/GAME FISH
			ANIMAL BREEDER/WORMS
			AQUACULTURIST (FISH GROWER)
			BEEKEEPER
			BOATBUILDER
			BUILDING MOVING/DEMOLITION CONTRACTOR
			CARPENTER
			CARPETS AND RUGS/DYEING
			CARPETS AND RUGS/LAYING
			CEILING REPAIR
			COMPUTER/REPAIR AND MAINTENANCE
			COMPUTER/ROOM INSTALLATION
			CONCRETE FENCE BUILDER
			CONSTRUCTION CONTRACTOR/AIR-CONDITIONING
			CONSTRUCTION CONTRACTOR/CONCRETE
			CONSTRUCTION CONTRACTOR/STUCCO/MASONRY
			DRIVER/AUTO TEST
			ELECTRICIAN/ELECTRICAL CONTRACTOR
			ELEVATOR CONTRACTOR
			ENAMELING REPAIR
			FENCE CONSTRUCTION
			FIRE SAFETY CONSULTANT
			FIREWORKS DISPLAY PRODUCER
			FISHERMAN, COMMERCIAL
			FOUNTAIN PEN REPAIR
			FURNACE INSTALLER AND REPAIRER
			GAME BIRD PROPAGATOR

FIRST	SECOND	THIRD	CAREER OR BUSINESS
BUILDER	LEADER	PROBLEM SOLVER	GEMOLOGIST
			GLASS/ETCHING
			GROWER/CHRISTMAS TREE
			GROWER/FRUIT TREE
			GROWER/NURSERY
			GROWER/ORCHID
			GROWER, SPECIALTY FOODS/EDIBLE FLOWERS
			GROWER, SPECIALTY FOODS/GINSENG
			GROWER, SPECIALTY FOODS/HERBS
			GROWER, SPECIALTY FOODS/MUSHROOM
			GROWER, SPECIALTY FOODS/SPROUTS
			GUIDE/ALPINE
			HANDYMAN SERVICE
			HARPSICHORD MAKER
			HEATING AND AIR-CONDITIONING CONTRACTOR
			HOT-AIR BALLOONIST
			ICE CARVER
			INSTALLER/AIR-CONDITIONING
			INSTALLER/WOOD STOVE
			KAYAK BUILDER
			KITCHEN/REMODELING
			KITE DEALER
			KITE MAKER
			LAUNDRY SERVICES
			LAWN AND YARD CARE, MOWING, RAKING, MULCHING, SNOW RMVAL
			LAWN CARE SERVICE
			LEAK DETECTION SERVICE
			LIGHTING CONSULTANT
			LIVESTOCK AGENT
			LIVESTOCK BUYER/BROKER/DEALER
			PACKAGING AND SHIPPING SERVICE
			PAINTER/SIGN
			PLUMBER
			RACE CAR DRIVER
			REPAIR SERVICES/AIRCRAFT
			REPAIR SERVICES/BICYCLES
			REPAIR SERVICES/BOATS
			REPAIR SERVICES/CAMERAS
			REPAIR SERVICES/GUN
			REPAIR SERVICES/LAWN MOWER
			REPAIR SERVICES/MOBILE HOMES
			REPAIR SERVICES/SEWING MACHINES

FIRST	SECOND	THIRD	CAREER OR BUSINESS
BUILDER	LEADER	PROBLEM SOLVER	REPAIR SERVICES/SNOW BLOWERS
			REPAIR SERVICES/VACUUM CLEANER
			REPAIR SERVICES/VCR
			REPAIR SERVICES/WATCHES
			SANDBLASTER
			SCUBA DIVING INSTRUCTOR
			SEPTIC TANK PUMPING/INSTALLING
			SHEET-METAL WORKER
			SHELLFISH FISHER/GROWER
			SNOW REMOVAL
			SOUND TECHNICIAN
			STUCCO MASON
			TREE SURGEON/INJECTOR
			TROPHY/ENGRAVING
			TROPHY/MAKING
			TROPICAL FISH CARE
			TUGBOAT OPERATOR
			WELDING AND SOLDERING
BUILDER	ORGANIZER	IMPROVER	BLUEPRINT SERVICE
			CARPET/WEAVER
			COURT REPORTER
			FORM DESIGNING
			FURNITURE/RESTORER
			GLASS CREATOR
			HOUSE-SITTER
			INSTALLER/FURNITURE GLASS
			INSTALLER/WATER PURIFIERS AND SOFTENERS
			MOBILE/PET GROOMING
			PET SERVICES/BOARDING: DOGS, HORSES, ETC.
			PET TAXI SERVICE
			PET WALKER
			PET-SITTER
			PET-SITTING FOR UNUSUAL ANIMALS
			REPAIR SERVICES/TELEPHONE
			REUPHOLSTERER
			REWEAVER
			SHOE POLISHING SERVICE
			SOUND MIXER
			UPHOLSTERY/INSTALLATION AND REPAIR
			WASHING AND LAUNDRY SERVICES
			WINDOW SIGN PAINTER
			ZIPPER REPAIR

FIRST	SECOND	THIRD	CAREER OR BUSINESS
BUILDER	ORGANIZER	LEADER	AFFIXING COMPANY LOGOS TO BASEBALL CAPS
			AUDIO/VIDEO/DUPLICATION
			AUTO/DETAILING
			AUTO/GLASS INSTALLER
			BUILDING INSPECTION SERVICE
			CAMERA REPAIR
			CLEANING SERVICE/RV'S AND VANS
			CLEANING SERVICES/HOME RESTORATION SERVICE
			CLEANING SERVICES/SIGNS
			CLOSET/CONSTRUCTION
			COMPUTER/CD-ROM MASTERING
			COMPUTER/DISK DUPLICATING SERVICE
			COMPUTER/DISK FORMATTING
			CRAFTS/KNITWEAR
			CRAFTS/WOOL SPINNING AND DYEING
			CUSTOMER SERVICE CONSULTANT
			DISK COPYING SERVICE
			DISK FORMATTING SERVICE
			DUPLICATING SERVICE/AUDIOTAPES
			DUPLICATING SERVICE/COMPUTER MEDIA
			DUPLICATING SERVICE/SLIDES/OVERHEADS
			DUPLICATING SERVICE/VIDEOTAPES
			ENGRAVER
			FOOD/ROADSIDE FRUIT STAND
			FURNITURE/REPAIRER
			GEM AND DIAMOND CUTTER
			GIFT/WRAPPING SERVICE
			KEY SERVICE
			KNITTING/BY AUTOMATED MACHINE
			LASER CARTRIDGE REMANUFACTURING
			MIRROR/CUSTOM DESIGN AND INSTALLATION
			MOBILE/CAR WASH
			MOBILE/VEHICLE DETAILER
			MOBILE POWER WASHING SERVICE
			OPTICIAN
			PAPERHANGER
			PICTURE FRAMER
			PLAYGROUND EQUIPMENT ERECTOR
			PUSHCART VENDOR/STREET AND MALL
			REPAIR SERVICES/VENDING MACHINES
			ROTOTILLING SERVICE
			RUG MAKER

FIRST	SECOND	THIRD	CAREER OR BUSINESS
BUILDER	ORGANIZER	LEADER	SEWING AND TAILORING/DOLL CLOTHING
			SHARPENING SERVICES/KNIVES/SAWS/LAWN MOWERS
			SKIP TRACING/MISSING PERSONS
			STUFFED-ANIMAL VENDOR
			TAPE-DUPLICATING SERVICE
			TENNIS RACQUET RESTRINGING SERVICE
			TREE PRUNING
			VENDING MACHINE/REPAIR
			VIDEO/TRANSFER SERVICE
			WATER SOFTENER SERVICE AND INSTALLER
			WEAVER
BUILDER	ORGANIZER	PROBLEM SOLVER	ASSAYER
			BUILDING RESTORATION AND PRESERVATION
			COMPUTER-AIDED DESIGN SERVICE
			CONSTRUCTION CONTRACTOR/HOME RENOVATION
			DENTAL TECHNICIAN/DENTURIST
			DRAFTING SERVICE
			ELECTROCARDIOGRAPH TECHNICIAN
			ELECTROPLATING SERVICE
			GARDEN CARE
			GARDEN CARE/ROTOTILLING SERVICE
			HEAVY EQUIPMENT OWNER AND OPERATOR
			HOME/REPAIR SERVICES
			INSTALLER/SWIMMING POOL
			INVENTORY CONTROL SERVICES FOR BUSINESSES
			INVENTORY HOUSEHOLD EFFECTS
			PHOTO SEARCH SERVICE
			PLANT/CARE
			POSTMARK SERVICE
			RARE RECORDINGS AND VIDEOS SEARCH SERVICE
			RV'S AND VANS/CUSTOMIZING
			TELEPHONE REPAIR SERVICE
			VAN AND RV CUSTOMIZING
			VIDEO/DATA SERVICE
			VIDEO CLIPPING SERVICE
BUILDER	PROBLEM SOLVER	CREATOR	LASER LIGHT SHOW PRODUCER
			LIGHTING DESIGNER
			MOVIE LOCATION SCOUT
BUILDER	PROBLEM SOLVER	IMPROVER	ANTIQUE/REPAIR
			ANTIQUE/REFINISHING
			ANTIQUE/RESTORATION
			APPRAISER/PERSONAL COLLECTIONS

FIRST	SECOND	THIRD	CAREER OR BUSINESS
BUILDER	PROBLEM SOLVER	IMPROVER	APPRAISER/PRECIOUS METALS
			AUTO/MECHANIC
			BICYCLE/CUSTOM CONSTRUCTION
			BRONZE WORK
			CABINET MAKER/WOODWORKER
			DESKTOP PUBLISHING SERVICE
			FARMER
			FORESTER
			GOLF HANDICAPPING SERVICE
			HELICOPTER PILOT
			INSTALLER/MILK EQUIPMENT
			JEWELRY/APPRAISAL
			LANDSCAPING SERVICE
			MILK GRADER/SAMPLER/HAULER
			MOBILE/MECHANIC
			NUCLEAR IMAGING TECHNOLOGIST
			PLANT/PROPAGATOR
			PLANT/INTERIOR PLANT DESIGN
			SKI MAKER, CUSTOM
			SOIL-TESTING SERVICE
BUILDER	PROBLEM SOLVER	LEADER	AIRCRAFT MECHANIC
			APPLIANCE/REFINISHING
			APPLIANCE/REPAIR
			BASEMENT/FINISHING
			BASEMENT/WATERPROOFING
			BEER MICROBREWER
			BLACKSMITH
			BLASTER
			BROKER/SECONDHAND PRODUCTS
			CARPENTER
			CLOTHING ALTERATIONS
			COMPUTER-AIDED DESIGN SERVICE
			CROP DUSTER
			DRAFTING SERVICE
			DRIVER/DUMP TRUCK
			DRIVER/TRACTOR-TRAILER TRUCK
			ELECTRICIAN/ELECTRICAL CONTRACTOR
			GARAGE DOOR SERVICE
			INSTALLER/DRYWALL
			INSTALLER/STAINED GLASS
			INSTALLER/TELEPHONE
			INSTALLER/TV/RADIO

FIRST	SECOND	THIRD	CAREER OR BUSINESS
BUILDER	PROBLEM SOLVER	LEADER	INSTALLER/WINDOW
			MACHINIST
			MINE BLASTER
			MOBILE/COMMUNICATIONS SERVICE
			MOTORCYCLE REPAIR
			OFFICE AUTOMATION CONSULTANT
			PARENT GUIDANCE INSTRUCTION
			PARKING CONSULTANT
			PATTERN MAKER
			PET SERVICES/BLACKSMITH/HORSESHOEING SERVICE
			PILOT/AIRPLANE, COMMERCIAL
			PRINTER/QUICK
			RENTAL SERVICES/ROBOTS
			REPTILE FARMER
			RESTAURANT CONSULTANT
			SAILING INSTRUCTOR
			SEWING AND TAILORING/CLOTHING ALTERATIONS
			SHOEMAKER, CUSTOM
			SKYLIGHT INSTALLATION
			SOUND STUDIO
			SPECIAL-EFFECTS TECHNICIAN
			TAILOR/ALTERATION
			TRADE SHOW EXHIBIT BUILDER
			WELL DRILLER
			WINE MAKER
			WOODWORKER
BUILDER	PROBLEM SOLVER	ORGANIZER	AUTO/BATTERY RECONDITIONING SERVICE
			BOILER INSTALLER/REPAIRER
			CONSTRUCTION COST ESTIMATOR
			CONSTRUCTION INSPECTOR
			HEALTH CARE CONSULTANT
			HOME/INSPECTOR
			LASER TECHNICIAN
			SIGN CONTRACTOR
			SIGN MAKER
			SOLAR ENERGY CONTRACTOR
CREATOR	BUILDER	IMPROVER	CHRISTMAS TREE DECORATOR
			CRAFTS/PET TOY CREATOR
			GIFT/BASKET SERVICE
			MUSEUM EXHIBIT DESIGNER
			STAGE MANAGER
CREATOR	BUILDER	LEADER	AUTO/BODY PAINTING

FIRST	SECOND	THIRD	CAREER OR BUSINESS
CREATOR	BUILDER	LEADER	CAKE DECORATING
			CRAFTS/DOLL HOUSES
			DESKTOP VIDEO SERVICES
			MINIATURE ITEMS FOR COLLECTORS
			MINIATURE SET CONSTRUCTOR
			PAINTER/HAND-PAINTED ITEMS
			TEXTILE DESIGN
CREATOR	BULIDER	ORGANIZER	CALLIGRAPHY
			CERTIFICATE AND AWARD CREATOR/COMPUTER GENERATED
			CERTIFICATE AND AWARD CREATOR/HAND LETTERED
			DOLL/HOUSE BUILDING
			HAND LETTERING
			MINIATURE ITEMS FOR COLLECTORS
CREATOR	BUILDER	PROBLEM SOLVER	CERAMIC DESIGNER
			HAIR COLORIST
			MODEL MAKING
			PET TOYS CREATOR
			POTTER
CREATOR	IMPROVER	BUILDER	CLOTHING DESIGNER/ATHLETIC
			CLOTHING DESIGNER/CHILDREN'S
			CLOTHING DESIGNER
			COMPUTER/ACCESSORIES, CUSTOMIZED
			COMPUTER/SPECIAL EFFECTS
			DESKTOP VIDEO/SPECIAL EFFECTS
			HAIRSTYLIST
			PAINTING RESTORER
			VIDEO BIOGRAPHER
			WALL COVERING TEXTURER
CREATOR	IMPROVER	LEADER	ACTING/DRAMA COACH
			ART/INSTRUCTOR
			ARTIST/COMPUTER
			ARTIST/COURTROOM
			ARTIST/HOME PORTRAITS
			ARTIST/STAINED GLASS
			ARTIST/TEXTILE
			ARTIST/WILDLIFE
			ATHLETIC CLOTHING DESIGNER
			CANTOR
			CARPET/SCULPTOR
			CHRISTMAS TREE ORNAMENT CREATOR
			COMPOSER
			CRAFTS/CHRISTMAS TREE ORNAMENTS AND WREATHS

FIRST	SECOND	THIRD	CAREER OR BUSINESS
CREATOR	IMPROVER	LEADER	DANCE INSTRUCTOR
			DANCING/INSTRUCTOR
			DISK JOCKEY SERVICE
			DRAMA COACH
			ENTERTAINER/COMEDIAN
			HOME/INSPECTOR
			HOUSE/PORTRAIT PAINTING
			HUMORIST
			INTERVIEW COACH
			INTERVIEWER—PRINT, RADIO, OR TV
			JOURNALIST
			LETTER WRITER
			LIBRETTIST
			LYRICIST
			MUSIC/ARRANGING AND COMPOSITION
			NEEDLEWORK ARTIST
			NEON ARTIST
			NEW AGE CRAFTS/CHANNELING
			PET PORTRAITS
			PHOTOGRAPHER/REAL ESTATE
			PLAYWRIGHT
			REAL ESTATE/PHOTOGRAPHER
			REPORTER
			SONGWRITER/SPECIAL OCCASIONS
			SPEAKER, PROFESSIONAL/HUMOROUS
			SPEECH COACH
			TRAVELOGUE CREATOR
			VOICE/COACH
CREATOR	IMPROVER	ORGANIZER	ARTIST/NEEDLEWORK
			BARBER
			CLIP ART SERVICE
			MUSIC/CONDUCTOR
CREATOR	IMPROVER	PROBLEM SOLVER	ARTIST/NEON
			BEAUTICIAN/HAIRSTYLISTS
			COPYWRITER/ADVERTISING
			COPYWRITER/BOOK COVER
			COPYWRITER/CORPORATE
			COPYWRITER/NEWSPAPER
			DANCE THERAPIST
			GHOSTWRITING SERVICE
			GRANT WRITER
			MUSICAL ACCOMPANIST

FIRST	SECOND	THIRD	CAREER OR BUSINESS
CREATOR	IMPROVER	PROBLEM SOLVER	MUSICIAN
			PAINTER/FINE ART
			PIANIST
			THERAPIST/DANCE
			WRITER/MANUALS
CREATOR	LEADER	BUILDER	ATHLETIC EQUIPMENT REPAIR
			BRIDAL/MAKEUP SERVICE
			DANCER
			MAKEUP ARTIST/CONSULTANT
			SCULPTOR
CREATOR	LEADER	IMPROVER	ACTOR
			ADVERTISING/AGENCY
			ARCHIVIST
			ART/CRITIC
			ART/HISTORIAN
			ARTIST/AIRBRUSH
			ARTIST/CARICATURE
			ARTIST/CARTOONIST
			AUCTIONEER
			AUDIO/VIDEO/EDITING
			BALLOON DECORATOR
			BANDLEADER/CONDUCTOR
			BRIDAL/CONSULTING
			CARTOONIST
			CHILDREN'S BOOKS ILLUSTRATOR
			CHILDREN'S BOOKS WRITER
			CHORAL DIRECTOR
			CHOREOGRAPHER
			COLOR CONSULTING
			COMEDIAN
			CRAFTS/PRINTMAKER
			CRAFTS/WORKSHOP ORGANIZER
			CREATIVITY CONSULTANT
			CRITIC/ART
			CRITIC/BOOKS
			CRITIC/FASHION
			CRITIC/MOVIES
			CRITIC/TV
			DESIGNER/INDUSTRIAL
			DESIGNER/LIGHTING
			DESIGNER/RESIDENTIAL
			DESIGNER/TEXTILE

FIRST	SECOND	THIRD	CAREER OR BUSINESS
CREATOR	LEADER	IMPROVER	DESIGNER/TOOL
			DESKTOP PUBLISHING SERVICE
			DIRECTOR/PHOTOGRAPHY
			DIRECTOR/THEATER
			EDITOR/BOOKS
			EDITOR/FILM
			ENTERTAINER/AMUSEMENT PARK
			ENTERTAINER/BELLY DANCER
			ENTERTAINER/DANCER
			ENTERTAINER/GLASSBLOWER
			ENTERTAINER/MUSICIAN
			ENTERTAINER/SINGER
			ENTERTAINER/VENTRILOQUIST
			FASHION/MERCHANDISING CONSULTANT
			FASHION/CRITIC
			FASHION/EDITOR
			FASHION/WRITER
			FURNITURE/DESIGNER
			GRAPHIC DESIGNER
			GREETING CARD/ARTIST/DESIGNER
			GREETING CARD/WRITER
			ILLUSTRATOR/CATALOGS
			ILLUSTRATOR/CHILDREN'S BOOKS
			ILLUSTRATOR/FASHION
			ILLUSTRATOR/MANUALS
			ILLUSTRATOR/MEDICAL
			IMPERSONATOR
			INTERIOR DECORATOR
			INTERIOR DESIGNER
			LANGUAGE INSTRUCTION
			LECTURER/PUBLIC SPEAKING/MOTIVATIONAL
			LIVESTOCK AUCTIONEER
			MAGICIAN
			MANUSCRIPT EDITING
			MEETING PLANNER
			MILLINER/HAT MAKER
			MURALS
			MUSIC/TEACHER
			PHOTOGRAPHER/MOVIES, VIDEO
			PHOTOGRAPHER/UNIQUE LOCAL LANDMARKS
			PHOTOGRAPHER/WEDDING
			PIANO TEACHER

FIRST	SECOND	THIRD	CAREER OR BUSINESS
CREATOR	LEADER	IMPROVER	PLAY/THERAPIST
			POET
			PORTRAIT ARTIST
			PRINTMAKER
			RADIO TALK SHOW HOST
			REAL ESTATE/AUCTIONEER
			REAL ESTATE/BROCHURE SERVICE
			RÉSUMÉ WRITING/PORTFOLIO PREPARATION SERVICE
			REUNION PLANNER
			ROMANCE NOVELIST
			SCRIPT READER
			SCRIPTWRITER
			SET DECORATOR
			SET DESIGNER
			SINGER
			SINGING TELEGRAM SERVICE
			SPEECHWRITER
			SQUARE DANCE CALLER
			THERAPIST/PLAY
			TV CAMERA OPERATOR
			TYPEFACE DESIGNER
			VENTRILOQUIST
			VOICE-OVER ARTIST (LOOPING)
			WARDROBE CONSULTING
			WEDDING CONSULTANT
			WEDDING PLANNING
			WRITER/CHILDREN'S BOOKS
			WRITER/COMEDY
			WRITER/COMPANY NEWSLETTERS
			WRITER/FICTION
			WRITER/FOREIGN CORRESPONDENT
			WRITER/GHOST
			WRITER/GREETING CARDS
			WRITER/MEMOIRS
			WRITER/NONFICTION
			WRITER/PLAYWRIGHT
			WRITER/ROMANCE
			WRITER/SCREENWRITER
			WRITER/SCRIPTWRITER
CREATOR	LEADER	ORGANIZER	FABRIC DESIGNER
			NEW AGE CRAFTS/PSYCHIC READING
			PERSONAL BUSINESS MANAGER

FIRST	SECOND	THIRD	CAREER OR BUSINESS
CREATOR	LEADER	ORGANIZER	PHOTOJOURNALIST
			REUNION PLANNER
			TATTOO ARTIST
CREATOR	LEADER	PROBLEM SOLVER	ENTERTAINER/MAGICIAN
			ENTERTAINER/MIME
			ENTERTAINER/PUPPETEER
			FASHION/ILLUSTRATOR
			FASHION/DESIGNER
			IMAGE CONSULTANT
			PACKAGE DESIGN AND DEVELOPMENT
			PACKAGING PRINTING CONSULTANT
			PUPPETEER
			SCREENWRITER
CREATOR	ORGANIZER	IMPROVER	CATERER
			CATERING/BOX LUNCH CREATOR
			CATERING/CUSTOM WEDDING CAKE CREATOR
			CATERING/FILM LOCATION
			GRAPHOLOGIST
			HANDWRITING ANALYST
			OFFICE LUNCH SERVICE
			PARTY/ENTERTAINMENT
CREATOR	PROBLEM SOLVER	BUILDER	ARCHITECTURAL/SALVAGE
			ARCHITECTURAL/DESIGNER
			ARCHITECTURAL/MODEL MAKER
			LANDSCAPE ARCHITECT
			LANDSCAPE DESIGNER
			SOFTWARE WRITER/DEVELOPER, GAME
			TENNIS COURT/DESIGN
			VIDEO/EDITING
CREATOR	PROBLEM SOLVER	IMPROVER	COMPUTER-AIDED DESIGN SERVICE
			GAME DESIGNER/EDUCATIONAL
			MARKET MAPPING SERVICE
			RESTORATION SERVICES/PAPER AND PRINTS
CREATOR	PROBLEM SOLVER	LEADER	ARCHITECT
			ARTIST/COMPUTER
			COMPUTER/ANIMATION
			COMPUTER/ARTIST
			COMPUTER/GRAPHICS
			DESKTOP VIDEO/ANIMATION
			GAME DESIGNER/COMPUTER
			ILLUSTRATOR/MEDICAL
			ILLUSTRATOR/TECHNICAL

FIRST	SECOND	THIRD	CAREER OR BUSINESS
CREATOR	PROBLEM SOLVER	LEADER	KITCHEN/DESIGN
			MEDICAL ILLUSTRATOR
			PRESENTATION GRAPHICS SPECIALIST
			SET DESIGNER
IMPROVER	BUILDER	LEADER	AEROBICS CLASSES
			BOAT/INSTRUCTOR
			EXECUTIVE RECRUITER
			FITNESS TRAINER
			FLYING/INSTRUCTOR
			FURNITURE/REFINISHER
			FURNITURE/STRIPPER
			GOLF COACH
			GYMNASTICS INSTRUCTOR
			ICE-SKATING/COACH
			MANTEL REPAIR
			MUSIC/LIBRARIAN
			NEEDLEPOINT INSTRUCTOR
			OCCUPATIONAL THERAPIST
			OPTICIAN
			PILOT/INSTRUCTOR
			REHABILITATION COUNSELOR
			TENNIS/COACH
			TENNIS/INSTRUCTOR
			WIG AND HAIRPIECE MAKER
IMPROVER	BUILDER	ORGANIZER	ART/REPAIRS
			ERRAND SERVICE
			REPAIR SERVICES/ART OBJECTS
			REPAIR SERVICES/FINE CHINA
			REPAIR SERVICES/LAMPSHADES
			REPAIR SERVICES/NECKLACE RESTRINGING
			REPAIR SERVICES/STATUARY
			REPAIR SERVICES/VINTAGE BOOKS
			RESTORATION SERVICES/ANTIQUES
			RESTORATION SERVICES/AUTO
			RESTORATION SERVICES/FLOORING
			VENDING MACHINE/OPERATION
IMPROVER	BUILDER	PROBLEM SOLVER	NAVIGATIONAL INSTRUCTOR
IMPROVER	CREATOR	LEADER	ACTING/DRAMA COACH
			IMAGE CONSULTANT
			READING SERVICE
IMPROVER	CREATOR	ORGANIZER	FACIALIST/SKIN CARE SPECIALIST
			HOME HEALTH AIDE

FIRST	SECOND	THIRD	CAREER OR BUSINESS
IMPROVER	CREATOR	PROBLEM SOLVER	DENTAL HYGIENIST
			LIBRARY MANAGER/FILM
			LIBRARY MANAGER/TAPE
			PASTORAL COUNSELOR
			PSYCHOTHERAPIST/PASTORAL COUNSELOR
			SPECIALTY INFORMATION PROVIDER
			SPEECH INSTRUCTOR
			SPEECH PATHOLOGIST
IMPROVER	LEADER	BUILDER	SELF-DEFENSE INSTRUCTOR
			CHILDBIRTH INSTRUCTOR
			COMPANION/PERSONAL
			DRIVING/INSTRUCTOR
			EXERCISE AND PHYSICAL FITNESS INSTRUCTION
			FITNESS INSTRUCTOR
			FURNITURE/RENTAL CONSULTANT
			HAIRSTYLIST
			IN-HOME HEALTH CARE
			MARTIAL ARTS INSTRUCTOR
			MOBILE/HAIRSTYLIST
			PET SERVICES/ANIMAL REMOVER
			RENTAL SERVICES/OFFICE EQUIPMENT
			RESEARCH ANALYSIS
			RESEARCH AND DEVELOPMENT CONSULTANT
			RESEARCH SERVICE
			SCUBA DIVING/INSTRUCTOR
			YOGA INSTRUCTOR
IMPROVER	LEADER	CREATOR	ADOPTION ADVOCATE
			ARBITRATOR
			ART/CORPORATE ART CONSULTANT
			ART/DEALER
			ART/GALLERY OWNER
			BEAUTICIAN/HAIRSTYLISTS
			BOOKING AGENCY/ENTERTAINERS
			BOOKING AGENCY/MODELS
			CASTING DIRECTOR
			CONSULTANT/TALENT
			COOKING TEACHER
			COSMETOLOGIST
			DATING SERVICE
			DIRECT MAILING CONSULTANT
			DIRECT MARKETING CONSULTANT
			DIRECTOR/TV

FIRST	SECOND	THIRD	CAREER OR BUSINESS
IMPROVER	LEADER	CREATOR	DIRECTOR/VIDEO
			FACIALIST/SKIN CARE SPECIALIST
			HOME/ECONOMIST
			MOBILE/BEAUTICIAN
			PARALEGAL
			PSYCHOTHERAPIST/SOCIAL WORKER
			RENTAL SERVICES/PICTURES
			SOCIAL WORKER/PSYCHIATRIC
			TALENT/COORDINATOR
			TALENT/SCOUT
			TV DIRECTOR
			WEDDING MAKEUP ARTIST
IMPROVER	LEADER	ORGANIZER	ADDICTION/SUBSTANCE ABUSE COUNSELOR
			ASTROLOGER, FINANCIAL
			BABY-SITTING/AU-PAIR/NANNY/AGENCY
			BABY-SITTING/AU-PAIR/NANNY/REFERRAL SERVICE
			BARTENDER
			CAMP CONSULTANT
			CHARTERING SERVICE/AIRPLANES
			CHARTERING SERVICE/YACHTS
			CHILD CARE PROVIDER/DAY CARE
			COMPUTER/TRAINER
			COMPUTER/TUTOR
			DAY CARE/ADULTS
			DEED INVESTIGATOR
			DENTAL PRACTICE MANAGEMENT CONSULTING
			DIRECTOR/CASTING
			DIRECTOR/MOTION PICTURE
			EDUCATIONAL/THERAPIST
			EMPLOYMENT AGENCY
			ESCORT SERVICE
			ETIQUETTE CONSULTANT
			EXPORT AGENT
			EXPORTER
			FAMILY CHILD-CARE PROVIDER
			FIRE SAFETY CONSULTANT
			FOSTER PARENT
			FUND-RAISER, PROFESSIONAL
			HOME/SCHOOLING CONSULTANT
			HOME/SCHOOLING GRADER
			HOME/TUTOR
			HORSE TRAINER

FIRST	SECOND	THIRD	CAREER OR BUSINESS
IMPROVER	LEADER	ORGANIZER	IMPORTER
			IN-HOME HEALTH CARE
			LAW/OFFICE MANAGEMENT CONSULTANT
			LIBRARY MANAGER/LAW
			LITIGATION SUPPORT
			NEW AGE CRAFTS/ASTROLOGY
			NEW AGE CRAFTS/NUMEROLOGY
			NURSE/LICENSED PRACTICAL
			PACKAGING AND SHIPPING SERVICE
			PARTY/PLANNING
			PERSONAL SERVICES BROKER
			PSYCHOTHERAPIST/HYPNOTHERAPIST
			RECREATIONAL THERAPIST
			RETIREMENT COUNSELING
			SCOUT/PROFESSIONAL SPORTS
			TRAINER/COMPUTER
			TRAVEL CONSULTANT/GUIDE/PACKAGER
			TUTORING/ACADEMIC/ACHIEVEMENT TESTS
			WEIGHT LOSS INSTRUCTION
			WIG DRESSER
IMPROVER	LEADER	PROBLEM SOLVER	ART/HISTORIAN
			CHILDREN'S TELEVISION PRODUCER
			CHILDREN'S THEATER DIRECTOR
			DIETITIAN
			HISTORIAN/ART
			HISTORIAN/FAMILY
			HISTORIAN/HOUSE
			HISTORIAN/ORGANIZATIONAL
			HISTORIAN/PERSONAL
			HOME/HISTORIAN
			INSURANCE ADJUSTER
			MARRIAGE AND FAMILY COUNSELOR/THERAPIST
			MATH TUTOR
			NEW AGE CRAFTS/FOLK HEALER
			NURSES' REGISTRY
			PARTY/PRODUCTION
			POLITICAL CAMPAIGN CONSULTANT
			PRODUCER/RADIO BROADCAST
			PRODUCER/TV BROADCAST
			PSYCHOLOGIST/INDUSTRIAL-ORGANIZATIONAL
IMPROVER	LEADER	PROBLEM SOLVER	SOCIAL SECURITY CLAIMANT REPRESENTATIVE
			TV PRODUCER

FIRST	SECOND	THIRD	CAREER OR BUSINESS
IMPROVER	ORGANIZER	CREATOR	RENTAL SERVICES/BOOKS/TAPES
			SIGN PAINTING AND STENCILER
IMPROVER	ORGANIZER	LEADER	APPRAISER/REAL ESTATE
			EDUCATION/CONSULTANT
			INTERPRETER/SIGN LANGUAGE
			SIGN LANGUAGE/INTERPRETER
			SMALL-BUSINESS CONVENIENCE SERVICES
			STUNT PERFORMER
IMPROVER	ORGANIZER	PROBLEM SOLVER	PACKAGING MACHINERY CONSULTANT
			PACKAGING STRUCTURAL DESIGN CONSULTANT
			VISITING SERVICE FOR SHUT-INS
IMPROVER	PROBLEM SOLVER	BUILDER	MIDWIFE
			PODIATRIST
			REFERRAL SERVICE/TRADESPEOPLE
			RESPIRATORY THERAPIST
IMPROVER	PROBLEM SOLVER	CREATOR	COMPUTER/TECHNICAL SUPPORT SERVICE
			CONCIERGE SERVICES
			DESKTOP PUBLISHING SERVICE
			FOCUS GROUP RESEARCH
			HUMAN REPRODUCTION CONSULTANT
			INTERNATIONAL OPERATIONS CONSULTANT
			MARRIAGE BROKER
			MATCHMAKER
			MEDIATOR/MARITAL
			MEDIATOR
			PSYCHOLOGIST/CLINICAL
			PSYCHOTHERAPIST/MARRIAGE AND FAMILY COUNSELOR
IMPROVER	PROBLEM SOLVER	LEADER	CAREER COUNSELING
			COLLEGE/COUNSELING SERVICE
			DIET COUNSELING
			DIETITIAN
			ELDER CARE/ADULT DAY CARE
			HOME/HEALTH AIDESOLVER
			INVESTMENT/ADVISOR REFERRAL SERVICE
			NUTRITION COUNSELOR
			NUTRITIONIST
			PHYSICAL THERAPIST
			REFERRAL SERVICE/CHILD CARE
			REFERRAL SERVICE/DENTAL
			REFERRAL SERVICE/HOUSING SWAP SERVICE
			REFERRAL SERVICE/MEDICAL
			REFERRAL SERVICE/PHYSICIAN

FIRST	SECOND	THIRD	CAREER OR BUSINESS
IMPROVER	PROBLEM SOLVER	LEADER	REFERRAL SERVICE/ROOMMATES
			REFERRAL SERVICE/SECOND MEDICAL OPINION
IMPROVER	PROBLEM SOLVER	ORGANIZER	EVENT CLEARINGHOUSE
			REFERRAL SERVICE/BED-AND-BREAKFAST INNS
LEADER	BUILDER	CREATOR	ANTIQUE/DEALER
LEADER	BUILDER	IMPROVER	ALARM SERVICE
			APPRAISER/AUTOMOBILE DAMAGE
			BOUQUET DELIVERY SERVICE
			BREAKFAST-IN-BED SERVICE
			DELIVERY SERVICE
			DELIVERY SERVICES/CANDY
			DELIVERY SERVICES/FIREWOOD
			DELIVERY SERVICES/FLOWERS
			DELIVERY SERVICES/GROCERIES
			DELIVERY SERVICES/PARCELS
			DISASTER RECOVERY CONSULTANT
			DISASTER/EMERGENCY PREPAREDNESS
			DRIVER/BOTTLED-WATER DELIVERY
			DRIVER/BREAKFAST DELIVERY
			DRIVER/COFFEE DELIVERY
			DRIVER/DELIVERY ROUTE
			DRIVER/GROCERY DELIVERIES
			FIREWOOD DELIVERY AND STACKING
			FLYING/INSTRUCTOR
			LUNCH TRUCK SERVICE
			MOBILE HOME PARK OPERATOR
			PHOTO SERVICES
			PHOTOGRAPHY/BLOWUP SERVICE
			PHYSICAL DISTRIBUTION AND LOGISTICS CONSULTANT
			PILOT/MARINE
			RADIO TIME SALES REPRESENTATIVE
			RELOCATION CONSULTING
			SALES REPRESENTATIVE
			SANDWICH SNACK ROUTE
			SEWING AND TAILORING/INSTRUCTOR
LEADER	BUILDER	PROBLEM SOLVER	BAIL BOND AGENT
			COMPUTER/SALES AND SERVICE
			LIVESTOCK AUCTION OPERATOR
LEADER	CREATOR	BUILDER	LOBBYIST
			MAIL ORDER BUSINESS
LEADER	CREATOR	IMPROVER	AUDIOTEXT (900) PROVIDER
			FASHION/CONSULTANT

FIRST	SECOND	THIRD	CAREER OR BUSINESS
LEADER	CREATOR	IMPROVER	FASHION/COORDINATOR
			FOREIGN CORRESPONDENT
			MODELING AGENCY
			PUBLIC RELATIONS SPECIALIST
			PUBLICITY SERVICE
			SALES TRAINER
LEADER	CREATOR	ORGANIZER	CLOWN FOR PARTIES, PROMOTIONS
			CONTEST ORGANIZER
LEADER	CREATOR	PROBLEM SOLVER	BOOK/PACKAGER
LEADER	IMPROVER	BUILDER	ANTIQUE/LOCATING SERVICE
			APARTMENT FINDERS
			ASSOCIATION MANAGEMENT SERVICE
			BED-AND-BREAKFAST INN
			BODY MAKE-UP ARTIST
			BUSINESS NETWORK ORGANIZER
			CLAIMS ADJUSTER
			CLEANING SERVICES/COMMERCIAL OR INSTITUTIONAL
			CONSULTANT/CORPORATE BENEFITS
			COUNSELOR/ALCOHOL, DRUG, AND SUBSTANCE ABUSE
			DRUG AND ALCOHOL COUNSELOR
			EMPLOYEE TRAINER
			EQUIPMENT EVALUATION AND SELECTION CONSULTANT
			EXECUTIVE DIRECTOR SERVICES
			FINANCIAL CONSULTANT
			FINANCIAL PLANNER
			FOOD/SERVICE MANAGEMENT
			FUNERAL DIRECTOR
			HAULING SERVICE
			HOME/SECURITY ANALYSIS SERVICE
			HOME/SECURITY PATROL SERVICE
			HOUSING CONSULTANT
			HUMAN RELATIONS COUNSELOR
			HUMAN RESOURCES CONSULTANT
			LANDSCAPE CONTRACTOR
			MANAGEMENT TRAINING
			MARKSMANSHIP INSTRUCTOR
			MATERIALS MANAGEMENT CONSULTANT
			NEEDLEPOINT SUPPLIES SALES
			NEWSLETTER COPYWRITING
			NEWSLETTER PUBLISHER
			OUTPLACEMENT CONSULTANT
			PAYROLL PREPARATION SERVICE

FIRST	SECOND	THIRD	CAREER OR BUSINESS
LEADER	IMPROVER	BUILDER	PERSONAL SHOPPER
			PERSONNEL CONSULTING
			PERSONNEL/HUMAN RESOURCES CONSULTANT
			PET IDENTIFICATION SERVICE
			REAL ESTATE/AGENT
			REPOSSESSION SERVICE
			RETIREMENT PLANNING CONSULTANT
			SECURITY CONSULTANT
			SELLING/CLOSEOUT AND SURPLUS
			SOFTWARE PUBLISHER
			SPORTS/AGENT
			SPORTS/INSTRUCTOR
			SPORTS EVENTS ORGANIZER
			SURVIVAL SPECIALIST
			TEMPORARY HELP AGENCY
			TIME MANAGEMENT CONSULTANT
			TOUR OPERATOR/FOOD
			TRAFFIC AND TRANSPORTATION CONSULTANT
			TRAINER/DISABLED
			TRAINER/DRIVING
			TRAINER/EMPLOYEE
			UMPIRE/REFEREE
LEADER	IMPROVER	CREATOR	ATHLETIC RACE/MEET ORGANIZER/PROMOTER
			ATTORNEY
			BROKER/LOAN
			BUSINESS CARD SALES/PHOTOGRAPHIC/HOLOGRAPHIC/POP-UPS
			CHEF/PERSONAL
			CHILDREN'S TELEVISION PRODUCER
			CHILDREN'S THEATER DIRECTOR
			COLLECTION AGENCY
			CONFERENCE PLANNER
			EMPLOYEE TRAINER
			ENTERTAINER/CHARACTER IMPERSONATOR
			ENTERTAINER/CRUISE SHIP
			ENTERTAINER/HOSPITAL
			ENTERTAINER/IMPERSONATOR
			ENTERTAINER/NURSING HOME
			ENTERTAINER/STORYTELLER
			EXECUTIVE DIRECTOR SERVICES
			FASHION MERCHANDISING/CONSULTANT
			FAX-ON-DEMAND SERVICE
			FILM PRODUCER

FIRST	SECOND	THIRD	CAREER OR BUSINESS
LEADER	IMPROVER	CREATOR	FRANCHISING CONSULTANT
			FUND-RAISER, PROFESSIONAL
			GENERATING SALES LEADS
			GOVERNMENT ADMINISTRATION CONSULTANT
			HEALTH ENHANCEMENT PRODUCT SALES
			INTERPRETING SERVICE/LANGUAGES
			KNITTING/SELLING SUPPLIES
			LEGAL VIDEO SERVICES
			LINGERIE SALES
			LITERARY/AGENT
			LITERARY AGENT
			LOAN/PACKAGER
			MANUFACTURER'S AGENT/REPRESENTATIVE
			MARKETING/CONSULTANT
			MARKETING CONSULTANT
			MUSIC TOUR COORDINATOR
			NAME CREATION CONSULTANT
			PARTY SALES/CANDLE
			PARTY SALES/CLOTHING
			PARTY SALES/COOKWARE
			PARTY SALES/HOUSEWARES
			PARTY SALES/JEWELRY
			PARTY SALES/LINGERIE
			PARTY SALES/MAKEUP
			PHOTOGRAPHER'S REPRESENTATIVE
			PRODUCER/DOCUMENTARIES
			PRODUCER/FILM
			PRODUCER/THEATER
			PRODUCER/VIDEO
			PRODUCT DEMONSTRATOR
			PROMOTIONS/IN-STORE
			PURCHASING AGENT SERVICE
			PURCHASING CONSULTANT
			RETAIL CLOTHING BUYER
			SCHOLARSHIP MATCHING
			SECURITIES/BROKER
			SECURITIES AGENT
			SECURITIES INVESTMENT ADVISER
			SELLING/OLD CURRENCY AND STOCK
			SEMINAR/LEADER
			SEMINAR/PRODUCER
			SEMINAR/PROMOTER

FIRST	SECOND	THIRD	CAREER OR BUSINESS
LEADER	IMPROVER	CREATOR	SHOW ORGANIZER/PROMOTER/ART SHOWS
			SHOW ORGANIZER/PROMOTER/TRADE SHOWS
			SIGN LANGUAGE/INSTRUCTOR
			SPEAKER, PROFESSIONAL/KEYNOTE
			SPEAKER, PROFESSIONAL/MASTER OF CEREMONIES
			SPEAKER, PROFESSIONAL/MOTIVATIONAL
			STOCKBROKER
			STORYTELLER
			TALENT/AGENT
			TELEMARKETING CONSULTANT
			TICKET BROKER
			TOUR OPERATOR/MUSIC
			TRAINER/SALES
			VIDEO/PRODUCTION
			YELLOW PAGE/CONSULTANT
LEADER	IMPROVER	ORGANIZER	ACCOUNTANT, CPA
			ACCOUNTANT, PUBLIC
			ADMINISTRATIVE SERVICES CONSULTANT
			ASSET PLANNING CONSULTANT
			AUTO/DRIVING INSTRUCTOR
			BODYGUARD
			BUSINESS BROKER
			CONDOMINIUM MANAGER
			COUPON NEWSPAPER PUBLISHING
			DISPATCHER/TAXI
			DRIVING SCHOOL OPERATOR
			DUDE WRANGLER
			FAMILY HISTORIAN
			GENEALOGY RESEARCH SERVICE
			GIFT/BUYING SERVICE
			GOVERNMENT ADMINISTRATION CONSULTANT
			HOTEL MARKETING/CONSULTANT
			IN-STORE PROMOTIONS SERVICE
			INSURANCE ADJUSTER
			INSURANCE AGENT
			INSURANCE BROKER
			INSURANCE CONSULTANT
			INSURANCE INSPECTION AND AUDITS
			INSURANCE SOLICITOR
			INSURANCE THIRD PARTY ADMINISTRATOR
			INVESTMENT/BANKER
			MOBILE/MANICURIST

FIRST	SECOND	THIRD	CAREER OR BUSINESS
LEADER	IMPROVER	ORGANIZER	MYSTERY SHOPPER
			NETWORKING/ORGANIZATION
			PROCESS SERVER
			PROFESSIONAL PRACTICE CONSULTANT/MEDICAL/DENTAL
			SECURITY ESCORT SERVICE
			SIGHTSEEING/GUIDE
			SPEAKER, PROFESSIONAL/CONTENT EXPERT
			TELEPHONE SALES
			TOUR OPERATOR/OUTLET SHOPPING MALLS
			TOUR OPERATOR/SHOPPING TOUR
			TOUR OPERATOR
			TRADE ASSOCIATION OPERATOR
			TRAVEL/GUIDE
LEADER	IMPROVER	PROBLEM SOLVER	ACCIDENT INVESTIGATOR
			ADVERTISING/AGENCY
			ADVERTISING/BROKER
			ADVEDRTISING/SALES
			ART/CONSERVATIONIST
			ART/THERAPIST
			BEAUTICIAN/HAIRSTYLIST
			CAMP DIRECTOR
			CONSULTANT/SAFETY
			DEBT NEGOTIATION SERVICE
			EMPLOYEE TRAINER
			ESTATE-PLANNING SERVICE
			FIREWORKS DISPLAY
			INVESTIGATOR, PRIVATE
			LABOR CONTRACTOR
			LOST PET LOCATION SERVICE/(PET DETECTIVE)
			MOBILE/PARAMEDIC
			MUSIC/THERAPIST
			NETWORKING/CLASSES
			OCCUPATIONAL THERAPIST
			ORGANIZATIONAL DEVELOPMENT CONSULTANT
			PRIVATE INVESTIGATOR
			PRODUCER/LASER LIGHT SHOW
			PROPERTY MANAGEMENT SERVICE/CONDOMINIUMS
			PUBLISHING RIGHTS NEGOTIATOR
			SEMINAR/LEADER
			SMALL AND START-UP BUSINESS CONSULTANT
			TEACHER/ADULT EDUCATION
			THERAPIST/ART

FIRST	SECOND	THIRD	CAREER OR BUSINESS
LEADER	IMPROVER	PROBLEM SOLVER	THERAPIST/MUSIC
			URBAN PLANNER
LEADER	ORGANIZER	BUILDER	EVENT PLANNER/SPORTS EVENTS
			LIQUIDATED-GOODS BROKER
LEADER	ORGANIZER	CREATOR	ART/SHOW PROMOTER
			EVENT PLANNER/ART SHOWS
LEADER	ORGANIZER	IMPROVER	ART/SHOW PROMOTER
			AUTO/BROKER
			BOAT/BROKER
			BROKER/BAIL BONDS
			BROKER/BULK FOOD
			BROKER/CEMETERY REAL ESTATE
			BROKER/EXPERT WITNESS
			BROKER/FURNITURE
			BROKER/GOVERNMENT SURPLUS
			BROKER/IMPORT/EXPORT
			BROKER/INTERNATIONAL FOOD
			BROKER/LIVESTOCK
			BROKER/MANUFACTURED HOMES
			BROKER/MONEY
			BROKER/MOTORCYCLE
			BROKER/RECYCLING
			BROKER/RESTAURANT FOOD
			BROKER/RV'S AND VANS
			BROKER/SALVAGE
			BROKER/SCRAP
			BROKER/SOLAR EQUIPMENT
			BROKER/VACATION HOMES
			BROKER/VENTURE CAPITAL
			BROKER/VINTAGE AUTOS
			BROKER/VINTAGE CLOTHING
			CONFERENCE PLANNER
			CONSULTANT/BROKER
			ESCROW TEMPORARY AGENCY
			ESTATE SALE COORDINATOR
			EVENT PLANNER/CHILDREN'S PARTIES
			EVENT PLANNER/FUND-RAISERS
			EVENT PLANNER/SPOUSE PROGRAMS
			EXPERT BROKER
			EXPOSITION MANAGER
			FRANCHISE BROKER/DEALER
			FREE CLASSIFIED ADVERTISING NEWSPAPER

FIRST	SECOND	THIRD	CAREER OR BUSINESS
LEADER	ORGANIZER	IMPROVER	INCOME TAX SERVICE
			MOTORCYCLE BROKER
			PRINTING/BROKER
			PRINTING BROKER
			REAL ESTATE/BROKER
			REAL ESTATE/BROKER
			REAL ESTATE/SALES
			SHOW ORGANIZER/PROMOTER/ANTIQUE CARS
			TRAINING/BROKER
			TRAVEL AGENT
			USED-COMPUTER BROKER
			WEDDING GOWN RENTAL/BROKERING
			WEDDING GOWN BROKER
			YACHT/BROKER
			YELLOW PAGE/BROKER
LEADER	ORGANIZER	PROBLEM SOLVER	ART/SHOW PROMOTER
			EVENT PLANNER/CONFERENCES
			EVENT PLANNER/CONVENTIONS
			EVENT PLANNER/TRADE SHOWS
			GOVERNMENT/PROCUREMENT CONSULTANT
			MULTIMEDIA PRODUCER
LEADER	PROBLEM SOLVER	BUILDER	ACCIDENT INVESTIGATOR
			COMMUNICATIONS CONTRACTOR/HOME SECURITY SYSTEM INSTLATION
			CONSTRUCTION CONTRACTOR/DRYWALL
			CONSTRUCTION CONTRACTOR/EARTHWORK/PAVING
			CONSTRUCTION CONTRACTOR/FIRE PROTECTION SYSTEMS
			CONSTRUCTION CONTRACTOR/GENERAL
			CONSTRUCTION CONTRACTOR/GREENHOUSES
			CONSTRUCTION CONTRACTOR/HOMES
			CONSTRUCTION CONTRACTOR/SMART HOUSE SYSTEMS
			CONSTRUCTION CONTRACTOR/SWIMMING POOLS
			ENGINEER/INDUSTRIAL
			INSULATION AND ACOUSTICAL CONTRACTOR
			UNION GRIEVANCE MEDIATOR
LEADER	PROBLEM SOLVER	CREATOR	DATABASE MARKETING SERVICE
			PSYCHOLOGIST/FORENSIC
			PUBLISHER/BOOKS
			PUBLISHER/CATALOGS
			PUBLISHER/DIRECTORIES
			PUBLISHER/GUIDES
			PUBLISHER/NEWSLETTER
			PUBLISHER/SMALL LOTS

FIRST	SECOND	THIRD	CAREER OR BUSINESS
LEADER	PROBLEM SOLVER	IMPROVER	COMPUTER BACKUP SERVICE
			INFORMATION TECHNOLOGY AND SYSTEMS CONSULTANT
			TRAINING BROKER
LEADER	PROBLEM SOLVER	ORGANIZER	COMMODITIES TRADER
ORGANIZER	BUILDER	IMPROVER	ARBORIST
			CANING REPAIR
			CRAFTS/STUFFED TOYS
			CRAFTS/TOYS
			MONITORING TV, RADIO
			MONOGRAMMING
			MUSIC/COPYIST
			ORDER FULFILLMENT SERVICE
			PROFESSIONAL ORGANIZER
			REPAIR SERVICES/CANE CHAIRS
			REPAIR SERVICES/SAILS
			REPAIR SERVICES/UMBRELLAS
			REPAIR SERVICES/WINDOW SCREENS
			SEWING AND TAILORING/DRAPERIES
			SEWING AND TAILORING/SLIPCOVERS
			SPORTS EQUIPMENT REPAIRER
ORGANIZER	BUILDER	LEADER	BOOKKEEPING SERVICE
			BROKER/BEADS
			CRAFTS/DRIED FLOWER ARRANGEMENTS CREATOR
			CRAFTS/STUFFED TOYS
			CRAFTS/TOYS
			DOLL/REPAIR
			ELECTROLOGIST/ELECTRIC HAIR REMOVAL
			FLOWER-ARRANGING SERVICE
			FRAMER/PICTURES, MIRRORS
			GLAZIER
			KNITTING/INSTRUCTION
			MANUFACTURING SPECIALTY PRODUCTS/CUSTOM PARTY FAVORS
			PLASTICS/RECYCLING
			SEWING AND TAILORING/CUSTOM PATCHES
			TYPESETTING
ORGANIZER	BUILDER	PROBLEM SOLVER	COMPUTER/SCANNING SERVICE
			MEDICAL TRANSCRIPTION SERVICE
			SCOPIST
ORGANIZER	IMPROVER	BUILDER	BRAILLE TYPIST
			COLLECTION AGENCY
			EMBROIDERY
			MEDICAL BILLING SERVICE

FIRST	SECOND	THIRD	CAREER OR BUSINESS
ORGANIZER	IMPROVER	BUILDER	MEDICAL CLAIMS PROCESSING SERVICE
			RECORD-SEARCHING SERVICE
			RECORD-KEEPING SERVICE
ORGANIZER	IMPROVER	LEADER	ANSWERING SERVICE
			BEAUTY SUPPLIES/HOME DELIVERY
			BOOKKEEPING SERVICE
			CALENDAR SERVICE
			DATA/ENTRY OVERLOAD
			DATABASE ENTRY AND MAINTENANCE
			GOVERNMENT/FORM-FILLING SERVICE
			LEGAL SECRETARIAL SERVICES
			LEGAL TRANSCRIPTION SERVICE
			MEDICAL RECORDS REVIEW
			MOBILE/NOTARY
			NOTARY SERVICE
			OFFICE SUPPORT SERVICES
			OUT-OF-TOWN BUSINESS SERVICE
			PAGING SERVICE
			POLLING AND SURVEYING
			REMINDER SERVICE
			SCRIPT PREPARATION SERVICE
			SECRETARIAL SERVICES
			SPACE PLANNING
			SPEAKERS' BUREAU
			TELEPHONE ANSWERING SERVICE
			TICKET AGENT
			TRANSCRIBING/COURT REPORTER NOTES
			TRANSCRIBING/RADIO AND TV PROGRAMS
			WAKEUP SERVICE
			WORD-PROCESSING/OFFICE SUPPORT
ORGANIZER	IMPROVER	PROBLEM SOLVER	ABSTRACTING SERVICE
			EDUCATIONAL/RECORD-KEEPING SERVICE
			GOVERNMENT/BID NOTIFICATION SERVICE
			PROOFREADER
			PROPERTY TAX REDUCTION SERVICE
			REAL ESTATE/ABSTRACT SEARCHER
			RED-TAPE WRANGLER
ORGANIZER	LEADER	BUILDER	BILL-PAYING SERVICE
			BILLING AND INVOICING SERVICE
			BOOKKEEPING SERVICE
			PAINTER/JEWELRY
			ACCOUNTANT, CPA

FIRST	SECOND	THIRD	CAREER OR BUSINESS
ORGANIZER	LEADER	IMPROVER	ACCOUNTANT, PUBLIC
			BARTERING SERVICE
			BOOKKEEPING SERVICE
			CAR POOL SERVICE
			DELIVERY SERVICE
			DELIVERY SERVICE/MEALS
			DRIVER/COURIER SERVICE
			DRIVER/DELIVERY ROUTE
			EMPLOYMENT APPLICATION CHECKING
			FIRE SAFETY CONSULTANT
			FLOWER DELIVERY SERVICE, WEEKLY
			FOOD/SPECIAL DIET DELIVERY
			MESSENGER SERVICE
			MOBILE/LUNCH WAGON
			TAX PREPARER/CONSULTANT
ORGANIZER	PROBLEM SOLVER	BUILDER	COMPUTER/PROGRAMMER-BUSINESS
			DATA/PROCESSING SERVICE
			FREIGHT TRAFFIC CONSULTANT
			SOFTWARE WRITER/DEVELOPER, BUSINESS
ORGANIZER	PROBLEM SOLVER	IMPROVER	BOOK/INDEXING SERVICE
			CONSOLIDATION SERVICES/FREIGHT
			CONSOLIDATION SERVICES/ODD-LOT
			INDEXING SERVICE
			MEDICAL CLAIMS ASSISTANCE
			MOVING CONSULTANT
			POLYGRAPH EXAMINER
			VOICE STRESS ANALYST
ORGANIZER	PROBLEM SOLVER	LEADER	BUDGET ANALYST
PROBLEM SOLVER	BUILDER	CREATOR	CONSULTANT/SATELLITE COMMUNICATIONS
			DEBUGGING SOFTWARE
			INVENTOR
			SURGEON
PROBLEM SOLVER	BUILDER	IMPROVER	AGROLOGIST
			AGRONOMIST
			ANIMAL BREEDER/SHEEP
			ANIMAL BREEDER/WILD ANIMALS
			COPYWRITER/TECHNICAL
			CURATOR
			DETECTIVE
			ECOLOGY CONSULTANT
			EMERGENCY MEDICAL TECHNICIAN
			GRANT WRITER

FIRST	SECOND	THIRD	CAREER OR BUSINESS
PROBLEM SOLVER	BUILDER	IMPROVER	HORTICULTURIST
			INDOOR ENVIRONMENTAL TESTER
			MEDICAL PHYSICIST
			MICROBIOLOGIST
			ORGAN TRANSPLANT COORDINATOR
			ORTHODONTIST
			PLANT/BREEDER
			PLANT/DOCTOR
			PROPOSAL AND GRANT WRITER
			PROSTHODONTIST
			RADIOLOGIST
			STRUCTURAL ENGINEER
			TAXIDERMIST
			VETERINARIAN
			WRITER/COMPUTER DOCUMENTATION
			WRITER/TECHNICAL
			WRITER/TEXTBOOKS
			WRITER/TRADE PUBLICATIONS
			X-RAY TECHNICIAN
PROBLEM SOLVER	BUILDER	LEADER	ANIMAL BREEDER/BIRDS, EXOTIC
			ANIMAL BREEDER/CATS
			ANIMAL BREEDER/CATTLE
			ANIMAL BREEDER/CHICKENS
			ANIMAL BREEDER/DOGS
			ANIMAL BREEDER/FISH FARMER
			ANIMAL BREEDER/FUR BEARING
			ANIMAL BREEDER/HORSES
			ANIMAL BREEDER/LLAMAS
			ANTHROPOLOGIST
			APPRAISER/INSURANCE
			ARCHAEOLOGIST
			ARTIFICIAL INSEMINATOR OF ANIMALS
			ARTIFICIAL INTELLIGENCE CONSULTANT
			ASBESTOS ABATEMENT SERVICES
			COMPUTER/CONSULTANT
			COMPUTER/PROGRAMMER-SCIENTIFIC
			COMPUTER/SECURITY CONSULTANT
			COMPUTER-AIDED DESIGN SERVICE
			CROSS-CULTURAL TRAINING CONSULTANT
			DRAFTING SERVICE
			DRIVER/TAXI
			ELECTRICAL ENGINEER

FIRST	SECOND	THIRD	CAREER OR BUSINESS
PROBLEM SOLVER	BUILDER	LEADER	ENERGY MANAGEMENT CONSULTANT
			ENGINEER/ACOUSTICS
			ENGINEER/CERAMIC DESIGN
			ENGINEER/CHEMICAL RESEARCH
			ENGINEER/COMMUNICATIONS
			ENGINEER/COMPUTER
			ENGINEER/ELECTRICAL AND ELECTRONIC
			ENGINEER/NUCLEAR
			ENVIRONMENTAL PLANNER
			ENVIRONMENTAL SERVICES/HAZARDOUS WASTE REMOVAL
			ETHNOGRAPHER
			FOREST SERVICE TRAIL CONTRACTOR
			GEOLOGIST
			INDOOR ENVIRONMENTAL TESTER
			IRRIGATION SYSTEM/CONSULTANT
			PILOT/AIRPLANE
			SOFTWARE WRITER/DEVELOPER, SCIENTIFIC
			SOIL CONSERVATIONIST
			SPORTS LEAGUE STATISTICS
			STATISTICIAN
			TAXI DRIVER
			TELECOMMUNICATIONS CONSULTANT
			UNDERGROUND STORAGE TANK SERVICES
PROBLEM SOLVER	BUILDER	ORGANIZER	COMPUTER/BULLETIN BOARDS SERVICE
			COMPUTER/DATA RECOVERY
			COMPUTER/DEBUGGING
			COMPUTER-AIDED DESIGN SERVICE
			DATA/CONVERTING SERVICE
			DRAFTING SERVICE
			FORENSIC RECONSTRUCTION SPECIALIST
			HERB GROWER
PROBLEM SOLVER	CREATOR	IMPROVER	APPRAISER/ART
			APPRAISER/GEMSTONES
			APPRAISER/JEWELRY
			CLOSET/DESIGN
			ECONOMICS RESEARCH
			WRITER/PROPOSAL AND GRANT
PROBLEM SOLVER	CREATOR	LEADER	BUSINESS INTELLIGENCE CONSULTANT
			BUSINESS PLAN WRITER
			COMPUTER/SHAREWARE DEVELOPER
			ELECTRONIC MARKETER
			SPECIALTY INFORMATION PROVIDER

FIRST	SECOND	THIRD	CAREER OR BUSINESS
PROBLEM SOLVER	IMPROVER	BUILDER	ACUPRESSURIST
			AUDIOLOGIST
			CHIROPRACTOR
			DENTIST
			EYESIGHT TRAINER
			FOOD/CRAFTING
			FOOD/SPECIALTY JAMS AND PRESERVES
			FOOD/STYLIST
			INSURANCE PARAMEDICAL EXAMINER
			MOBILE/PHLEBOTOMISTS
			NAPRAPATH
			NATUROPATH
			NURSE/REGISTERED
			OPHTHALMOLOGIST
			OPTOMETRIST
			OSTEOPATHIC PHYSICIAN
			PHLEBOTOMIST
			PHYSICIAN
			SAFETY/CLOTHING DEVELOPER
			SAFETY/ENGINEER
			SAFETY/EQUIPMENT DEVELOPER
PROBLEM SOLVER	IMPROVER	CREATOR	INSTRUCTIONAL DESIGNER
			NURSE PRACTITIONER
			NURSE/PSYCHIATRIC
			PHYSICIAN ASSISTANT
			PSYCHIATRIST
			PUBLIC OPINION/ANALYSIS
			PUBLIC OPINION/POLLING AND SURVEYS
			VIDEOGRAPHY/EDUCATIONAL
			VIDEOGRAPHY/INSURANCE DOCUMENTATION
			VIDEOGRAPHY/LITIGATION DOCUMENTATION
			VIDEOGRAPHY/PERSONAL EVENTS
			VIDEOGRAPHY/SPECIAL EVENTS
			VIDEOGRAPHY/YEARBOOKS
			WEDDING PHOTOGRAPHER
			GLASS/STAINED
PROBLEM SOLVER	IMPROVER	LEADER	ACUPUNCTURIST
			COMPUTER/BULLETIN BOARD SERVICE
			FURNITURE/REPRODUCER
			FURNITURE/CUSTOM MADE
			INVESTMENT/COUNSELOR
			PEDIATRICIAN

FIRST	SECOND	THIRD	CAREER OR BUSINESS
PROBLEM SOLVER	IMPROVER	ORGANIZER	COMPUTER/BULLETIN BOARD SERVICE
			FINDOLOGIST
			MARKETING RESEARCH
			PARALEGAL
			SIGHTSEEING GUIDE SERVICE
			TRANSCRIPT DIGESTING
PROBLEM SOLVER	LEADER	BUILDER	AUDIO/VIDEO/ENGINEERING
			AUDIO/VIDEO/PRODUCTION
			ENGINEER/BROADCAST
			ENGINEER/INDUSTRIAL
			ENGINEER/RECORDING
			ENGINEER/STRESS TESTING
			ENGINEER/TEST
			EXPLORER
			MANAGEMENT/CONSULTANT
			MANAGEMENT CONSULTANT
			POLLUTION CONTROL ENGINEER
			VOICE INSTRUCTOR
PROBLEM SOLVER	LEADER	CREATOR	FINANCIAL INFORMATION SERVICE
			INFORMATION BROKER
			LAND SURVEYOR
PROBLEM SOLVER	LEADER	IMPROVER	ANIMAL SHOW JUDGE/BIRDS
			ANIMAL SHOW JUDGE/CATS
			ANIMAL SHOW JUDGE/DOGS
			ANIMAL SHOW JUDGE/FISH, TROPICAL AND EXOTIC
			ANIMAL SHOW JUDGE/HORSES
			ART/CRITIC
			BIRTH PARENTS SEARCH SERVICE
			EDUCATIONAL/THERAPIST
			EXPERT WITNESS IN YOUR SPECIALTY
			HOMEOPATH
			JOB PLACEMENT AND REFERRAL SERVICE
			LECTURER/PUBLIC SPEAKING/INFORMATIONAL
			PHARMACIST
			PSYCHOLOGIST/EDUCATIONAL
			STOCK MARKET ANALYSIS
			STOCK PORTFOLIO MANAGEMENT
			TEAM-BUILDING CONSULTANT
PROBLEM SOLVER	LEADER	ORGANIZER	AUDITING AND EXPENSE REDUCTION SERVICE
			DATABASE CONSULTANT
			EXPERT LOCATION SERVICE
			BOAT/NAVIGATIONAL INSTRUCTOR

FIRST	SECOND	THIRD	CAREER OR BUSINESS
PROBLEM SOLVER	ORGANIZER	BUILDER	INFORMATION BROKER
			MAILING LIST BROKER
			MAILING LIST SERVICE
			MAILING LIST SERVICES/BULK MAILING
			MAILING LIST SERVICES/COMPILATION AND RENTAL
			MAILING LIST SERVICES/MAINTENANCE
			MAILING SERVICE/FULFILLMENT SERVICE
			MAILING SERVICE/HANDWRITTEN ADDRESSING
			MAILING SERVICE/PRESORTING
PROBLEM SOLVER	ORGANIZER	CREATOR	AUDITING AND EXPENSE REDUCTION SERVICE
PROBLEM SOLVER	ORGANIZER	IMPROVER	AUDITING MORTGAGES
			CLIPPING SERVICE
			CLOSET/ORGANIZING
			MEDICAL TRANSCRIPTION SERVICE
			PET SERVICES/GROOMER
			SOFTWARE/LOCATION SERVICE
PROBLEM SOLVER	ORGANIZER	LEADER	BROKER/MORTGAGE
			EXPENSE REDUCTION SERVICE
			PRICING AND ESTIMATING CONSULTANT
			RISK MANAGEMENT CONSULTANT

AVE QUESTIONS OR FEEDBACK?

.uthors of this book, Paul and Sarah Edwards, want to answer you ques-
. They can respond to you directly, usually within twenty-four hours, if you
.ave a message for them on the Working From Home Forum in CompuServe Information Service.

If you have a computer and access to CompuServe, simply type "GO WORK"
at any "!" prompt; their ID is 76703,242. If you do not now have access to CompuServe, you can obtain a complimentary Compuserve membership and receive
$15 of free connect time by calling (800) 524-3388. Ask for Operator 395. You
can also obtain a CompuServe starter kit in many stores.

If you do not have a computer, you can write to Paul and Sarah in care of
"Q&A," Home Office Computing magazine, 730 Broadway, New York, NY 10003.
Your question may be selected to be answered in their monthly column or they
may respond to it on their radio or TV show. However, they cannot respond to
every letter.

Use the table below to locate other books that contain the information you n... your business interests.

SUBJECT	Best Home Businesses for the 90s	Getting Business to Come to You	Making It on Your Own	Making Money with Your Computer at Home	Worki... from Home
ADVERTISING		Yes			
BUSINESS OPPORTUNITIES					Yes
BUSINESS PLANNING				Yes	
CHILDREN & CHILDCARE					Yes
CLOSING SALES		Yes	Yes		
CREDIT					Yes
EMPLOYEES					Yes
ERGONOMICS				Yes	Yes
FAILURE			Yes		
FAMILY AND MARRIAGE ISSUES					Yes
FINANCING YOUR BUSINESS			Yes	Yes	Yes
FRANCHISE NAMED					Yes
GETTING REFERRALS		Yes			Yes
HANDLING EMOTIONAL/ PSYCHOLOGICAL ISSUES				Yes	
HOUSECLEANING					Yes
INSURANCE					Yes
LEGAL ISSUES					Yes
LONELINESS, ISOLATION					Yes
MANAGING INFORMATION				Yes	Yes
MARKETING	Specific techniques by business	Yes Focus of book	Yes Attitude	Yes Technology tools	Yes
MARKETING MATERIALS		Yes		Yes	
MONEY			Yes	Yes	Yes
NAMING YOUR BUSINESS		Yes			
NETWORKING		Yes			Yes
OFFICE SPACE, FURNITURE, EQUIPMENT					Yes
OUTGROWING YOUR HOME					Yes
PRICING	Yes Specific			Yes Specific	Yes Principles
PROFILES OF SPECIFIC BUSINESSES	Yes			Yes	
PUBLIC RELATIONS AND PUBLICITY		Yes			Yes
SELECTING A BUSINESS	Yes			Yes	Yes
SOFTWARE				Yes	Yes
SPEAKING		Yes			
START-UP COSTS	Yes			Yes	
SUCCESS ISSUES			Yes		
TAXES					Yes
TIME MANAGEMENT			Yes	Yes	Yes
ZONING					Yes

Jeremy P. Tarcher, Inc.	For Canadian orders:
Mail Order Department	PO Box 25000
PO Box 12289	Postal Station 'A'
Newark, NJ 07101–5289	Toronto, Ontario M5W 2X8

			PRICE
_____	Working from Home	0-87477-764-X	$15.95
_____	The Best Home Businesses for the 90s	0-87477-784-4	$12.95
_____	Making It on Your Own	0-87477-636-8	$11.95
_____	Getting Business to Come to You	0-87477-629-5	$11.95
_____	Making Money with Your Computer at Home	0-87477-736-4	$12.95

Subtotal	_____
Shipping and handling*	_____
Sales tax (CA, NJ, NY, PA)	_____
Total amount due	_____

Payable in U.S. funds (no cash orders accepted). $15.00 minimum for credit card orders.
*Shipping and handling: $2.50 for one book, $0.75 for each additional book. Not to exceed $6.50

Payment method:
- ☐ Visa   ☐ Mastercard   ☐ American Express
- ☐ Check or money order
- ☐ International money order or bank draft check

Card # _____   Expiration date _____

Signature as on charge card _____

Daytime phone number _____

Name _____

Address _____

City _____ State _____ Zip _____

Please allow six weeks for delivery. Prices subject to change without notice. Source key WORK